The Language of Ramesses: Late Egyptian Grammar

François Neveu

Translated from the French by
Maria Cannata

Oxbow Books
Oxford & Philadelphia

Published in the United Kingdom in 2015 by
OXBOW BOOKS
10 Hythe Bridge Street, Oxford OX1 2EW

and in the United States by
OXBOW BOOKS
908 Darby Road, Havertown, PA 19083

Paperback Edition: ISBN 978-1-78297-868-8
Digital Edition: ISBN 978-1-78297-869-5

A CIP record for this book is available from the British Library
Library of Congress Cataloging-in-Publication Data

Neveu, François, author.
[Grammaire du néo-égyptien. English]
The language of Ramesses: late Egyptian grammar / François Neveu; translated from the French by Maria Cannata.
pages cm
Includes index.
ISBN 978-1-78297-868-8
1. Egyptian language--Grammar. I. Title.
PJ1135.N4813 2015
493'.15--dc23
2015001998

Printed in the United Kingdom by Berforts Information Press

For a complete list of Oxbow titles, please contact:

UNITED KINGDOM
Oxbow Books
Telephone (01865) 241249, Fax (01865) 794449
Email: oxbow@oxbowbooks.com
www.oxbowbooks.com

UNITED STATES OF AMERICA
Oxbow Books
Telephone (800) 791-9354, Fax (610) 853-9146
Email: queries@casemateacademic.com
www.casemateacademic.com/oxbow

Oxbow Books is part of the Casemate Group

Front cover: Extract from
The Tale of the Two Brothers
(Papyrus D'Orbiney, 19th dynasty)

To Pascal Vernus

P. Anastasi III, 5, 4.

Contents

Introduction XV
Aim of the book XV
Late Egyptian XV
General organisation of the book XVI
Notes on the transliteration and the passages cited XVI
Acknowledgments XVII
Translator's note XVII
Bibliographical orientation XVIII
Abbreviations XIX

Part one: Morphology 1

1. Nouns 3
1.1 Morphology 3
1.2 Syntax 3

2. Articles 4
2.1 The definite article 4
2.2 The indefinite article 5

3. Demonstratives 7
3.1 First paradigm 7
3.1.1 Forms 7
3.1.2 Usage 7
3.1.3 Remark 8
3.2 Second paradigm 8
3.2.1 Forms 8
3.2.2 Usage 8

4. Possessives 10
4.1 Forms 10
4.2 Usage 10

5. Numbers 12
5.1 Cardinal numbers 12
5.1.1 Number one 12
5.1.2 Number two 12
5.1.3 Numbers 3 to 9 12
5.1.4 Numbers from 10 onward 13
5. 2 Ordinal numbers 14
5.2.1 'First' 14

5.2.2 From the 'second' 14

6. The indefinites 16
6.1 *nb* 16
6.2 *ky* 16
6.2.1 Used as adjective 17
6.2.2 Used as pronoun 17
6.3 *nkt* 17

7. Personal pronouns 19
7.1 Suffix pronouns 19
7.1.1 Spellings 19
7.1.2 Usage 19
7.2 Dependent pronouns 20
7.2.1 Spellings 20
7.2.2 Usage 20
7.3 The new direct object pronouns 21
7.3.1 Spellings 21
7.3.2 Origin 21
7.3.3 Usage 21
7.4 Independent pronouns 22
7.4.1 Spellings 22
7.4.2 Usage 23

8. Prepositions 24

9. Adverbs 26

10. Particles 27
10.1 *ḫr* 27
10.2 *ỉr* 27
10.3 *pꜣwn* 27
10.4 *yꜣ* 27
10.5 *mk* (old), or *ptr* (new) 27

11. Other common morphemes 28
11.1 Negative morphemes 28
11.2 Interrogative morphemes 28
11.2.1 Interrogative particles 28
11.2.2 Interrogative pronouns 28
11.2.3 Interrogative adverb 28
11.3 Converters 29

Part two: syntax 31

12. Fundamental notions 33
12.1 Autonomy 33

12.2 Initiality ... 33
12.3 The enunciation ... 33
12.3.1 Tools of the enunciation: narrative and non-narrative forms ... 34
12.3.2 The register of the enunciation: narrative and discourse ... 34
12.3.2.1 The narrative ... 34
12.3.2.2 The discourse ... 34
12.4 The strategy of the enunciation ... 35
12.4.1 The theory of the three points of view ... 35
12.4.2 The strategic or enunciative point of view ... 35
Terminology ... 35
Marked and unmarked utterances ... 36

The verbal system ... 39

13. The infinitive ... 41
13.1 Morphology ... 41
13.2 Syntax ... 41
13.3 Aspectual value ... 41
13.4 Usage ... 41
13.4.1 Predicative usage ... 42
13.4.1.1 Perfective ... 42
13.4.1.2 Imperfect ... 43
13.4.2 Non-predicative usage ... 43
13.4.2.1 Noun phrase ... 43
13.4.2.1.1 Perfective ... 43
13.4.2.1.2 Imperfect ... 44
13.4.2.2 Prepositional phrase ... 44

14. The pseudo-participle ... 46
14.1 Morphology ... 46
14.2 Values ... 46
14.3 Usage ... 47
14.3.1 With a proper subject, in grammaticalised verbal forms ... 47
14.3.2 With a subject already playing a role in a preceding clause ... 47
14.4 Remarks ... 48

Independent verbal forms ... 49

15. The perfective *sḏm.f* ... 51
15.1 The active perfective *sḏm.f* ... 51
15.1.1 Usage ... 51
15.1.2 Negation ... 52
15.1.2.1 Origin ... 52
15.1.2.2 Morphology ... 52
15.1.2.3 Usage ... 53
15.2 The perfective *sḏm.f* called 'passive' ... 53
15.2.1 Affirmative Forms ... 53
15.2.2 Negation ... 55

16. The First Present 56
16.1 Introduction 56
16.1.1 Subject 56
16.1.2 Predicate 56
16.2 The predicate is an adverb 57
16.3 The predicate is a prepositional phrase 58
16.4 The predicate is the *ḥr* + infinitive form 59
16.4.1 The immediate present 60
16.4.2 The habitual present 61
16.4.3 The general present 61
16.4.4 Negation 61
16.5 The predicate is the *m* + infinitive form 63
16.5.1 Excursus: the first future 63
16.6 The predicate is a pseudo-participle 63
16.6.1 Transitive verbs (except *rḫ*) 63
16.6.2 Intransitive verbs 64
16.6.2.1 Verbs of motion 64
16.6.2.2 Other intransitive verbs 66
16.7 Special case: the verb *rḫ* 67
16.7.1 *rḫ* + noun (or pronoun) 68
16.7.2 *rḫ* + infinitive 68
16.8 Summary: the main forms of the First Present 69

17. The negative aorist 70
17.1 Introduction 70
17.2 Values 70
17.3 *bw sḏm.n.f* 70
17.4 *bw sḏm.f* 70
17.5 *bw ỉrỉ.f sḏm* 71
17.6 Excursus: the *ḫr-sḏm.f* form 72

18. The expression 'not yet' 74
18.1 Active voice 74
18.2 Passive voice 74

19. The Third Future 76
19.1 Introduction 76
19.2 Pronominal subject 76
19.3 Nominal subject 77
19.4 Remarks 78

20. The independent prospective *sḏm.f* 80

21. The imperative 83
21.1 Affirmative forms 83
21.2 Negative forms 85
21.2.1 General case 85
21.2.2 Special case: the verb *rdỉ* 86

22. The existential predication 88
22.1 Affirmative Forms 88
22.2 Negative Forms 89
22.3 Remarks 89

23. Second tenses 91
23.1 Introduction 91
23.2 How second tenses work 91
23.3 How to translate second tenses 92
23.4 The second tenses periphrased 93
23.4.1 Affirmative Forms 93
23.4.2 Negative Forms 94
23.5 Modal second tenses (non-periphrased) 95
23.6 Other second tenses 96

24. Independent forms: recapitulation 99
24.1 Table of the main independent forms 99
24.2 Conjugation of transitive verbs 100
24.3 Conjugation of intransitive verbs 101
24.3.1 Verbs of motion 101
24.3.2 Other intransitive verbs 102
2.4.4 Final remarks 102

Non-independent verbal forms 105

25. The continuative forms 107
25.1 Introduction 107
25.2 The sequential 107
25.2.1 Leaning onto an independent form 107
25.2.2 Leaning onto an adverbial clause 108
25.2.3 Leaning onto a non-verbal circonstant 108
25.2.4 Excursus: other continuative-narrative forms 109
25.3 The conjunctive 110

26. The non-independent prospective *sḏm.f* 113
26.1 In complement clauses following all forms of the verb *rdỉ* 113
26.2 In purpose clauses 113
26.3 In subordinate clauses introduced by a preposition or a conjunction 113

27. The participles 115
27.1 Active participles 115
27.1.1 Morphology 115
27.1.2 Syntax 115
27.1.3 Values 115
27.1.4 Usage 115
27.2 Passive participles 116
27.2.1 Morphology 116
27.2.2 Syntax 116
27.2.3 Usage 117

28. The relative forms ... 119
28.1 Morphology ... 119
28.2 Syntax ... 119
28.3 Values ... 119
28.4 Usage ... 119
28.4.1 As attributive adjective ... 119
28.4.2 As noun ... 121

29. Relative clauses introduced by *nty* ... 123
29.1 Syntax ... 123
29.2 Temporal values ... 123
29.3 Usage ... 123
29.4 *nty* + First Present, affirmative forms ... 123
29.4.1 The antecedent is the same as the subject of the relative clause ... 123
29.4.2 The antecedent is different from the subject of the relative clause ... 124
29.5 *nty* + First Present, negative forms ... 125
29.6 *nty* + Third Future ... 126
29.7 *nty* + *bwpwy.f sḏm* ... 127
29.8 *nty* + varia ... 127

30. Relative clauses introduced by (*ỉ*).*wn* or (*ỉ*).*wn.f* ... 129
30.1 Introduction ... 129
30.2 Relative clauses introduced by the participle (*ỉ*).*wn* ... 129
30.3 Relative clauses introduced by the relative form (*ỉ*).*wn.f* ... 130

31. Table of relative clauses (defined antecedent) ... 131

32. Adverbial clauses introduced by *ỉw* ... 132
32.1 Introduction ... 132
32.2 Used as adverbial clauses ... 133
32.2.1 The circumstantial is placed after the main clause (unmarked order) ... 133
32.2.1.1 General case ... 133
32.2.1.2 Special cases ... 135
32.2.1.2.1 The adverbial clause is focalised by a second tense ... 135
32.2.1.2.2 The adverbial clause is marked by the particle *ḫr* ... 135
32.2.2 The adverbial clause is placed before the main clause (marked order) ... 135
32.3 Used in place of a relative clause ... 136
32.4 Used in place of a complement clause ... 137
32.5 Excursus: the construction of verbs called 'operators' ... 138
32.5.1 Verb + direct object pronoun + pseudo-verbal predicate ... 138
32.5.2 Verb + direct object pronoun + adverbial clause ... 138
32.5.3 Verb + adverbial clause (without direct object pronoun) ... 139
32.5.4 Verb + *r-ḏd* + independent form ... 139
32.6 Remarks ... 139

33. Adverbial clauses introduced by *ỉr* ... 140
33.1 The particle *ỉr* ... 140
33.2 Correlative systems introduced by *ỉr* ... 140

33.2.1 The protasis incorporates *ỉr* + independent verbal form 140
33.2.1.1 The protasis incorporates *ỉr* + First Present 141
33.2.1.1.1 The predicate of the First Present is a prepositional phrase...... 141
33.2.1.1.2 The predicate of the First Present is (*ḥr*) + infinitive............... 141
33.2.1.1.3 The predicate of the First Present is *m* + infinitive 142
33.2.1.1.4 The predicate of the First Present is a stative........................... 142
33.2.1.2 The protasis incorporates *ỉr* + *sḏm.f* 142
33.2.1.2.1 *ỉr* + perfective *sḏm.f*.. 142
33.2.1.2.2 *ỉr* + prospective *sḏm.f*.. 143
33.2.1.3 The protasis incorporates a Third Future 143
33.2.1.4 The protasis incorporates an existential sentence............................... 143
33.2.2 The protasis incorporates *ỉr* + non-independent verbal form 143
33.2.2.1 The protasis incorporates a sequential 143
33.2.2.2 The protasis incorporates a circumstantial First Present..................... 144
33.2.2.3 The protasis incorporates *m-ḏr sḏm.f* or *m-ḫt sḏm.f*.......................... 144
33.2.2.4 Remarks 145
33.2.3 The protasis incorporates the ambiguous syntagma *ỉw.f* (*?*) *sḏm* 146
33.3 Conclusion 146
33.4 Excursus A: thematisations with *ỉr* 147
33.4.1 Thematisation of the subject 147
33.4.2 Thematisation of the direct object pronoun 147
33.4.3 Thematisation of a noun (or equivalent) object of a preposition 148
33.4.4 Thematisation of the subject of a complement clause.................................... 148
33.5 Excursus B: *ỉr* + adverb / verbal form.. 148
33.6 Excursus C: *ỉr* + prepositional phrase / verbal form.. 149

34. Adverbial clauses introduced by *wnn* 150
34.1 Introduction.. 150
34.2 Examples.. 151
34.3 Remark: another use of *wnn*... 152

35. Adverbial clauses introduced by *ỉnn* 153
35.1 Introduction 153
35.2 Usage.. 153

36. Adverbial clauses introduced by *hn*, *bsỉ* and *ḥl* (*ḥnr*) 155
36.1 Introduction.. 155
36.2 The conditional introduced by *hn*... 155
36.3 The conditional introduced by *bsỉ*.. 156
36.4 The conditional introduced by *ḥl* (*ḥnr*) 157

37. The *i.ỉrỉ.t.f sḏm* form 158
37.1 Introduction 158
37.2 Examples 158
37.3 Remarks 158

38. Recapitulation 160
38.1 The morpheme *ỉw* in the synchrony of Late Egyptian 160
38.2 The different values of *sḏm.f* 161
38.3 Uses of the prosthetic yod 161
38.4 The morphemes *wnn* and *wn* 161
38.5 The negative morphemes 162

Nominal forms 165

39. The nominal sentence with nominal predicate 166
39.1 Introduction 166
39.2 Classification predication 166
39.2.1 Examples in the first two persons 167
39.2.1.1 General case: the predicate is a noun 167
39.2.1.2 Special case: the predicate is an interrogative pronoun 169
39.2.2 Examples in the third person 169
39.2.2.1 Examples of the form *B Ø* 169
39.2.2.2 Examples of the form B *pꜣy* 171
39.2.2.3 Extensions of previous constructions 171
39.2.2.3.1 Examples of the form *B Ø pꜣ A* 172
39.2.2.3.2 Examples of the form *ỉr pꜣ* A B *pꜣy* and variants 172
39.3 Identification predication 174
39.3.1 Examples in the first two persons 175
39.3.2 Examples in the third person 177
39.3.2.1 Examples of the unmarked paradigm 177
39.3.2.1.1 Examples of the form *pꜣ B Ø* 178
39.3.2.1.2 Examples of the form *pꜣ B pꜣy* 178
39.3.2.1.3 Examples of the form *ỉr pꜣ* A *pꜣ* B *Ø* 179
39.3.2.1.4 Example of the form *pꜣ* A *pꜣ* B *Ø* 180
39.3.2.2 Examples belonging to the marked paradigm 180
39.4 Important remark 181

40. The nominal sentence with adjectival predicate 182
40.1 Introduction 182
40.2 *nfr Ø* 182
40.3 *nfr Ø se* 183
40.4 *nfr Ø (pꜣ) A* 183
40.5 Special case 185

41. Expressing possession 186
41.1 The possessor is represented by a name (or an interrogative pronoun) 186
41.2 The possessor is represented by a personal pronoun 188
41.2.1 Examples with the new independent pronoun 188
41.2.2 Examples with the traditional independent pronoun 189
41.3 Examples using both modes of expressing possession 190
41.4 Remark: the independent pronoun used as an attribute 190

42. Cleft sentences 192
42.1 Introduction 192
42.1.1 What is a cleft sentence? 192
42.1.2 Cleft sentences in Late Egyptian 193
42.1.2.1 The (true) cleft sentence (type I) 193
42.1.2.2 The pseudo-cleft sentence (type II) 195
42.2 Rhematisation the subject of the predicative plain verbal sentence 199
42.2.1 The phrase is in the active voice (type I or II) 199
42.2.1.1 Past (type I) 199
42.2.1.2 Present (type II) 201
42.2.1.3 Imperfect (type II) 203
42.2.1.4 Aorist (type I) 204
42.2.1.5 Future (type I) 205
42.2.2 The sentence is in the passive voice (type II) 206
42.3 Rhematisation of the direct objet of the predicative plain sentence (type II) 207
42.3.1 Past 207
42.3.2 Present 209
42.3.3 Future 209
42.4 Rhematisation of the verb of the predicative plain sentence (type II) 210
42.4.1 Past 210
42.4.2 Imperfect 210
42.4.3 Future 211
42.5 Special cases 211
42.5.1 The relative clause of the second member is strictly verbal 212
42.5.2 The relative clause of the second member is non verbal 212
42.6 Conclusion 213

Part Three: appendices 217

43. Appendix one: interrogative syntagmas 218
43.1 Introduction 218
43.2 Syntagmas introduced by an interrogative particle 218
43.2.1 Syntagmas introduced by *ỉn* 218
43.2.1.1 *ỉn* + *sḏm.f* 218
43.2.1.1.1 *ỉn* + perfective *sḏm.f* 219
43.2.1.1.2 *ỉn* + prospective *sḏm.f* 219
43.2.1.2 *ỉn* + *bwpwy.f sḏm* 220
43.2.1.3 *ỉn* + Third Future 220
43.2.1.4 *ỉn* + First Present 220
43.2.1.5 *ỉn* + *bw ỉrỉ.f sḏm* (negative aorist) 221
43.2.1.6 *ỉn* + Second Tense 221
43.2.1.7 *ỉn* + existential predication 221
43.2.1.8 *ỉn* + nominal sentence with substantival predicate 222
43.2.1.9 *ỉn* + nominal sentence with adjectival predicate 222
43.2.1.10 *ỉn* + cleft sentence 222
43.2.1.11 Special case 223
43.2.1.12 Remarks 223
43.2.2 Sentences introduced by *ỉst* 223

43.2.2.1 *ỉst* + *bw ỉrỉ.s sḏm* (negative aorist) 223
43.2.2.2 *ỉst* + First Present 224
43.2.2.3 *ỉst* + Second Tense 224
43.2.2.4 *ỉst* + nominal sentence with substantival predicate 225
43.2.2.5 *ỉst* + nominal sentence with adjectival predicate 225
43.2.3 Syntagmas introduced by *ỉs-bn* 225
43.2.3.1 Possible examples 225
43.2.3.2 Probable examples 225
43.2.3.3 Examples certain 226
43.3 Syntagmas incorporating an interrogative pronoun 226
43.3.1 Syntagmas with *ỉḫ* 227
43.3.1.1 Nominal sentences 227
43.3.1.2 Cleft sentences 228
43.3.1.2.1 Past 229
43.3.1.2.2 Present 229
43.3.1.2.3 Future 229
43.3.1.3 Verbal sentences 229
43.3.1.3.1 *ỉḫ* subject 229
43.3.1.3.2 *ỉḫ* direct object 230
43.3.1.3.3 *ỉḫ* object of a preposition 231
43.3.2 Syntagmas with *nỉm* 231
43.3.2.1 Nominal sentences 232
43.3.2.2 Cleft sentences 233
43.3.2.2.1 Past 233
43.3.2.2.2 Future 233
43.3.2.3 Verbal sentences 233
43.3.2.3.1 *nỉm* subject 233
43.3.2.3.2 *nỉm* genitive 233
43.3.2.3.3 *nỉm* object of a preposition 234
43.3.3 Syntagmas with *ỉṯ* 234
43.3.4 Syntagmas with *wr* 234
43.3.5 Remarks 235
43.4 Syntagmas incorporating an interrogative adverb 235
43.5 Questions without interrogative morphemes 236

44. Appendix two: Syllabic Writing 239
44.1 Introduction 240
44.2 Usage 240
44.2.1 Writing foreign words 240
44.2.2 Writing words of foreign origin (loan words) 241
44.2.3 Writing Egyptian words 241

Indexes 243
Grammar index 245
Egyptian grammar index 248
Coptic index 250
Index of texts cited 252
List of figures 267

Introduction

Aim of the book

This book is designed for people with a good knowledge of Middle Egyptian who wish to read texts written in Late Egyptian, the language in use in Egypt during the New Kingdom.

The result of ten years of teaching Late Egyptian grammar at the *École pratique de hautes études* and the *Kheops Institute* (Paris), this book is not a comprehensive grammar, which remains to be written, but aims to be a pedagogical tool,[1] which objective will be achieved if it allows its readers to study and understand 90-95% of texts. The remainder corresponds to very rare constructions with incomprehensible expressions, either because our knowledge of the language is still lacking, or because the text is incorrect or damaged.[2]

Although a teaching tool, this book is resolutely 'modern' and reflects the most recent work. In order to make it accessible to a wide audience, every attempt has been made to avoid departing from the linguistic terminology traditionally used in grammars of Egyptian without very strong reasons.

Late Egyptian

Late Egyptian corresponds to the language spoken from the 17th to the 24th dynasty. During the Amarna period (circa 1364 BC) Late Egyptian was adopted as a written language (in private letters, administrative, legal and literary texts, and some official inscriptions). Essentially, this is the common language of the Ramesside age.[3]

Together with demotic and Coptic, this stage of the language belongs under the 'second phase' of the Egyptian idiom.

Here are briefly summarised its main features:

- gender and number are indicated by determiners (articles, demonstratives, possessives) prefixed to nouns, rather than by endings;
- the opposition defined – undefined is morphologically marked by the definite and indefinite articles (or their lack thereof);
- the disappearance of the copula *pw* results in the replacement of Middle Egyptian three-member nominal sentence, having a substantival predicate, with a two-member sentence;
- the conjugation increasingly favours the Svo[4] order. This shift results from the evolution of verbal forms – such as the First Present or the Third Future – which were developed on the model of the nominal sentence with adverbial predicate, and eventually absorb it completely. At the same time, the suffix conjugation simplifies and declines in importance – the prospective is the only one to survive out of the four Middle Egyptian *sḏm.f* forms, while the *sḏm.n.f* loses the *n* thus becoming the perfective *sḏm.f*.[5] Finally, it is possible to observe the establishment of a precise temporal system that facilitated the development of the periphrastic conjugation with the auxiliary *ỉrỉ*, and the use of the past converter *wn*;
- the free morpheme *ỉw* imroduces henceforth a non-independent, non-initial sentence, basically taking on the role of an adverbial clause.

---

[1] This is the reason for the deliberate omissions and the repetitions that one cannot fail to note in this work.

[2] It is clear that in the Ramesside Period scribes and students did not always understand what they recopied.

[3] Gardiner, *EG*, p. 5; Vernus, *Les langues dans le monde ancien et moderne*, Paris, 1988, p. 162; Winand, *Morphologie*, p. 3-17.

[4] Subject + verb + object.

[5] Therefore, only two *sḏm.f* forms remain in Late Egyptian: the prospective and the perfective.

To these traits, which distinguish Late Egyptian from the 'first phase' stages of the language, can be added some of its evolutionary trends:

– as Egypt opens to the outside world, there develops, next to the traditional graphic system, the so-called syllabic writing, used whenever the scribe does not feel linguistically driven (see Appendix 2);
– the orthography (or the writing) tries to follow the evolution of the pronunciation. To confine this to a single example: *mdt* 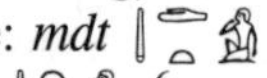 'word' becomes through the loss of the final *t* and the passage from *d* to *t*, *mty*  ;[6]
– in terms of lexicon a number of 'outdated' words are replaced with more 'modern' ones having the same meaning: *mꜣꜣ* 'see' becomes *ptr*, *sꜣ* 'son' becomes *šrỉ*, *ḥnꜥ* 'with' becomes *ỉrm*, etc.;
– but there is also a semantic shift affecting certain words: for example, the word *mdt* (or *mty*) 'word,' quoted above, very often takes on the meaning of 'case, matter,' etc.

General organisation of the book

The first part covers most of the fundamental notions on the different categories of morphemes, with the exception of the verb. The second part is devoted to the syntax. After a chapter on the basics of Late Egyptian forms, the verbal system is introduced, which is then followed by a study of 'nominal forms.' Two appendices, one devoted to interrogative constructions and one to syllabic writing, complete the work.

Note on the transliteration and the passages cited

The many examples used to illustrate the grammatical notions discussed, although for the most part derived from original hieratic texts, are reproduced in hieroglyphs, written from left to right, using MacScribe programme. No attempt has been made to reproduce the original text exactly (in terms of forms, arrangement of signs and minor lacunes), unnecessary in a teaching grammar, for which the reader should refer to the original sources or to their latest editions systematically referenced for each example. Note the use of the abbreviation v° for 'verso,' while, if no abbreviation is used, the passage is inscribed on the 'recto.'

The transliteration used is primarily that adopted by J. Černý-S. Groll in *A Late Egyptian Grammar*. The only notable exception being the use of *se* to transliterate the pronouns of the third person singular whenever the script does not correspond to the theoretical spelling (see *infra* §7.2.1).

[6] *Cf.* the coptic ⲘⲦⲀⲨ(B). The same evolution for *bdt* 'wheat' and *šndt* 'Nile acacia.'

Acknowledgments

This book would never have been written if Vernus Pascal, director of studies at the *École pratique de hautes études* in Paris, had not entrusted me with the teaching of Late Egyptian at this institution. It is to him that I owe the greatest debt – it was him who taught me the language, taught me to love it and, through it, all who spoke and/or wrote it.

I also owe much to Robert Navailles, my longtime friend, with whom I meticulously discussed every issue of 'grammatical doctrine.' His criticisms and suggestions were invaluable to me.

I would also like to thank Patricia Cassonnet for allowing me access to her research on the second tenses in Late Egyptian, which was taken into account in writing the corresponding chapter of this grammar.

Christine Gallois, director of the Kheops Institute, who willingly took the odds of publishing this book, is ensured my deep gratitude.

Marie-Claire Cuvillier and Jean-Louis Chassaing took upon themselves the burden of reading the manuscript, and correct the countless clerical errors as well as the inevitable careless mistakes, they also offered many improvements to the text, and to them I am extremely grateful.

Farout Dominique inserted the hieroglyphic text, and Olivier Cabon formatted the volume.

Finally, I cannot forget the warm and demanding public that represent the students and audience of the EpHE and of the Kheops courses, whose encouragement never failed me.

François Neveu, Paris, 1996

Translator's note

The scope of translating this grammar into English is to offer an additional learning tool to students who wish to learn this stage of the Egyptian language, but do not feel entirely at home with French.

In producing this translation, I have strived to keep it as close as possible to the original French, which, in some instances, has meant choosing a more literal translation in preference to one in good English style. In particular, I have attempted to render the French translation of the Egyptian passages as closely as possible in English, although I am aware that I may not have succeeded in every instance.

In typesetting the volume I have maintained, as far as possible, the layout of the original publication. The hieroglyphic passages were all rewritten using Inscribe Saqqara Technology with the exception of a small number of examples which particular sign arrangement could not be reproduced with the programme used. For the linguistic terminology I have relied mostly on the online *SIL International French-English Glossary of Linguistic Terms*, although, in a small number of cases I have preferred to give also the original French term, in brackets, next to its English translation.

Finally, I would like to express my deep gratitude to my friends and colleagues who kindly helped with my queries on English, French and Egyptian grammar, linguistics and translations – Leire Olabarria, Christina Adams, Liz McKillop and Cisco Bosch-Puche. I would also like to express my sincerest gratitude to OxbowBooks/Casemate, and especially the Publishing Director, Clare Litt, for entrusting to me the translation of this work, and for patiently waiting for its completion, which was delayed by my prolonged period of illness.

Bibliographical notes

A complete bibliography can be found in recent literature, for example J. Winand cited below. The following works are a good starting point for beginner students of Late Egyptian.

In terms of grammars, the works of J. Černý and S. Groll, P. Frandsen, H. Satzinger and J. Winand are essential. A. Erman's and M. Korostovtsev's grammars are surpassed as regards the verbal system, but they are still useful for studying different categories of morphemes (clauses, particles, adverbs, etc.).

In the lexicographic field, the only dictionary specifically dedicated to Late Egyptian, by L. Lesko, is rather mediocre. One should, therefore, consult the traditional dictionaries (for example the recent one by R. Hannig, which is excellent), and the *Année lexicographique* by D. Meeks (three volumes published), and, for the words of Semitic origin, the recent book by J. Hoch.

S. Allam, *Hieratische Ostraka und Papyri aus der Ramessidenzeit*, Tübingen, 1973.

A. M. Bakir, *Egyptian Epistolography from the Eighteenth to the Twentyfirst Dynasty*, Cairo, 1970 (= *BdE* 48).

R. Caminos, *Late Egyptian Miscellanies*, Oxford, 1953.

J. Černý, *A Community of Workmen at Thebes in the Ramesside Period*, Cairo, 1973 (= *BdE* 50).

J. Černý, *The Valley of the Kings*, Cairo, 1973 (= *BdE* 61).

J. Černý, *Late Ramesside Letters*, Brussels, 1939.

J. Černý, *Papyrus hiératiques de Deir el-Medineh I* and *II*, Cairo, 1978-1986.

J. Černý-S. Groll, *A Late Egyptian Grammar*, 3rd ed., Rome, 1984.

A. Erman, *Neuägyptische Grammatik*, Leipzig, 1933.

P. Frandsen, *An Outline of the Late Egyptian Verbal System*, Copenhagen, 1974.

A. Gardiner, *Late Egyptian Stories*, Brussels, 1932.

A. Gardiner, *Late Egyptian Miscellanies*, Brussels, 1937.

A. Gardiner, *Ramesside Administrative Documents*, London, 1948.

S. Groll, *The Negative Verbal System of Late Egyptian*, London, 1970.

S. Groll, *Non Verbal Sentence Patterns in Late Egyptian*, London, 1967.

J. Hoch, *Semitic Words in Egyptian Texts of the New Kingdom and Third Intermediate Period*, Princeton, 1994.

R. Hannig, *Großes Handwörterbuch Ägyptisch-Deutsch*, Mayence, 1995.

J. Janssen, *Commodity Prices from the Ramessid Period*, Leiden, 1975.

J. Janssen, *Late Ramesside letters and Communications*, London, 1991.

K. Kitchen, *Ramesside Inscriptions*, 8 volumes published, Oxford, 1968-1990.

M. Korostovtsev, *Grammaire du néo-égyptien*, Moscow, 1973.

J.-M. Kruchten, *Études de syntaxe néo-égyptien*, Brussels, 1982.

L. Lesko, *A Dictionary of late Egyptian*, 5 volumes, Berkeley, 1982-1990.

A. G. MacDowell, *Jurisdiction in the Workmen's Community of Deir el-Medina*, Leiden, 1990.

T. E. Peet, *The Great Tomb Robberies of the Twentieth Dynasty*, Oxford, 1930.

H. Satzinger, *Neuägyptische Studien*, Vienna, 1976.

D. Valbelle, *Les ouvriers de la Tombe*, Cairo, 1985 (= *BdE* 96).

P. Vernus, *Chants d'amour de l'Égypte antique*, Paris, 1992.

P. Vernus, *Affaires et scandales sous les Ramses*, Paris, 1993.

E. Wente, *Late Ramesside Letters*, Chicago, 1959.

E. Wente, *Letters from Ancient Egypt*, Atlanta, 1990.

J. Winand, *Études de néo-égyptien I, La morphologie verbale*. Liege. 1992.

Abbreviations

Allam, *HOP*	S. Allam, *Hieratische Ostraka und Papyri*, 3 vols., Tübingen, 1973.
BIFAO	*Bulletin de l'Institut français d'archéologie orientale*, Cairo.
CdE	*Chronique d'Égypte*, Brussels.
CED	J. Černý, *Coptic Etymological Dictionary*, Cambridge, 1976.
Černý, *Community*	J. Černý, *A Community of Workmen at Thebes in the Ramesside Period*, Cairo, 1973.
CLEM	R. Caminos, *Late Egyptian Miscellanies*, Oxford, 1963.
Crossroad I	*Crossroad, Conference on Egyptian Grammar*, Copenhagen, 1987.
DE	*Discussion in Egyptology*.
Doret, *Narrative*	E. Doret, *The Narrative Verbal System of Old and Middle Egyptian*, Geneva, 1986.
Festschrift Westendorf	*Studien zu Sprache und Religion Ägyptens I*, Göttingen, 1984.
Frandsen, *LEVS*	P. J. Frandsen, *An Outline of the Late Egyptian Verbal System*, Copenhagen, 1974.
Gardiner, *EG*	A. Gardiner, *Egyptian Grammar*, 3rd ed., Oxford, 1957.
GM	*Göttinger Miszellen*, Göttingen.
Groll, *Negative*	S. Groll, *The Negative Verbal System of Late Egyptian*, London, 1970.
Groll, *Non Verbal*	S. Groll, *Non Verbal Sentence Patterns in Late Egyptian*, London, 1967.
HO	J. Černý-A. Gardiner, *Hieratic Ostraca*, I, Oxford, 1957.
IFAO	*Institut français d'archéologie orientale.*
JEA	*The journal of Egyptian Archaeology*, London.
JNES	*Journal of Near Eastern Studies*, Chicago.
Janssen, *CP*	J. Janssen, *Commodity Prices from the Ramessid Period*, Leiden, 1975.
Janssen, *Ship's logs*	J. Janssen, *Two Ancient Egyptian Ship's Logs*, Leiden, 1961.
Johnson, *DVS*	J. Johnson, *The Demotic Verbal System*, Chicago, 1976.
Korostovtsev, *Grammaire*	M. Korostovtsev, *Grammaire du néo-égyptien*, Moscow, 1973.
KRI	K. Kitchen, *Ramesside Inscriptions*, 8 vol., Oxford, 1968-1990.
LÄ	Lexikon der Ägyptologie, Wiesbaden.
Lefebvre, *Grammaire*	G. Lefebvre, *Grammaire de l'égyptien classique*, 2nd ed., Cairo, 1955.
LEG	J. Černý-S. Groll, *A Late Egyptian Grammar*, 3rd ed., Rome, 1984.
LEM	A. Gardiner, *Late Egyptian Miscellanies*, Brussels, 1937.
LES	A. Gardiner, *Late Egyptian Stories*, Brussels, 1932.
LingAeg	*Lingua Aegyptia*, Göttingen.
LRL	J. Černý, *Late Ramesside Letters*, Brussels, 1939.
NÄG	A. Erman, *Neuägyptische Grammatik*, 2nd ed., Leipzig, 1933.
Or.	*Orientalia*, Rome.
RAD	A. Gardiner, *Ramesside Administrative Documents*, London, 1948.
RdE	*Revue d'égyptologie*, Paris.

SAK	*Studien zur Altägyptische Kultur*, Hamburg.
Satzinger, *NÄS*	H. Satzinger, *Neuägyptische Studien. Die Partikel ir. Das Tempussystem*, Vienna, 1976
SEAP	*Studi di egittologia e di antichità puniche*, Pisa.
Valbelle, Ouvriers	*Les ouvriers de la Tombe*, Cairo, 1985.
Vernus, Future	P. Vernus, *Future at Issue. Tense, Mood and Aspect in Middle Egyptian*, New Haven, 1990.
Wenre, *LRL*	E. Wente, *Late Ramesside Letters*. Chicago, 1967.
Winand, Morphologie	J. Winand, *Études de néo-égyptien I, La morphologie verbale*, Liege, 1992.
ZDMG	*Zeitschrift für morgenländischen*, Wiesbaden.

() Indicates the restoration of a morpheme which omission does not constitute an 'error;' for example: *ỉw.f* (*r*) *sḏm* (Third Furure), (*ỉ*).*wn* (participle);

‹ › Indicates the restitution of a morpheme mistakenly left out by the scribe; for example *sḏm.‹f›*;

[ ] Indicates a passage in *lacuna*, a restoration may be included;

{} Indicates an incorrect morpheme in the text and should not be taken into consideration;

* precedes examples constructed for the purpose of grammatical demonstration but are not actually attested.

PART ONE

MORPHOLOGY

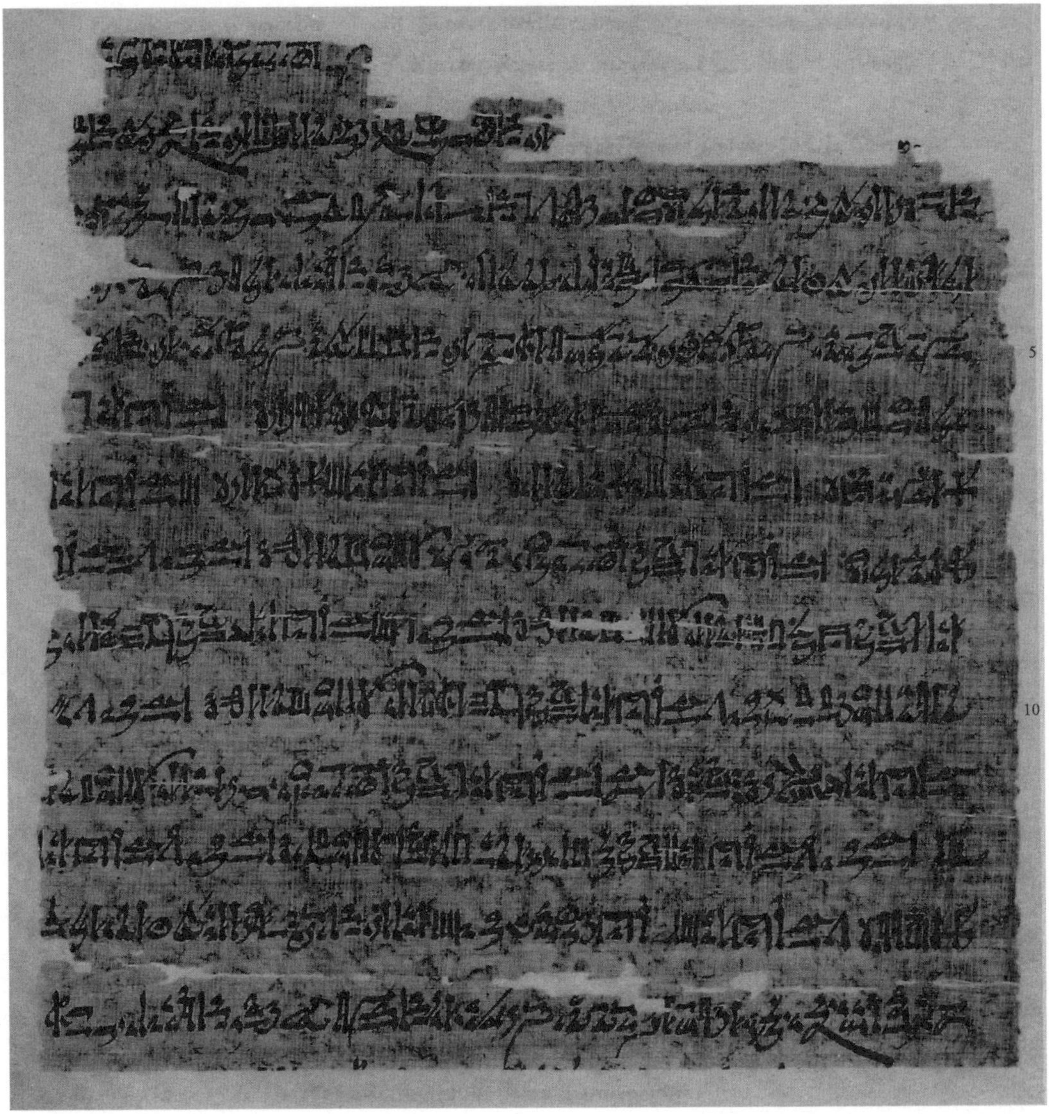

P. Cairo J 65739, 1-14 (*cf.* p. 11, 60, 111).

1. Nouns

In Late Egyptian there are two genders, masculine and feminine; as well as two numbers, singular and plural.

▪ Unlike classical Egyptian, Late Egyptian expresses the neuter by means of the masculine, the dual having practically disappeared from the current stage of the language.

1.1 Morphology

Theoretically, masculine nouns have no special endings, while feminine nouns take a *.t* ending. The plural is marked, for both genders, with a *.w*, with three short strokes, or both.

In practice, gender and number are indicated by the definite article, the demonstrative or the possessive. The endings, no longer pronounced, lost their significance and no longer need to be taken into account. Indeed, it is not uncommon to find masculine nouns with a *.t* ending, feminine ones without endings, as well as singular nouns marked with the endings of the plural (see *infra* §2).

▪ The feminine *.t* ending may have been retained in the pronunciation, and consequently writing, of Semitic loan words:  *mrkbt* 'chariot,'[1] and of nouns in the pronominal state (status pronominalis)  *psḏt.f* 'his Ennead.'[2]

1.2 Syntax

Nouns can be **defined** or **undefined**. **Defined** nouns are preceded by a definite article, a demonstrative adjective or a possessive adjective. In addition, nouns that do not fall into the above categories, but are followed by a suffix pronoun,[3] a proper name,[4] or by *nb*,[5] are treated as syntactically defined, and will be treated as such in the present study. **Undefined** nouns can be preceded by an indefinite article or by no morpheme at all.[6]

▪ The latter instance is frequent after the *m* (or the *r*) of predication,[7] as well as in some nominal forms, see infra §39.2 and §42.2.2.

---

[1] P. BM 10326, V° 6-7 (= *LRL*, 19, 10).

[2] P. BM 10375, 6 (= *LRL*, 44, 10).

[3] Unlike Middle Egyptian where a suffix is not defining. In Middle Egyptian, nouns with a suffix come under existential predication, which subject cannot be defined: *wn pr.f* 'there exists his house = he has a house.'

[4] Example: *wdpw nsw ny-se-ỉmn* 'the Royal Cupbearer Nesamun' – *cf.* English 'King Arthur.' See also *infra* §2, example 2.

[5] Because *rmṯ nb* designates men in their entirety (= mankind), it is a defined noun; similarly, *rmṯ nb n pꜣ tꜣ*, denotes the country's population.

[6] Also defined 'bare noun' *Ø A*.

[7] Example: *X (ỉ).wn m ḥry pḏt* 'X who had been chief of the archers,' P. BM 10052, 7, 11 (= *KRI* VI, 784, 13-14).

2. Articles

2.1 The definite article

The definite article derives from the late demonstrative pronoun of the classical stage of the language. It is placed before the noun it determines.

Masculine singular	 , var.  ,  [8]	*p3*
Feminine singular		*t3*
Plural	 , var. 	*n3*

1. P. Mayer A, 3, 6 (= *KRI* VI, 808, 15-16).
'The fourth month of the summer season, day 17,
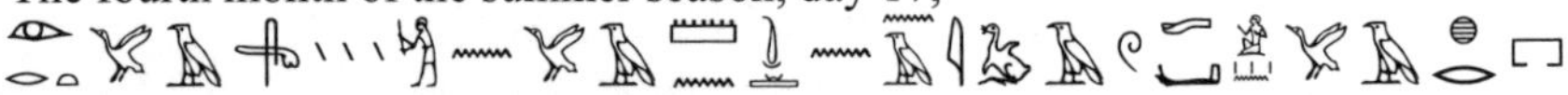
*ỉrt **p3** smtr n **p3** mn n **n3** ỉṯ3w n **p3** ḫr*
proceeding (to) the examination of the remaining thieves of the tomb.'

2. P. BM 10284, 7 (= *LRL*, 48, 16).

*ʿš ḥ3t n sš ṯry n **p3** ḫr*
'Be a pilot for the scribe of the tomb, Tjaroy.'

The form ***n3 n*** is still found during the 19th dynasty:

3. O. DM 554, v° 5 (fig. p. 103).

*ỉr **n3 n** rmww r(=ỉ).dỉ.k ỉn.tw.w (n).n*
'As for the fish (*lit.* fishes) that you had brought to us ...'

▪ In some rare instances *p3*, *t3*, *n3* keep the nuance of a demonstrative, as is the case with *p3 hrw* 'this day,' that is, 'today.'

Consequence 1. By this stage of the language it was the definite article that indicated the gender and number of nouns, rather than the endings ***.Ø***, ***.t***, ***.w***, ***.wt***, which were no longer pronounced.

4. P. DM V, 2 (= *KRI* VI, 266, 1).

***p3** sḫr*
'The position' (singular).

---

[8] Hieroglyphic texts.

5. O. Cairo 25589, 2 (= *KRI* V, 436, 7)

tꜣ iḥ(t)

'The cow' (feminine).

6. P. DM VII, 1.

pꜣ ꜥꜣ

'The donkey' (masculine).

Consequence 2. The difference between defined and undefined nouns, which was morphologically unmarked in classical Egyptian, becomes so from this stage of the language.

2.2 The indefinite article

In the case of the indefinite article, there is no longer a distinction between masculine and feminine in the singular, while the spelling used does not always correspond to the gender of the nouns:

Singular	 or 	***wꜥ (n)***	a, an
Plural		***nh(ꜣ)y n***	some

7. P. DM VI, v° 2-3 (= *KRI* VI, 267, 7-8)

yꜣ i.iri.s iy r ꜥḥꜥ m-bꜣḥ nfrt-iry ꜥ.w.s. ḥr wꜥ qd (i).ptr.s

'Because if she came to consult (Ahmose)-Nefertari l.p.h., it is about a dream she had' (*lit.* 'came to stand in front ... a dream that she has seen') (Second Tense).

8. P. Turin 1973, v° 5 (= *LRL*, 4, 6).

wꜥ šꜥt

'A letter.'

The form ***wꜥ n*** is encountered, above all, in texts of the 19th dynasty:

9. O. DM 587, 5-6.

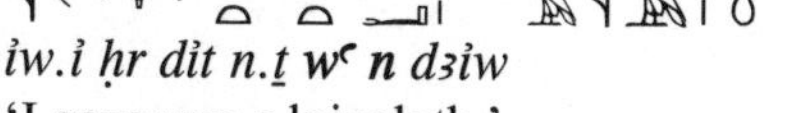

iw.i ḥr dit n.ṯ ***wꜥ n*** *dꜣiw*

'I gave you a loincloth.'

The plural, which is very rare, derives from a word meaning ‘some:’

10. P. BN 197, V, 3 (= *LRL*, 35, 13).

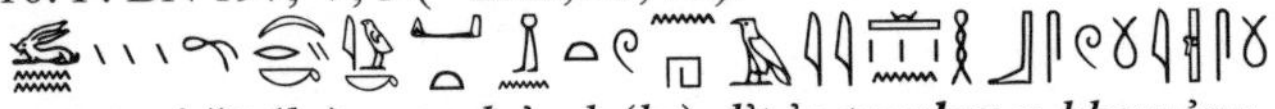

wnn tꜣy.ỉ šꜥt (ḥr) spr r.k ỉw.k (ḥr) dỉt ỉn.tw ***nhꜣy n*** *ḥbsw ỉsw*
‘As soon as my letter will reach you, you will have some (or ‘a few’) old garments sent.’

▪ In Egyptian, like in French and German, but unlike English, there is no distinction between the singular indefinite article and the numeral one.

3. Demonstratives

In Late Egyptian there are two paradigms of demonstratives.

3.1 First paradigm

3.1.1 Forms

Masculine singular		***pꜣy***
Feminine singular		***tꜣy***
Plural		***nꜣy***

3.1.2 Usage

These demonstratives are used above all as **adjectives**, and they correspond to **this**, **that**, **these**, **those**.

1. P. Mayer A, 4, 4 (= *KRI* VI, 811, 4-5).

ḏd n.f ṯꜣty i̓.ḏd my n.i̓ pꜣ di̓.k ***pꜣy*** *ḥḏ i̓m*

'The vizier said to him "Tell me, please, the place where you put this silver."'

However, they can also serve as pronouns, in which case they are translated as **this one**, **that one**, **these ones, those ones**:

2. P. Mayer A, 10, 22-3 (= *KRI* VI, 823, 12-13).

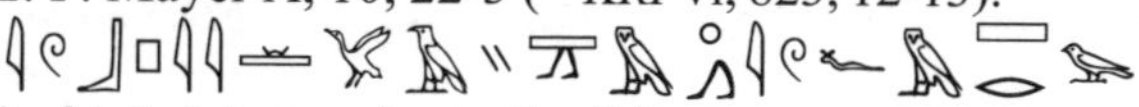

i̓w b(w)p(w)y ***pꜣy*** *šm i̓w.f m šri̓*

'But this one did not go since he was a child' (*lit.* 'because he was a child').

3. P. BM 10054, v° 1, 6 (= *KRI* VI, 490, 9-10).

m ḥsbt 13 n pr-ꜥꜣ ꜥ.w.s. 4 rnpt r ***tꜣy***

'In year 13 of Pharaoh l.p.h. four years ago' (*lit.* 'four years until that one').

This demonstrative is also employed as subject in nominal sentences of the (*pꜣ*) *B pꜣy* type (see *infra* §39.2.2.2 and §39.3.2.1.2):

4. Doomed Prince, 4, 8-9 (= *LES*, 2, 5).

i̓w.f (ḥr) ḏd n.f ṯsm ***pꜣy***

'He said to him "it is a dog."'

3.1.3 Remark

There is also a neuter form  ***p3w***, translated as **this**, **that**, which is used mainly as pronoun:

5. P. Salt 124, 2, 1 (= *KRI* IV, 410, 12-13).

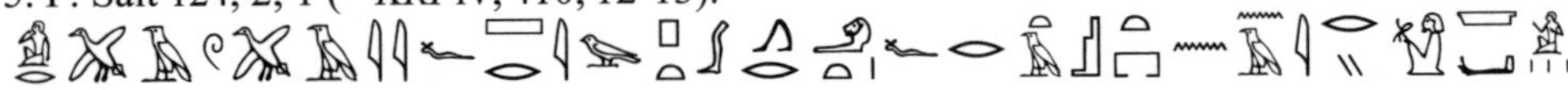

sḫ3 r ***p3w*** *p3y.f šri pt r-ḥ3t.f r t3 st n n3 iryw-ˁ3*

'Denunciation concerning this: his son ran before him to the lodge (lit. 'place') of the porters.'

▪ One can still find some vestiges of the old paradigm – *pn, tn* – in set expressions; the main ones being *hrw pn* 'this day'[9] (not to be confused with *p3 hrw* 'today') and *st tn* 'this place.'[10]

3.2 Second paradigm

3.2.1 Forms

Masculine singular	, var. 	***p(3)-n***, var. ***p3-(n)***
Feminine singular	, var. 	***t(3)-nt***, var. ***t3-(nt)***
Plural	, var. 	***n3y-(n)***, var. ***n3(y)-(n)***

▪ **Note**: the *n* is but very rarely written, and it is important not to confuse these forms with the definite articles.

3.2.2 Usage[11]

These demonstratives are always used as pronouns with the meaning of **this of**, **that of**, **these of**, **those of**:

6. P. DM XXVIII, 9-10.

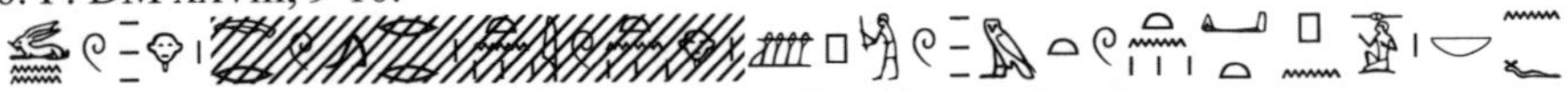

wnn.w ḥr [spr r.tn iw.tn ḥr] šsp.w mtw.tn dit ***p(3)-n*** *s nb n.f*

'When they will reach you, you will receive them and you will give each man his (own)' (lit. 'that of each man to him').

7. Wenamun, 2, 75 (= *LES*, 75, 1)

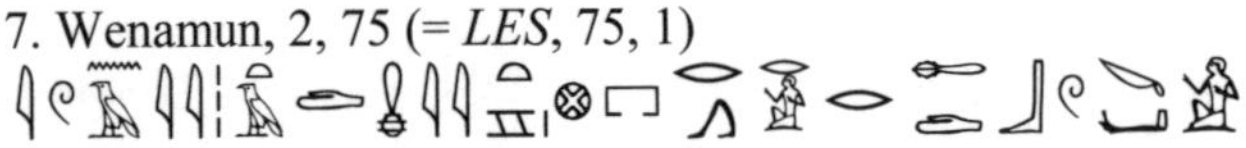

iw ***n3y-(n)*** *t3 dmit (ḥr) pr r.i r ḏdb.i*

'Those of the city came out against me to kill me.'

---

[9] O. Cairo 25530, 1 (= *KRI* V, 542, 10), cited in §13.4.1.1, example 1.

[10] P. Turin 1880, 1, 5 (= *RAD*, 53, 3), cited in §13.4.1.2, example 5.

[11] For this paradigm see Vernus, *Or* 50 (1981), 435-437.

They are also used in the construction of personal names, both masculine and feminine:

8. O. DM 364, 2-3 (= *KRI* v, 475, 2-3).

ꜥnh n nb ꜥ.w.s. ỉn kl r dỉt ꜥꜣ n ***p(ꜣ)-n****-tꜣ-wrt*

'Oath by the Lord l.p.h. (spoken) by Kel to give a donkey to Pentawer.'[12]

9. Wenamun, 1, 4 (= *LES*, 61, 5).

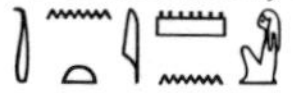

t(ꜣ)-nt*-ỉmn*

'Tanetamun.'

[12] 'He of the Great (fem.) one.'

4. Possessives

4.1 Forms

Possessives are formed by the addition of a suffix pronoun to the demonstratives.

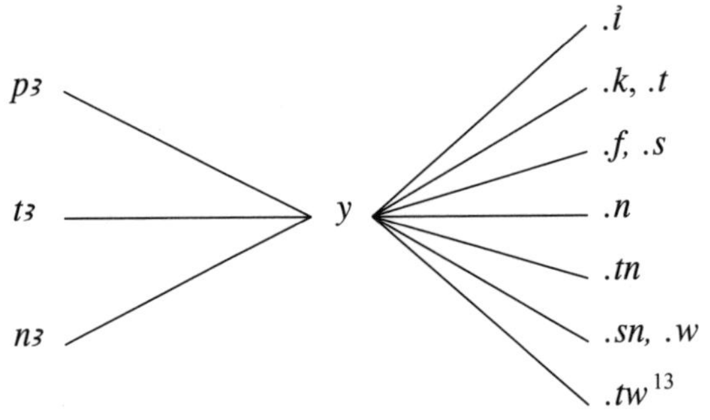

Agree in gender and number with what is **possessed**

Agree in person with the **possessor**

4.2 Usage

The possessives are, above all, used as adjectives:

1. P. Turin 2021, 3, 6-8 (= *KRI* VI, 740, 16-741, 4).

nꜣ snw ꜥꜣyw (n) ***nꜣy.f*** *ḫrdw … ḏd.w m r(ꜣ) wꜥ mꜣꜥtw* ***pꜣy.n*** *ỉt*

'The elder brothers among his children ... they said with one voice: "Our father is justified."'

2. P. Orbiney, 5, 2 (= *LES*, 14, 6).

ỉs bn ỉnk ***tꜣy.k*** *mwt*

'Am I not your mother?'

Much more rarely they are used as pronouns:

[13] For *pꜣy.tw*, with the impersonal suffix, see Vernus *Or* 50 (1981), 435 and n. 17. Example: P. Salt 124, v° 1, 11 (= *KRI* IV, 413, 14): *sḫꜣ r pꜣy.tw šm r smꜣ-tꜣ n N* 'Denunciation concerning the fact that one went for the burial of N.'

3. P. BM 10054, 3, 6 (= *KRI* VI, 494, 7).[14]

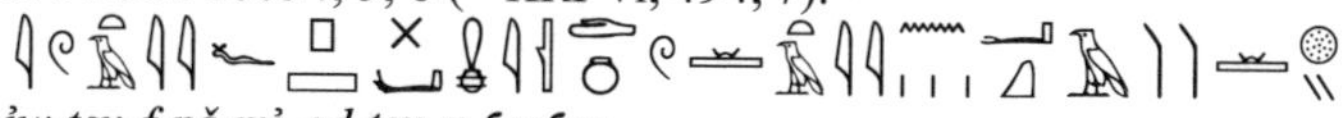

ỉw tꜣy.f pš mỉ-qd ***tꜣy.n*** *ꜥqꜣꜥqꜣ*

'Given that his share is very exactly the same as ours.'

▪ The classical method of expressing possession by means of a suffix continues to be used for some nouns designating elements intimately relating to an individual, or any other being: body parts, name, health, location, price ...[15] Note that such nouns are considered as defined.[16]

4. P. Cairo J 65739, 5 (= *KRI* II, 800, 9-10).

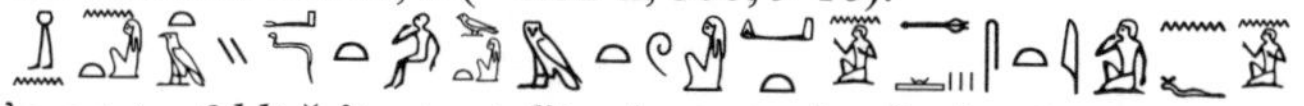

ỉn n.ṯ tꜣy ꜥḏdt šrỉt mtw.ṯ dỉt n.ỉ ***swnt.s*** *ỉ.n.f n.ỉ*

'"Buy for yourself this little girl and pay me her price," he said to me.'

[14] Another example is found in Wenamun, 2, 10 (= *LES*, 68, 3-4).

[15] A detailed list can be found in Černý-Groll, *LEG*, §4.2.9, p. 60-66.

[16] See *supra* §1.2.

5. Numbers

5.1 Cardinal numbers

With the exception of the number one, cardinal numbers are never written phonetically.

5.1.1 Number one

wꜥ stands before the noun and its spellings are the same as those of the indefinite article (see *supra* §2.2). As with the latter, the distinction between genders is lost.

1. P. BM 10052, 5, 23 (= *KRI* VI, 781, 6); see also example n. 2.

wꜥ st *wꜥty tꜣ wn.n*

'It is one, (and only) one, tomb that we opened' (Cleft sentence).

5.1.2 Number two

It is always placed after the noun. The latter remains in the singular, as do its determinatives, which agree in gender with it.

2. P. BM 10052, 6, 12-13 (= *KRI* VI, 782, 15-16).

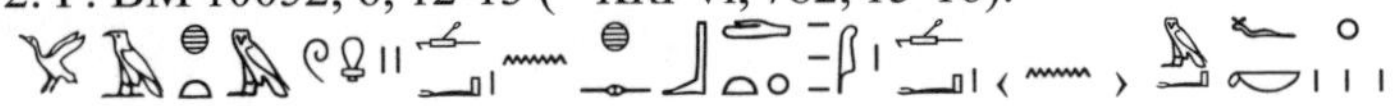

pꜣ ḫtm 2 *wꜥ n ḫsbd mꜣꜥ wꜥ ‹n› mfk(t)*

'The two seals, one of real lapis lazuli, and one of turquoise.'

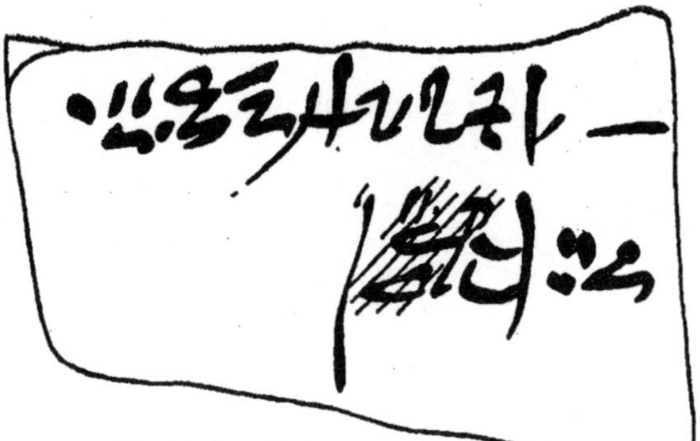

O. Brussels E 317 (*cf.* p. 218)

5.1.3 Numbers 3 to 9

They are often placed before the noun. The latter remains in the singular, as do its determinatives, which agree in gender with it.

3. P. Turin 1880, v° 6, 4-5 (= *RAD*, 48, 12).

*bn i.in.tw **tзy.i 3 ẖrd** ḥr.i*

'If one wants to bring my three daughters (to appear before a court), it will not be because of me' (Negative modal second tense).

It is not uncommon to find that, with feminine nouns, the number itself shows gender agreement:

4. P. BM 10052, 3, 7-8 (= *KRI* VI, 773, 8-9).

*iw.f (ḥr) dit n.n **4.t dnyt** m pз 4 gr inn*

'He gave us four shares for the four of us too' (*lit.* 'namely the four us also').

5.1.3 Numbers from 10 onward

Up to number 299 the rule is the same as above, except that the number is linked to the noun by means of the indirect genitive:

5. Amenemope, 27, 7.

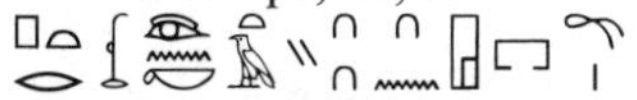

*ptr n.k **tзy 30 n ḥwt***

'Look, for you(rself), at these thirty chapters.'

6. P. BM 10383, 2, 2 (= *KRI* VI, 835, 1).

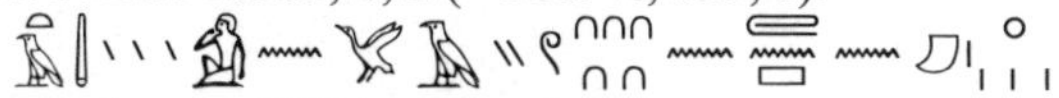

*tз mdt n **pзy 150 n dbn** n ḥmt*

'The matter of these 150 deben of copper.'

With numbers between 300 and 999 the determinatives of the noun are always feminine:[17]

7. P. Chester Beatty V, v° 5, 1.

tз 377 n nṯr

'The 377 gods.'

8. P. Mallet, VI, 4 (= *KRI* VI, 67, 15).

*ḫr di.i šʿd.tw **kt 700 n ẖt***

'And I have had another 700 logs cut.'

Afterwards, they are all masculine.[18]

[17] On the construction of cardinal numbers see Černý, *JEA* 23 (1937), 57-59.

[18] Example: P. Mallet, 5, 7 (= *KRI* VI, 67, 8-9): *imi grg pзy* 1000 *n ẖt* 'Have these thousand logs prepared.'

5.2 Ordinal numbers

5.2.1 'First'

The classical term ***tpy*** is still used at this time, and it is placed after the noun:

9. P. Abbott, 4, 14 (= *KRI* VI, 474, 5-6) (fig. p. 106).

ḥm nṯr ***tpy*** *n imn-rʿ nsw nṯrw*

'The high priest of Amun-Ra, king of the gods' (*lit*. 'The first servant of god').

Another term used is ***ḥ3wty*** 'that which is at the head:'

10. P. Orbiney, 5, 8 (= *LES*, 15, 1).

t3 iḥt ***ḥ3wty***

'The first cow.'

5.2.2 From the 'second'

These numbers are written using the participle of the verb ***mḥ***, 'completing:'

11. P. BM 10052, 15, 7 (= *KRI* VI, 800, 12).

iw.i (m) ***mḥ 4*** ***ḥmt***

'Given that I am the fourth wife' (*lit*. 'that which completes four women').

12. P. BM 10052, 8, 1 (= *KRI* VI, 785, 10).

ḥsbt 1 3bd 4 šmw sw 7 ***mḥ hrw 3*** *n smty*

'Year 1, 4th month of the summer season, day 7, 3rd day of examination.'

The participle of *mḥ* can have a prosthetic *yod*, sometimes written as *r*, as in the following example:

13. P. Abbott, 3, 10 (= *KRI* VI, 472, 1-2) (fig. p. 104).

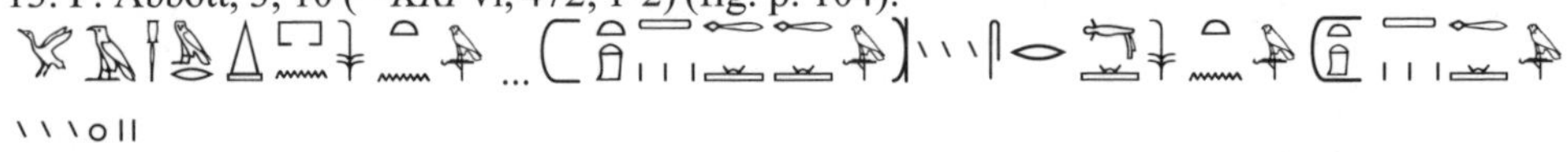

p3 mr n nsw … t3-ʿ3-ʿ3 ʿ.w.s. ***r(=i).mḥ nsw t3-ʿ3 ʿ.w.s 2***

'The pyramid of the king … Tao the elder l.p.h. who is a second king Tao l.p.h.'

14. P. Mayer A, 1, 23 (= *KRI* VI, 806, 3).

ỉw.‹ỉ› (ḥr) gm pꜣy 5 rmṯ ỉnk ***mḥ* 6**

'I met these five men, me being the sixth.'

In some set expressions (such as titles), it is possible to find the old ordinal formed with *nw*, although it is quite rare:

15. P. Leopold-Amherst, 4, 12 (= *KRI* VI, 489, 9).

ḥm-nṯr **2-*nw*** *n ỉmn-rꜥ nsw nṯrw*

'The second prophet of Amun-Ra, king of the gods.'

6. The indefinites

6.1 *nb*

nb, 'each, every, all' in an affirmative context, 'any' in a negative context, is used solely as an adjective. The two spellings, ***nb*** and  ***nbt***, are used indistinctly, since the word had become invariable.

1. P. BM 10417, v° 6-7 (=*LRL*, 28, 8-9).

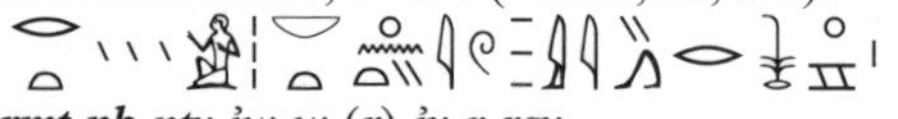

***rmṯ nb** nty iw.w (r) iy r rsy*

'All the people who will come to the south'

▪ In the example above, *rmṯ nb* is the antecedent of a relative clause introduced by *nty*. Given that the antecedent of such a clause should always be defined, its use here shows that a noun followed by *nb* is treated syntactically as defined (see *supra* §1.2 and *infra* §29.1).

2. P. Abbott, 7, 13-14 (= *KRI* VI, 481, 4-5): narrative.

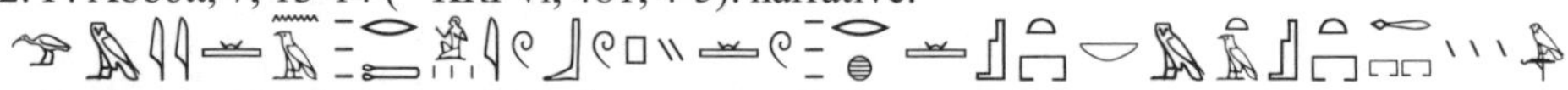

*gmy.Ø nꜣ rmṯ iw bwpw.w rḫ **st nb** m tꜣ st pr-ꜥꜣ ꜥ.w.s*

'It was found that people did not know of any tomb in the necropolis of Pharaoh l.p.h.' (*lit.* 'one found the people, even though they did not know…').

3. P. BM 10326, v° 10-11 (=*LRL*, 19, 15-16).

*mtw.k hꜣb n.i **pꜣ nty nb** iw.k (r) irt.f*

'And you will write to me (about) all that you will do.'

6.2 *ky*

Masculine singular	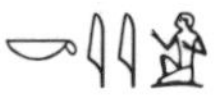	***ky***
Feminine singular	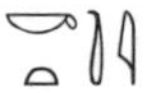	***kt***
Plural		***ktḫw***

ky can be employed as pronoun or as adjective. In the latter instance, contrary to the general rule, it is placed before the noun. Although its meaning is generally 'other, the other, another,' sometimes *ky* does not refer back to someone or something like that already mentioned, in which case it is translated as 'some, any.'[19]

[19] Erman, *NÄG*, §240; Černý, *CED*, p. 51; Vernus, *DE* 6, 81, n. e.

6.2.1 Used as adjective

4. Hittite Treaty, 15 (= *KRI* II, 228, 3).

ỉr ỉw ***ky ḫrwy*** *r nꜣ tꜣw n wsr-mꜣꜥt-rꜥ stp.n-rꜥ*

'If any enemy comes to the lands of Usermaatra-Setepenra.'

5. P. BM 10052, 5, 12 (= *KRI* VI, 780, 3).

nꜣ ***ktḫw ỉṯꜣw***

'The other thieves.'

6.2.2 Used as pronoun

6. P. BM 10052, 15, 7 (= *KRI* VI, 800, 12).

ỉw.ỉ (m) mḥ 4 ḥmt tꜣ 2.t mwt.tw ***kt*** *ꜥnḫ.tw*

'Given that I am the fourth wife; the (first) two are dead, another is alive.'

7. P. Louvre E 27151, 8 (= *JEA* 64 (1978), pl. XIV).

ỉnn m ***ky*** *r(=ỉ).dỉ se n.k ỉmỉ ptr.f se*

'If it is someone else who supplied it to you, let him see it.'

8. P. DM XXVIII, 10-11.

p[tr ỉw.ỉ (r) dỉt] ỉn.tw n.tn nꜣ ***ktḫw*** *nty ỉw.ỉ (r) šsp.[w]*

'Look, I will have sent to you the others that I will receive.'

6.3 *nkt* 

Originally the meaning of this word was 'thing, matter.' In Late Egyptian its meaning became '(a) bit of,' before a noun, and, after a verb, 'something,' if the sentence is affirmative, or 'nothing, anything,' if the sentence is negative.

9. P. Valençay I, v° 6-7 (= *RAD*, 73, 6-7) (fig. p. 30).

ỉw.w (ḥr) skꜣ pꜣ ***nkt*** *n ꜣḥt r(=ỉ).gm.w ỉm.f*

'They cultivated the little field that they found there.'

10. P. ESP, A, 9-10 (= *KRI* VI, 517, 12-13).[20]
'As soon as my letter will reach you,

iw.tn ḥr wḫꜣ n.i m ***nkt*** *n msḏmt*
you will seek out for me a bit of galena.'

11. Hittite treaty, 13 (= *KRI* II, 227, 15).

iw bw iri pꜣ wr ꜥꜣ n ḫtꜣ th r pꜣ tꜣ n kmt r nḥḥ r iṯꜣ ***nkt*** *im.f*
'Without that the great chief of Hatti could ever invade the country of Egypt to take possession of anything there.'

12. P. BM 10053, v° 3, 12 (= *KRI* VI, 760, 3).[21]

bw iri.tn dit n.i ***nkt***
'You never give me anything.'

13. P. Turin 1887, v° 1, 5 (= *RAD*, 78, 12-13).

iw bwpw[y.f] ir(t) ***nkt*** *r.w*
'Without him having done anything against them.'

14. P. DM XVI, v° 1 (= *KRI* VI, 268, 4).
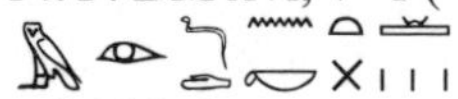
m ir ḏd ***nkt***
'Do not say anything!'

[20] Parallel example: O. Berlin P 11247, v° 1 (= *KRI* III, 533, 5).
[21] Parallel example: O. Prague 1826, 6 (= *HO*, 70, 2).

7. Personal pronouns

7.1 Suffix pronouns

7.1.1 Spellings

Singular	1st	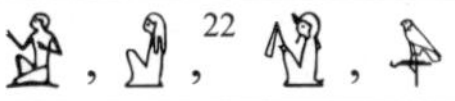 [22] or Ø (rare)	*.i*
	2nd masc.	 , rarely  [23]	*.k*
	2nd fem.	 [24] or	*.ṯ*
	3rd masc.		*.f*
	3rd fem.	 [25] [26]	*.s*
Plural	1st	 [27] Ø [28]	*.n*[29]
	2nd	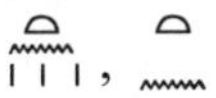	*.tn*
	3rd (old form)	 (very rare) [30]	*.sn*
	3rd (new form)	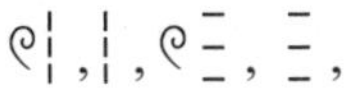	*.w*
Impersonal			*.tw*
		Ø	*.Ø*

7.1.2 Usage

After nouns: this usage is limited to some names where the suffix replaces the possessive;[31]

After prepositions;

After verbs: **subject** of verbal forms except the infinitive; **direct object** of the infinitive;[32]

[22] Note the two values – *.i* and *.ṯ* – of  .
[23] O. DM 554, 4.
[24] Note the two values – *.i* and *.ṯ* – of  .
[25] Often employed after the dative:  *n.s.*
[26] P. BM 10052, 14.
[27] Not to be confused with *n.n* (dative + pronoun).
[28] Following a word ending in *n*: P. BM 10052, 5, 13: *in.‹n› tꜣ swḥt n ḥḏ m tꜣ st* 'We carried away the silver sarcophagus from the tomb.'
[29] Sometimes, following a feminine noun, it can be written as *tn*.
[30] P. Turin 1887, 2, 9.
[31] Listed in Černý-Groll, *LEG*, §4.2.9, p. 60-66.

After converters: *ỉw* (circumstantial), ***wn*** (past), ***wnn*** (nominalisation).

7.2 Dependent pronouns

7.2.1 Spellings

Singular	1st	𓏲𓀀, 𓅱𓀀, rarely 𓀀, or **Ø**	***wỉ***
	2nd masc.	𓏏𓏲, 𓏏𓅱	***tw***
	2nd fem.	𓍿𓇋, 𓍿𓇋𓁐 [33]	***tỉ***
	3rd masc.	𓇓𓏲, 𓇓𓅱	***sw***
	3rd fem.	𓋴𓏏	***st***
Plural	1st	𓈖𓏥	***n***
	2nd	𓏏𓏲𓏏𓈖𓏥	***twtn***
	3rd	𓋴𓈖𓏥, 𓇓𓏲𓋴𓈖𓏥 (very rare) [34]	***sn***
	3rd	𓋴𓏏𓏥, 𓋴𓏏	***st***

Note: all dependent pronouns of the third person, singular and plural, were pronounced ***se*** and the spellings 𓇓𓏲, 𓋴𓏏, 𓋴𓏏𓏥, 𓋴𓈖𓏥, etc. were employed indistinctly. These pronouns will be transliterated ***se*** whenever the writing encountered does not correspond to the theoretical spelling.

Do not confuse 𓀀 = (*w*)*ỉ* with the suffix *.ỉ*, nor 𓋴𓏏 = *se* is with the suffix *.s*.

Do not confuse *sw*, *st*, dependent pronouns with *sw*, *st*, the proclitic pronouns of the first present, see *infra* §16.1.1.

7.2.2 Usage

Direct object pronoun of all verbal forms, except the infinitive;

Subject of a number of nominal sentences with adjectival predicate (see *infra* §40.3), and of constructions of the same type expressing possession (see *infra* §41).

[32] In this latter usage the suffix tends to be replaced by the new direct object pronouns, see §7.3.
[33] O. Petrie 62, 1.
[34] P. ESP, A, 12.

7.3 The new Direct Object pronouns[35]

7.3.1 Spellings

Singular	1st		*tw.ỉ*
	2nd masc.		*tw.k*
	2nd fem.	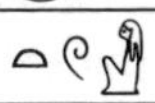	*tw.ṯ*
	3rd masc.		*tw.f*
	3rd fem.	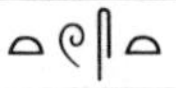	*tw.s*
Plural	1st		*tw.n*
	2nd		*tw.tn*
	3rd		*tw.w*

7.3.2 Origin

The new direct object pronouns derive from the combination of the morpheme *tw*, found after the determinative in the infinitive of some verbs when they are in the pronominal state (mark of the feminine *t*, or mark of the change of the last radical from *d*, *ḏ* or *ṯ* to *t*), with the suffix pronoun indicating the direct object. As a result, the combination *tw.f* came to be perceived as constituting the direct object pronoun itself, and its use was extended to other verbs.

In the imperative, the frequent presence of the reinforcing particle *tw*[36] led the dependent pronoun to be replaced by the new direct object pronoun to indicate the direct object.

7.3.3 Usage

Direct object after the infinitive. The following is an example with a strong verb which root does not end in *t*:

1. P. BM 10326, v° 14 (= *LRL*, 20, 4-5).[37]

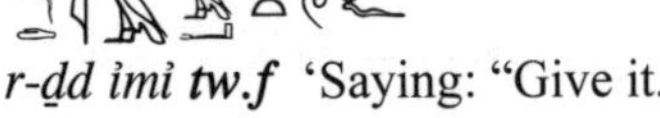

ỉw.tn (r) ḥ3p.tw.f r.ỉ

'You will conceal it from me.'

Direct object after the imperative. It is used especially with *rdỉ*, rarely with other verbs:

P. Cairo 58057, 6 (= *KRI* I, 238, 11-12).

r-ḏd ỉmỉ ***tw.f*** 'Saying: "Give it."'

3. Wenamun, 1, 37-38 (= *LES*, 65, 1).

ỉ.rwỉ3 ***tw.k*** *(m) t3y.ỉ mr(yt)*

'Remove yourself from my port.'

---

[35] See in the last instance Winand, *o. l.*, p. 98-100.

[36] Originally a second person singular, masculine, dependent pronoun. See Winand, *o. l.*, p. 156-160.

[37] On this passage see Wente, *LRL*, p. 41, n. ac, with additional examples with strong verbs.

7.4 Independent pronouns

There are two series of independent pronouns that, with some exceptions, are not distinguished in writing in Late Egyptian, but become so in Coptic:
- the **tonic series**, which is **complete** and is employed in marked constructions (thematisations, cleft sentences, marked nominal sentences, and so on);
- the **atonic series**, which is limited to the **first two persons** and is used in unmarked constructions (unmarked nominal sentences, and so on).

In addition, some very old forms are still used in the 2nd and 3rd person singular to express possession.

7.4.1 Spelling

Old forms

2nd *person singular common*	〔hieroglyphs〕	*twt*
3rd *person singular common*	〔hieroglyphs〕	*swt*

New forms[38]

		Tonic Serie			Atonic Serie	
Singular	1st	*ink*	(ⲀⲚⲞⲔ)	〔hieroglyphs〕 [39]	*ink*	(ⲀⲚⲄ̄)
	2nd masc.	*ntk*	(Ⲛ̄ⲦⲞⲔ)	〔hieroglyphs〕	*ntk*	(Ⲛ̄ⲦⲔ̄)[40]
	2nd fem.	*ntṯ*	(Ⲛ̄ⲦⲞ)	〔hieroglyphs〕 [41]	*ntṯ*	(Ⲛ̄ⲦⲈ)
	3rd masc.	*ntf*	(Ⲛ̄ⲦⲞⳈ)	〔hieroglyphs〕	//////	
	3rd fem.	*nts*	(Ⲛ̄ⲦⲞⲤ)	〔hieroglyphs〕	//////	
Plural	1st	*inn*	(ⲀⲚⲞⲚ)	〔hieroglyphs〕	*inn*	(ⲀⲚⲚ̄)
	2nd	*nttn*	(Ⲛ̄ⲦⲱⲦⲚ̄)	〔hieroglyphs〕	*nttn*	(Ⲛ̄ⲦⲈⲦⲚ̄)[42]
	3rd	*ntw*	(Ⲛ̄ⲦⲞⲞⲨ)	〔hieroglyphs〕	//////	

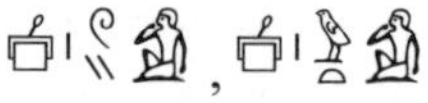

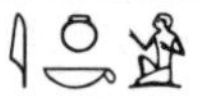

[38] The spellings used in the table are those of the tonic series. They are homogeneous and all persons are represented therein.

[39] Variants: 〔hieroglyphs〕, etc.

[40] Rare atonic form: 〔hieroglyphs〕 (P. BN 197, VI, 8 = *LRL*, 64, 10). Note the similarity with the spelling of the conjunctive.

[41] Rare anomalous spellings: 〔hieroglyphs〕 (O. Petrie 61, 3 = *HO*, 23, 4), 〔hieroglyphs〕 (O. Nash 1, 7 = *KRI* IV, 315, 16).

[42] Rare atonic forms: 〔hieroglyphs〕 (P. Turin 2026, 4 = *LRL*, 71, 14), and 〔hieroglyphs〕 (*KRI* II, 110, 3).

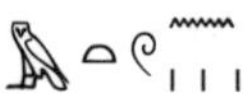

7.4.2 Usage

Subject or predicate of a nominal sentence (see *infra* §39);

predicate of a sentence expressing possession (see *infra* §41);

attribute (with the sense of 'to me, to you, etc.' (see *infra* §41.4);

marked rheme in nominal sentences (see *infra* §39.3), **or cleft sentences** (see *infra* §42);

marked theme (see *infra* §33.4.1, example 21, and §39.2.1.2, examples 2, 3 and 4);

strengthener of another pronoun, often preceded by ***gr***:

4. P. Mayer B, 5-6 (= *KRI* VI, 515, 12-13).

*ỉw.n (ḥr) ḏd n.f ỉw.n (r) ỉṯꜣy.**k** ‹r› pꜣ gm.n st ỉm mtw.**k** ỉn n.**k** gr **ntk***

'We said to him: "We will take you there where we found (the silver objects) and you will carry away (some) for you(rself), too."'

8. Prepositions

Below are listed the typical Late Egyptian prepositions, and those with slightly confusing spellings. For the others the reader should refer to the conventional grammars and dictionaries.

	***ỉrm***	'with, and, together with,' replaces ***ḥnꜥ***
	***wỉꜣ.tw***	'apart from, not to say, besides'
	***m***	'in,' var.: ; before a suffix:  ,  or 
	***m-ḫmt***	'without, without the knowledge of'
	***m-dỉ***	'with, in possession of' derives from  ***m-ꜥ***, and can be written  ; note: ***m-ḏr*** is still used and can be written 
	***m-ḏrt***	'through'
	***mỉ-qd***	'as, like'
	r	'towards;' before a suffix: 
	***r-ỉwd***	'between, since, in charge of'
	***r-ꜥqꜣ***	'opposite, vis-à-vis'
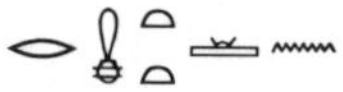	***r-mỉtt-n***	'in accordance with'
	***r-šꜣꜥ-m***	'since, for, from'[43]
	***r-šꜣꜥ-r***	'until'[44]
	***r-qr-n***	'next to, near, against (jur.)' var.: 
	***r-ḏbꜣ***	'in exchange for, in place of, against'
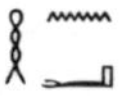	***ḥnꜥ***	'with, and;' var.:  old form replaced by ***ỉrm***

[43] Not to be confused with the following preposition.
[44] Not to be confused with the previous preposition.

	*ḥr*	'on;' before a suffix: 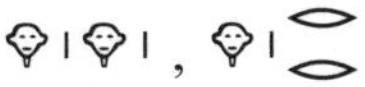 or 
	*ḥr-ˁwy*	'in charge of;' abbreviated as 
	*ḥr-ḏ3ḏ3-n*	'on top of'
	*ẖr*	'under;'  before a suffix
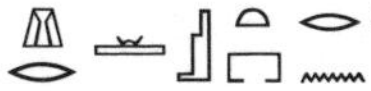	*ẖr-st-r(3)-n*	'because, due to, instead of'
	*ẖr-ḏrt*	'under the responsibility of'

9. Adverbs

Below are listed the most common adverbs and adverbial phrases.

	*ꜣs*	'quickly, immediately'[45]
	*ỉm*	'there, down there, from there' var. 
	*ꜥn*	'once more, again, already, more, also, further'[46]
	*ꜥqꜣ*	'exactly, precisely, correctly'
	*m-mỉtt*	'likewise, similarly, in the same way'
	*m-rꜥ*	'again, also'
	*m-dwn*	'regularly, usually'[47]
	*mỉnꜣ*	'like this, in this way'
	*r-ỉqr*	'very'
	*r-bl*	'outside'[48]
	*r-mỉtt*	'likewise, similarly, in the same way'
	*gr*	'again, further, also'
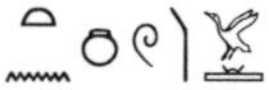	*tnw*	'where? where from?'
	*dy*	'here, there (new form)'
	*ḏrỉ*	'completely, conscientiously, severely, carefully, thoroughly'

[45] Often with *sp-sn*.
[46] Coptic ⲟⲛ.
[47] Often with *sp-sn*.
[48] Coptic ⲉⲃⲟⲗ.

10. Particles

Particles are distinguished from prepositions by their position, almost always a proclitic one, before various forms (verbal or nominal, independent or not). They are never found before a simple nominal syntagma.

10.1 *ḫr*

It coordinates an utterance with the preceding one, and it is never found in an initial position. It is translated by a coordinating conjunction 'and, but, or, so ...'[49]

10.2 *ỉr*

Signals a marked order (fronting of a syntagma or of a clause) and can be found in an initial position. It is either left untranslated or rendered by 'as for, if ...'[50]

10.3 *pꜣwn*

It has, above all, an explanatory or causal value ('because, since, for'). It is no longer found in texts after the nineteenth dynasty, and it never appears in an initial position.

10.4 *yꜣ*; var.: , , , etc.

It is used to strengthen a clause, and has two main uses:

- to reinforce a question, usually introduced by *ỉḫ*, and can be found both in initial and non-initial position (it is rendered as 'truly, indeed');
- to reinforce an assertion, having, most often, an explanatory or supporting value (rendered as 'because, since, for'), and it is found in non-initial position, especially in the twentieth dynasty after the disappearance of *pꜣwn*.[51]

10.5 *mk* (old), or *ptr* (new)

'See, look:' awakens or maintains the attention of the message's recipient ('phatic' function), while presenting him this message as immediately verifiable.

▪ Only *ḫr* and *ỉr* are found in a narrative context;
- *ḫr* can precede *ỉr*, *ptr*, or *mk*, but not *yꜣ*;
- *yꜣ* can precede *ỉr*, but not *ḫr*, *ptr* or *mk*;
- only *ỉr* can be preceded by *ptr* or *mk*.

---

[49] See Neveu, *SAK* Beihefte, Band 3 (1989), 99-110.
[50] See *infra* §33.1.
[51] See Neveu, *SEAP* 11 (1992), 13-30.

11. Other common morphemes

11.1 Negative morphemes[52]

Classical Egyptian		*Late Egyptian*		*Coptic*
	n	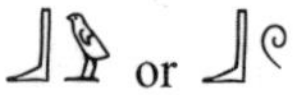	*bw*	M̄
	*nn*		*bn*	N̄
	(*n*...*is*)[53]		*bn* ... *iwnꜣ*	N̄...ⲁN
	*tm*		*tm*	TM̄

11.2 Interrogative morphemes[54]

11.2.1 Interrogative particles

in, common spelling: ; rarer spellings:  ,  or 

***is*(*ṯ*)**:  ,  or 

11.2.2 Interrogative pronouns

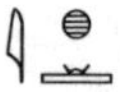	***iḫ***	what? (things)
	***nim***	who? (persons)
	***iṯ***	which? (very rare)

11.2.3 Interrogative adverb

 ***ṯnw*** or ***tnw*** where? whence?

[52] See *infra* §38.5.
[53] This is only the 'functional' predecessor of the discontinuous negative morphemes *bn* ... *iwnꜣ*, not its ancestor.
[54] See *infra* §43.

11.3 Converters

Past[55]	𓃹𓈖𓏲	***wn***
Circumstantial[56]	𓇋𓅱 or 𓇋𓏲	***ỉw***
Relative converter[57]	𓈖𓏏𓏭	***nty***
Nominalisation converter[58]	𓃹𓈖𓈖	***wnn***

[55] See *infra* §38.4.
[56] See *infra* §32.
[57] See *infra* §29.
[58] See *infra* §34 and §38.4.

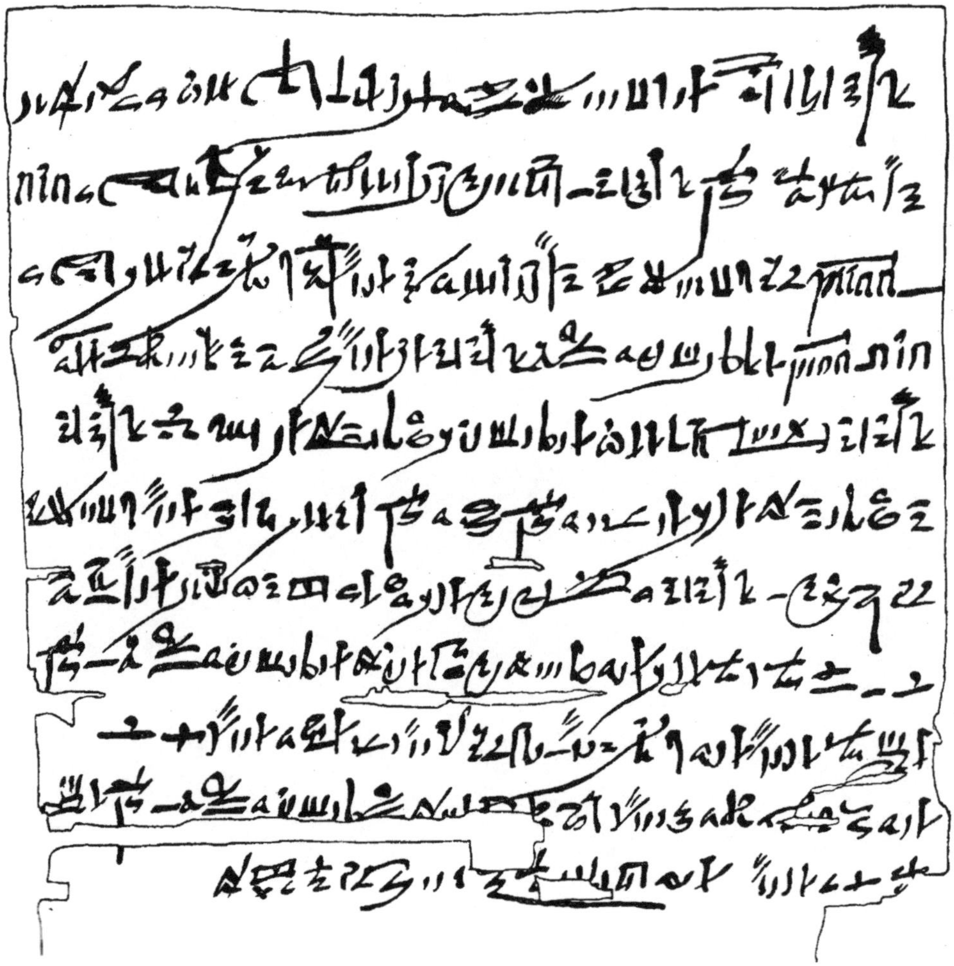

P. Valençay I, v° (*cf.* p. 17)

PART TWO

SYNTAX

P. Adoption, r° II, 15-26 (*cf.* p. 178)

12. Fundamental notions

A Late Egyptian utterance consists of units called 'forms' that can be nominal or verbal.[59]

12.1 Autonomy

A Late Egyptian form, verbal or nominal, is called **independent** if it **can** constitute in itself a complete sentence. It takes its temporal value, if it has one, from the register where the utterance[60] is found, and from its morphological characteristics.

A Late Egyptian form, verbal or nominal, is called **subordinate (non-autonomous)** if it **cannot** constitute, in itself, a complete sentence. It has to lean on another form, independent or not, that most often precedes it, but may also follow it.

Its temporal value depends both on the register of the utterance and on the other forms with which it is necessarily connected.

▪ Although some forms are (intrinsically) non-independent, it is also possible to convert an independent form into a non-independent one by using a specific morpheme, called 'converter,' placed at the beginning of the form. For example: *ỉw*, *wnn*, *nty*, *m-ḏr*, *ỉnn*, etc.

▪ Two subordinate forms that depend on one another can constitute an independent utterance (of higher order). For example, the correlative systems *wnn.f ḥr sḏm* / *ỉw.f ḥr* (*tm*) *sḏm*, see *infra* §34.

12.2 'Initiality'[61]

A Late Egyptian form, either verbal or nominal, is called **initial** if it is ***can*** to stand in an initial position, that is to say, at the beginning of a text, or after various expressions (often using the verb *ḏd*) indicating the beginning of direct speech, which are called direct indicators of initiality: *r-nty*, *r-ḏd*, *ḥnʿ ḏd*, *ky-ḏd*, *ḏd.f*, *ỉw.f ḥr ḏd*, etc.

A Late Egyptian form, either verbal or nominal, is called **non-initial** if it **can never appear** in an initial position, or after direct indicators of initiality.

▪ Any independent form is an initial one, but the converse is not true, since there are initial non-independent forms (for example the construction *wnn.f ḥr sḏm* cited above §12.1).

12.3 The enunciation[62]

The enunciation is a complex phenomenon that testifies to the way in which the speaker 'appropriates the language' to organise it into a discourse. In so doing, he is led to place himself in relation to his ***interlocutor***, in relation to ***his surroundings***, and in relation to ***what he states***.

In Late Egyptian, the enunciation is crossed by two oppositions, one affecting its tools, and the other its registers.

---

[59] 'Un énoncé est ou nominal ou verbal.' Benveniste, *Problèmes de linguistique générale,* I, p. 157.
[60] See *infra* §12.3.2.
[61] Černý-Groll, *LEG*, 10, p. 154-179, especially §10.10-11, p. 164-169.
[62] See Benveniste, *Problèmes de linguistique générale,* I, 1966, p. 238-243 and 255-256; Doret, *Narrative*, 1986, p. 13-14; Vernus, *DE* 9 (1987), 100-102.

12.3.1 The tools of the enunciation: narrative and non-narrative forms

Among the forms constituting an enunciation, some are objective, limited, and, if they possess a specific temporality, they express the past. They thus allow, in their succession, to **relate past events in an objective, punctual[63] and chronological manner, and this without relation to the time of the enunciation**. The events thus reported are, therefore, presented as being outside the sphere of the speaker's immediate interest, or, if one prefers, as not belonging to his *hic et nunc* (= *here and now*).

Such forms will be called '**narrative forms**,' and the sentences, of which they constitute the framework (and within which can be placed parenthetical clauses), that satisfy all the characteristics listed above, will be called '**narrative passages**' or '**narrative**.'[64]

The narrative forms include: the *sḏm.f* perfective, the sequential, the forms *wn.ỉn.f ḥr sḏm*, *ʿḥʿ.n.f ḥr sḏm*, and *ʿḥʿ.n sḏm.f*, some forms of the first present, and so on.[65]

Forms that do not possess the above properties, and/or that are employed with marks of the *hic et nunc*, will be called '**non-narrative forms**,' and the utterances in which they figure will be called '**non-narrative passages**.'

Among the non-narrative forms, while some are objective – third future, first present, *sḏm.f* perfective, etc. – others are subjective – prospective, negative aorist, imperative, conjunctive, second tense, cleft sentences, etc.

▪ As can be seen from the above list, some objective, punctual forms expressing the past, such as the perfective *sḏm.f*,[66] or the first present having as predicate the pseudo-participle of an intransitive verb,[67] can function as either narrative or non-narrative forms. It is the context that allows one to determine the nature of the passage.[68] For example, *sw ỉw* is rendered as 'he came,' if it is accompanied by other narrative forms (such as the sequential), but it is translated as 'he has come' (and he is still there) within the construction *ptr sw ỉw*, which shows a mark of the *hic et nunc*.

12.3.2 The registers of the enunciation: narrative and discourse

12.3.2.1 The narrative

The (historical) narrative is an utterance that recounts past events **without any intervention by the speaker**. Its framework consists of a succession of **narrative forms in the third person**.[69] It may, of course, contain parenthetical clauses and discourse quotations.

12.3.2.2 The discourse

The discourse is an utterance in which a **speaker addresses a listener** (real or imagined) whom he seeks to influence in some way. **Non-narrative forms** (non-narrative passages)[70] and

---

[63] 'Punctual' understood here as 'specific to a point in time.'

[64] The use of this term is complex: the narration is not in opposition to the narrative or the discourse, which belong to another type of opposition, but to the 'non narration,' that is to say, to the 'non-narrative' passages.

[65] Narrative forms, being punctual, cannot be used to describe repeated or habitual events, for which non-narrative forms, like the conjunctive, are used. For example, the beginning of the 'Story of the two brothers' (P. Orbiney, 1, 3-9). See Wente, *JNES* 21 (1961), 304-311.

[66] See below §15.

[67] See below §16.6.2.

[68] Presence of other narrative forms or narrative indicators, like *hrw pn* 'this day,' *ḥr ỉr ḥr-sꜣ 10 n hrw* 'and, ten days later,' in the case of narrative passages; presence of non-narrative forms or marks of the *hic et nunc* as *pꜣ hrw* 'today,' *10 n hrw r pꜣy* 'ten days ago,' and *ptr* 'look,' in the other case.

[69] Or better to the 'non person,' see Benveniste *o.c.*, p. 256.

[70] Or 'narrative in discourse.'

narrative forms (narrative passages) are found in **all persons**. The discourse can be introduced by specific expressions called direct indicators of initiality (see above §12.2), and be closed by other, equally specific, indicators called 'verbs of discourse closure:' *ỉ.n.f* (past), *kꜣ.f* (future), *ẖr.f* (temporally neutral).

▪ While the framework of the narrative is always a narration in the third person, the discourse may contain narrative passages (narration within a discourse, without restriction on persons) or non-narrative passages.
▪ Some narrative forms are common to both discourse and narration (sequential, some forms of the first present), while others are specific to the narrative (*wn.ỉn.f ḥr sḏm*, *ꜥḥꜥ.n sḏm.f*, etc.).
▪ The use of non-narrative forms in narration, such as the conjunctive, is an effect of style. For example in P. Salt 124 (denunciation of the misdeeds of Paneb), and P. Turin 1887 (Elephantine's scandal), where some of the past events are denounced subjectively.

12.4 The strategy of the enunciation

12.4.1 The theory of the three points of view[71]

A sentence, that is to say, an utterance that is grammatically complete, meaningfully interpretable and delimited by intonation,[72] may be regarded from three points of view:

- **morphosyntactic** point of view: according to the functions fulfilled by the terms of the sentence, we can distinguish a **subject** (even a zero subject), a **predicate** and, where required, complements;
- **semantic** point of view: the sentence consists of one or more **participants** (agent, patient), of a **process**, and optionally of beneficiaries, and/or of circonstants;
- **strategic** point of view or **enunciative**: the sentence always contains only two parts, which do not convey the same amount of information: the **theme** is presented as the **least informative** element, while the **rheme** is presented as the **most informative** element of the sentence.

Example: *The lion roars*. In this sentence, *the lion* is at the same time subject, actor (agent) and theme, while *roars* corresponds to the predicate, the process and the rheme.

It should be noted that even if a correspondence frequently exists between subject, actor and theme on the one hand, and predicate, process and rheme on the other, it is not always so.

12.4.2 The strategic or enunciative point of view

Terminology

If theme and rheme are primarily defined as the former being less informative than the latter, other properties contrast them in general terms. Thus the theme is often presented as 'that about which one is going to say something,' the 'support' or the 'given,' the rheme then being 'what is said about the theme,' the 'apport' or the 'new information.' The following are the main terms used to designate theme and rheme:

---

[71] See Hagège, *La structure des langues,* 1982, p. 27-54; *L'homme de paroles,* 1985, p. 207-233.
[72] Thus excluding 'emotional' statements like 'Get out!' 'Cheers!' etc.

Theme	Rheme
Support	Apport (contribution)
Presupposed	Comment(ary)
Dictum	Modus
Given	New
Topic	Focus

▪ It was thought preferable to reserve the last two terms to marked theme and marked rheme respectively (see below).

Marked and unmarked utterances[73]

An utterance is said **unmarked** if it satisfies the statistical affinities subject-theme and predicate-rheme, and is devoid of any syntactic wording **explicitly** designating one of its components as the theme or the rheme. Such an utterance is described as plain sentence (*Fr.* phrase plane). See the following examples in English and Late Egyptian:

– 'I have my meals at the restaurant.'
– **dỉ.ỉ ḥmt dbn 40 r pꜣy.ỉ ꜥꜣ*: 'I paid (lit. 'gave') 40 copper debens for my donkey.'

An utterance is said to be **marked** if the statistical affinities subject-theme and predicate-rheme are not satisfied (the subject then corresponds to the rheme and the predicate to the theme), or if either the theme or the rheme are explicitly designated by an *ad hoc* syntactic process.[74]

The term '**topic**' is used to designate a **marked theme**, and the entire syntactic process establishing an element of the plain sentence as topic or marked theme will be called '**topicalisation**' or '**thematisation**:'

– 'My meals, I have them at the restaurant' → Topicalisation of the direct object pronoun;
– 'Me, I have my meals at the restaurant' → Topicalisation of the subject.

In Late Egyptian the topicalisation of any nominal element in a plain sentence *can be done* by anteposing the element in question and having the particle *ỉr* precede it. The element thus topicalised is then referred back to by a pronoun in the 'comment' (see *infra* §33.4 and §39):

– * *ỉr ỉnk / dỉ.ỉ ḥmt dbn 40 r pꜣy.ỉ ꜥꜣ*
'As for me, I have paid 40 copper debens for my donkey' → Topicalisation of the subject;
– *ỉr pꜣy.ỉ ꜥꜣ / dỉ.ỉ ḥmt dbn 40 r.f*[75]
'As for my donkey, I paid 40 copper debens for it' → Topicalisation of a noun object of a preposition.

[73] See Vernus, *LingAeg* 1 (1991), 334-335.
[74] Since Late Egyptian is a dead language, nothing will be said here about processes involving intonation.
[75] O. Berlin P 1121, v° 1 (= *KRI* v, 525, 1).

Note that such a process results in an embedded construction. For example: *ỉr pꜣy.ỉ ꜥꜣ* (marked theme 1 = topic) / *dỉ.ỉ ḥmt dbn 40 r.f* (rheme 1 or comment), the rheme 1 *dỉ.ỉ ḥmt dbn 40 r.f* being itself structured in theme 2 reduced to the suffix *.ỉ*, while all the rest constitutes the rheme 2.[76]

Similarly, the term '**focus**' will apply to the **marked rheme**, and the entire syntactic process setting up an element of the plain sentence as focus, or marked rheme, will be referred to as '**focalisation**' or '**rhematisation**:'

– 'It is in the restaurant that I have my meals' → Focalisation of the adverbial;

– 'It is I who has (my) meals at the restaurant' → Focalisation of the subject;

– 'It is my meals that I have at the restaurant' → Focalisation of the direct object pronoun.

In Late Egyptian, the focalisation of an adverbial element (adverbial) of a plain sentence is achieved by means of the **second tenses** (see *infra* §23):

– **ỉ.ỉrỉ.ỉ dỉt ḥmt dbn 40 / r pꜣy.ỉ ꜥꜣ*
'It is for my donkey that I paid 40 copper debens' → Focalisation of the adverbial.

On the other hand, the focalisation of a nominal element is achieved by means of **cleft sentences** (see *infra* §42):

– **ỉnk / ỉ.dỉ ḥmt dbn 40 r pꜣy.ỉ ꜥꜣ*
'It is I who paid 40 copper debens for my donkey' → Focalisation of the subject;

– ** ḥmt dbn 40 / pꜣ dỉ.ỉ r pꜣy.ỉ ꜥꜣ*
'It is 40 copper debens that I paid for my donkey' → Focalisation of the direct object pronoun.

Remark. Topicalisation and focalisation are by no means mutually exclusive:

– 'My Brother won the race' → Plain sentence;

– 'My brother, it is him who won the race' → Topicalisation and focalisation of the subject;

– 'The race, it is my brother who won it' → Topicalisation of the direct object pronoun and focalisation of the subject;

– 'The race, my brother, it is him who won it' → Topicalisation of the direct object pronoun first, then of the subject, and focalisation of the subject.

[76] See Hagège, *L'homme de paroles,* p. 226.

The same is true in Late Egyptian:

– *ir pꜣw iryt nb ntw i.iri se*[77]

'As for all that has been done, it is they who have done it: → Topicalisation of the direct object pronoun and focalisation of the subject of a verbal sentence.

The structure of the passage is the following: *ir pꜣw iryt nb* (marked theme 1 = topic) / *ntw i.iri se* (rheme 1 = comment), the latter being subdivided into *ntw* (marked rheme 2 = focus) / *i.iri se* (theme 2).

– *ir imn-rꜥ nsw nṯrw ntf pꜣ nb n pꜣ ꜥnḫ snb*[78]

'As for Amun-Ra, king of the gods, it is him, the lord of life and health' → Topicalisation and focalisation of the subject of a nominal sentence.

As before: *imn-rꜥ nsw nṯrw* (marked theme 1 = topic) / *ntf pꜣ nb n pꜣ ꜥnḫ snb* (rheme 1), with rheme 1 consisting of: *ntf* (marked rheme 2 = focus) / *pꜣ nb n pꜣ ꜥnḫ snb* (theme 2).

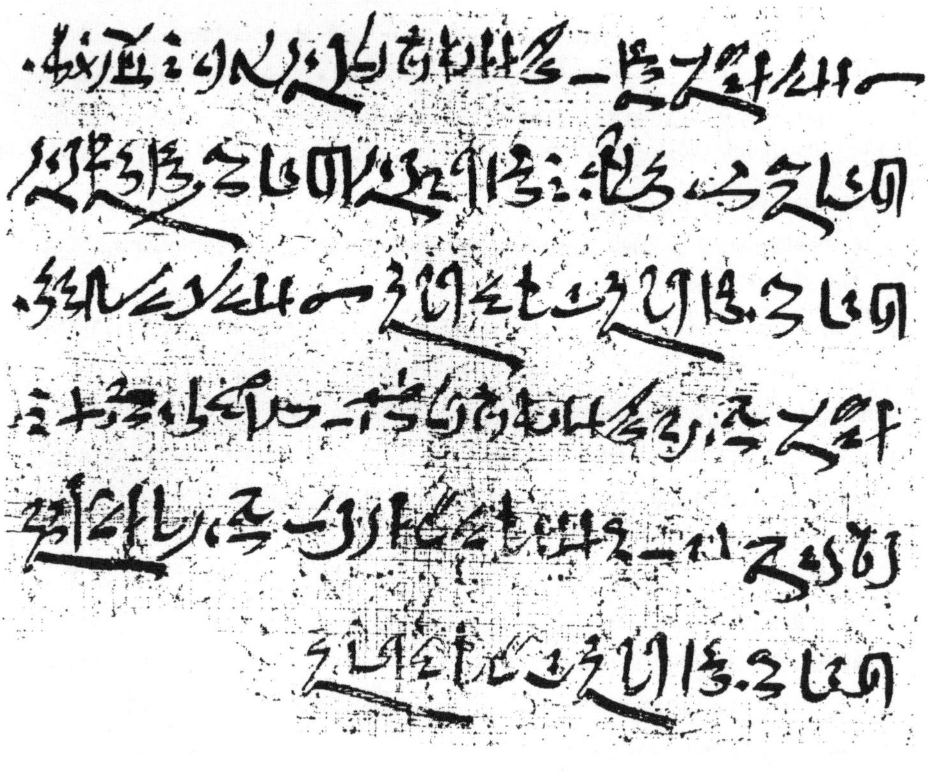

P. Northumberland I, v° 3-8 (*cf.* p. 110)

[77] P. Turin 1875, 3, 1 (= *KRI* v, 351, 6-7). Plain sentence: **iri.w pꜣw iryt nb*.

[78] Wenamun, 2, 30-31 (= *LES*, 70, 1-2). A sentence simply topicalised: **ḫr ir imn-rꜥ nsw nṯrw / pꜣ nb n pꜣ ꜥnḫ snb pꜣy* (the plain sentence is uncommon).

VERBAL SYSTEM

P. Adoption, v° II, 1-13 *(cf.* p. 82)

13. The infinitive

The infinitive is the nominal form of the verb, and is neutral with regard to the diathesis.[79]

13.1 Morphology[80]

Infinitives of verbs that were feminine in Middle Egyptian (3ae-*inf.*, caus. 2-*lit.*, *rdỉ*, *ỉw*, *ỉy*, *ỉnỉ*) generally retain the *t*. Sometimes a *t* is added without reason to the infinitives of verbs that were masculine in the classical stage of the language.

In the absolute[81] and the construct[82] state the 𓏏 *t* is placed before any determinative.

In the pronominal[83] state, the ending takes the form 𓏏𓏲 *tw*,[84] and is placed after the determinative. When combined with a suffix, the resulting morpheme is *tw.f*, which is at the origin of the 'new direct object pronoun' (see *supra* §7.3).

13.2 Syntax

Infinitives are almost always treated as masculine regardless of their class.[85]

The direct object of the infinitive, if there is one, and it is pronominal, is indicated by a suffix,[86] which tends to be replaced by the 'new direct object pronoun.'

The infinitive is negated with the negative verb *tm*.

If the agent of the process is expressed, it can be introduced by the preposition *ỉn* (see *infra* §13.4.1.2); it can correspond to the subject of the relative form of the verb *ỉrỉ*, if the infinitive is periphrased (see *infra* §13.3, 13.4.1.1, 13.4.2.1.1); or it can be expressed by a possessive (see *infra* §13.4.2.2.2).

Important remarks: verbs with four (4-*lit.*) or more radicals, have only the infinitive (and, possibly, the pseudo-participle), while in all other forms, these verbs are periphrased using the auxiliary *ỉrỉ*, which is conjugated in the correct form and is followed by the infinitive of the verbal expression.

13.3 Aspectual value

The infinitive takes the marked aspectual value of a **perfective** when it is periphrased using the perfective relative form of the verb *ỉrỉ*: *ỉ.ỉrỉ.f* or *ỉ.ỉrỉ N* (that sometimes is still found in its old form: *ỉr.n.f* or *ỉr.n N*). Otherwise, the infinitive has the unmarked value of an **imperfect**.

13.4 Usage

The infinitive is employed mainly in **grammaticalised verbal forms**, such as the first present, the third future, the second tense, the continuative forms, the negative aorist, and so on (see *infra*), and in some cleft sentences (see *infra* §42). Besides the abovementioned forms, it is also found in predicative and non-predicative usages.

---

79 Or 'voice' (active or passive).
80 See Winand, *Morphologie*, p. 90-101.
81 An infinitive not immediately followed by a direct object.
82 An infinitive followed by a nominal direct object.
83 An infinitive followed by a pronominal direct object.
84 Variant *tỉ*.
85 Rare exceptions: *h3b, ỉṯ3* ... they can be preceded by the article *t3*.
86 Rare exceptions in the 3rd person masculine; Gardiner, *EG*, §300.

13.4.1 Predicative usage

The infinitive can be employed as an independent narrative[87] form within the narrative framework. It is found in the perfective and the imperfect.

13.4.1.1 Perfective

The process, in which the agent is expressed by the subject of the relative form, is identified as perfective by the speaker.

P. Northumberland I, 2 *(cf.* p. 59)

1. O. Cairo 25530, 1-3 (= *KRI* V, 542, 10-11);[88] *cf.* example 1 above.

ḥsbt 29 ꜣbd 2 prt sw 10 hrw pn n ***sn ỉr.n tꜣ ỉst*** *tꜣ ỉnb*(*t*) *ḥr pꜣy.w dỉw*

'Year 29, second month of the winter season, day 10, this day when the wall was crossed[89] by the crew, because of its[90] rations' (*lit.* 'this day of crossing that the crew did (of) the wall ...'). Note the old relative form.

2. Wenamun, 1, 2 (= *LES*, 61, 3-5).

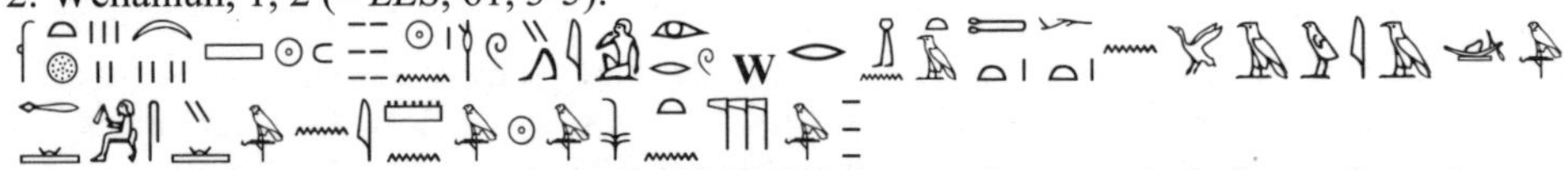

ḥsbt 5 ꜣbd 4 šmw sw 16 hrw (pn) n ***wḏ ỉ.ỉrỉ W*** *r ỉn tꜣ ṯt-ḫt n pꜣ wỉꜣ ꜥꜣ špsy n ỉmn-rꜥ nsw nṯrw*

'Year 5, fourth month of the summer season, day 16, (this) day when W set off to fetch the timber for the great and noble barque of Amun-Ra, king of the gods' (*lit.* 'this day of departing that W did ...'). The structure is as follows:[91]

Infinitive + *ỉr.n / ỉ.ỉrỉ* + agent [92] + (direct object pronoun) + (prepositional phrase)

[87] Gardiner, *EG*, §306, 2.

[88] Another example is found in a Graffito of year 47 of Ramses II (= *KRI* III, 148, 4-6).

[89] *sn* became *sš* following the confusion in hieratic between the signs , and on one hand, and on the other.

[90] *Lit.* 'their' agreeing, semantically, with the collective *ỉst* 'crew.'

[91] For the origin of this sentence see Gardiner, *EG*, §392: *sḏm pw ỉr.n.f.*

[92] Identical to the subject of the relative.

13.4.1.2 Imperfect

The speaker takes no position in the fulfilment of the process.

3. P. Turin 1880, 1, 1 (= *RAD*, 52, 14-15); *cf.* example 1 above.

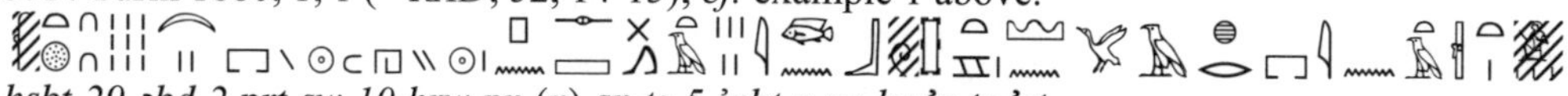

ḥsbt 29 ꜣbd 2 prt sw 10 hrw pn (*n*) ***sn** tꜣ 5 inbt n pꜣ ḫr **in tꜣ ist***

'Year 29, second month of the winter season, day 10, this day, (of) passing the five guard posts of the Tomb by the crew' (*lit.* 'this day (of) passing the five booths …').

4. Graffito of regnal year 34 of Ramses II, 3 (= *KRI* III, 436, 8-9).

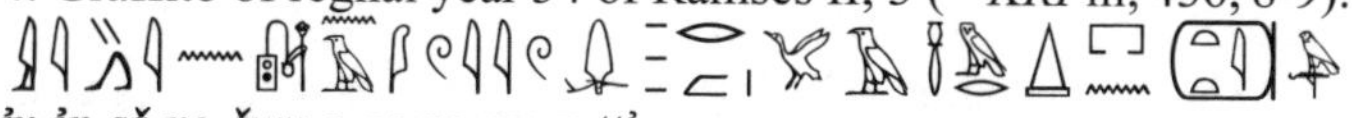

***iy in sš nꜣ-šwy** r-gs pꜣ mr n tti*

'Arrival of the scribe Neshuy near the pyramid of Teti' (*lit.* 'Coming by the scribe Neshuy ...').

The structure this time is:

Infinitive + (direct object pronoun) + *in* + agent + (prepositional phrase)

The agent can be unexpressed:

5. P. Turin 1880, 1, 5 (= *RAD*, 53, 2-3).[93]

***wrš** m st tn*

'Spending the day in this place.'

Remark. A clause having an infinitive as predicate can function as the direct object of a verb.

6. Qadesh Bulletin, 65-67 (= *KRI* II, 115, 9-14), Luxor text:

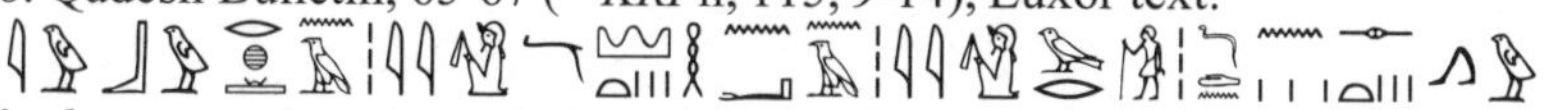

*iw bw rs nꜣy.i mr ḫꜣswt ḥnꜥ nꜣy.i wrw **ḏd n.n** st iw*

'Without that neither my chiefs of foreign countries nor my officials were able to say to us: "They have come."'

13.4.2 Non-predicative usage

13.4.2.1 Noun phrase

13.4.2.1.1 Perfective

The infinitive, defined by the article, is periphrased by the relative form of *iri* which subject denotes the agent of the process.[94]

[93] Another example is P. Mayer A, 3-6 (= *KRI* VI, 808, 15-16).

[94] If, which is very rare, the agent is unexpressed, the passive participle replaces the relative form. Example: P. Turin 1887, 1, 7 (= *RAD* 74, 15) *sḫꜣ r pꜣ ṯꜣwt i.iry*(*t*) *wꜥ wḏꜣ* 'Denunciation concerning the theft that was perpetrated of an udjat-eye.'

pꜣ sḏm i.iri.f   *pꜣ sḏm i.iri N*[95]

7. Abydos Osireion, Hieratic ostraca n. 2 (= *KRI* I, 128, 14).

ir pꜣ ḏd ir.n n.i pꜣ-nfr

'As for the statement that Panefer made to me ...' or 'As for what Panefer said to me …'
Note again the classical relative form.

8. P. DM VIII, 1 (= *KRI* VI, 671, 5).

ḥr ir pꜣ hꜣb i.iri.k ḥr tꜣ mdt n tꜣ mꜣst

'And, as for what you have written (*lit.* 'the sending which you did') concerning the matter of the maset[96]…'

9. P. DM IX, 3 (= *KRI* VI, 672, 8).

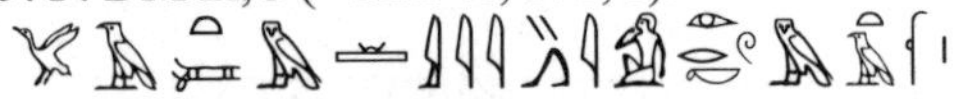

pꜣ tm iy i.iri.k *m tꜣ rnpt*

'The fact that you have not come this year' (*lit.* 'The not coming that you have done ...').

13.4.2.1.2 Imperfect

The infinitive is defined by the possessive adjective, which also denotes the agent of the process; there is no nominal agent:

pꜣy.f sḏm

10. O. DM 552, v° 1-2 (fig. p. 45).

ḥr ir ***pꜣy.k ḏd***

'And, as for what you say ...' (*lit.* And, as for your saying ...').

11. O. Ashmolean 1945-37, 15 (= *KRI* II, 381, 11-12).

yꜣ iḫ ***pꜣy.s wstn*** *pꜣ wḏꜣ n pr-ꜥꜣ ꜥ.w.s. m-ḫm.se*

'Well, what is the meaning of her striding freely the warehouse of Pharaoh l.p.h. without their knowledge?'[97] (*lit.* 'Now, what is her act of walking freely …?').

13.4.2.2 Prepositional phrase

The prepositions most often encountered are *r*, *ḥr*, *m*.

---

[95] Or *pꜣ sḏm ir.n.f*, *pꜣ sḏm ir.n N*, relative forms of the classical type.

[96] See Černý, *JEA* 31 (1945), 39.

[97] Unbeknownst to the officials of the warehouse.

12. Graffito of regnal year 47 of Ramses II, 1 (= *KRI* III, 148, 4-6).

ḥsbt 47 ꜣbd 2 prt sw 25 ỉy ỉr.n sš pr-ḥḏ hd-nḫt sꜣ swl mwt.f tꜣ-wsr(t) ***r swtwt sḏꜣy-ḥr*** *ḥr ỉmntt mn-nfr*

'Year 47, second month of the winter season, day 25, arrival of the treasury scribe Hednakht son of Sul, whose mother is Tawesert, to walk and enjoy himself in the west of Memphis' (*lit.* 'coming that the treasury scribe Hednakht did ... his mother is Tawesert …').

13. P. Turin 1887, 1, 13 (= *RAD*, 75, 12-13).

ỉw.tw (ḥr) dỉt n.f ꜥnḫ n nb ꜥ.w.s. ***r tm ꜥq*** *r ḥwt-nṯr*

'An oath by the Lord l.p.h. was imposed on him to not enter the temple.'

14. P. DM II, 1 (= *KRI* VI, 259, 13): statement heading.

r[98] ***dỉt*** *rḫ.tw pꜣ dỉw ỉ.dỉ.f n.ỉ*

'List of the rations that he gave to me' (*lit.* 'To cause that one knows the ration …').

15. P. Phillipps, v° 6-7 (= *LRL*, 30, 8-9).

ḥr bw ỉrỉ.ỉ nnỉ ***m ỉṯꜣ*** *n.f mw*

'And I never neglect to take water to him' (*lit.* 'And I am never negligent in bringing water to him').

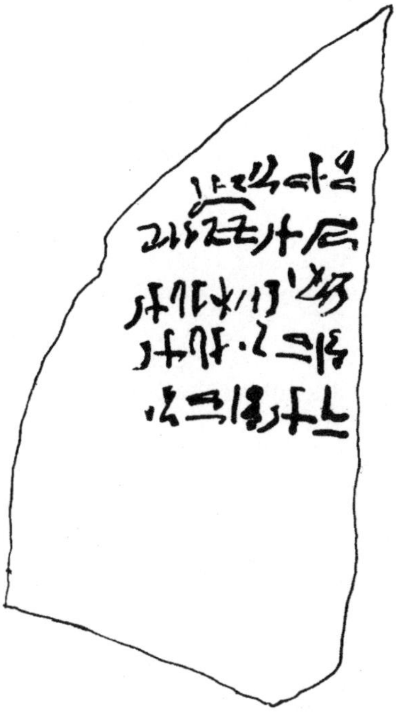

O. DM 552, v° *(cf.* p. 44)

[98] Read 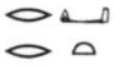.

14. The Pseudo-participle

The pseudo-participle[99] is the adverbial form of the verb.

14.1 Morphology[100]

In Late Egyptian the pseudo-participle is only used in sentences where it is always preceded by its subject. As a result, the endings are no longer pertinent, and tend to be simplified, or even disappear.

– Thus one goes from a system with five suffixes in use during the 19th dynasty: ***k*** (1st sg.); ***tw*** (2nd sg. and pl.); ***tỉ*** (3rd f. sg.); ***n*** (1st pl.); ***Ø*** (3rd m. sg. and pl.);

– to a system with three suffixes in the 20th dynasty: ***k*** (1st sg.); ***tw*** (1st pl. and 2nd sg. and pl.); ***Ø*** (3rd sg. and pl.);

– to a system with only two suffixes during the 21st dynasty: ***tw*** (1st and 2nd sg. and pl.); ***Ø*** (3rd sg. and pl.).

Table of suffixes and spellings

Singular	1st	***k*** 𓎡𓏲𓀀 or 𓎡[101], later ***t*** 𓏏𓏲 , (***Ø*** rare)
	2nd masc.	***t*** 𓏏𓏲 or 𓏏𓇋 (rare), (***Ø*** rare)
	2nd fem.	***t*** 𓏏𓏲
	3rd masc.	***Ø*** or ***y*** 𓇌 (3rd inf.), (***t*** 𓏏𓏲 very rare)
	3rd fem.	***t*** 𓏏𓇋 or 𓏏𓏲 , (***Ø*** rarer)
Plural	1st	***n*** 𓈖𓏥 or 𓏲𓈖𓏥 , later ***t*** 𓏏𓏲 or ***Ø***
	2nd	***t*** 𓏏𓏲 (or 𓏏𓇋), or ***Ø***
	3rd	***Ø*** or ***y*** 𓇌 (3rd inf.), (***t*** 𓏏𓏲 rare)

14.2 Values

The fundamental value of the pseudo-participle is that of a **resultative perfective**.

– In the case of **intransitive verbs**, it describes a durable **state**, resulting from the completion of a preceding process, and has full **resultative** value.[102]

▪ This nuance contrasts, in adjective verbs (*Fr.* verbes de qualité), with the stative value expressed by the adjectival construction. Thus: **sw nfr* 'it has become good; it has improved; it has been improved,' but **nfr sw* 'it is good' (intrinsically). In practice, the difference tends to disappear because the adjectival construction fell into disuse, being no longer used except with a very small number of adjectives.

---

[99] Also called 'old perfective, stative or qualitative.'

[100] See Winand, *o.l.*, p. 103-149, especially 123-124.

[101] The full form predominates in the 19th dynasty, while the short form is used mainly in the 20th.

[102] Except in a narrative context, see *infra* §16.6.2.

– In the case of **transitive verbs,**[103] it expresses a **passive perfective**.

▪ This is not a simple passive. The distinction is important in the case of verbs with a non-terminative *Aktionsart*:[104] 'he is questioned' is equivalent to 'he is being questioned' (**tw.tw ḥr smtr.f*) and does not have the same value as 'he has been questioned' (**sw smtr*). In other cases the nuance is barely perceptible: 'he is found' ≈ 'he has been found.'

14.3 Usage

The pseudo-participle is always employed in the context of the nominal sentence with adverbial predicate: **subject + pseudo-participle**.

14.3.1 With a proper subject, in grammaticalised verbal forms

The pseudo-participle can be employed as predicate in the first present or the third future.[105] In these sentences it always has a proper subject. See *infra* §16.6 and §19.4.

14.3.2 With a subject already playing a role in a preceding clause

Examples are quite frequent after 'operator' verbs,[106] such as *gmỉ* 'find' (see *infra* §32.5), and the semi-auxiliaries: *ꜥḥꜥ, ḥmsỉ, sḏr, ḫpr*.[107]

1. P. Leopold-Amherst, 2, 9-10 (= *KRI* VI, 484, 5-6).

*ỉw.n (ḥr) gm **pꜣy nṯr sḏr** m pḥ tꜣy.f st qrs*

'We found this god lying (*lit.* 'being stretched out') at the back of his grave.' In this example ***pꜣy nṯr*** is both direct object of *gmỉ* and subject of *sḏr*.

2. P. Mayer A, 3, 17 (= *KRI* VI, 809, 16).

***sw** gmy **wꜥb** ḥr nꜣ ỉṯꜣw dd.tw n.f ṯꜣw*

'He was found innocent concerning the thieves, (and) he was freed' (*lit.* 'He was found pure[108]... one gave him the air'). Here *sw* is both subject of *gmy* (first present) and then of *wꜥb*.

3. P. Pushkin 127, 4, 12-13.[109]

*dỉ.f ꜥḥꜥ.ỉ **šww.tỉ** (m) nꜣy.ỉ šsy*

'He caused that I found myself deprived of my grain (*lit.* grains)' (*lit.* 'that I stood being deprived ...'). The suffix *.ỉ* is the subject of both the semi-auxiliary *ꜥḥꜥ* in the independent prospective *sḏm.f* form, and of *šww.tỉ*.

---

[103] An exception is the verb *rḫ* 'learn, seek to know' which pseudo-participle retains, as in Middle Egyptian, an active value: *rḫ sw* 'he knows' (= he achieved seeking knowledge).

[104] Do not confuse the **Aktionsart**, which is part of the semantic (internal) value of the verb, for example: *search* (Aktionsart non-terminative) ≠ *find* (Aktionsart terminative), and the **aspect**, which is a value conferred by particular grammatical markings (external).

[105] And their derivates obtained using the past converter *wn* or the circumstantial *ỉw*.

[106] Verbs that can introduce a complement clause. Verbes «opérateurs» in French. See Vernus, *Orientalia* 50 (1981), 432-433 and n. 10.

[107] On these verbs see Krutchen, *Études de syntaxe néo-égyptienne,* 1982, p. 43-44 and 69-71.

[108] *Cf.* the French expression 'lavé de tout soupçon' (= 'cleared of all charges').

[109] Another example with *ḫpr*: P. BM 10403, 3, 5-6 (= *KRI* VI, 831, 11-12).

4. P. Orbiney, 2, 1-2 (= *LES*, 10, 15-16).

*ꞽw **nꜣ ꞽḥw(t)** nty r-ḥꜣt.f ḥr ḫpr **nfr** r-ꞽqr sp-sn*

'The cows that were under his responsibility became extremely fine.' ***nꜣ ꞽḥw(t)*** is both the subject of the sequential *ḥr ḫpr* and of *nfr*.

5. Truth and Falsehood, 4, 5 (= *LES*, 32, 6).

ꞽw.s (ḥr) ꜥḥꜥ ***ꞽwr.tꞽ*** *‹m› pꜣy grḥ m wꜥ ꜥḏd šrꞽ*

'She became pregnant that night with a child.' Here again the subject *.s* of the sequential is also the subject of the pseudo-participle *ꞽwr.tꞽ*.

6. O. Nash 2, v° 8-9 (= *KRI* IV, 319, 8-9).

ꞽw.ꞽ ꜣꜥꜥ.k(wꞽ) ***m pꜣy.ꞽ pr ḏd*** *r pr-ꜥꜣ ꜥ.w.s.*

'I will have become a stranger[110] in my house (it being) given[111] to Pharaoh l.p.h.' In the latter example, it is a noun phrase, which forms part of the adverbial complement of the preceding clause, which functions as subject of the pseudo-participle.

14.4 Remarks

Some verbs are not attested in the pseudo-participle and appear not to have had this form. The following are some examples of these verbs:

swr	drink	*ptr*	see	*mrꞽ*	love, desire
wnm	eat	*sḏm*	hear	*wḫꜣ*	seek
ḏd	say	*ꜥmꜣ*	learn	*qn*	achieve
mdw	speak	*sṯnꞽ*	distinguish	*rmꞽ*	cry

[110] Third Future with a pseudo-participle as predicate; *cf. infra* §19.4.

[111] *ḏd* is a well attested spelling of the pseudo-participle of *rdꞽ* in the 3rd person masculine singular. On the other hand, examples of the passive participle with the same spelling are not known from the 19th dynasty. See Winand, *o.l.*, p. 149 and 370, who, unfortunately, does not discuss the passage. It should be understood that the house will be forfeited to the State.

INDEPENDENT VERBAL FORMS

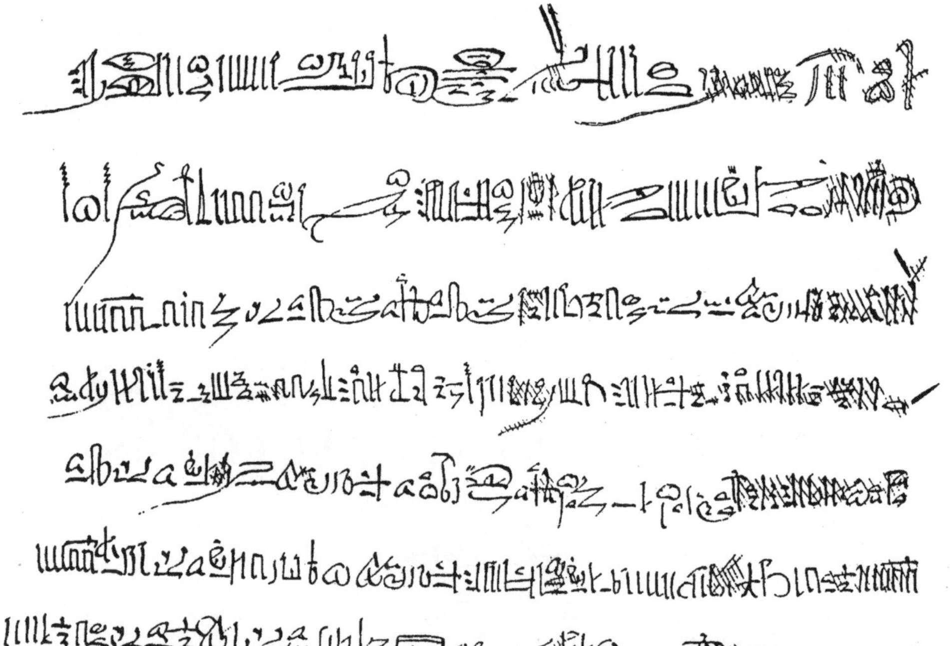

P. Abbott 1

15. The perfective *sḏm.f*

15.1 The active perfective *sḏm.f*

The use of this form is limited to transitive verbs, and expresses the **past**. It derives from the *iw sḏm.n.f* form of Middle Egyptian.

▪ By transitive verb is to be understood verbs that can have a direct object. It is possible, though, to encounter the perfective *sḏm.f* employed 'intransitively,' that is, without direct object.

15.1.1 Usage

The *sḏm.f* perfective is found both in the discourse, either in a narrative context or not, and in the narrative. In a narrative context, it allows one to describe events in the past in an **objective** and **punctual** manner.

▪ Given that the perfective *sḏm.f* is morphologically similar to the prospective *sḏm.f*, both possibilities should be considered whenever an independent *sḏm.f* form is encountered in a discourse context.

1. P. Gardiner 4, 5-6 (= *KRI* VII, 339, 8-9): letters, discourse, non-narrative context.

*ptr **hꜣb** n.ỉ **pꜣ ḥm-nṯr n ḥwt-ḥr** r-ḏd my r šsp se*

'See, the prophet of Hathor has written to me saying: "Come to take them"' (*lit.* 'to receive them').

2. P. Bologna 1086, 20-21 (= *KRI* IV, 81, 1-2): letter, discourse, non-narrative context.

*m dy ḥꜣty.k m-sꜣ pꜣ ṯs-prt **ỉrỉ.ỉ** smtr.f **gm.ỉ** s 3 mnḥ 1 dmḏ 4 ỉr.n ḫꜣr 700 **mdw.ỉ** m-dỉ nꜣ ḥryw sꜣw sšw n tꜣ šnwt*

'Do not worry about the seed-sowing form, I have examined it. I have found three men and a helper, total: 4, which makes 700 bags. I have reprimanded the chief archivists of the granary.' Note the periphrasis of the verb *smtr* (*4 lit.*) using the auxiliary *ỉrỉ* (see *supra* §13.2, Remark).

3. P. DM XVIII, 6 (= *KRI* VII, 384, 3-4): letter, discourse, non-narrative context.

***ỉrỉ.ỉ** ỉḫ r.ṯ*

'What have I done against you?'

4. P. BM 10052, 7, 5-7 (= *KRI* VI, 784, 4-8): official report, narrative and discourse.

ỉr.Ø smtr.f *m bdn* ***ḏd.tw*** *n.f ỉ.ḏd p3 sḫr (n) p3 ḥḏ ỉ.ptr.k m-dỉ p3(y) nb twt* ***ḏd.f ptr.ỉ*** *nhy n ḥḏ m-dỉ.f ỉw.w ‹m› wmt n ṯ(3)bw n ḥmt ỉw b(w)p(w)y.ỉ dgs t3y st m rdwy.ỉ*

'(He) was questioned with a staff. They said to him: "Relay (*lit.* 'say') the aspect of this silver that you saw in the possession of this master of yours." He said: "I saw in his possession some silver (objects) that were the size (*lit.* 'thickness') of vases[112] in copper, although I did not soil this place with my feet.'[113]

During the 19th dynasty it is still possible to find rare vestiges of the *sḏm.n.f* form:

5. P. Anastasi IX, 1-2 (= *KRI* III, 505, 3-4): letter, discourse, non-narrative context.

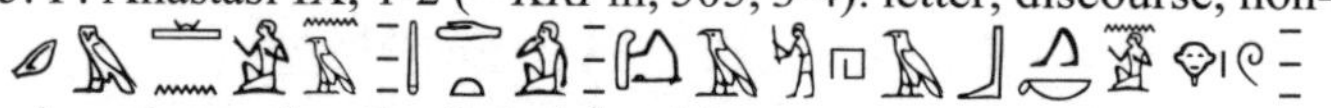

sḏm.n.ỉ *n3 mdwt ꜥḥ3 (ỉ).h3b.k n.ỉ ḥr.w*

'I have learnt of the litigation cases about which you have written to me' (*lit.* 'I heard of the litigation matters about which you have sent to me').

Remark: intransitive verbs can, sometimes, have a *sḏm.f* with a past meaning. This represents a Second Tense deriving from the 'emphatic' *sḏm.n.f* of the classical language.[114] See *infra* §23.6.

15.1.2 Negation

The perfective *sḏm.f* is negated with the *bwpwy.f sḏm* form.

15.1.2.1 Origin

The *bwpwy.f sḏm* form derives from Middle Egyptian *n p3.f sḏm*;[115] which is the ancestor of Coptic **ⲘⲠϤⲤⲰⲦⲘ̄**:

***n p3.f sḏm* ► *bwpwy.f sḏm* ► ⲘⲠϤⲤⲰⲦⲘ̄**

15.1.2.2 Morphology

– current spellings: 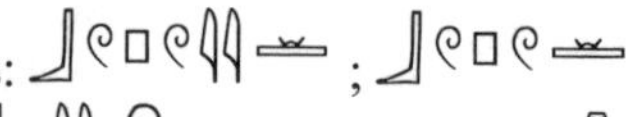

– late spellings:  ; rare spellings:[116] 

112 Perhaps 'cups;' see Janssen, *CP*, p. 433-434.

113 That is: 'Although I have not set foot in this tomb.'

114 Groll, *JNES* 28 (1965), 189; Winand, *Morphologie*, p. 261-264.

115 Where the auxiliary *p3* 'to come into being for the first time,' an indicative *sḏm.f*, is followed by the infinitive of the auxiliary. Grandet-Mathieu, *Cours d'égyptien hiéroglyphique*, II, §37.4, p. 76.

116 P. Bulaq X, 7.

15.1.2.3 Usage

As negative correlate of the active perfective *sḏm.f*.

6. P. Turin 2026, v° 1 (= *LRL*, 73, 7): letter, discourse, non-narrative context.

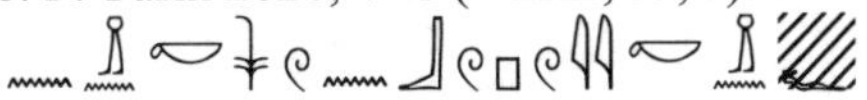

(ỉ)n ỉn.k se (ỉ)n ***bwpwy.k ỉn.***[*f*]

'Have you brought him (or) have you not brought him?'

7. Wenamun, 1, 22 (= *LES*, 63, 4-5): discourse, non-narrative context.

mk ***bwpw.k gm*** *pꜣy.ỉ ḥḏ*

'See, you have not found my silver.'

An example with a nominal subject:

8. P. Abbott, 2, 15 (= *KRI* VI, 470, 15-16): narrative.

bwpw nꜣ ỉṯꜣw rḫ *pḥ.f*

'The thieves were not able to reach it.'

Remarks

1. The use of the *bwpwy.f sḏm* form is not limited to the negation of the past of transitive verbs, it is also used as negative correlate of the 'passive' perfective *sḏm.f* (see below) and of the forms of the first present expressing the past of intransitive verbs (see *infra* §16.6.2.1) .
2. There is also another, infrequent, negation of the perfective *sḏm.f*, the *bw sḏm.f* form, which is the new spelling of *n sḏm.f*, the negative correlate of the traditional *ỉw sḏm.n.f*. The paucity of occurrences of this form to negate the perfective is probably due to the risk of confusion between this and another morphologically similar form, the *bw sḏm.f* form, which represents a stage in the evolution of the negative aorist *n sḏm.n.f* (see *infra* §17).

15.2 The perfective *sḏm.f* called 'passive'

15.2.1 Affirmative forms

It derives from Middle Egyptian 'passive' *ỉw sḏm.f*. In Late Egyptian, it is employed only with a limited number of verbs. The following are the most frequent, shown here with their more common spellings: *ỉrỉ*  ; *rdỉ*  ; *ỉnỉ*  ; *gmỉ*  .

▪ The relative rarity of this form is due to the fact that it competed with the active form with an impersonal subject *sḏm.tw* + noun (not to be confused with the second tense passive *sḏm.tw.f*), and later with the active *sḏm.w* with the third person plural as subject.[117]

It is in reality, just like its ancestor, an active form with an unexpressed subject (zero subject).

When, as in almost all cases, the patient of the process is nominal, it can be interpreted (or

[117] *Cf.* the English usage to express the neuter: *they say*, French 'on dit.'

perceived) as the subject of a passive form, or the direct object of an active form with zero subject.

9. P. Turin 1875, 6, 2 (= *KRI* V, 360, 3-4): narrative.

ḥrw ꜥꜣ pꜣy-bs (ỉ).wn m wdpw ***ỉrw.Ø*** *n.f* ***tꜣy sbꜣyt*** *ỉw.tw (ḥr) wꜣḥ.f ỉw.f (ḥr) mtw n.f ḏs.f*
'The great enemy Paybes, who had been cup-bearer, this punishment was applied to him: one is to leave him (and) he is to (cause) death to himself.' In this example, *tꜣy sbꜣyt* could be considered as the subject of a passive, or the direct object of an active form with Ø subjet, but note that the text continues with an active construction, not a passive one, which would be **sw wꜣḥ*.

Parallel examples:

11. P. BM 10052, 4, 22 (= *KRI* VI, 777, 15-16): narrative.

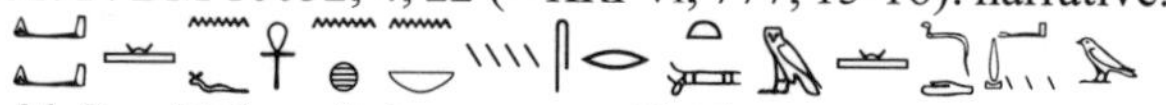

ḏd.Ø *n.f* ***ꜥnḫ n nb*** *ꜥ.w.s. r tm ḏd ꜥḏꜣ*
'An oath by the lord l.p.h. was imposed on him not to lie.'

11. P. Abbott, 7, 13-14 (= *KRI* VI, 481, 4-5) (fig. p. 245): narrative; *cf.* example 17.

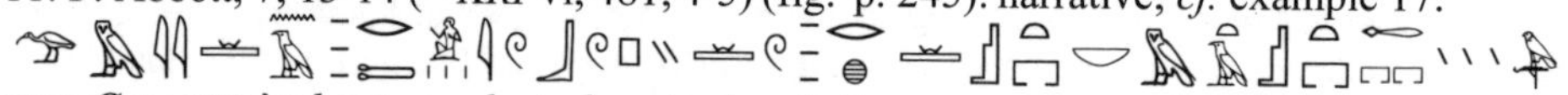

gmy.Ø nꜣ rmṯ *ỉw bwpw.w rḫ st nb m tꜣ st pr-ꜥꜣ ꜥ.w.s.*
'It was found that the people did not know of any tombs in the necropolis of Pharaoh l.p.h.' (*lit.* 'people were found, though they knew not ...').

However, if the patient of the process is pronominal (which rarely happens), and the form is not periphrased, a dependent rather than a suffix pronoun is used. Consequently, this is an active construction.

12. P. Turin 1880, 2, 17 (= *RAD*, 55, 13-14): discourse, non-narrative context.

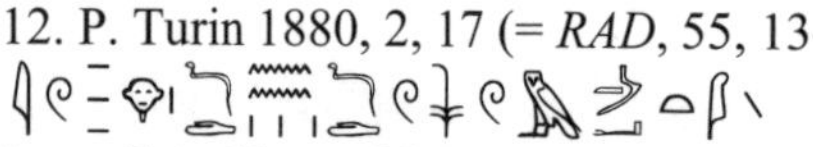

ỉw.w (ḥr) ḏd n.n ***ḏd.Ø*** *se m mꜣꜥt*
'They told us: "It was said in truth."'

13. O. DM 554, v° 3-4 (fig. p. 103): discourse, narrative context.

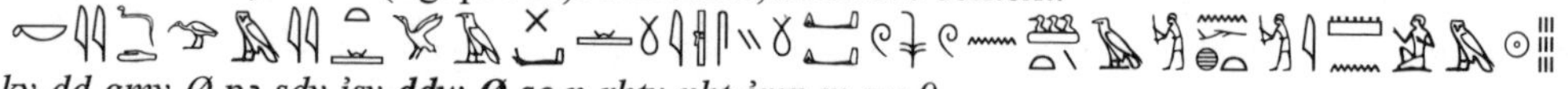

ky ḏd gmy.Ø pꜣ sḏy ỉsy ***ddw.Ø se*** *n rḫty nḫt-ỉmn m sw 9*
'Another thing: the used loincloth was found (and) it was given to the washerman Nakhtamun on day 9.'

If the form is periphrased (in the case of *4 lit.* verbs) the pronominal patient is represented by a suffix attached to the infinitive, as is the norm with a direct object, and not to the auxiliary, as it would have been the case if the patient had been the subject of a passive syntagma.

14. P. Leopold-Amherst, 3, 16 (= *KRI* VI, 487, 6): narrative.

ỉr.Ø smtr.w

'One questioned them.' Periphrased active form with zero subject, improperly called 'passive,' where *.w* is the direct object.

Compare with example 4 above, and with the following:

15. P. Mayer A, v° 9, 10-11 (= *KRI* VI, 821, 1-2): narrative.

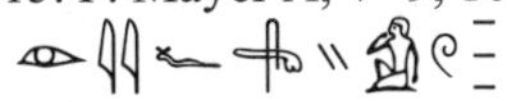

ỉr.f smtr.w

'He questioned them.' Periphrased, active form with expressed subject *.f*, and which also has *.w* as direct object.

▪ The real passive form employs the first present with a pseudo-participle as predicate: *sw smtr* 'he was questioned' (P. BM 10052, 10, 9 = *KRI* VI, 789, 12), see *infra* §16.6.1. It is also the construction more frequently used when the patient of the process is pronominal.

▪ In principle, one would not expect to find examples of the passive perfective *sḏm.f* with a suffixal subject. A few cases have been identified, but they are all debatable.[118]

15.2.2 Negation

There is no special form, instead, the forms *bwpwy.tw sḏm*[119] with an impersonal subject, or *bwpwy.Ø sḏm* with zero subject, are used, which are also employed as negation of the first present with a pseudo-participle as predicate, and of the active perfective *sḏm.tw* + noun.

Example with nominal patient:

16. Doomed Prince, 4, 1 (= *LES*, 1, 1-2): narrative.

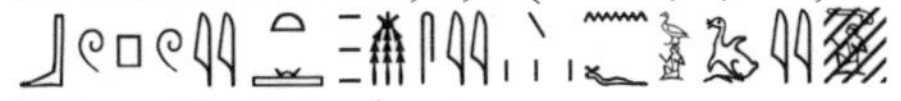

***bwpwy.Ø msy** n.f sꜣ ṯꜣy*

'No male son had been born to him' (*lit.* 'One had not given birth to a male son for him').

Example with pronominal patient:

17. P. Abbott, 5, 5-6 (= *KRI* VI, 475, 4-5) (fig. p. 216): narrative; *cf.* example 11.

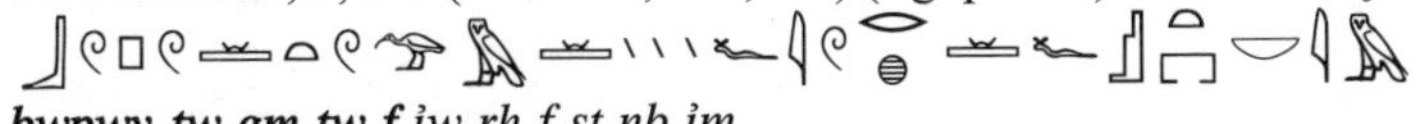

***bwpwy.tw gm.tw.f** ỉw rḫ.f st nb ỉm*

'It was not found (out) that he had known of any tomb there' (*lit.* 'One did not find that he knew of any tomb there'). This example can also be interpreted as negation of the first present:[120] **sw gmy ỉw rḫ.f st nb ỉm*.

[118] See Winand, *o.l.*, p. 306; Satzinger, *NÄS*, §2.3.10.2.2, n. 2, p. 294; Wente *LRL*, p. 77, n. b. Add to the dismissed examples: P. Bologna 1086, 26-27, where it is very probably a second tense (successor of Middle Egyptian *sḏm.n.tw.f*) and which is undoubtedly to be read *dd.(tw).f*.

[119] And other rarer variants, see Winand, *o.l.*, p. 308.

[120] In this papyrus there are seven examples of *sw gmy* against one anomalous *gmỉ.f*; see Winand, *o.l.*, example 718, p. 306.

16. The First Present

16.1 Introduction

The first present is a bipartite construction based on the model of the nominal sentence with adverbial predicate, also called 'location predication' (= location sentence).

rˁ (subject) ***im*** (predicate)

16.1.1 Subject

The subject, or first member, can be a noun (or noun equivalent), most often defined,[121] or a special type of pronoun used only in this construction:

Proclitic pronouns of the first present

Singular	1st	***tw.i***	
	2nd masc.	***tw.k***	
	2nd fem.	***tw.ṯw***	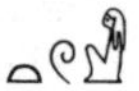
	3rd masc.	***sw***	
	3rd fem.	***st***	
Plural	1st	***tw.n***	, rarely 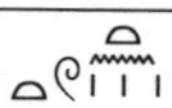
	2nd	***tw.tn***	
	3rd	***st***	, very rarely 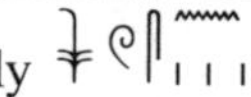
Impersonal		***tw.tw***	, or 

▪ Beware of the confusion between the pronouns of the third person singular and plural, all pronounced *se*, and to the double value, *tw.i* and *tw.ṯ*, of .

When the converters *iw* (circumnstantial) and *wn* (past) are employed, they are combined with the suffixes and not with the proclitic pronouns: *iw.f* ; *wn.k* 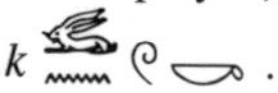.

16.1.2 Predicate

The predicate, or second member, consists of an adverbial phrase that can be:

- an **adverb**,
- a **prepositional phrase** (preposition + noun or pronoun),
- ***ḥr*** **+ infinitive**,
- ***m*** **+ infinitive** (verbs of motion only),

[121] The exceptions are rare: for *wˁ* A a few examples are known. However, *Ø* A is not attested apart from Middle Egyptian aphorisms inserted in Late Egyptian texts (*cf.* 'A rolling stone gathers no moss'). See in the latter instance Winand, *CdE* 64 (1989), 159-171.

– a **pseudo-participle** (some verbs do not have one).

16.2 The predicate is an adverb

The syntagma describes a situation contemporary to the statement (non-narrative passages), or to the events narrated (narrative passages). The use of the converter *wn* indicates a time prior to the point of reference.

sw ỉm

1. Qadesh Bulletin, 27 (= *KRI* II, 108, 6-9): narrative.
'Now, the Hittite enemy had come with all the chiefs of all foreign countries,
 *ỉw n rḫ ḥm.f r-ḏd* ***st ỉm***
without his majesty knowing that they were there' (*lit.* 'without that his majesty knew "they are there"'). In this narrative the point of reference is the time when the events unfolded.

Interrogative example:

2. Qadesh Bulletin, 12 (= *KRI* II, 105, 2): non-narrative passage.

ḏd.ỉn ḥm.f n.sn ***st tnw*** *nꜣy.tn snw*
'Then his majesty said to them: "Where are they, your brothers?"'

Example with the converter *wn*:

3. P. Mayer A, 2, 12 (= *KRI* VI, 807, 6-7): non-narrative passage.

ḏd.f ***wn pꜣy.ỉ ỉt ỉm*** *n(=m) mꜣꜥt*
'He said: "My father was there, in truth."'

Sometimes the adverbial predicate shares its subject with one or more other predicates (*ḥr* + infinitive, pseudo-participle, prepositional phrase).

4. P. Northumberland I, v° 1 (= *KRI* I, 239, 15): non-narrative passage.
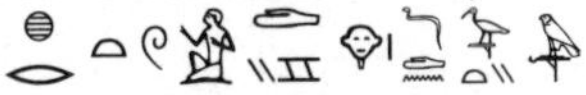
ḫr ***tw.ỉ dy ḥr ḏd*** *n ḏḥwty*
'And I am here, saying to Thoth.'

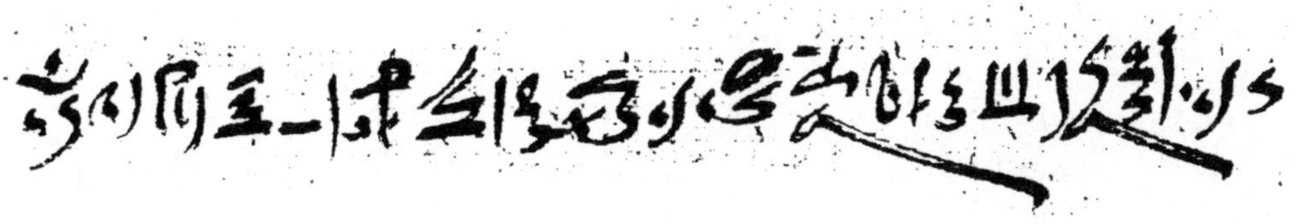

P. Northumberland I, v° 1

5. P. Berlin 10494, 6 (= *LRL*, 23, 11).

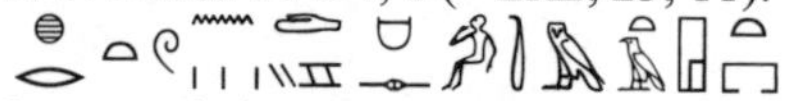

***ḥr tw.n dy ḥms.tỉ** m tꜣ ḥwt*

‘And we are here, installed in the temple.’

The construction is **negated** using the negative morpheme *bn*:

bn sw ỉm

6. P. DM VIII, 3 (= *KRI* VI, 671, 7).

***bn nꜣy.k ỉryw ỉm** r-ḏr.w*

‘Your companions are not all there’ (*lit.* ‘they are not in their totality’).

▪ In the negative form the adverb is frequently implied, the predication is thus taken on by *bn*[122] alone (see *infra* §22.3).

7. Wenamun, 2, 27-28 (= *LES*, 69, 12-13).

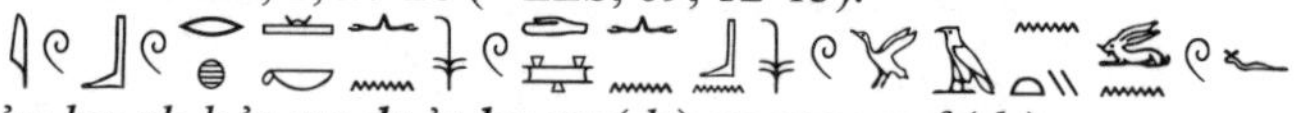

*ỉw bw rḫ.k ỉn **sw dy** ỉn **bn sw** (dy) pꜣ nty wn.f (dy)*

‘Without your knowing whether he was here, or if (he) was not (here), the one who had been (present)’ (*lit.* ‘without that you tried to know: is he here? Is he not (here) the one who had been (here)?’ – but who is no longer here).

16.3 The predicate is a prepositional phrase

The construction has the same values as before.

sw m pꜣ pr ***sw ỉm.f***

8. P. Cairo 58057, 7 (= *KRI* I, 238, 12).

pꜣ ʿꜣ m-dỉ.ỉ

‘The donkey is in my possession.’

9. Graffito of regnal year 34 of Ramses II, 4 (= *KRI* III, 436, 11).

tw.ỉ r-gs.tn

‘I am at your (pl.) side.’

10. Qadesh Bulletin, 14 (= *KRI* II, 105, 3-4): response to example 2 above.

st m pꜣ nty pꜣ wr ẖsỉ n ḫtꜣ ỉm

‘They are there where the wretched chief of Hatti is’ (*lit.* ‘in the (place) that the wretched chief of Hatti is in’).

---

[122] See Vernus, *RdE* 36 (1985), 153-168.

Note the two embedded first present constructions, one with a prepositional phrase as predicate (*m pꜣ* A, with A = *nty pꜣ wr ẖsỉ n ḫtꜣ ỉm*), the other, relativised by *nty*, with the adverb *ỉm* (*pꜣ wr ẖsỉ n ḫtꜣ ỉm*).

Examples with the converter *wn*:

11. P. Abbott, 4, 16 (= *KRI* VI, 474, 8-9) (fig. p. 106).

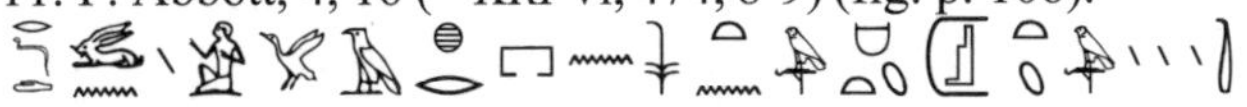

r-ḏd wn.ỉ m pꜣ ḫr n ḥmt nsw ꜣst ꜥ.w.s.

'Saying: "I was in the tomb of the royal wife Isis l.p.h."'

12. P. BM 10052, 2, 1 (= *KRI* VI, 769, 11-12).

r-ḏd wn.w m tꜣy.f ṯt ỉṯꜣw

'Saying: "They were in his group of thieves."'

Interrogative example:

13. P. Northumberland I, 2 (= *KRI* I, 239, 4) (fig. p. 42).

***tw.k mỉ ỉḫ** sp-sn sp-sn*

'How are you then?' (*lit.* 'You are like what?').

The construction is **negated** with the discontinuous negative morpheme(s) *bn…(ỉwnꜣ)*:

bn sw m pꜣ pr (ỉwnꜣ) ***bn sw ỉm.f (ỉwnꜣ)***

14. P. Leiden I, 369, v° 4 (= *LRL*, 2, 8).

*ḥr **bn** tw.ỉ m pꜣy.ỉ sḫr **ỉwnꜣ***

'Because I am not in my (normal) condition.'

Example with *wn*:

15. P. Mayer A, 3, 28 (= *KRI* VI, 810, 13).

bn wn.f** ỉrm.ỉ **ỉwnꜣ

'He was not with me.'

16.4 The predicate is the *ḥr* + infinitive form

This form is always found in a non-narrative context where it can convey multiple values:[123]

---

[123] With the exception of the verbs of motion, which use a specific construction to express the immediate present: first present with *m* + infinitive as predicate.

a. immediate present. It can be 'synchronic' – the event is simply presented as (almost) concomitant to the time of the statement: '(Come) to the table, we eat;' or 'unmarked' (progressive), the event is presented in the process of realisation: 'One is eating;'

b. habitual present (consuetudinal present or iterative) – the syntagma describes the repetition of the process without any specific temporal reference: 'One eats three times a day;'

c. general present (or gnomic) – the event is described in general terms, in its universality, without any temporal reference: 'One eats to live.'[124]

sw ḥr sḏm

Over time, and with increasing frequency, the preposition *ḥr* is omitted. In this case it should be inserted in brackets.

16.4.1 The immediate present

16. O. DM 607, 2.

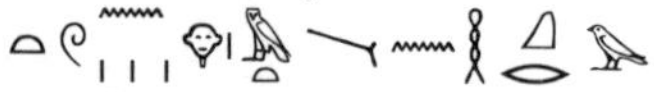

***tw.n ḥr** mwt n ḥqr*

'We are dying of hunger.' Unmarked present.

17. O. OIC 16991, 11- v° 3 (= *KRI* V, 560, 3-5).[125]

***tw.ỉ ḥr b3k** m n3 ḥrw n msw nsw r(=ỉ).sḥn p3y.ỉ nb r ỉrt.w*

'I am working on the tombs of the royal children that my master has commanded to make' (*lit.* 'that my master has given orders to make them'). Unmarked present.

18. O. Berlin P 11247, v° 7 (= *KRI* III, 533, 8).

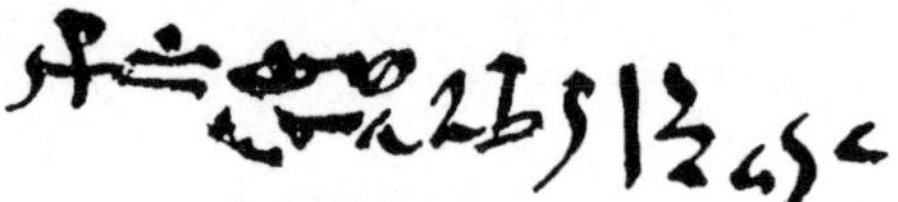

O. Berlin P 11247, v° 7

***tw.ỉ ḥr wḫ3** ỉrty.ỉ nn se*

'I am looking for my eyes (but) they are no longer (there)!' Unmarked present.

19. P. Cairo J 65739, 6 (= *KRI* II, 800, 11).[126]

*ḥr ptr **tw.ỉ ḥr ḏd** t3 swnt ỉ.dỉ.ỉ r.s m-b3ḥ n3 srw*

'And see, I state the price I paid for her before the officials.'[127] Synchronic present.

[124] The last two values are sometimes grouped under the term **aorist**.
[125] Parallel example: P. DM IX, 4-5 (= *KRI* VI, 672, 9).
[126] Parallel example: P. Anastasi V, 22, 7-8 (= *LEM*, 69, 1-2).
[127] There follows a list of objects representing the price of the slave.

20. P. Turin 2021, 2, 11-12 (= *KRI* VI, 740, 5-7).

tw.ỉ* (*ḥr*) *dỉt *pꜣ ỉrỉ.‹ỉ› nb ỉrm ꜥnḫ nw nỉwt ỉnk-se-nḏm tꜣ st-ḥmt nty m pꜣy.ỉ pr n.s m pꜣ hrw*
'I bequeath, on this day, all that I have acquired together with the lady Ineksenedjem, the woman who lives with me, to her' (*lit.* 'I give everything that I have made with the citizen Ineksenedjem, the woman who is in my house, to her, on this day'). Synchronic present.

16.4.2 The habitual present

21. P. Cairo 58057, 8 (= *KRI* I, 238, 14-15).

ḫr ***tw.tw ḥr šd*** *bꜣkw.f m-dỉ.ỉ rnpt n rnpt*
'And one exacts from me its work (from) year to year.'

22. P. Leiden I 366, 2-3 (= *KRI* II, 910, 11-12).

tw.ỉ ḥr ḏd *n pꜣ-rꜥ-ḥr-ꜣḫty m pꜣy.f wbn m pꜣy.f ḥtp*
'I say to Pre-Horakhty, at his rising, at his setting ...'

The use of the past converter *wn* allows one to describe past habitual events that are no longer occurring at the time of the statement.

23. P. Turin 1887, v° 3-7 (= *RAD*, 82, 3).

ḫr ***wn.f* (*ḥr*) *ỉr*(*t*).*f*** *m-dwn sp-sn*
'And he was doing it very often.'

24. Wenamun, 2, 28-29 (= *LES*, 69, 14-15).

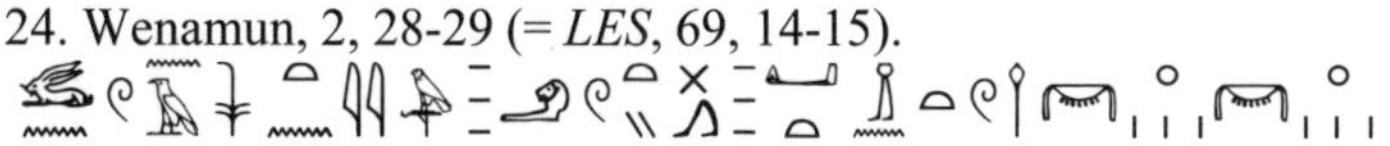

wn nꜣ nsyw ḥꜣwtyw* (*ḥr*) *dỉt *ỉn.tw ḥḏ nbw*
'Former kings had silver and gold brought.'

16.4.3 The general present (examples are rare)

25. P. Turin 2021, 3, 4 (= *KRI* VI, 740, 13-14): legal deed.

ḫr ***pr-ꜥꜣ ꜥ.w.s.* (*ḥr*) *ḏd*** *ỉmỉ sfr n stn b*(*t*) *n.s*
'But Pharaoh l.p.h. said: "Give each woman her *sefer*"' (*lit.* 'the *sefer* of each woman to her').

16.4.4 Negation

The construction is negated with *bn*. This, contrary to what is stated in some grammars,[128] can

[128] Černý-Groll, *LEG*, §20.1, p. 303-304.

negate both the immediate present (unmarked or synchronic), and the habitual, or general, present:

bn sw ḥr sḏm

26. O. Ashmolean Museum 1945-37 + 1945-33, 13-14 (= *KRI* II, 381, 10).

ḥr tw.tw m-sꜣ.s m-rꜥ ***bn tw.tw ḥr ḫꜣꜥ.s***

'And one is always in her pursuit (lit. 'after her'), one does not leave her.' Unmarked present.

27. O. OIC 16991, v° 4-7 (= *KRI* V, 560, 6-7).

m dy di͗t pꜣy.i͗ nb ḥꜣty.f m-sꜣ.w yꜣ tw.i͗ ḥr bꜣk r-i͗qr sp-sn ***bn tw.i͗ ḥr nni͗*** *m-kfꜣ sp-sn*

'Do not let my lord be concerned (*lit.* 'put his heart after') about them (= the tombs), for I am working very, very well, and I am not going to be idle at all.' Note the use of the two forms of the unmarked present, affirmative first and then negative.

28. P. Bologna 1094, 2, 4-5 (= *LEM,* 2, 13-14): prayer to Amun, the vizier of the poor.

bn sw ḥr šsp *{ḥr} fqꜣw n ꜥḏꜣw* ***bn sw ḥr ḏd*** *{n} i͗n mtrt* ***bn sw ḥr nw*** *r šꜥr*

'He does not accept a wine-jar from the guilty, he does not say: "Bring evidence," and he does not take into account the pressures.' Negation of habitual activities.

29. P. Anastasi III, v° 3, 2-3 (= *LEM,* 30, 16-31, 1).

st ḥr i͗rt tꜣy.sn i͗pt (n) dbt m-mnt ***bn tw.i͗ ḥr nni͗*** *m bꜣkw m pꜣ pr n mꜣwt*

'They are making their quota of bricks daily, and I am not negligent with regard to the work in the new house.' Description of habitual activities, with two syntagmas, one affirmative and the other negative.[129]

30. P. Anastasi II, 7, 6-7 (= *LEM*, 17, 1-3).

pꜣ wꜥb ḥr i͗rt ḥnw i͗.i͗ri͗.f nw i͗w wn 3.t r ṯḫb.f m ‹pꜣ› i͗trw ***bn sw ḥr sṯn*** *r prt r šmw*

'The pure priest performs divine services and, since there are three of them, he spends the time plunging himself in the river. He does not distinguish between winter and summer.' Note the two habitual presents, affirmative and negative.[130]

---

[129] For another interpretation see Groll, *Negative*, p. 100-101 and example 209.

[130] The parallel passage in P. Sallier I, 7, 7 (= *LEM*, 85, 1-2) uses, in place of the present, a negative aorist; see *infra* §17.5, example 6.

Very important remark: to emphasise the fact that the process **never** takes place, or that it cannot be completed, either because it is **unrealisable**, or because the agent is **incapable** of doing so, a marked form is used: the **negative aorist** (see *infra* §17).

16.5 The predicate is the *m* + infinitive form

This form is used exclusively with verbs of motion.[131] It expresses only the unmarked (or progressive) present:

sw m ꜥq: 'he is entering'

31. O. DM 446, v° 6-7 (= *KRI* II, 383, 15-16).

yꜣ ***sw m ḫd*** *r pꜣ ḥb-sd*

'Because he is travelling north for the Sed festival.'

The form is **negated** with the negative morpheme *bn* too:

bn sw m ꜥq

32. P. BM 10375, 26 (= *LRL*, 46, 10-11).

(ỉ)n ***bn tw.k m nꜥy*** *ỉrm nꜣ ḥbsw*

'Are you not transporting (*lit.* 'going with') the clothes?'

16.5.1 Excursus: The first future

The verb *nꜥỉ* 'go, navigate, traverse,' is employed in the above example with its full meaning. In Coptic (**ⲚⲀ, ⲚⲞⲨ**) it becomes the auxiliary of the first future that expresses the immediate future. Some examples of this usage can already be found in Late Egyptian.

subject + *m* + *nꜥỉ* + *r/m* + infinitive

33. P. BN 197, V, v° 2, 3 (= *LRL*, 35, 15).

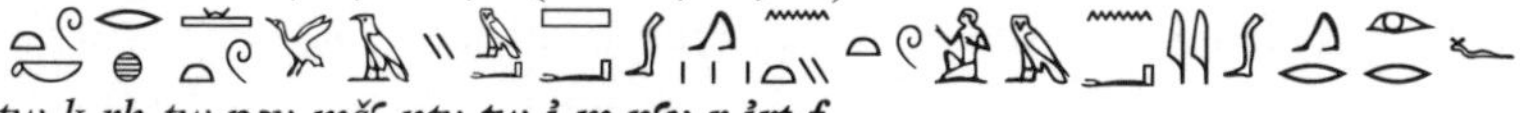

tw.k rḫ.tw pꜣy mšꜥ nty ***tw.ỉ m nꜥy r ỉrt.f***

'You are aware of this journey that I am about to make.'

16.6 The predicate is a pseudo-participle

16.6.1 Transitive verbs (except *rḫ*)

The construction has the value of a passive perfective. If the agent of the process is expressed, it is introduced by the preposition *ỉn* (cf. example 36 below).

sw wꜣḥ: 'He has been placed'

▪ This passive value is only an effect of the meaning deriving from the fundamental value of the pseudo-

[131] Except *šm*; see Satzinger, *NÄS*, p. 143.

participle: the construction means that the subject is in the position resulting from the completion of the action of placing.

34. Wenamun, 1, 13 (= *LES*, 62, 4-5).

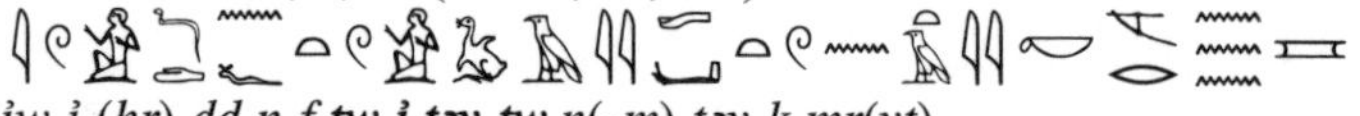

ỉw.ỉ (ḥr) ḏd n.f ***tw.ỉ ṯꜣy.tw*** *n(=m) tꜣy.k mr(yt)*
'I said to him: "I have been robbed in your harbour."'

35. P. Cairo 58057, 3 (= *KRI* I, 238, 7).

pꜣwn ***sw dỉ.tw*** *n.f*
'Because it (= the donkey) has been allocated to him' (*lit.* 'given').

36. P. Abbott, 2, 7 (= *KRI* VI, 470, 3-4) (fig. p. 98).

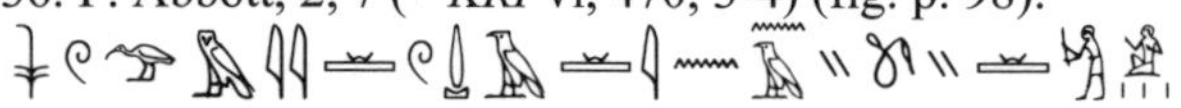

sw gmy *wḏꜣ ỉn nꜣy rwḏw*
'It (= the tomb) was found intact by these inspectors.'

37. O. UCL 19614, 5-6 (= *KRI* V, 2, 3-4).

ỉw.tw ḥr ḫꜣꜥ.f r-ḏd bỉn ỉw.ỉ ḥr ḏd.tw.f n.s m-mỉtt r-ḏd ***sw ḫꜣꜥ***
'It was rejected saying: "It is bad." I repeated it to her in these terms: "It has been rejected."'

The isomorphic **negation** by means of the negative morpheme *bn* is rare. In the three examples listed,[132] the form is preceded by the circumstantial *ỉw*.

38. P. Berlin P 10496, 12-13 (= *KRI* V, 477, 6-7).

ỉw.w ḥr gm wꜥ wt ỉw.f nꜥꜥ ỉw ***bn sw mtn.tw*** *ḥr rn n rmṯ nb*
'They found a coffin that was plain, and that had not been inscribed with the name of anybody.'

▪ The construction *bwpwy.tw sḏm.f* can also be used, see *supra* §15.2.2, example 17.

16.6.2 Intransitive verbs

16.6.2.1 Verbs of motion

The value of the syntagma depends on the nature of the passage:
– **in narrative passages**, the action is presented in an active and punctual manner, unrelated to the time of the statement, to which it is anterior. It is the equivalent, for this category of verbs, of the perfective *sḏm.f* of transitive verbs;
– **in non-narrative passages**, the construction describes the situation resulting from the

[132] Other examples are found in P. Anastasi IV, 12, 6 (= *LEM*, 48, 5), and O. Gardiner 67, 4 (= *KRI* III, 542, 14).

completion of the action, still persisting at the time of the statement. Therefore, it has full resultative value.[133]

sw **ꜥ*q***: 'he entered' (narrative context), 'he has entered' (non-narrative context)

39. Qadesh Bulletin, 78-79 (= *KRI* II, 118, 8 and 9): narrative passage (narrative).
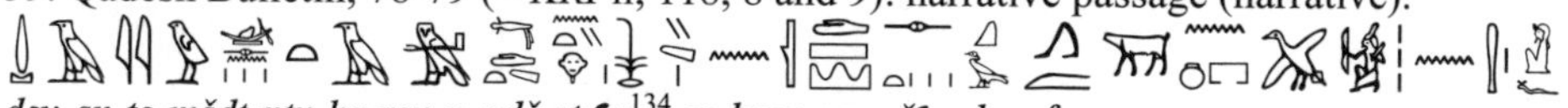
ḏꜣy.sn tꜣ mšdt nty ḥr rsy n qdš ***st ꜥq***[134] *m-ẖnw pꜣ mšꜥ n ḥm.f*
'They crossed the channel that is south of Qadesh, they penetrated in (amongst) the army of his majesty.' Note the parallelism between *ḏꜣy.sn*, perfective *sḏm.f* of a transitive verb, and *st ꜥq*, a first present having as predicate the pseudo-participle of a verb of motion.

40. P. Bologna 1086, 14-15 (= *KRI* IV, 80, 5-7): discourse, narrative passage.
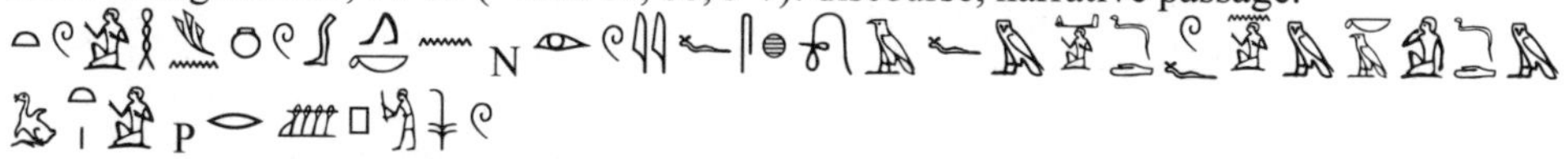
tw.ỉ ḥn.k(wỉ) *n N ỉrỉ.f sẖwn.f m-dỉ.ỉ ḏd.f n.ỉ m kꜣ-ḏd m ṯꜣty P r(=ỉ).šsp se*
'I ran to N, he contested it with me (= the fact of having taken a slave); in short,[135] he said to me: "It is the vizier P who took him." Note also the use of the first present for the verb of motion, and the perfective (either periphrased or not) for transitive verbs.

41. Qadesh Bulletin, 40 (= *KRI* II, 111, 2): discourse, non-narrative passage.

ptr pꜣ wr ḥsỉ n ḫtꜣ ỉw
'See, the wretched chief of Hatti has arrived' (*lit.* 'has come' — and is still there). Note (as below) the presence of the particle *ptr*, mark of the *hic* and *nunc*.

42. P. Turin 2021, 2, 8-9 (= *KRI* VI, 740, 1-2): discourse, non-narrative passage.

ḥr ptr ***tw.ỉ ỉw.k(wỉ)*** *m-bꜣḥ ṯꜣty [nꜣ] srw n tꜣ qnbt m pꜣ hrw*
'And see, I am come here today before the vizier and the magistrates of the court' ('and I am here at this moment').

The isomorphic **negation** (with *bn*) is not used;[136] the form *bwpwy.f ꜥq* is used instead.

43. P. Mayer A, 5, 18-19 (= *KRI* VI, 814, 12-13): discourse, non-narrative passage.
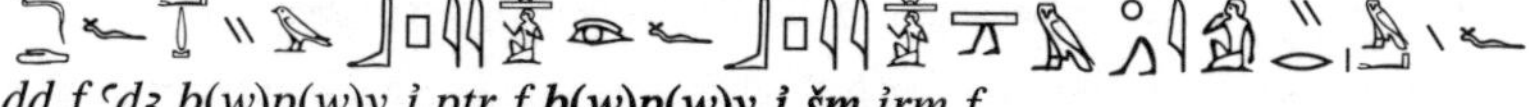
ḏd.f ꜥḏꜣ b(w)p(w)y.ỉ ptr.f ***b(w)p(w)y.ỉ šm*** *ỉrm.f*
'He said: "It is false, I did not see him, I did not go with him."'

This example illustrates the fact, already pointed out, that the form *bwpwy.f sḏm* serves as negation of the perfective *sḏm.f* of transitive verbs **and** of the first present having as predicate

[133] Satzinger, *o.c.*, p. 133-144.
[134] Variant: *ꜥḥꜥ.n.sn ꜥq*.
[135] See Gardiner, *JEA* 24 (1938), 243-244.
[136] A resultative example: P. Turin A, v° 4, 7-8 (= *CLEM* 509, 11).

the pseudo-participle of verbs of motion. The affirmative form would have been: **ḏd.f mꜣꜥtw ptr.ỉ se tw.ỉ šm.k(wỉ) ỉrm.f* 'He said: "It is true, I saw him, I went with him."'

16.6.2.2 Other intransitive verbs (locative verbs, adjective verbs, to die, to live, etc.)

They substantially convey the same values as the verbs of motion.[137]

Narrative passages (active, punctual, equivalent to the perfective *sḏm.f* of transitive verbs):

sw sḏr	'he laid (down)'	*sw mwt*	'he died'
wn.f sḏr	'he (had) laid (down)'		

Non-narrative passages (resultative stative (or stative) linked to a present situation):

sw sḏr	'he is laid (down)'	*sw mwt*	'he is dead'
wn.f sḏr	'he was laid (down)'	*wn.f mwt*	'he was dead'

This dual value is illustrated by the following example, where the verb *mwt* is used in a narrative context first (presence of sequentials) and a non-narrative one after:

44. O. DM 126, 5-6 (= *KRI* III, 532, 6-7).

pꜣy rmṯ mwt *m pr n ḥr-m-ḥb ỉw.f ḥr hꜣb n.ỉ r-ḏd* ***ḥr-ms mwt*** *ỉw.ỉ ḥr šm ḥnꜥ mḥy*

'This man **died** in the house of Horemheb, he (= Horemheb) wrote to me saying: "Harmose **is dead**." I went with Mehy...'

45. O. Cairo 25556, 4-5 (= *KRI* IV, 302, 15-303, 1): discourse, narrative passage.

ỉr ỉnk ***tw.ỉ sḏr.kwỉ*** *m tꜣy.ỉ ỉsb(t) ỉw p(ꜣ)-n-ỉmn (ḥr) pr ḥnꜥ nꜣy.f rmṯ ỉw.sn (ḥr) ḏd ḫnw m-dỉ ꜥꜣ n pr-ꜥꜣ ꜥ.w.s. r ḥꜣy*

'As for me, I was laying (down) in my hut. Penamun went out with his people, they made accusations of lese-majesty (*lit.* 'concerning the greatness of Pharaoh l.p.h.') against Hay.'

[137] Satzinger, *o.c.*, p. 149-162.

46. P. Mayer A, 6, 21-22 (= *KRI* VI, 816, 12-14): discourse, narrative passage.

ḏd.f wn.i ḥms.k(wi) *r s3w nhy n it irm 3ˁˁ qr ẖr ir tw.i m {n} iy r-ẖry iw.i (ḥr) gm wˁb t3t3-šri*

'He said: "I was sitting guarding (*lit.* 'sat to guard') some grain (pl.) together with the foreigner Qar; now, as I came down (*lit.* 'went downwards'), I met the pure priest Tatasheri."'

47. P. Gardiner 4, v° 1 (= *KRI* VII, 339, 11): discourse, non-narrative passage.

tw.i wˁ.kwi *ẖr p3y.i sn mr*

'I am alone (*lit.* 'lonely') because my brother is sick.'

48. P. Leiden I 366, 7 (= *KRI* II, 911, 1-2): discourse, non-narrative passage.

tw.i ˁnḫ.k(wi) *m p3 hrw bw rḫ.i ˁ.i n dw3w*

'I am alive today (but) I do not know my condition of tomorrow.'

49. P. Northumberland I, v° 1 (= *KRI* I, 239, 15): discourse, non-narrative passage.

tw.i ḥqr.k(wi) *m ptr.k*

'I am famished to see you' (= I have much desire to see you).

The isomorphic **negation** (with *bn*) is only attested in non-narrative contexts, and it is not uncommon with adjective verbs like *nfr* or *nḏm*.

50. O. IFAO 1296, 7 (Černý-Groll, *LEG*, example 847): discourse, non-narrative passage.

bn tw.k ḥqr.tw

'You are not famished' *cf.* example 49 above.

51. O. DM 554, 6 (fig. p. 87): discourse, non-narrative passage.

nn sw nfr *p3 r(=i).ir.n.k*

'It is not good what you have done.'

Note the traditional spelling of the negation and of the relative form, but especially the adverbial value of the pseudo-participle that contrasts the adjectival value of the form *bn nfr iwn3*: 'It (= the donkey) is not good' (O. Petrie 14 = *KRI* V, 524, 8), negation of *nfr sw* 'it is good.'

16.7 Special case: the verb *rḫ*[138]

This verb, which Aktionsart is non-terminative, and which first meaning is 'to seek to know,'

[138] *Satzinger, NÄS,* §2.3.12, p. 184-191; Frandsen, *LEVS,* §24 (2), P. 37-38; Černý-Groll, *LEG*, §20.5.4-10, p. 311-313. Its analysis here is limited to the present and the past tenses.

must be studied apart. While it is transitive, it possesses, as in Middle Egyptian, an active pseudo-participle, which negation takes, most of the time, a specific form: *bw rḫ.f*. Its direct object can be a noun (frequently) or an infinitive (rarer).[139]

16.7.1 *rḫ* + noun (or pronoun)

In almost all cases, the process is presented as completed; the construction thus has a resultative value, the meaning being 'to know, to have knowledge (of).'

Present	affirmative	***sw rḫ***	'he knows'[140]
	negative	***bw rḫ.f***	'he does not know'[141] (very frequent; negation of the process: 'He has not learned')
		bn sw rḫ	'he does not have knowledge of' (rare;[142] negation of the result)
Past	affirmative	***rḫ.f***	'he knew'[143]
	negative	***bwpwy.f rḫ***	'he did not know'[144]

▪ The unmarked imperfective aspect 'learn, get to know' does not appear to be used. Indeed *sw ḥr rḫ* 'he learns,' and *bn sw ḥr rḫ* 'he does not learn' are not attested. Note, however, an example of the negative aorist (*cf.* §17): *bw ỉri.f rḫ* 'he cannot learn:' P. Chester Beatty IV, v° 4, 4.

16.7.2 *rḫ* + infinitive

This is a rather infrequent construction. The meaning is: 'try to, seek to, have the will to' (imperfective), 'be able to, can' (perfective).

Present	affirmative[145]	***sw ḥr rḫ stp***	he tries to choose[146]
	negative	***bw rḫ.f stp***	he is not able to choose'[147]
		bn sw ḥr rḫ stp	he does not try to choose[148]
Past	negative[149]	***bwpwy.f rḫ stp***	he has not been able to choose'[150]

[139] The verb can also be constructed with *r-ḏd* + independent form (see *infra* §32.5.4). For an example with the perfective see P. Bologna 1086, 6-7, cited in §23.4.1, example 2.
[140] P. BN 197 V, v° 2-3 (= *LRL*, 35, 15 = example 33 above).
[141] Qadesh Bulletin, 27 (= example 1 above); P. Leiden I 366, 7 (example 48 above).
[142] Two examples: P. Leiden I 371, v° 26 and 37, and P. Anastasi V, 26, 4 (= *LEM*, 71, 7-8) with *ỉs bn*.
[143] With the circumstantial *ỉw*: P. Abbott, 5, 5-6 (example 17, §15.2.2 *supra*).
[144] With the circumstantial *ỉw*: P. Abbott, 7, 13-14 (example 11, §15.2.1 *supra*).
[145] The pseudo-participle (**sw rḫ stp*) is not attested in this construction.
[146] In a clause relativised by *nty*: P. Gurob, 2, 5-6 (= *RAD*, 14, 10-11).
[147] With the circumstantial *ỉw*: Qadesh Bulletin, 65-67 (example 6, §13.4.1.2 *supra*).
[148] Horus and Seth, 3, 1 (= *LES*, 39, 14-15).
[149] The affirmative form is not attested.
[150] P. Abbott, 2, 15 (= *KRI* VI, 470, 15-16).

16.8 Summary: the main forms of the First Present

affirmative		negative
sw dy	he is here	***bn sw (dy)***
sw m pꜣ pr	he is in the house	***bn sw m pꜣ pr (ỉwnꜣ)***
sw ḥr wꜣḥ	he places	***bn sw ḥr wꜣḥ***
		(bw ỉrỉ.f wꜣḥ)[151]
sw m ꜥq	he enters	***bn sw m ꜥq***
sw wꜣḥ	he is placed	***bn sw wꜣḥ***
		bwpwy.tw wꜣḥ.f sw[152]
sw ꜥq	he entered *or* he has entered	***bwpwy.f ꜥq***
sw mwt	he died *or* he has died	**?**
sw ḥms	he sat *or* he is seated	**?**
sw ḥqr	he is famished	***bn sw ḥqr***
sw nfr	he is good *or* he is well	***bn sw nfr***
sw rḫ	he knows	***bw rḫ.f*** (frequent)
		bn sw rḫ (rare)

[151] 'He never places, he is unable to place,' negative aorist, see *infra* §17.5.
[152] See Frandsen, *o.c.*, §42.4, p. 76.

17. The negative aorist

17.1 Introduction

This is the descendant of the Middle Egyptian *n sḏm.n.f* form, which later developed into *bw sḏm.n.f*, which is very rare. Following the disappearance of *n*, it developed into *bw sḏm.f*, a transitional and ambiguous form that could be confused with the, outwardly, similar negation of the perfective *sḏm.f* deriving from *n sḏm.f* (see above §15.1.2.3, n. 2). Finally, with the periphrasis of the verb by the auxiliary *ỉrỉ*, it developed into the construction most commonly employed: *bw ỉrỉ.f sḏm*.

***n sḏm.n.f* ► *bw sḏm.n.f* ► *bw sḏm.f* ► *bw ỉrỉ.f sḏm* ► ⲘⲈϤⲤⲰⲦⲘ̄**

17.2 Values

It is, as its classic ancestor, a form that negates the **realisation** of the process without any temporal reference.

As the negation applies only to the **realisation** of the process, without excluding attempts at realisation, obviously unsuccessful, the construction often conveys a nuance of inability or impossibility.

The negative aorist is, thus, a **marked form**, without temporal value, used to specify that the process:

– was not, is not, or will **never** (or never again) be **accomplished,**[153]

– and, possibly, that it **cannot** be accomplished, because it is impossible, or the agent is incapable of doing so.

17.3 *bw sḏm.n.f* (very rare)

1. P. Anastasi IV, 6, 9 (= *LEM,* 41, 7-8):[154] school text.

'The country of Hatti is in his power (that of Ramses), isolated;

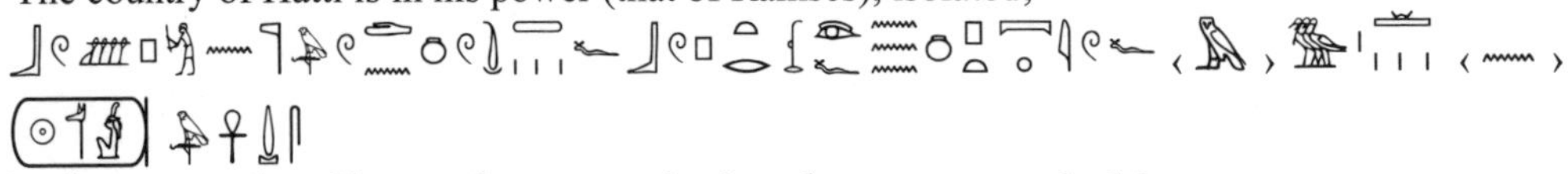

***bw šsp.n nṯr** wdnw.f **bw ptr.f** mw nw pt ỉw.f ‹m› bꜣw ‹n› wsr-mꜣꜥt-rꜥ ꜥ.w.s.*

'the (Hittite) god no longer receives (or 'can no longer receive') its offerings (and consequently) he never sees (or 'can no longer see') the rain, being that it is in the power of Usermaatra l.p.h.'

17.4 *bw sḏm.f* (quite frequent in school texts)

2. P. Anastasi III, 7, 8 (= *LEM,* 29, 1-2): school text.

*ḏr ptr.w pꜣ ḥqꜣ ꜥ.w.s. ꜥḥꜥ ḥr ꜥḥꜣ **bw ꜥḥꜥ** ḏww r-ḥꜣt.f*

'Since they saw the sovereign l.p.h. fighting, the mountains cannot stand before him.'[155]

[153] Note that the traditional form *n sp sḏm.f* (Gardiner, *EG*, §106 and 456) does not have a Late Egyptian successor.

[154] The parallel P. Anastasi II, 2, 4 (= *LEM*, 13, 3) shows the form without *n*, *bw sḏm.f*.

[155] For this expression, see Yoyotte, *Kémi* 10, p. 67.

3. P. Anastasi II, 9, 3-4 (= *LEM,* 18, 1-3): hymn to Amun, school text.

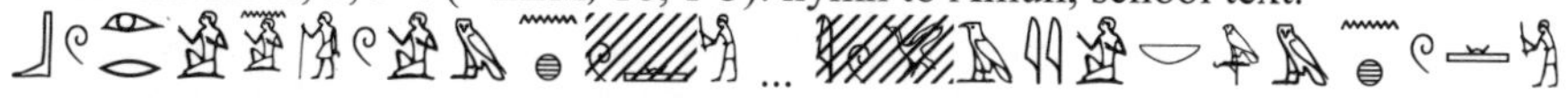

***bw ỉrỉ.ỉ** n.ỉ sr m nḫw* … *[ỉw p]ꜣy.ỉ nb m nḫw*
'I never take an official as protector ... because my lord (*i.e.* Amun) is a protector.'

17.5 *bw ỉrỉ.f sḏm*

4. P. Phillipps, v° 6-7 (= *LRL,* 30, 8-9).

*ḫr **bw ỉrỉ.ỉ nnỉ** m ỉṯꜣ n.f mw*
'And I never neglect to take water to him.'

5. P. BM 10053, v° 3, 12 (= *KRI* VI, 760, 2-3).

ḫr ỉr hrw ỉw pꜣ-mnỉw pꜣy.n ḥry (*ḥr*) *ṯṯṯ ỉrm.n r-ḏd **bw ỉrỉ.tn dỉt** n.ỉ nk*[*t*]
'Now, one day, Pameniu, our superior, quarrelled with us saying: "You never give me anything!"'

6. P. Sallier I, 7, 6-7 (= *LEM,* 84, 17-85, 2).

*pꜣ wꜥb ḥr ỉrt ḥnw ỉw ỉ.ỉrỉ.f nw ỉw wn 3 tḫb.f m pꜣ ỉtrw **bw ỉrỉ.f sṯn** r prt šmw*
'The pure priest performs divine services and, since there are three of them, he spends the time plunging himself in the river. He cannot distinguish between winter and summer.' [156]

7. P. DM v, 4 (= *KRI* VI, 266, 3).
Write to me, please, of the state of your heart so that I (may) enter it, because, (despite) my being with you since I was a child until today,

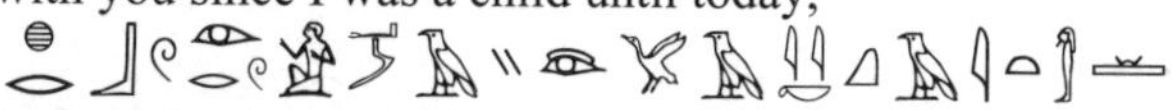

*ḫr **bw ỉrỉ.ỉ ꜥm** pꜣy.k qỉ*
'I cannot understand your nature.'[157]

8. O. Berlin P 10627, 6-8 (= *KRI* VI, 155, 12-13).

*bn ntk rmṯ ỉwnꜣ yꜣ **bw ỉrỉ.k dỉt** ỉwr tꜣy.k ḥmt mỉ-qd pꜣy.k ỉry*
'You are no man, because you are not able to impregnate your wife like everybody else' (*lit.* 'like your similar').

---

[156] *Cf.* the parallel example with a negative first present (§16.4.4, example 30).
[157] For this passage, see Neveu, *SAK* Beihefte 3 (1988), 103.

17.6 Excursus: the *ḫr-sḏm.f* form

The negative aorist is also used to negate a form rare in Late Egyptian, the *ḫr-sḏm.f*. This construction, which derives from the *sḏm-ḫr* and *ḫr.f sḏm.f* forms of classical Egyptian, is the ancestor of the Demotic aorist *ḫr ỉr.f sḏm* and Coptic **ϣⲁϥⲥⲱⲧⲙ̄**. It can be found in an initial position, after a topicalisation or in the apodosis of a correlative system. It denotes something that must necessarily happen, or that has to be done in the given circumstances. The *ḫr-sḏm.f* form occurs in aphorisms, proverbs, instructions, or in descriptions of habitual facts – all of the applications are exactly those of the aorist in demotic.[158]

***sḏm-ḫr.f* ► *ḫr.f sḏm.f* ► *ḫr-sḏm.f* ► *ḫr ỉr.f sḏm*► ϣⲁϥⲥⲱⲧⲙ̄**

In initial position:

9. P. Leiden I 350, VI, 9: hymn to Amun-ra, beginning of stanza.

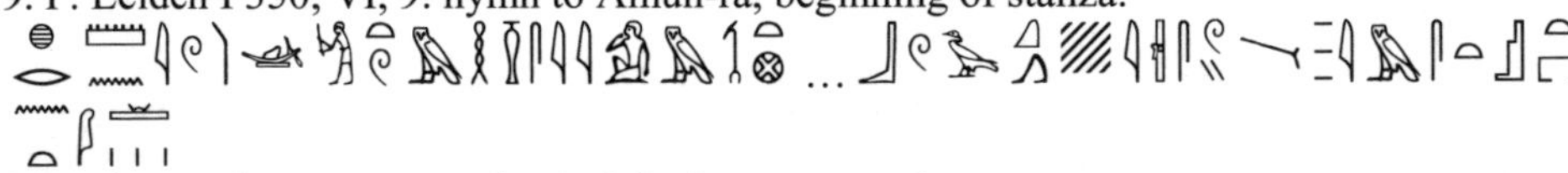

ḫr-mnỉ.tw *m ḥsy m wꜣst ... bw ꜥq ỉsfty ỉm.s st nt mꜣꜥt*

'One lands like a blessed one in Thebes ... the fisherman never enters (or 'cannot enter therein') (in) the Place of Truth.' In this example, the initial form *ḫr-sḏm.f* is followed by a negative aorist.

After topicalisation:

10. O. Berlin P 10627, 9-11 (= *KRI* VI, 155, 14-156, 1).

tw.k ꜥšꜣ m ḏrỉw r-ỉqr bw ỉrỉ.k dỉt nkt n wꜥ ỉr pꜣ nty ỉw[159] *mn m-dỉ.f ꜥḏd* ***ḫr-ỉn.f*** *n.f ky nmḥ sḫpr.f (se)*

'You are too rich, (but) you never give anything[160] to anybody. As for he who has no child, he should[161] adopt some[162] orphan to raise him up.'

In the apodosis of a correlative system:

11. Pentawer poem, 202 (= *KRI* II, 65, 1-4): epic narrative; synthesis of engraved texts.

ỉr pḥ.ỉ r ḥḥ ỉm.sn bw ỉrỉ rdwy.w smn ***ḫr-wꜥr.sn***

'If I attack millions among them, their legs cannot stand firm, they must flee.' It should be noted that the apodosis consists of two directly parallel aorists, first as a negative form and then as an affirmative one.

---

[158] See Johnson, *DVS*, p. 137.

[159] The presence of *ỉw* after *nty* is not necessary, it heralds a demotic usage.

[160] Or 'you are not able to give anything.'

[161] The aorist retains here the nuance of obligation that it had in classical Egyptian, see Vernus, *Future*, p. 78-82 and 98.

[162] *ky* does not necessarily refer to something or somebody already mentioned, see *supra* §6.2.

12. P. Turin A, v° 1, 6-7 (= *CLEM,* 507, 4-5): school text, passage from a letter addressed to an apprentice scribe that one cannot prevent from sneaking out.

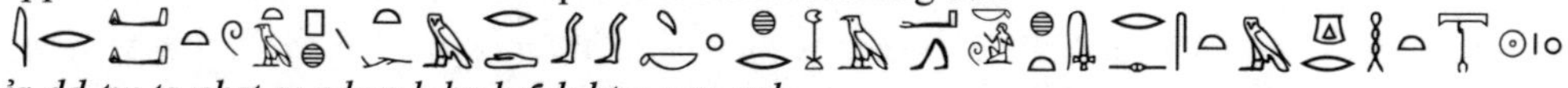

ỉr dd.tw tꜣ pẖꜣt m rdwy.k ḥr-ẖꜣʿ.k ẖt r.s m grḥ

'If a fetter is put to your feet ('if a fetter is placed on your feet'), you set it on fire in the night.'

18. The expression 'not yet'

This expression is articulated, both with active and negative meaning, by the successors of Middle Egyptian perfective *n sḏm.t.f* form 'he has not yet heard.'[163]

18.1 Active Voice

From Middle Egyptian to Coptic its evolution is as follows:

n sḏm.t.f ► *bw sḏm.t.f* ► *bw ỉrỉ.t.f sḏm* ► Ⲙ̄ⲠⲀⲦϤ̄ⲤⲰⲦⲘ̄

Whereas the *bw sḏm.t.f* form is rare and is employed only with a small number of verbs (*rdỉ*, *ỉrỉ*, *šm*, *rḫ*) in texts of the 19th dynasty, *bw ỉrỉ.t.f sḏm*, is much more frequent, and is encountered with a greater variety of verbs. In both cases, the *t* is often written out using the full grapheme: 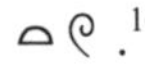.[164]

1. O. Turin 57093, v° 4.

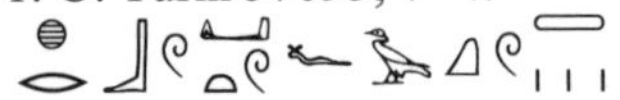

ḫr bw dỉ.t.f *ʿqw*

'And he has not yet given provisions.'

2. P. Anastasi V, 21, 2-3 (= *LEM,* 67, 15-16).

bn tw.k ḥr h3b n.ỉ nfr m-r-pw bỉn ***ḫr bw ỉrỉ.t rmṯ m n3 nty tw.k (ḥr) h3b.w {ḥr} snn*** *ḥr.ỉ ḏd.f n.ỉ ḥr ʿ.k*

'You do not send to me any news, good or bad, because none of the people among those you send has yet come to me to give me your news' (*lit.* 'that he can tell me of your condition').

3. P. Nevill, v° 3-4 (= *JEA* 35 (1949), 70 and pl. VI): letter to the oracle.

ḫr bw ỉrỉ.t.k h3b *n.ỉ nfr bỉn*

'But, you have not yet answered me, favourably or unfavourably' (*lit.* 'You have not yet sent to me, good or bad').

18.2 Passive Voice

The 'not yet' expression in the passive voice is articulated through the form *bw sḏmy.t N* 'N has not yet been heard,' never periphrased, where the patient of the process is always nominal. This is a construction in the decline, which use is limited to three verbs: *ỉrỉ*, *rdỉ*, *ỉnỉ*.[165]

---

[163] Gardiner, *EG*, §402-405.

[164] See Winand, *o.l.*, §458-462, p. 289-292.

[165] See Winand, *o.l.*, §519-521, p. 329-331.

4. P. Anastasi IV, 8, 1-2 (= *LEM*, 42, 14-16): a *skty* boat has broken in the water.

wnn ***bw dy.t*** *n.f* ***nhy n ḥryt qꜣy n šnty*** *ḫr* ***bw dy.t*** *n.f* ***nhy n ḥryt qꜣy n ỉm*** *gr mḥ.sn m pꜣ skty*

'It turns out that it had not yet been laid with high gunwales in acacia, any more than it had been laid with high gunwales in *ỉm*-wood so that they might keep the boat in good repair' (*lit.* 'The fact being that it had not yet been laid with high gunwales in acacia and it had not yet been laid with high gunwales in *ỉm*-wood either'[166]).

5. P. Anastasi VI, 42 (= *LEM*, 75, 13-14).

ḫr bw dy.[t n.ỉ] prt dỉw *r-šꜣʿ-(r) pꜣ hrw*

'And neither seed nor rations have yet been supplied (*lit.* 'given') to me until today.'

[166] It is an explanatory gloss in which *wnn* nominalises the verbal sentence containing the following *bw sḏmy.t N* form. The resulting one is a nominal sentence of the type *B Ø*, in Middle Egyptian *B pw*, see *infra* §34.3 and §39.2.2.1, Remark.

19. The Third Future

19.1 Introduction

The third future is the Late Egyptian successor of the Middle Egyptian construction subject + *r* + infinitive.[167] Like its predecessor, it expresses the '**objective future,**' which contrasts with the 'modal future' expressed by the prospective *sḏm.f*. It often conveys a '**deontic**' nuance, the subject being pressed into action by a transcendent obligation.[168] From a practical point of view there are morphological differences, since the subject of the third future is either pronominal or nominal.[169]

19.2 Pronominal subject

The suffixal subject is necessarily attached to the morpheme *ỉw*, which is an integral part of the construction. The construction is negated by means of the negative morpheme *bn*.

ỉw.f r sḏm 'he will hear' ***bn ỉw.f r sḏm*** 'he will not hear'

▪ The *ỉw* (see *supra* §12.2) of the third future is the only *ỉw* that can appear in an initial position, or after the direct indicators of initiality, and the particles *ḫr*, *mk*, or *ptr*.
▪ The preposition *r*, like *ḥr* in the case of the first present, can be omitted, and, thus, it is to be restored in brackets.

1. P. Turin 1880, 3, 4-5 (= *RAD,* 56, 6-7).

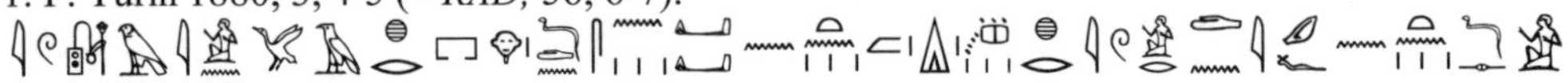

ỉw sš ḥrỉ n pꜣ ḫr ḥr ḏd n.sn dd n.tn gs dỉw ḫr ***ỉw.ỉ r dnỉ.f*** *n.tn ḏs.ỉ*

'The scribe of the tomb, Hori, said to them: "It has been allocated to you (pl.) half ration(s), and I shall share it out to you myself."'

2. P. Gurob, 2, 1-2 (= *RAD,* 14, 5-6).

ỉw.ỉ r dỉt *ỉrỉ.tw swhꜣ n.ỉ ḥr.w* ***bn ỉw.ỉ r dỉt*** *ṯꜣy.tw n.ỉ*

'I will cause that one congratulate me because of them (= the students entrusted by Pharaoh), I will not let that one attack me.[170] It can also be translated with a 'deontic' nuance: 'it is necessary that I ensure ...'

3. P. Leiden I 368, 11 (= *KRI* II, 895, 11): concerning prisoners.

'I wrote to inform my lord in these terms: "that one write to me to give me instructions:

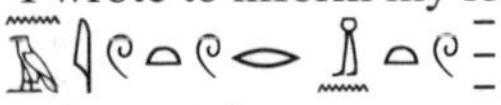

in ***ỉw.tw r ỉn.tw.w***

will they be brought?"'

[167] Gardiner, *EG*, §332, p. 253-254.
[168] See Vernus, *Future*, 1990, p. 9-15.
[169] See the excellent chapter by Winand on the third future, *o.l.*, p. 481-517.
[170] Or 'that fault is found with me;' for this expression see Caminos, *JEA* 49 (1963), 32.

4. P. Abbott, 5, 18 (= *KRI* VI, 476, 9) (fig. p. 216).
'The scribe of the interior of the proscribed Tomb Hori-the-young, son of Amennakht, and the scribe of the Tomb Paybes, have reported to me against you (pl.) concerning five very serious crimes, punishable by death,

ḥr ỉw.ỉ (r) hꜣb *ḥr.w m-bꜣḥ pr-ꜥꜣ ꜥ.w.s. pꜣy.ỉ nb ꜥ.w.s.*
and I must write about them to Pharaoh l.p.h., my lord l.p.h.' In this example the 'deontic' value is clearly marked.

The use of the past converter *wn* before the third future gives it, in addition to a past temporal value, a nuance of unreality rendered in English by the conditional. This usage is frequent in the apodosis of correlative systems introduced by *hn* (see *infra* §36.2).

5. P. BM 10052, 4, 11-12 (= *KRI* VI, 776, 13-14).

ḏd.f b(w)p(w)y.ỉ ptr rmṯ nb hn ptr.ỉ ***wn ỉw.ỉ (r) ḏd.tw.f***
'He said: "I did not see anyone, if I had seen (someone), I would have said it."'

6. Wenamun, 2, 29-30 (= *LES,* 69, 15-16).
'As for what you said: "Former kings had silver and gold sent,"

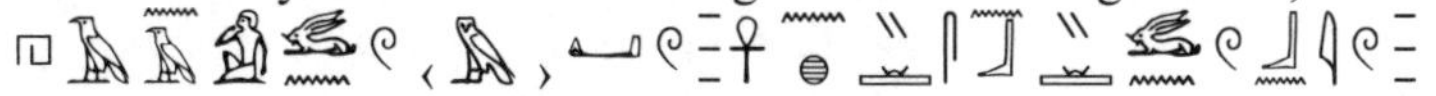

hn wn ‹m›-dỉ.w ꜥnḫ snb ***wn bn ỉw.w (r) dỉt*** *ỉn.tw nꜣ ḫtw*
if they had had life and health (see *infra* §22.1), they would not have caused material goods to be sent.'

19.3 Nominal subject

In this case, *ỉw* is, in principle, substituted with *ỉrỉ*  , thus the construction is:

ỉrỉ N r sḏm ***bn ỉrỉ N r sḏm***

7. O. Nash 1, v° 12 (= *KRI* IV, 317, 9-10).

ỉrỉ pꜣy.ỉ nb r dỉt *ỉry.tw sbꜣyt n tꜣy st-ḥmt r(=ỉ).ỉṯꜣy pꜣ ḫl*
'My lord will cause a punishment to be inflicted on this woman who stole the pick.' Or, with a 'deontic' nuance: 'It is necessary that my lord causes a punishment to be inflicted...,' on the evidence of the passage ending: 'so that no other woman of her kind acts so again.'

8. Hittite Treaty 22 (= *KRI* II, 229, 4): extradition clause for defectors.

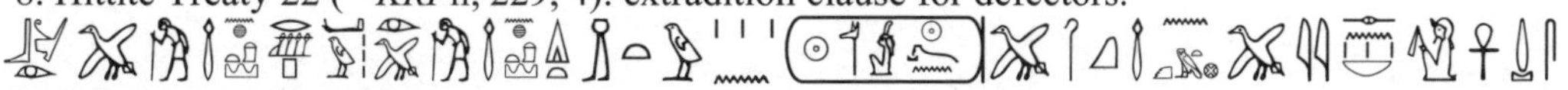

bn ỉrỉ pꜣ wr ꜥꜣ n ḫtꜣ r šsp.w
ỉrỉ pꜣ wr ꜥꜣ n ḫtꜣ (r) dỉt *ỉn.tw.w n wsr-mꜣꜥt-rꜥ stp.n-rꜥ pꜣ ḥqꜣ ꜥꜣ n kmt pꜣy.sn nb ꜥ.w.s.*
'The great chief of Hatti will not welcome them, the great chief of Hatti will have them brought back to Usermaatra Setepenra, the great ruler of Egypt, their lord l.p.h.' The 'deontic' value of the construction is still clearly perceptible, since the sovereign must act in accordance with

external norms specified in the treaty.

The interrogative pronoun *nỉm* is also constructed with *ỉrỉ*:

9. P. Turin 2021, 3, 10 (= *KRI* VI, 741, 7-8).

ỉr pꜣ ỉrỉ.f ***ỉrỉ nỉm (r) rḫ*** *mdw ỉm.f*

'As for what he has done, who will be able to contest it?'

It is, however, possible to find syntagmas, affirmative or negative, where the subject, though nominal, is introduced by *ỉw*.[171]

Affirmative example:

10. P. ESP, A, 7 (= *KRI* VI, 517, 10).

r-ḏd ***ỉw pꜣy.ỉ ḥry (r) ỉy*** *mtw.tn* [*dỉt*] *fꜣy.tw ỉ.n.ỉ*

'Saying: "My superior will come and you will have it loaded," so I said.'

In this example, one will have noted the presence of *ỉw* after *r-ḏd*. A dependent form cannot appear after *r-ḏd*, the sequential and the circumstantial first present are excluded, thus the only other possibility is the third future, hence the restoration of the preposition *r* in brackets. This interpretation is reinforced by the presence of a conjunctive, a very frequent construction after a third future.

Negative example:

11. O. Petrie 61, 7- v° 3 (= *HO,* 23, 4).

ỉw.ṯ (r) ḥms m tꜣ ꜥryt m pꜣy.ỉ wḏꜣ pꜣwn ỉnk ỉ.ỉrỉ se ***bn ỉw rmṯ nb n pꜣ tꜣ [r] ḫꜣꜥ.ṯ*** *ỉm r-bl*

'You will stay in the vestibule of my storehouse because it is I who built it (*lit.* made), and no one at all will throw you out from there.'

19.4 Remarks

It is possible to encounter, especially in wills and oaths, the third future with a **prepositional phrase** or a **pseudo-participle** as predicate.

12. O. DM 108, 4-5 (= *KRI* I, 409, 5-6): will.

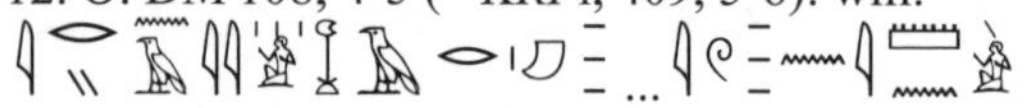

*ỉr nꜣy.ỉ ḫl …***ỉw.w n ỉmn-ms**

'As for my picks ... they will be for Amenmose.'

[171] See Winand, *o.l.*, §776, p. 498-500.

13. O. Gardiner 55, v° 4-6 (= *HO*, 66, 2): testamentary dispositions.

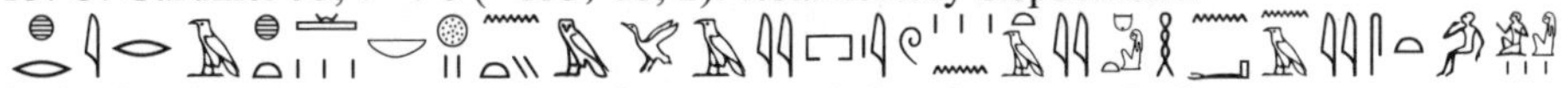

ḫr ỉr ꜣḫt nb sp-sn nty m pꜣy.‹ỉ› pr ***ỉw.w n tꜣy.‹ỉ› ḥmt*** *ḥnꜥ nꜣy.s ẖrdw*

'As for all possessions, without exception, that are in my house, they will be for my wife and her children.'

14. P. Cairo J 65739, 17 (= *KRI* II, 801, 12): oath.

'If witnesses accuse me, and some property belonging to the lady Baketmut is found among this silver that I have given for this slave, and that I have concealed it,

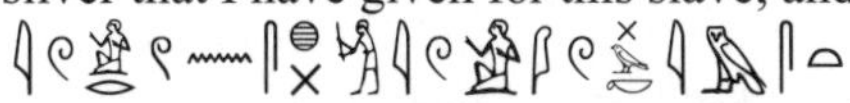

ỉw.ỉ r 100 n sḫt – ỉw.ỉ šw.k(wỉ) ỉm.s

I will receive a hundred blows (with a stick) and I will be deprived of her (= she will be confiscated from me).'

15. P. BM 10053, v° 3, 5 (= *KRI* VI, 758, 16-759, 1).

ỉry.f ꜥnḫ n nb ꜥ.w.s. ỉw bn mꜣꜥt pꜣ ḏd.tw.ỉ nb ***ỉw.ỉ dỉ.k(wỉ)*** *tp ḫt*

'He swore an oath by the lord l.p.h.: "And,[172] if everything I said is not true, I will be put on the stake."'

[172] The beginning of the oath has not been transcribed by the scribe, only the essential clause was noted down.

20. The independent prospective *sḏm.f*

The prospective *sḏm.f* is the successor of the prospective *sḏm.f* of classical Egyptian. In its independent usage,[173] it is a **subjective, modal** form that is only found in non-narrative contexts where it conveys various modalities, such as the will of the speaker (volitive), a wish (optative), or a polite command (jussive); while the future temporal value is only secondary.[174] It is negated by means of the negative morpheme *bn*.[175]

sdm.f 'he will hear, may he hear ...' ***bn sḏm.f***

- Unlike the perfective *sḏm.f*, limited to transitive verbs, the prospective *sḏm.f* is used in all categories of verbs.
- The non-independent prospective (see *infra* §26) is not a modal form. It is found:
  - in complement clauses following *rdỉ* (frequent);
  - by itself, in purpose clauses, where it is negated by *tm* (quite frequent);
  - after various prepositions and particles (quite rare).

The following example illustrates clearly the difference between the prospective and the third future:

1. P. BM 10052, 8, 21-22 (= *KRI* VI, 787, 10-13): the vizier questions a thief.

ḏd n.f ṯꜣty...ỉr ỉw ky(?)[176] *ỉy mtw.f sꜥḥꜥ.k* ***ỉry.ỉ*** *— ḏd.f ỉr ỉw ky(?)*[176] *ỉy mtw.f sꜥḥꜥ.(ỉ)* ***ỉw.k (r) ỉrt*** *n.ỉ sbꜣyt nbt bỉn(t)*

'The vizier said to him: "... if someone comes and accuses you, I am determined to act." — He (= the thief) said: "If someone comes and accuses me, you will inflict on me all sorts of severe punishments."' Using the prospective, the vizier states his willingness to act if the thief is found guilty, while the latter, using the third future, simply acknowledges the decision of the vizier.

A volitional modality is found in the following three examples:

2. O. Turin 57173, 3-5 (= *KRI* V, 458, 1-3): a man has sold a donkey.

ỉry.f ꜥnḫ n nb ꜥ.w.s. r-ḏd wꜣḥ ỉmn wꜣḥ pꜣ ḥqꜣ ***bn mdw.ỉ*** *m pꜣy ꜥꜣ* ***bn mdw ky*** *ỉm.f mtw.Ø ỉrỉ.f ỉw.f r.ỉ m q(ꜣ)b*

'He swore an oath by the lord l.p.h. in these terms: "As Amun endures, and as the sovereign l.p.h. endures, I have no intention of disputing about this donkey, and nobody will be able to dispute about it, and if that happens (*lit.* "and one does it"), it will cost me double (*lit.* "it will be

[173] Although forming a single morphological entity (Winand, *o.l.*, §343, p. 211), the prospective has, in Late Egyptian, both independent and non-independent applications. For purely pedagogical reasons, the two types of usages have been distinguished and treated separately in this grammar.

[174] See Vernus, *o.c.*, p. 15-26.

[175] It is still possible to find (in texts of the nineteenth dynasty) the classical spelling *nn*.

[176] On this ambiguous syntagma (circumstantial first present, third future or sequential), see *infra* §33.2.3.

double for me”).”’ By this oath, the seller, satisfied with the price paid, declares that he has no intention of challenging the sale in the future. In addition, he says that nobody else can do it, because he was the sole owner of the donkey just sold.

3. P. BM 10052, 1, 17 (= *KRI* VI, 768, 14-15).

ỉr.Ø smtr.f m bḏn ꜥn ḏd.f ỉ.wꜣḥ ***ḏd.ỉ***

‘He was questioned again with the aid of a staff; he cried (*lit.* ‘said’): “Stop, I will talk!”’

4. P. BM 10375, 13-14 (= *LRL*, 45, 5-6).

ỉw.ỉ (ḥr) ꜥš.s n.w ỉw.w (ḥ)r ḏd ***ỉry.n ỉry.n*** *m pꜣ ỉ.ḏd pꜣy.n nb*

‘I read it to them (= the letter of the general), they said: “We want to act, we want to act in accordance with what our lord has said.”’

The construction is frequently used in the second person to express a polite command. In this case, it is often preceded by the particle *ỉẖ*:

5. O. Berlin P 11247, v° 1 (= *KRI* III, 533, 5).

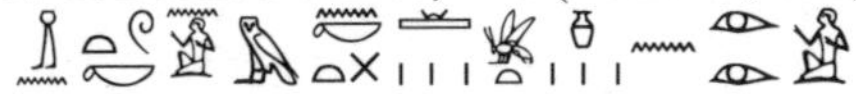

ỉn.tw.k *n.ỉ m nkt n bỉt n ỉrty.ỉ*

‘Will you bring me some honey for my eyes?’

The spelling shows that the *t* ending of the classical prospective of the verb *ỉnỉ* was still pronounced during the reign of Ramses II when the verb was used in the pronominal state.

6. P. Leiden I 369, 9 (= *LRL,* 2, 2).

ỉẖ ḏd.tn *n ỉmn*

‘Would you say to Amun ...?’

7. P. Northumberland I, v° 6 (= *KRI* I, 240, 4).

ỉẖ dỉ.k *ỉn.tw n.ỉ mry-ms wꜥ n ꜥw(ty) ḏmꜥ*

‘Will you get Merymose to bring me a roll of papyrus?’

It is this jussive nuance that is conveyed by the construction found at the end of letters sent by a superior to a subordinate:

8. P. BN 197, III, v° 3 (= *LRL,* 34, 14): from the general in chief to the scribe of the Tomb.

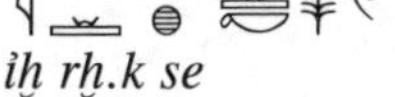

ỉẖ rḫ.k se

‘You will want to read carefully (the content of the letter).’ The meaning being: ‘Will you take into account?’ or ‘Will you take due note (of it)?’

O. Berlin P 11247, v° 1

The optative modality is often used in the third person in greetings, compliments, curses, and so on.

9. P. ESP, C, 16 (= *KRI* VI, 520, 11).

ḥsy twtn ***ỉmn-rꜥ*** *nsw* ***nṯrw*** *ḥsy twtn* ***mnṯw***

'May Amun-Ra, king of the gods reward you; may Montu reward you!'

10. P. BN 197, VI, 7-8 (= *LRL*, 64, 9-10).

ḫr ꜥš n.k ***ỉmn*** *ḥȝt*

'And may Amun be a pilot for you!'

11. P. Ashmolean Museum 1945.96 (= P. Adoption), v° 6-7 (= *KRI* VI, 738, 1-3).

nk *sw ꜥȝ* ***nk*** *ꜥȝ ḥmt.f pȝ nty ỉw.f (r) dd bȝk r wꜥ ỉm.w*

'May a donkey violate him, may a donkey violate his wife, whoever will treat as a slave one among them!' (*lit.* 'who will say "this is a slave" against one of them').

Greetings at the end of a letter to an equal or a superior:

12. P. Turin 1974 + 1945, v° 7 (= *LRL*, 40, 6).

nfr ***snb.k***

'May your health be good!'

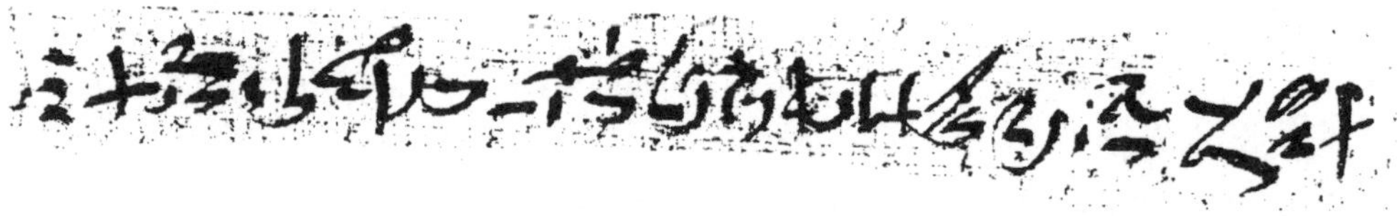

P. Northumberland I, v° 6

21. The imperative

21.1 Affirmative forms

Regular forms are constructed directly from the root, which is quite frequently preceded by a prosthetic yod almost always written as [hieroglyphs], but sometimes with the sign for the mouth. In principle, there is no gender or number ending.[177]

***ỉ.sḏm* (*sw*)** 'listen (to) (sg. and pl.) (it)'

There are two irregular forms:

– the imperative form of the verb *ỉy* / *ỉw* 'come' is [hieroglyphs] *my* 'come' (sg. and pl.);
– the imperative form of the verb *rdỉ* 'give' is [hieroglyphs] *ỉmỉ* 'give' (sg. and pl.).

The direct object, when pronominal, is expressed by a dependent pronoun, which allows one to distinguish the imperative from the infinitive. In some cases, above all with the verb *rdỉ*, the dependent pronoun can be replaced by the 'new direct object pronoun.'[178]

▪ In practice, it is not always easy to distinguish between dependent and suffix[179] pronouns, given the ambiguity of some spellings. In particular, care must be taken not to confuse the dependent pronoun *wỉ*, written simply [hieroglyph], with the suffix *ỉ*.

1. P. BM 10052, 1, 17 (= *KRI* VI, 768, 14-15).

ỉrỉ.Ø smty.f m bḏn ꜥn ḏd.f ***ỉ.wꜣḥ*** *ḏd.ỉ ḏd n.f ṯꜣty* ***ỉ.ḏd*** *pꜣ* ***ỉ.ỉrỉ.k***

'He was questioned again by means of a staff. He said: "Stop, I will talk!" The vizier said to him: "Relate what you did."'

2. O. Gardiner 54, 5 (= *KRI* V, 473, 11): concerning a jenny.

r-ḏd ***ỉ.ỉn*** *se*

'Saying: "Bring it."'

3. P. Gardiner 4, 5-6 (= *KRI* VII, 339, 8-9): concerning grain.

hꜣb n.ỉ pꜣ ḥm-nṯr n ḥwt-ḥr r-ḏd ***my*** *r šsp se*

'The prophet of Hathor has written to me saying: "Come to take them"' (*lit.* 'to receive them').

---

[177] See, however, example 14 below.

[178] See Winand, *o.l.*, §263-265, p. 156-160.

[179] See Winand, *o.l.*, §262, p. 155-156.

4. O. UCL 19614, 4 (= *KRI* V, 2, 2).

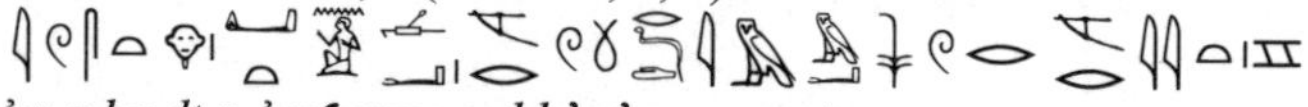

ỉw.s ḥr dt n.ỉ wꜥ mrw r-ḏd ***ỉmỉ se*** *r mryt*

'She gave me a sash[180] saying: "Put it on the shore"' (*lit.* 'Place it on the bank').

However, the dependent pronoun can be replaced by the new direct object pronoun:

5. O. DM 563, 4 (fig. p. 128): concerning an ox.

r-ḏd ***ỉmỉ tw.f***

'Saying: "Give it."'

The verb *rdỉ* can have as direct object a complement clause with a non-independent prospective. The resulting construction is *ỉmỉ sḏm.f*:

6. O. DM 446, 8-9 (= *KRI* III, 383, 13).

ỉmỉ ỉn.tw *nꜣ ṯbwt m tꜣ wnwt*

'Have the sandals brought within the hour!' (*lit.* 'Cause that one brings ...').

In the foregoing syntagma, the complement clause can employ the verb *rdỉ*:

7. P. Turin 1977, 4-6 (= Bakir, *Epistolography,* pl. 26 and XXXIII).

ḥr ỉr pꜣ hꜣb (ỉ).ỉrỉ.k ḥr tꜣy.k mwt r-ḏd se mwt ỉw.k ḥr ḏd ***ỉmỉ dỉ.tw*** *pꜣ ḥtr (ỉ).wn ḥr pr n.s n tꜣy.ỉ snt*

'And, as for what you wrote about your mother saying: "She is dead," you requested: "Let that the income that was paid to her (*lit.* 'went out for her') be given to my sister."'

The imperative can be reinforced by various expressions, which are:

– the particle *tw* – in reality the dependent pronoun whose origin was forgotten;
– the 'ethical' dative *n.k* or *n.tn*, especially in literary texts;
– the particle  *my*, during the second half of the 20th dynasty.

8. P. BM 10052, 6, 9 (= *KRI* VI, 782, 11).

ỉw.w (ḥr) ḏd n.ỉ ***ỉmỉ tw*** *pꜣy ḥḏ*

'They said to me: "Give then this silver."'

[180] See Janssen, *CP*, p. 286.

9. Wenamun, 2, 73 (= *LES,* 74, 14).

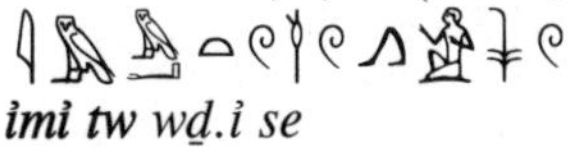

imi tw *wḏ.i se*
'Allow then that I send him (off).'

10. Horus and Seth, 3, 12 (= *LES,* 41, 2-3).

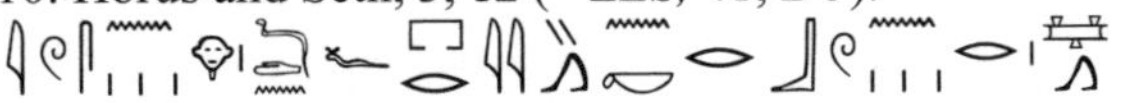

iw.sn ḥr ḏd n.f ***pry n.k*** *r-bl*
'They said to him: "Go out then!"' (*lit.* 'Go, for yourself, outside').

11. P. BM 10403, 3, 27 (= *KRI* VI, 833, 3).

i.ḏd my *n.i rmṯ i.ptr.ṯ*
'Tell me, please, whom you saw' (*lit.* 'the people that you saw').

12. P. DM V, 2-3 (= *KRI* VI, 266, 1).

iḫ r.k ***h3b my*** *n.i p3 sḫr ḥ3ty.k ʿq.i im.f*
'What's up with you? Tell me, please, your thoughts that I may understand them' (*lit.* 'It is what about you? Send to me, please, (about) the state of your heart so that I (may) enter therein').

21.2 Negative forms

21.2.1 General case

The negation of *i.sḏm* (*se*) 'listen (to it)' is:

m iri sḏm.(f) 'do not listen (to) (sg. and pl.) (it)'

where *m* is the imperative of the negative verb *imi*, *iri* the negative verbal complement (or infinitive) of the auxiliary *iri*, and *sḏm.(f)* the infinitive of the verbal expression, followed sometimes by a pronominal direct object.[181]

13. P. Berlin P 8523, 8-11 (= Allam, *HOP,* pl. 76).

m iri nḥm *t3y 3ḥt m-di p3y.(i)-nb-m-ʿḏd* — ***swḏ se*** *n.f* ***imi*** ***sk3.f*** *se*
'Do not take this field away from Paynebemadjed; entrust it to him, let him cultivate it.'

[181] See Gardiner, *EG*, §340.2 and §341, p. 260-261.

14. P. BM 10052, 12, 5 (= *KRI* VI, 793, 7-8).

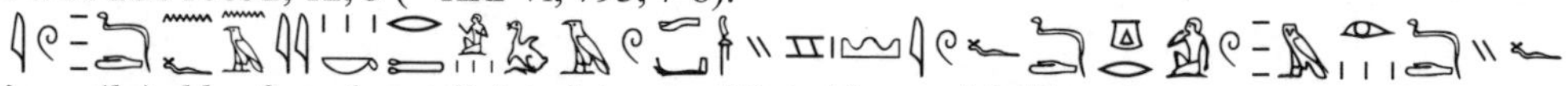

iw.w (*ḥr*) *ḏd n.f nꜣy.k rmṯ* (*ḥr*) *tꜣ imntt iw.f* (*ḥr*) *ḏd* ***gr m iri ḏd.tw.f***

'They said to him: "Your people plunder the West." He replied: "Shut up, do not say it!"'

Note the spellings of *gr* and of *m iri* that attempt to make the imperative plural.

15. P. Cairo 58057, 6-7 (= *KRI* I, 238, 12).

m iri *iṯꜣ.*(*i*) *r tꜣ qnbt*

'Do not drag (me) to the court.'

21.2.2 Special case: the verb *rdi*

Most often, the negative imperative of the verb *rdi* is not periphrased:[182]

m dy 'do not give' 'do not place'

16. P. Bologna 1086, 20-21 (= *KRI* IV, 80, 16-81, 2).

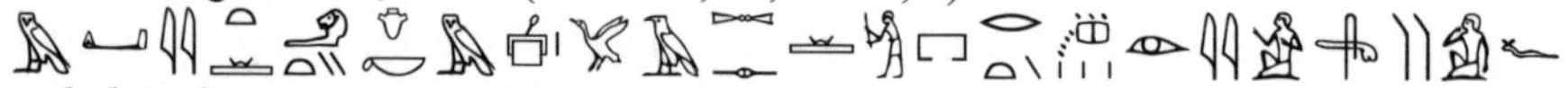

m dy ***ḥꜣty.k*** *m-sꜣ pꜣ ṯs-prt iri.i smtr.f*

'Do not worry about (*lit.* 'do not put your heart behind') the seed-sowing form: I have examined it.'

Consequently, the negation of *imi sḏm.f* 'have him hear, let him hear' is:

m dy sḏm.f 'do not let him hear'

where ***m*** is the imperative of the negative verb *imi*, ***dy*** the negative verbal complement of the verb *rdi*, and ***sḏm.f*** the non-independent prospective having the role of a direct object (complement clause).

17. P. Turin 1972, 4 (= *LRL,* 8, 7-8): concerning recruits.

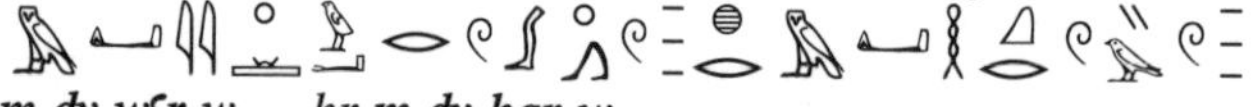

m dy wꜥr.w — *ḫr* ***m dy ḥqr.w***

'Do not let them escape and avoid them becoming hungry' (*lit.* 'Do not let that they run away and do not let that they are hungry').

Remark: It is possible to find examples where this construction is periphrased, in which case the resulting construction is the general case: *m iri dit sḏm.f.*

---

[182] On the numerous spellings' variants see Černý-Groll, *LEG*, §25.2.5, p. 358.

18. Wenamun, 2, 53 (= *LES,* 72, 8-9).

m ỉrỉ dỉt ptr.ỉ *se*

'Do not make me see it (= the grave).'

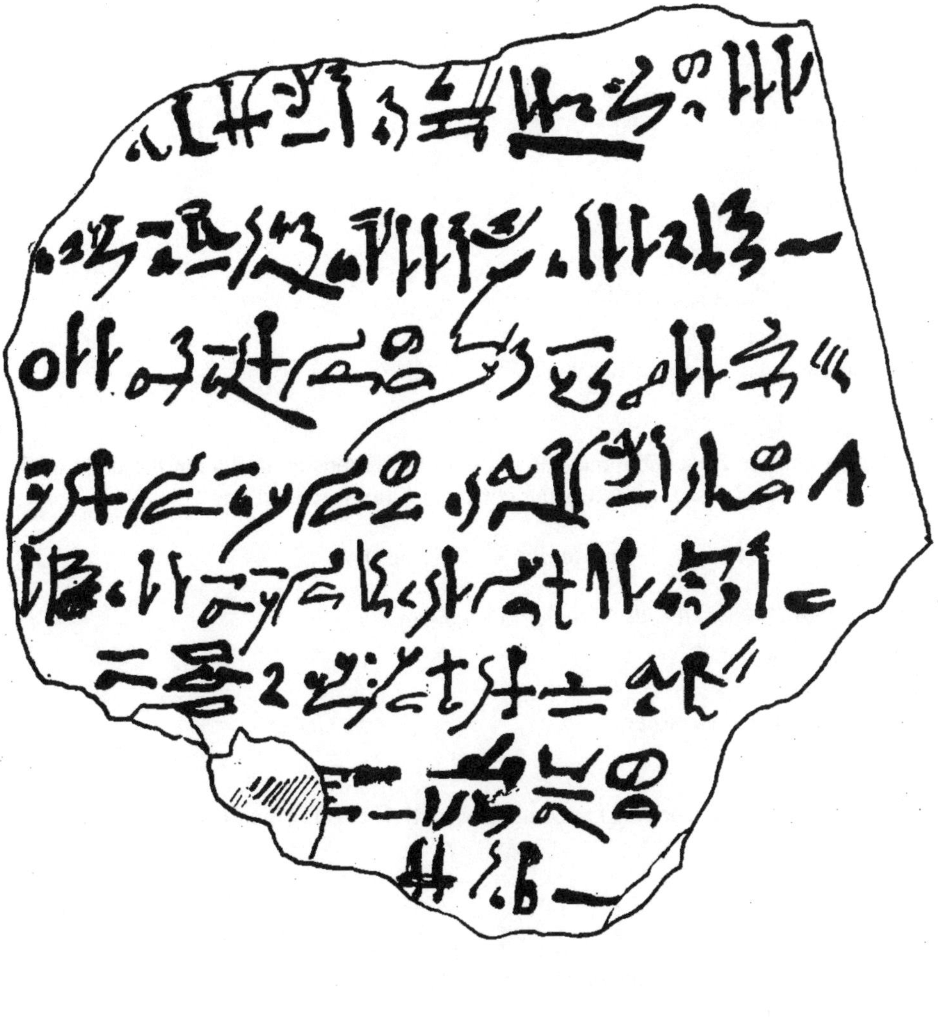

O. DM 554, r° (*cf.* p. 67, 185, 198, 223, 228)

22. The existential predication

22.1 Affirmative forms

These use the verb *wnn* 'to exist,' which in this case retains its full meaning. The verb is always in the form *wn*, and its subject, always nominal, is never defined, because its definition presupposes its existence. Such forms have no temporality. The theoretical minimal sentence, which is always accompanied by an adverbial and/or prepositional expansion, is:

wn A 'A exists,' 'there exists an A,' 'there is an A'

1. P. Orbiney, 3, 5-6 (= *LES,* 12, 8).

wn pḥty* [*ꜥꜣ*] *ỉm.k
'There is great strength in you.'

2. P. Leiden I, 370, 18 (= *LRL,* 10, 8-9).

yꜣ ***wn hrw*** *dy r-ḥꜣt.tn*
'Because there is a day, there, before you (pl.).'

The syntagma is more frequently encountered with the preposition *m-dỉ* 'in the hand of, in the possession of,' which is used to express our concept of **having** something:[183]

***wn m-dỉ.f* A** 'He has an A'

3. O. Prague 1826, 6-7 (= *HO,* 70, 2): letter to a woman.

ḫr wn m-dỉ.ṯ snw
'And you have brothers and sisters.'

This syntagma can be preceded by the composite particle *ỉs-bn*, which is used to pose rhetorical questions:

4. P. Anastasi V, 11, 4-5 (= *LEM,* 61, 12-13).

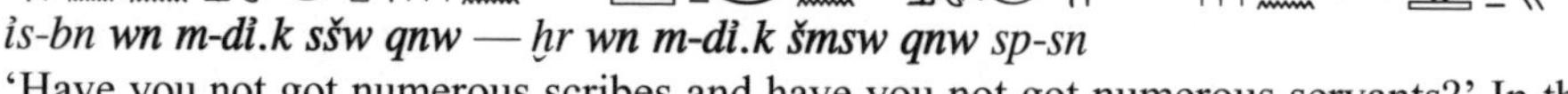

ỉs-bn ***wn m-dỉ.k sšw qnw*** — ***ḫr wn m-dỉ.k šmsw qnw*** *sp-sn*
'Have you not got numerous scribes and have you not got numerous servants?' In this example, the presence of *ỉs-bn* is understood after the *ḫr* particle.

[183] The concept of having a non-defined object (Paul has a dog), which means that Paul is the owner of a dog, is not to be confused with the notion of ownership of a defined object (this dog belongs to Paul), see *infra* §41.

22.2 Negative forms

The negation of *wn* is 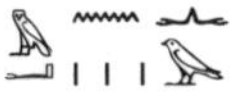 (and variants) *mn* 'it does not exist, there is not,' which is the successor of the traditional construction *nn wn* sometimes still encountered in texts from the nineteenth dynasty. The minimal sentence with zero subject is also attested:

5. P. Anastasi V, 11, 6 (= *LEM*, 61, 14-15).

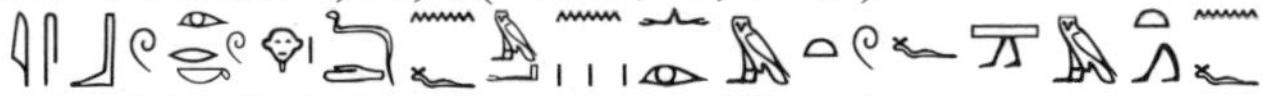

ỉs bw ỉrỉ.k {ḥr} ḏd n.f ***mn Ø*** *mtw.f šm n.f*

'Can you not say to him: "there is nothing" and let him go?'

6. P. Turin 1880, 2, 2-3 (= *RAD*, 53, 15-54, 1): discourse of workers on strike.

ỉ.ỉrỉ.n pḥ nꜣ r-ḥꜣt ḥqr r-ḥꜣt ỉb — ***mn ḥbsw mn sgnn mn rmw mn smw***

'If we have arrived here, it is because of hunger, it is because of thirst: there are no clothes, no oil, no fish, no vegetables!'

7. P. BM 10403, 3, 14-15 (= *KRI* VI, 832, 5-6).

ẖr ***mn rmṯ*** *ỉw ỉw.f (r) sꜥḥꜥ.[ỉ]*

'And there is no one who will accuse me.'

With *m-dỉ*, the negative correlate of the concept of **having** something is expressed as follows:

mn m-dỉ.f A 'He does not have A'

8. P. Turin 1887, v° 2, 10 (= *RAD*, 80, 16).

mn m-dỉ.f ỉt

'He does not have grain.'

22.3 Remarks

With defined nouns, the first present is normally used to express a concept similar to the non-existence: the **non-presence**.[184] Compare the following two constructions, which are extracts from same papyrus, with a line interval:

9. P. Turin 2009 + 1999, v° 1, 9 and 10 (= *KRI* VI, 564, 2 and 4).

mn *ẖꜣstyw*

'There are no foreigners.'

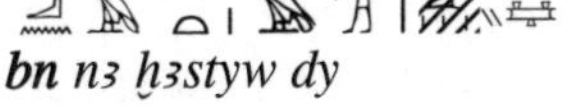

bn *nꜣ ẖꜣstyw dy*

'The foreigners are not there (anymore).'

[184] See Vernus, *Or.* 50 (1981), 440-442, and *RdE* 36 (1985), 153-168.

However, as noted above (§16.2), the adverb is often omitted and *bn* takes on the predication alone:

10. O. Berlin P 12630, 6 (= *KRI* V, 595, 3-4).

bn pꜣ wt* — *ḫr bn pꜣ ḥʿtỉ *r-šꜣʿ-(r) pꜣ hrw*

'Neither the coffin nor the bed are there today' (*lit.* 'until today').

11. P. Salt 124, v° 1, 9-10 (= *KRI* IV, 413, 11-13).

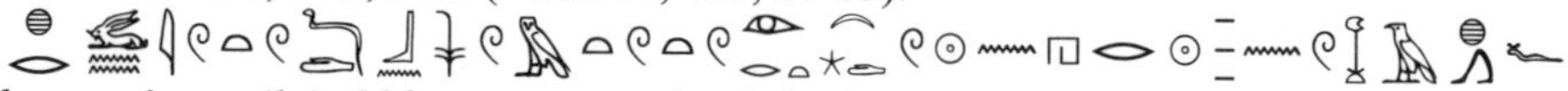

ḫr wnn ỉw.tw (ḥr) ḏd ***bn sw*** *mtw.tw ỉrt ꜣbd n hrw n wḫꜣ.f*

'and when one said: "It is not there" and one spent an entire month searching for it ...'

23. Second tenses

23.1 Introduction

Second tenses[185] are used in Late Egyptian to shift to marked rheme, that is to say, to bring to **focus**, an adverbial element or equivalent (circonstant) of a plain sentence (see *supra* §12.4.2). These modifiers may be:

- adverbs (example 8);
- prepositional phrases (preposition + noun or noun equivalent; examples 2, 6, 7);
- adverbial clauses introduced by *ỉw* (examples 3, 4, 9);
- subordinate clauses introduced by a conjunction (example 5).

The second tenses are only attested in discourse.
They are devoid of any temporal reference,[186] but can be imbued with modality.
They are characterised by the presence of a prosthetic yod.
Most often, they are periphrased by the auxiliary *ỉrỉ*:

theme marked rheme
ỉ.ỉrỉ.f sdm.(f) + **circonstant**

periphrased form where *sḏm* is an infinitive and (*f*) a possible pronominal direct object

but it can also be non-periphrased:

theme marked rheme
ỉ.sḏm.f (se) + **circonstant**

simple, non-periphrased, form, where (*se*) is a possible pronominal direct object

23.2 How second tenses work

Take the plain sentence: *King Henry II* ***had Thomas Becket murdered in his cathedral***, where *King Henry II* is the theme corresponding to the subject, while *had Thomas Becket murdered in his cathedral* is the rheme consisting of the predicate (had Thomas Becket murdered = predicate construction), followed by an adverbial (*in his cathedral*).

Supposing that the murder of the archbishop is already known and/or that one wants to emphasise the particularly scandalous circumstances in which the crime was committed, the **focus** will be on the **adverbial**, which will be rank-shifted to marked rheme. This is achieved by subjecting the sentence to a syntactic transformation resulting in a restriction of the rheme, which finds itself reduced to an adverb that carries all the rhematic weight, the rest of the sentence being reduced to the rank of theme. The method used consists of transforming the plain sentence in a *cleft sentence*:

It is in his cathedral *that King Henry II had Thomas Becket murdered*

where '***it is in his cathedral***' is the marked rheme, or focus, which conveys the essential

[185] Also called 'emphatic forms;' the term 'second tense' belongs to Coptic grammar.
[186] It is, however, possible to specify the tense thanks to the use (rare) of the converter *wn*, *cf.* example 6.

information, while '*that King Henry II had Thomas Becket murdered*' is only the theme conveying little or no new information.

The same is true in Late Egyptian, except that the restriction of the rheme is obtained through a second tense. Given the plain sentence:

tw.ỉ* ***ḥr dỉt dỉw m tꜣ ḥwt-nṯr*

'I give provisions in the temple' where, as in the English sentence, '*tw.ỉ*' is both theme and subject, while '***ḥr dỉt dỉw m tꜣ ḥwt-nṯr***' is the rheme consisting of a predicate '***ḥr dỉt dỉw***' (predicate construction) and of an adverbial ***m tꜣ ḥwt-nṯr***.

According to Polotsky and his school of thought,[187] the use of the second tense transforms the entire sentence into a noun, with the sole exception of the adverbial(s). Thus the result is a nominal sentence with an adverbial predicate of the type ***rꜥ m tꜣ pt***:

ỉ.ỉrỉ.ỉ dỉt dỉw* ***m tꜣ ḥwt-nṯr*

'The fact that I give provisions is **in the temple**' – '**it is in the temple** that I give provisions,' where '*ỉ.ỉrỉ.ỉ dỉt dỉw*' is a noun equivalent that serves as subject, thus corresponding to the theme, while '***m tꜣ ḥwt-nṯr***' plays the role of an adverbial predicate, transformed into **marked rheme**.[188]

Nowadays there is a tendency to reject the 'nominalisation' favoured by the proponents of Polotsky's theories or, at least, to think that, even if it was so originally, the second tense eventually came to be perceived as no more than a signal to focus the rhematic weight exclusively onto the adverbial(s).[189]

23.3 How to translate second tenses

Second tenses can be translated in English in several ways, the aim will be to choose one that best suits the sentence with which one is dealing. Thus the phrase **ỉ.ỉrỉ.ỉ ỉy* ***r ptr.k*** can be translated using a:

– a cleft sentence: '***It is*** *to see you* ***that*** *I came.*' This translation, although always possible, has the shortcoming of not respecting the word order of the original sentence;
– a correlative system:[190] '***If*** *I came,* ***it is*** *to see you*;'
– using a restriction like 'only...:'[191] '*I have come* ***only*** *to see you.*'

The last two phrases have the advantage of respecting the word order of the Egyptian sentence, but it is not always possible to use them.

---

[187] Bibliography in Frandsen, *LEVS*, notes to §85, p. 278-279.

[188] When there are several adverbials, it is, at least in theory, the last one that is rhematised; see Junge, *ZDMG* suppl. II (1972), 33ff. In reality, it seems that things are not so simple since, the set of adverbials, other than the last one, may well be focalised.

[189] The same type of evolution is found in French where, if etymologically the future is a compound tense: *je manger-ai* (infinitive + verb 'have'), in practice for centuries it has been felt as a simple tense.

[190] Polotsky, *Egyptian Tenses*, §18, p. 8.

[191] Others can also be used 'only ... for,' 'solely ... to,' etc.

23.4 The second tenses periphrased

i.iri.f sdm.(f) **+ circonstant**

They are attested in all verb forms without exception. They can also be imbued of modality, except for those that are employed also in the simple form, used for this purpose.

23.4.1 Affirmative forms

In the following examples the marked rheme is shown in bold.

1. P. Turin 1976, v° 1-6 (= *KRI* VI, 599, 9-11).

ptr ỉ.ỉrỉ.ỉ dỉt ỉn.(tw) n.k tꜣy.k ꜥꜣt ***m ḥsbt 6 ꜣbd 3 šmw sw 25***
ẖr ỉ.ỉrỉ.(ỉ) dỉt ỉn.tw n.k pꜣ ẖꜣr n ỉt ***ỉrm nꜣ ktẖw nty tw.(ỉ) ꜥḥꜥ.k(wỉ) ḥr ỉn.tw.w***
'See, it is in year 6, the third month of the summer season, day 25, that I have your jenny brought to you, and it is at the same time as I am sending you the other (things), that I have the sac of grain brought to you.'

This example shows that the second tenses are devoid of temporality. The first refers to the past, since the beginning of the letter indicates that the jenny has already been returned, while the second denotes the immediate present (or the immediate future).

2. P. Bologna 1086, 6-7 (= *KRI* IV, 79, 8-10).

ẖr bw rḫ.ỉ r-ḏd ỉrỉ pꜣy.ỉ ꜥḏd (r) pḥ r.k yꜣ ỉ.ỉrỉ.ỉ hꜣb.f ***r sḫm-pḥty***
'And I do not know if my boy will reach you, for I have (only) sent him to Sekhem-pehty.'

3. P. Berlin P 8523, 5-6 (= Allam, *HOP,* pl. 76).

ỉ.ỉrỉ.ỉ ỉy r nỉwt ***ỉw ḏd.ỉ n.k*** *bn ỉw.ỉ (r) dỉt skꜣ.k gr*
'It is after I said to you: "I will not let you plough anymore" that I returned to Thebes.'

4. Wenamun, 2, 19-22 (= *LES*, 68, 15-69, 4).

mk ỉ.ỉrỉ ỉmn ḫrw m tꜣ pt ***ỉw dỉ.f swtḫ m rk.f*** *– ḫr ỉ.ỉrỉ ỉmn grg {n} nꜣ tꜣw* ***(r)-ḏr.w***

ỉrỉ.f grg.w ***ỉw grg.f pꜣ tꜣ n kmt pꜣ ỉw.k ỉm ẖry-ḥꜣt*** *– ḫr ỉ.ỉrỉ mnḫt pr ỉm.f* ***r pḥ r pꜣ nty tw.ỉ ỉm*** *–*
ḫr ỉ.ỉrỉ sbꜣyt pr ỉm.f ***r pḥ r pꜣ nty tw.ỉ ỉm***
'See, it was only after having put Seth beside himself that Amun clashed in the sky. And, if it is in their totality that Amun has established the countries, he did not establish them until having first founded the country of Egypt, whence you have come; but it is to reach the place where I find myself that craftsmanship (= techniques) has come forth, and it is to reach the place where I am that learning (= education) has come forth.'

The particle *ḫr* is absent before the third second tense because the latter forms, together with what precedes it, a paratactic system, that is, a system in which the dependency relationship existing between the two, simply juxtaposed members is not explicited by a subordinating morpheme.

5. P. BM 10083, 2, 5 (= *KRI* VI, 835, 7-8).

ỉ.ỉrỉ.‹ỉ› pr m pꜣ pr n pr-ꜥꜣ ꜥ.w.s. ***m-ḏr ỉw pꜣy-nḥsy***
'It was only after Panehesy came that I left the palace of Pharaoh l.p.h.' or 'I did not leave the palace of Pharaoh l.p.h. until after the arrival of Panehesy.'

The use of the converter *wn* allows one to give the second tense an explicit past temporal reference:

6. P. BM 10052, 4, 21 (= *KRI* VI, 777, 13).

wn *ỉ.ỉrỉ.w pš pꜣ ḥḏ* ***m pr n A***
'**It was** in the house of A that they **shared** the silver.'

23.4.2 Negative Forms
There are several ways in which a second tense can be negated.

Given the affirmative construction:
– ****ỉ.ỉrỉ.ỉ ḏd.f n snḏ*** 'It is because of fear that I said it.'

If the negation affects the verb itself, the negative verb *tm* is used:
– ****ỉ.ỉrỉ.ỉ tm ḏd.f n snḏ*** 'It is because of fear that I did not say it.'

7. Horus and Seth, 15, 12-13 (= *LES,* 59, 6): question to Seth.
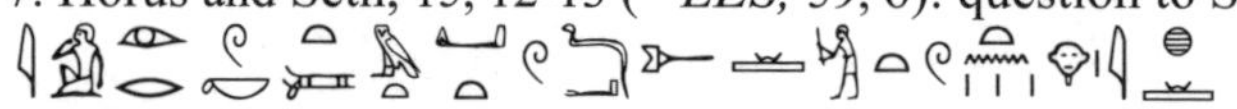
ỉ.ỉrỉ.k ***tm*** *dỉt wḏꜥ.tw.tn ḥr ỉḫ*
'Why have you not allowed you(rselves) to be judged?'

If the negation affects the 'nexus' (predicative link) between the nominalised verbal form functioning as subject and the adverbial playing the role of predicate, the negation *bn* is used, very often reinforced by *ỉwnꜣ* that can be rendered as 'definitely:'

– ***bn ỉ.ỉrỉ.ỉ ḏd.f n snḏ (ỉwnꜣ)*** ‘It is (definitely) not for fear that I said it.’

8. P. DM VII, v° 6.

*ḥr **bn** ỉ.ỉrỉ.ỉ ṯꜣy.w dy **ỉwnꜣ***
‘And it is certainly not here that I took them.’

The negation can affect both the verb and the nexus, in which case we have:
– ***bn ỉ.ỉrỉ.ỉ tm ḏd.f n snḏ*** ‘It is not because of fear that I did not say it.’

9. P. Turin 1880, 2, 20 (= *RAD*, 56, 2-3): *unique example.*

***bn** ỉ.ỉrỉ.ỉ **tm** ỉy ỉw mn nkt r ỉn.tw.f n.tn*
‘It was not because there was nothing to bring you that I did not come.’

23.5 Modal second tense (non-periphrased)

***ỉ.sdm.f** (se)* + **circonstant**

These second tenses are only attested with a limited number of verbs, such as: ***ỉw*** ‘come,’[192] ***ỉnỉ*** ‘bring,’ ***ỉrỉ*** ‘make,’ ***rdỉ*** ‘give,’ ***hꜣb*** ‘send,’ ***sbỉ*** ‘depart,’ ***šm*** ‘go,’ ***šdỉ*** ‘exact,’ ***ḏd*** ‘say.’ While these syntagmas are frequently called ‘prospective second tenses,’ it is preferable to retain the denomination ‘modal second tense,’ given that their essential characteristic is always that of conveying a modal nuance, which contrasts with periphrased forms of the same verbs that are (in principle) never imbued with modality.[193] This is clearly illustrated by the following example:

10. Wenamun, 2, 78-79 (= *LES,* 75, 7-9).
‘Say to your mistress that I have heard (say) as far as Thebes, the place where Amun is, that

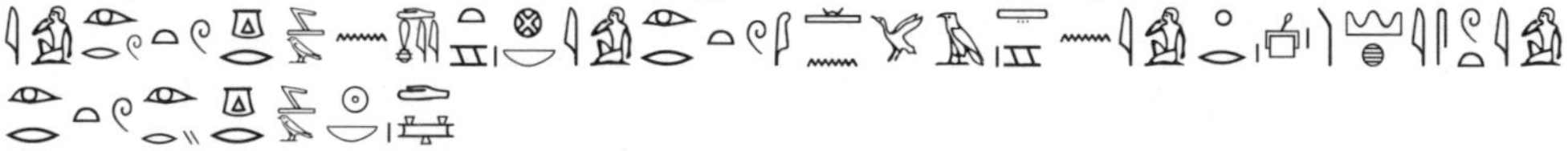

***ỉ.ỉrỉ.tw** grg n(=m) dmỉ nb* (modal second tense) – ***ỉ.ỉrỉ.tw** mꜣꜥt n(=m) pꜣ tꜣ n ỉls* (modal second tense) – *ỉst **ỉ.ỉrỉ.tw** ỉrỉ grg rꜥ nb dy* (periphrased second tense, non-modal)
evil is done everywhere, (and that) justice is done in the land of Alasya (only) (*lit.* ‘it is in every place that falsehood is practiced, it is in the land of Alasya that truth is done). Could it be that here injustice is (also) committed every day?’ (*lit.* ‘that one practices falsehood’).

Wenamun stresses the contrast between the reputation of Alasya (Cyprus), that reached the faraway Thebes, where it was said that it was the only place where one tried to do well, and his sad realisation on arriving there, that there was evil there as elsewhere. From the viewpoint of the syntax, it should be noted that the two modal second tenses form again a paratactic system.

---

[192] Note that the spelling is always *ỉw* not *ỉy*.
[193] *Cf.* Cassonnet, *LingAeg* 4 (1994).

11. P. Cairo J 65739, 27 (= *KRI* II, 802, 13-14).

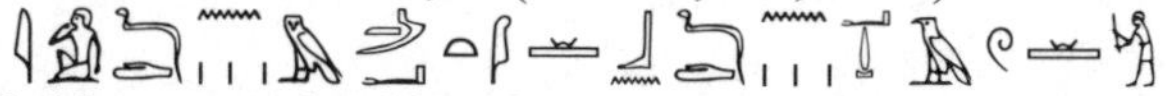

ỉ.ḏd.n *m mꜣꜥt bn ḏd.n ꜥḏꜣ*

'It is in accordance to the truth that we swear to speak: we are committed to not tell lies.'

12. O. Berlin P 10655, 5-7 (= *KRI* V, 573, 15-16): oath sworn by a debtor.

ỉw.f ḥr ỉrt 3 ꜥnḫ n nb ꜥ.w.s. r-ḏd ỉ.dỉ.ỉ ꜥq wpt-rnpt ỉw dỉ.ỉ pꜣ ḥḏ (*n*) *pꜣy rmṯ n.f*

'He took three oaths by the lord l.p.h. saying: "I have no intention of letting the New Year come than after having given to this man his money." In other words: "Indeed, the New Year will not come before I have paid this man!"

The construction is negated by means of the negative morpheme *bn*, although it is very rare:

bn ỉ.sdm.f (se) + **adverbial**

13. P. Turin 1880, v° 6, 4-5 (= *RAD*, 48, 11-12).

wꜣḥ ỉmn wꜣḥ pꜣ ḥqꜣ ꜥ.w.s. ***bn ỉ.ỉn.tw*** *tꜣy.ỉ 3 ẖrd ḥr.ỉ*

'As Amun endures, as the sovereign l.p.h. endures, if one wants to bring my three heirs (to appear before a court), it will not be because of me.'

23.6 Other second tenses

It is possible to find, especially in texts of the nineteenth dynasty, vestiges, more or less altered, of the second tenses in use in Middle Egyptian.[194]

Thus, when intransitive verbs – which cannot have a perfective *sḏm.f* – show a *sḏm.f* form with a **past** nuance[195] accompanied by an adverbial, this is classified as a second tense deriving from the 'emphatic' *sḏm.n.f* of classical Egyptian.

14. P. Chester Beatty VII, v° 1, 7.

ḥr ***sḏr.f*** *ḥr pꜣy.f ḥꜥtỉ m-ẖnw n pr.f*

'And it is on his bed, at home (*lit.* 'inside his house'), that he spent the night.'

15. Doomed Prince, 5, 10-11 (= *LES,* 3, 15-16).

ỉy.k *tnw pꜣ šrỉ nfr*

'From where have you come, beautiful child?'[196]

[194] See Winand, *o.l.*, §407-418, p. 258-265 and §487-494, p. 310-316.

[195] Beware of the confusion with the prospective, which can be found in all verb forms.

[196] *Cf. ỉy.n.tn tnw* 'Whence have you come?' (The Semnah Despatches, 2, 14 = *JEA* 31 (1945), pl. III): letter written under Amenemhat III.

Similarly, sometimes it is possible to find a *sḏm.tw.f* form with a past nuance, deriving from the traditional emphatic form *sḏm.n.tw.f*. This rare[197] form should not be confused with the passive prospective *sḏm.tw.f*, which is quite frequent in complement clauses after the verb *rdỉ*.

[197] Last occurrence under Ramses IV. See *infra* §28.14, example 3.

P. Abbott 2 (*cf.* p. 64)

24. Independent forms: recapitulation

24.1 Table of the main independent forms

Perfective[198]		**Third Future**	
sḏm.f	*bwpwy.f sḏm*	*ỉw.f r sḏm*	*bn ỉw.f r sḏm*
		ỉrỉ N r sḏm	*bn ỉrỉ N r sḏm*
First Present		**Prospective**	
sw dy	*bn sw dy*	*sḏm.f*	*bn sḏm.f*[199]
sw m pꜣ pr	*bn sw m pꜣ pr* (*ỉwnꜣ*)		
sw ḥr sḏm	*bn sw ḥr sḏm*		
sw m ꜥq[200]	*bn sw m ꜥq*	**Imperative**	
sw stp.Ø[201]	*bn sw stp.Ø*	(*ỉ*).*sḏm* (*sw*)	*m ỉrỉ sḏm.*(*f*)
	bwpwy.tw stp.f		
sw ꜥq.Ø	*bwpwy.f ꜥq*	**Predication of existence (to have)**	
sw nfr.Ø	*bn sw nfr.Ø*	*wn* (*m-dỉ.f*) *A*	*mn* (*m-dỉ.f*) *A*
Aorist		**Second tense**	
(*ḫr-sḏm.f*)	*bw ỉrỉ.f sḏm*	*ỉ.ỉrỉ.f sḏm.*(*f*) + adverbial	*ỉ.ỉrỉ.f tm sḏm.*(*f*) + adverbial[202] *bn ỉ.ỉrỉ.f sḏm.*(*f*) + adverbial (*ỉwnꜣ*)[203]
‘Not yet’			
	bw ỉrỉ.t.f sḏm	*ỉ.sḏm.f* + adverbial	*bn ỉ.sḏm.f* + adverbial
	bw sḏmy.t N		

[198] Limited to transitive verbs. Intransitive verbs express the past by means of the first present with a pseudo-participle as predicate: example *sw mwt.Ø* ‘he died,’ see *infra* §24.3.2.
[199] If the prospective is non-independent, the negation is *tm.f sḏm*.
[200] Only (intransitive) verbs of motion.
[201] Transitive verbs, expresses the passive.
[202] Negated verb.
[203] Negated nexus.

24.2 Conjugation of transitive verbs

Affirmative forms

Active voice

wꜣḥ.f	he placed (narrative context)
	he has placed (non-narrative context)
wn wꜣḥ.f	he had placed
sw ḥr wꜣḥ	he places (habitual)
	he is placing
wn.f ḥr wꜣḥ	he placed (habitual)
	he was placing
ỉw.f r wꜣḥ	he will place
wn ỉw.f r wꜣḥ	he would place
wꜣḥ.f	may he place

Passive voice

tw.tw ḥr wꜣḥ.f	he is placed (one places him)
wn.tw ḥr wꜣḥ.f	he was placed (one placed him)
sw wꜣḥ.Ø	he was placed (narrative context)
	he has been placed (non- narrative context)
wn.f wꜣḥ.Ø	he had been placed
ỉw.f wꜣḥ.Ø	he will be placed

Negative forms

Active voice

bwpwy.f wꜣḥ	he did not place (narrative context)
	he has not placed (non-narrative context)
bn sw ḥr wꜣḥ	he does not place (habitual)
	he is not placing
bw ỉrỉ.f wꜣḥ	he never places
	he cannot place
(bw wꜣḥ.f)	*id.*
bw ỉrỉ.t.f wꜣḥ	he has not yet placed
bw ỉw.f r wꜣḥ	he will not place
wn bn ỉw.f r wꜣḥ	he would not place
bn wꜣḥ.f	may he not place

Passive voice

bn tw.tw ḥr wꜣḥ.f	he is not placed (one does not place him)
bw ỉrỉ.tw wꜣḥ.f	he is never placed (one never places him) he cannot be placed (one cannot place him)
bn sw wꜣḥ.Ø	he was not placed (narrative context) he has not been placed (non-narrative context)
bwpwy.tw wꜣḥ.f	he was not placed (one did not place him) (narrative context) he has not been placed (one has not placed him) (non-narrative context)
bw wꜣḥy.t N	N has not yet been placed
bn ỉw.tw r wꜣḥ.f	he will not be placed (one will not place him)
bn ỉw.f wꜣḥ.Ø	he will not be placed

24.3 Conjugation of intransitive verbs

24.3.1 Verbs of motion

Affirmative forms

sw m ꜥq	he is entering
sw ḥr ꜥq	he enters (habitual)
wn.f ḥr ꜥq	he entered (habitual)
sw ꜥq.Ø	he entered (narrative context), he has entered (non-narrative context)
ỉw.f r ꜥq	he will enter
ỉw.f ꜥq.Ø	he would enter
ꜥq.f	may he enter

Negative forms

bn sw m ꜥq	he is not entering
bn sw ḥr ꜥq	he does not enter (habitual)
bwpwy.f ꜥq	he did not enter (narrative context) he has not entered (non-narrative context)
bw ỉrỉ.f ꜥq	he never enters, he cannot enter
bw ỉrỉ.t.f ꜥq	he has not yet entered
bn ỉw.f r ꜥq	he will not enter
bn ꜥq.f	may he not enter

24.3.2 Other intransitive verbs

sw ḥr ḥms	he sits down (habitual), he is sitting down
wn.f ḥr ḥms	he sat down (habitual), he was sitting down
sw ḥms.Ø	he sat down (narrative context), he is seated (non-narrative context)
wn.f ḥms.Ø	he was sitting down (narrative context), he was seated (non-narrative context)
ỉw.f r ḥms	he will sit down
ḥms	may he sit down

24.4 Final remarks

There is no exact symmetry between affirmative and negative forms:

- *bwpwy.f sḏm* can be used as negative correlate of the perfective *sḏm.f*, or of some forms of the first present having as predicate a pseudo-participle – particularly with verbs of motion;
- *bw ỉrỉ.f sḏm* (negative aorist) can negate the first present, habitual or general, when one wants to emphasise that the process never occurs or it is impossible, but this construction also serves as a negation of the *ḫr-sḏm.f* form;
- *bw ỉrỉ.t.f sḏm* does not have any affirmative correlate;
- *bw sḏm.f* is a heterogeneous form that could be the successor of *n sḏm.f* – thus representing a doublet of the *bwpwy.f sḏm* form – but also a successor of *n sḏm.n.f*, thus representing a doublet of the *bw ỉrỉ.f sḏm* form.

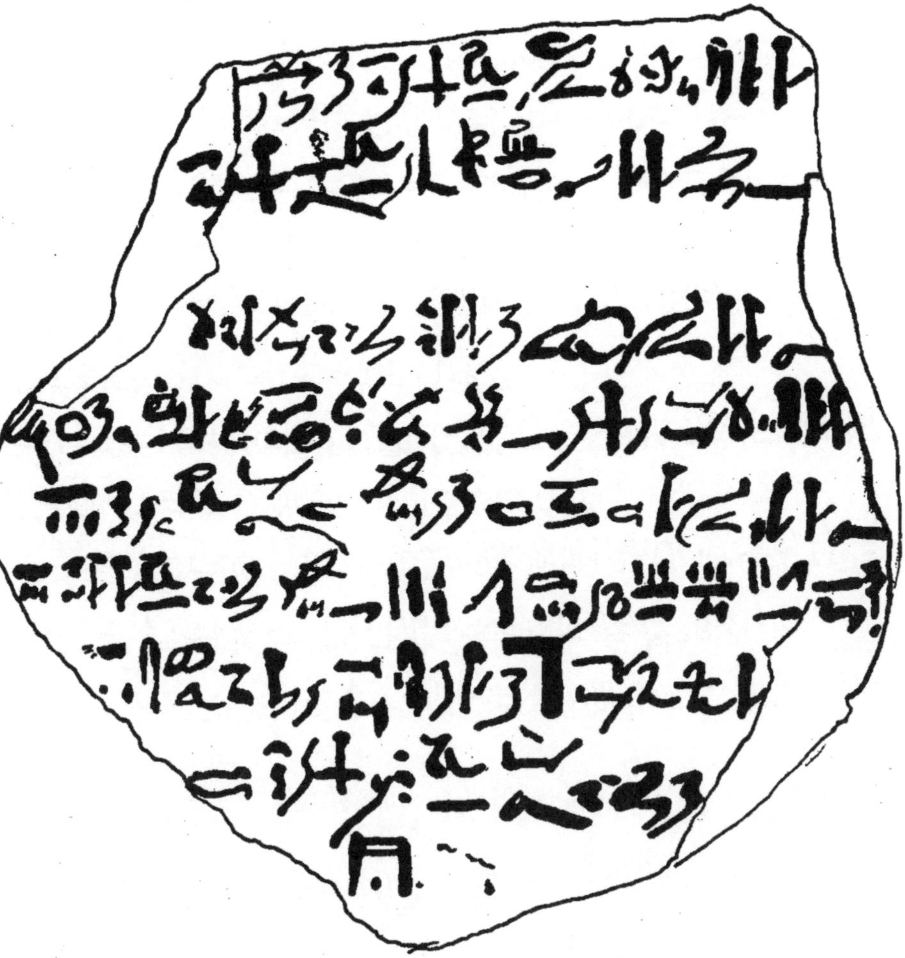

O. DM 554, v° (*cf.* p. 4, 54)

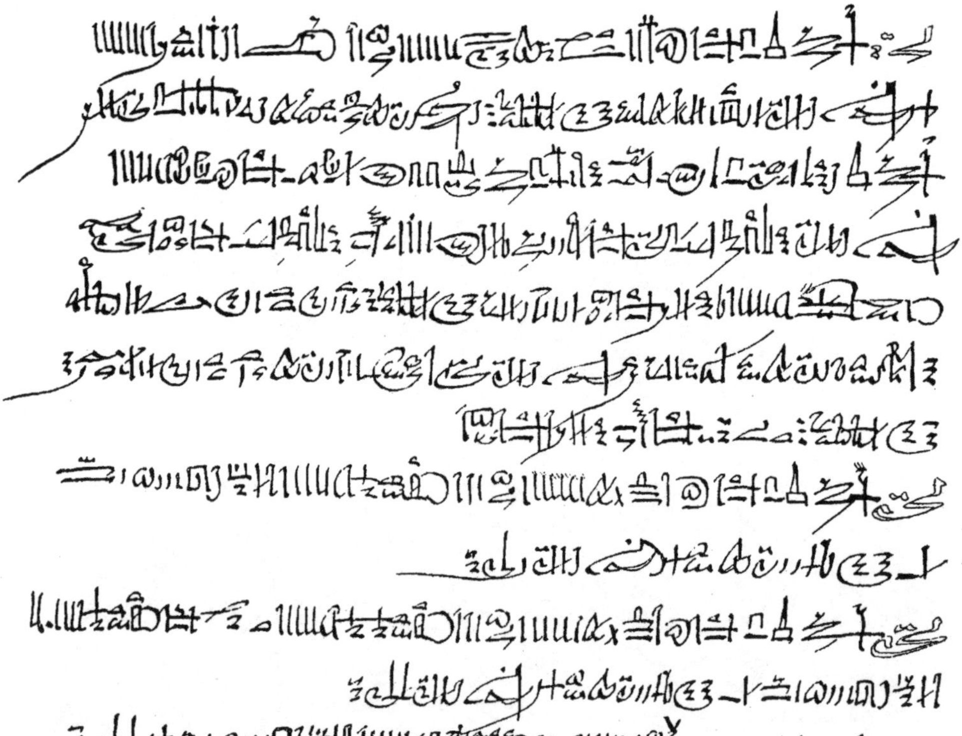

P. Abbott 3 (*cf.* p. 14)

NON-INDEPENDENT VERBAL FORMS

P. Abbott 4 (*cf.* p. 14, 59)

25. The continuative forms

25.1 Introduction

Sequential forms are non-independent forms which must lean on another form (independent or not), placed before them. These are, therefore, non-initial forms.
They always have the value of independent or main clauses (never subordinated).
They are devoid of temporality and simply continue the temporal nuance indicated either by the form preceding them, when the latter has one, or by the enunciation's register.
They are negated by means of the negative verb *tm*.[204]
In Late Egyptian there are two continuative forms: the sequential and the conjunctive.

25.2 The sequential[205]

This is a construction specific to Late Egyptian, since it has no predecessor in Middle Egyptian and disappears after the 21st dynasty. It can be considered as the 'functional' successor of the sequential *sḏm.n.f* of Middle Egyptian.

ỉw.f ḥr (tm) sdm ***ỉw N ḥr (tm) sḏm***

▪ The *ỉw* of the sequential, just like that of the third future, is an integral part of the construction, but, unlike the latter, it cannot appear in an initial position or after direct indicators of initiality.
▪ If the preposition *ḥr* is omitted, it should be restored in brackets in the transliteration.
▪ Unlike the first present (and the third future), the sequential can have only one type of predicate: *ḥr* + Infinitive

The sequential allows events to be related in an **objective and punctual** manner, in their chronological succession (excluding the repetition), making it a form essentially (but not exclusively) **narrative**.

The sequential can lean on various syntagmas, of which the main ones are the following:

25.2.1 Leaning onto an independent form

In this case, the sequential continues the temporal nuance of the independent form.

1. P. Mayer A, 1, 14-16 (= *KRI* VI, 805, 2-5): deposition before a court.

*ḏd.f **sḏm.‹ỉ›** r-ḏd n3 rmṯ ḥn.Ø r ỉrt h3w m p3y pr-n-sṯ3 **ỉw.ỉ (ḥr) šm ỉw.ỉ (ḥr) gm** p3y 6 rmṯ i.ḏd ỉṯ3y p3y-k3mn ʿq3*
'He said: "I learned that the men had left to seize this portable shrine," I went and found precisely these six individuals that the thief Paykamen named.' In this example, the initial form is a perfective *sḏm.f*.

---

[204] The negation, therefore, affects the verb, not the sentence, which remains affirmative; see Gilula, *JEA* 56 (1970), 212, n. 7.
[205] See Groll, *JEA* 55 (1969), 89ff.; Junge, *JEA* 72 (1986), 113ff.; Vernus, *DE* 9, 107, and especially Winand, *o.l.*, p. 442-457.

2. P. BM 10326, 5-8 (= *LRL*, 17, 10-12).

ḥnꜥ ḏd r-nty ***tꜣy šꜥt twt spr.Ø*** *r.ỉ m-ḏrt šmsw ḏḥwty-ḥtp m ḥsbt 10 ꜣbd 1 šmw sw 25* ***ỉw.ỉ (ḥr) šsp.s ỉw.ỉ (ḥr) nḏnḏ****.k m-dỉ.f* ***ỉw.f (ḥr) ḏd*** *n.ỉ tw.k ꜥnḫ.tỉ*
'Another matter: this letter of yours has reached me through the servant Djehutyhotep in year 10, first month of the summer season, day 25. I received it, I enquired about you with him, and he told me that you were alive.' This time the initial form is a first present having as predicate a pseudo-participle.

25.2.2 Leaning onto an adverbial clause

The sequential plays the role of apodosis in the correlative system thus obtained.

3. O. Cairo 25725, 1-3 (= *KRI* IV, 417, 6-8): deposition before a court.

ỉr ỉnk dỉ.‹ỉ› wꜥ n dꜣỉw n tꜣy.ỉ šrỉ(t) ỉw.s gb.[*tỉ*] *– ḫr ỉr st ḥr snb* ***ỉw.ỉ ḥr hꜣb*** *n.s ḥr ‹ḏd› ỉmỉ tw.f* ***ỉw.s ḥr tm dỉ.tw.f***
'As for me, I gave my daughter a skirt while she was ill, and, when she was recovering, I wrote to her saying: "So return it!" (*lit.* 'give it (back)!') She did not return it.'

The first sequential represents the apodosis of a correlative system, whose protasis contains a first present transformed into an adverbial by the particle *ỉr – ḫr* limits itself to coordinating all that precedes it (see *infra* §33.2.1.1). On the resulting system leans a second sequential (in this case, negative).

4. P. Gardiner 4, 4-5 (= *KRI* VII, 339, 6-8): discourse.

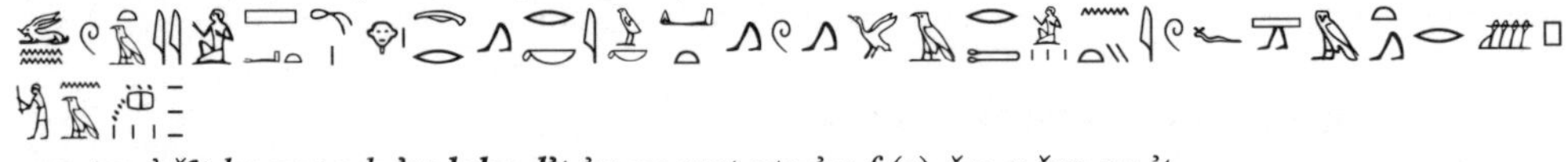

wnn tꜣy.ỉ šꜥt ḥr spr r.k ***ỉw.k ḥr dỉt*** *ỉw pꜣ rmṯ nty ỉw.f (r) šm r šsp nꜣ ỉt*
'As soon as my letter will reach you, you will cause the man who will go to take the grain (pl.) to come.' For this system, see *infra* §34.

25.2.3 Leaning onto a non-verbal circonstant

Most often, the sequential leans onto an adverbial phrase.[206] On these constructions, see *infra* §33.5 and §33.6.

5. P. Leiden I 350, v°, col. III, 13-14 (= *KRI* II, 810, 3-4).

ḥr ỉr ḥr-sꜣ ***ỉw.tw ḥr ḫꜣꜥ*** *sš ḥr-tl ḥr tr n mtrt*
'And then the scribe Hortel was released at noon' (*lit.* 'at noon time').

[206] Sometimes a noun with adverbial function.

6. P. Turin 1887, v° 1, 10 (= *RAD*, 79, 7-8).

ḥr ỉr m ḥsbt 1 *n nsw ḥqꜣ-mꜣꜥt-rꜥ stp.n-ỉmn ꜥ.w.s. pꜣ nṯr ꜥꜣ* ***ỉw.f (ḥr) ỉrt*** *wgg ꜥšꜣ m nꜣ ỉt*
'And in the year 1 of King Heqamaatra Setepenamun l.p.h. (Ramses IV), the great god, he committed many (cases of) misappropriations of grain (*lit.* 'in grains').'

25.2.4 Excursus: other continuative-narrative forms

– *wn.ỉn.f ḥr sḏm*: it is found almost exclusively in tales;[207]
– *ꜥḥꜥ.n sḏm.f*: derives from *ꜥḥꜥ.n sḏm.n.f* or from *ꜥḥꜥ.n sḏm N*;[208]
– *ꜥḥꜥ.n.f ḥr sḏm*: analytical form.[209]

The last two forms are found only in literary texts and some legal or administrative texts.[210]

▪ With regards to the relationship between these continuative forms and the sequential, opinions are divided. According to Satzinger, *wn.ỉn.f ḥr sḏm* is the literary equivalent of the sequential, whereas Winand sees *wn.ỉn* and *ꜥḥꜥ.n* as paragraphs markers – with *wn.ỉn* operating at a higher hierarchical level than *ꜥḥꜥ.n*.

7. Doomed Prince, 4, 3-6 (= *LES*, 1, 5-10): literary narrative.

ꜥḥꜥ.n msy *wꜥ n sꜣ ṯꜥy – ỉyt pw ỉr.n nꜣ n ḥwt-ḥr r šꜣ n.f šꜣy – ỉw.sn ḥr ḏd mwt.f n pꜣ msḥ m r-pw pꜣ ḥfꜣw mỉtt pꜣ ỉw*
ꜥḥꜥ.n sḏm *nꜣ n rmṯ nty r-gs pꜣ ẖrd –* ***wn.ỉn.sn ḥr wḥm****.sn n ḥm.f ꜥ.w.s. –* ***wn.ỉn ḥm.f ꜥ.w.s. ḥr ḫpr*** *ỉw ỉb.f ḏww r ꜥꜣt wrt –* ***wn.ỉn ḥm.f ꜥ.w.s. ḥr*** *dỉt* [*qd.tw n.f wꜥ n pr*] *n ỉnr ḥr ḫꜣst*
'Then a male child was born. The Hathors[211] came to assign him a destiny. They said: "It is by the crocodile, the snake or the dog that he will die!"[212] When the people who were with the child heard (these words), they repeated them to his majesty l.p.h. and the heart of his majesty l.p.h.

---

[207] Gardiner, *EG*, §470; Satzinger, *NÄS*, §2.7, p. 233ff.; Doret, *Narrative*, p. 114, example 17 and 22; Winand, *o.l.*, p. 474-475 and 479-480.
[208] Sometimes *ꜥḥꜥ.n sḏm.n.f* is still attested. Gardiner, *o.c.*, §478 and 481; Černý-Groll, *LEG*, §44.1, p. 452-453; Satzinger, *loc. cit.*
[209] Gardiner, *o.c.*, §482; Winand, *o.l.*, p. 474-478.
[210] For Example: P. BM 10355; O. Nash 1 and 2; P. Abbott; P. Adoption.
[211] *Lit.* 'It is a coming that the Hathors did;' it corresponds to the ancient form infinitive + relative form, which is only found in stories. *Cf.* Gardiner, *o.c.*, §392, and *supra* §4.1.1.
[212] Traditional second tense; *cf.* the Late Egyptian correlate *ỉ.ỉrỉ.s mwt ⟨n⟩ dm* 'it is by the sword that she will die' (P. Orbiney, 9, 9 = *LES*, 19, 11). See Winand, *o.l.*, §436, p. 277-278.

became very, very sad.[213] His majesty l.p.h. had a stone house built for him in the desert.'

8. Horus and Seth, 5, 2-3 (= *LES,* 42, 16-43, 1): literary narrative.

ꜥḥꜥ.n swtḫ ḥr ỉrt ꜥnḫ n nb r-ḏr r-ḏd

'Then Seth swore an oath by the Lord of the Universe as follows: ...'

25.3 The conjunctive

This is a continuative form which, according to Gardiner,[214] originated from a traditional theoretical construction: **ḥnꜥ sḏm ntf* (where *sḏm* is the infinitive), which became, between the end of the eighteenth and the beginning of the nineteenth dynasty *ḥnꜥ ntf sḏm.* Then, following the disappearance of *ḥnꜥ* and the revision of the independent pronoun: *mtw.f sḏm*. Therefore, we have:

Late XVIII – early XIX dynasty ***ḥnꜥ ntf (tm) sḏm***
current Late Egyptian ***mtw.f (tm) sḏm***

The conjunctive is a **subjective** form. It is very frequently, but not exclusively, employed in a **jussive context** and/or the **future**, as well as in oaths. It can also be used to describe past hypothetical[215] or habitual[216] events. Its use in the narrative allows one to achieve style effects.[217] Unlike the sequential, it cannot lean onto a non-verbal circonstant. Finally, its presence in the apodosis of correlative systems is debated.[218]

The following is an example from the beginning of the nineteenth dynasty, containing both forms of conjunctive in the same syntactic position, continuing *ỉḫ* + independent prospective *sḏm.f.*

9. P. Northumberland I, v° 3-8 (= *KRI* II, 240, 1-6) (fig. p. 38): letter.

*ky ḏd **ỉḫ dỉ.k** ḥr.k n mry-ms **mtw.k sḏm** tꜣ wpt (ỉ).hꜣb n.k pꜣ mr mšꜥ ḥr.s **mtw.k hꜣb** n.f ḥr rn.k **mtw.k hꜣb** n.ỉ ḥr snb.k nb ... **ỉḫ dỉ.k** ỉnt n.ỉ mry-ms wꜥ n ꜥw(ty) ḏmꜥ m-mỉtt nkt n ryt nfr sp-sn ỉw m dy ỉn.tw bỉn **ḥnꜥ ntk hꜣb** n.ỉ ḥr snb.k nb sp.sn*

'One more thing: Will you carefully take care of Merymes and take note of the commission about which the general wrote to you and send him (a report) in your signature (*lit.* 'in your name') and send me any (news) about your health ... Will you get Merymes to bring me (*lit.* 'cause that Merymes brings me') a roll of papyrus and a bit of very good ink – do not let bad one be brought – and send me any (news) about your health.'

---

213 *Lit.* 'and his majesty l.p.h. became so that his heart was very, very sad' (Satzinger, *NÄS*, p. 237).

214 *JEA* 14 (1928), 86-96; *EG*, §171 and 300 obs. See also Černý, *JEA* 35 (1949), 25-30. A comprehensive review of the theories on the origin of the conjunctive can be found in Winand, *o.l.*, p. 457-465.

215 See example 15 below.

216 See example 14 below.

217 Example: P. Salt 124, P. Turin 1887, see *supra* §12.3.4.

218 See besides the grammars, Borghouts *ZÄS* 106 (1979), 14-24, and Winand, *o.l.*, p. 466-473; however, note P. Anastasi VI, 38 (= *LEM*, 75, 9).

10. P. Cairo J 65739, 4-5 (= *KRI* II, 800, 9-10).

[iw.f ḥr] ḏd n.i ***in*** *n.ṯ tꜣy ʿḏdt šrit* ***mtw.ṯ*** *dit n.i swn(t).s*

'He told me: "Buy for yourself this young girl and pay me her price."' In this example, the conjunctive continues the imperative.

11. P. BM 10100, 14- v° 1 (= *LRL,* 50, 16-51, 3): letter of the general Piankh.

ḫr inn bwpwy.tn šsp.w ***iw.tn (r) šm*** *r pꜣ nty ḥrrt im* ***mtw.tn šsp.w*** *n.s* ***mtw.tn tm nni*** *n(=m) mdt nb(t) ink* ***mtw.tn sꜣw*** *tꜣy.i šʿt iry.s n.tn mtrt*

'And if you have not received them (the servants), you will go (and) find Hereret and you will receive them from her, and you will not be negligent about any matters of mine, and you will keep my letter so that it will serve you as proof.'

In this example, the conjunctive continues a correlative system which apodosis contains a third future.

The use of the conjunctive is particularly remarkable in the protasis of oaths where it continues the **truth value**[219] of the expression *wꜣḥ imn wꜣḥ pꜣ ḥqꜣ*:

12. O. Petrie 60, 1-v° 2 (= *HO,* 18, 2).

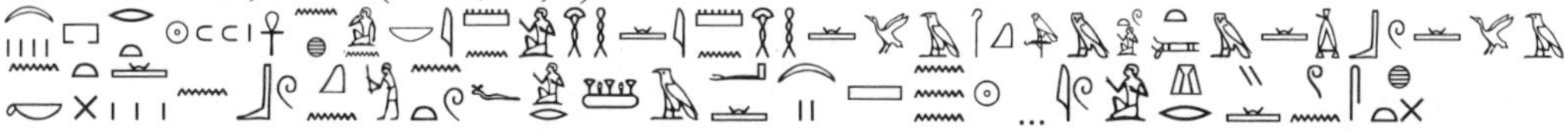

ꜣbd 4 prt sw 21 ʿnḫ n nb-imn wꜣḥ imn wꜣḥ pꜣ ḥqꜣ ***mtw.i tm ḏbꜣ*** *pꜣ nkt n bw-qn.tw.f r-šꜣʿ-(r) ꜣbd 2 šmw ... iw.i ḫr 100 n sḫt*

'Fourth month of the winter season, day 21. Oath (taken) by Nebamun: "As Amun endures, and as the sovereign endures, if I do not repay the goods of Bukentuf before the second month of the summer season ... I will receive a hundred blows."'

Lit. 'Amon endures (it is true), the sovereign endures (it is true) and I do not pay the goods of B. before the second month of the summer season (it is true), then I will receive one hundred blows (it is true).' The only thing to do to render false the realisation of the beating is to render false the non-payment, thus to pay by the deadline.

13. Mès, N 35 (= *KRI* III, 431, 6-7).

ḏdt.n ʿnḫ nt niwt t(ꜣ)-nt-pꜣ-iḥꜣy ***wꜣḥ imn wꜣḥ pꜣ ḥqꜣ mtw.i ḏd*** *ʿḏꜣ iw.i r pḥwy pr*

'What the lady Tanetpaihay said: "As Amun endures, and as the sovereign endures, if I tell lies, I will be relegated to the back of the house"' (that is to say, among the slaves).

[219] The *sḏm.f* in the expression is not the prospective but the **indicative** (old usage) because the endurance of Amun and of the sovereign could not be doubted by the Egyptians of the time.

The following is an example illustrating the use of the conjunctive to describe habitual events:[220]

14. P. Gurob, 2, 6-8 (= *RAD,* 14, 11-15, 2): concerning students.

ỉw.w m ḫꜣstyw mỉ-qd nꜣ (ỉ).wn.tw ḥr ỉn.tw.w n.n m hꜣw ***R mtw.w ḏd*** *n.n wn.n m ꜥḥꜥw m nꜣ prw n nꜣ srw* ***mtw.w ỉṯꜣ*** *mtrt* ***mtw.w rḫ*** *ỉrỉ pꜣ ḏd.tw n.w nb*

'Given that these are foreigners like those that were sent to us in the time of R(amses II), who told us: "We were in service in the houses of officials," (who) received (*lit.* 'taking') an education, and learned to do everything that they were told.'

The use of the conjunctive after a perfective *sḏm.f* should also be noted.[221] In the following example, the possible author of the denunciation having been killed, it was impossible to use the sequential, an objective form, to describe his conduct.

15. P. Mayer B, 8-9 (= *KRI* VI, 516, 2-4).

ỉw.f (ḥr) ḏd n.n ***ẖdb pꜣ ms-ḫr*** *ỉrm pꜣ bꜣk šrỉ ỉ.wn ỉrm.n* ***mtw.f tm dỉ.tw.n*** *r-bl ỉ.n.f n.n*

'He replied to us: "the native of the tomb, and the young servant that was with us, were killed, and (so) he could not denounce us," so he said to us.'

[220] See Wente, *JNES* 21 (1962), 304-311. Other examples: P. Orbiney, 1, 3-10 = *LES*, 9, 14-10, 15; Truth and Falsehood, 5, 4 (= *LES*, 32, 15), etc.

[221] Another example following *bwpwy.f sḏm*, where the conjunctive expresses feint outrage: P. Anastasi VI, 18 (= *LEM* 73, 15-16).

26. The non-independent prospective *sḏm.f*

In a functionally dependent role, the prospective *sḏm.f* ceases to be imbued with modality. Its main applications are:

26.1 In complement clauses following all forms of the verb *rdỉ*

1. P. BM 10052, 13, 17-18 (= *KRI* VI, 796, 12-13).

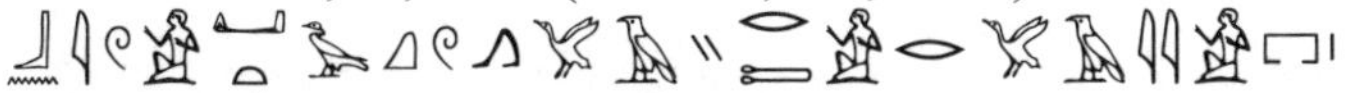

bn ỉw.ỉ (r) dỉt ***ꜥq pꜣy rmṯ*** *r pꜣy.ỉ pr*

'I will not let this man enter into my home (i.e. marry my daughter)' (*lit.* 'I will not allow that this man enters ...').

▪ No negation attested; if necessary, it is the verb *rdỉ* which is used in the negative form.

26.2 In purpose clauses

2. P. DM V, 2-3 (= *KRI* VI, 266, 1).

hꜣb my n.ỉ pꜣ sẖr ḥꜣtỉ.k ***ꜥq.ỉ*** *ỉm.f*

'Tell me, please, your thoughts that I may understand them.' (*lit.* 'Send to me, please, (about) the state of your heart so that I (may) enter therein').

The construction is negated by means of ***tm***:

3. O. Nash 1, v° 12-16 (= *KRI* IV, 317, 9-13).

ỉrỉ pꜣy.ỉ nb r dỉt ỉry.tw sbꜣ(yt) n tꜣy st-ḥmt r(=ỉ).ỉṯꜣy pꜣ ẖl m-mỉtt pꜣ wšb ***tm kt st-ḥmt mỉ-qd.s wḥm*** *ỉrt m-mỉtt*

'My lord will cause a punishment to be inflicted on this woman who stole the pick and the censer, so that another woman like her does not act so again.'

26.3 In subordinate clauses introduced by a preposition or a conjunction

The main prepositions governing these subordinate clauses are *m-ḏr*, *m-ẖt*, *r-tnw*.

4. P. Turin 1880, 2, 18-19 (= *RAD*, 55, 15-16).

ḫd ỉn ṯꜣty tꜣ ***m-ḏr ỉw.f*** *r ỉṯꜣ nꜣ nṯrw n ꜥ rsy r pꜣ ḥb-sd*

'Return to the north by the vizier Ta, after his coming to take the gods of the southern province to the Sed festival' (*lit.* 'Returning ... by the vizier Ta, after he came ...').

5. P. BM 10417, v° 3 (= *LRL*, 28, 4-5).

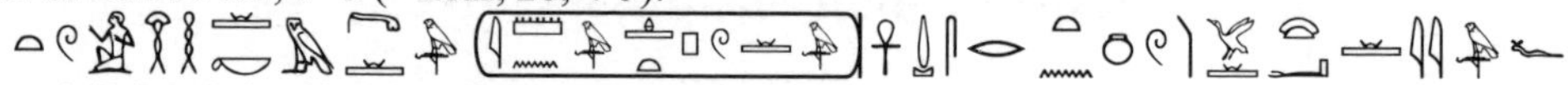

tw.ỉ (*ḥr*) *w3ḥ.k m-b3ḥ ỉmn-ḥtp ˁ.w.s.* ***r-tnw ḫˁy.f***

'I place you before Amenhotep l.p.h. each time that he appears.'

▪ No negative forms attested.

– Dependent clauses containing *m-ḏr* or *m-ḫt* may be found in the protasis of correlative systems introduced by *ỉr*, see *infra* §33.2.2.3.

– It is also possible to find the prospective after the particle *ỉr*, see *infra* §33.2.1.2.2, and in the *ḫr-sḏm.f* form, see *supra* §17.6.

27. The participles

These are adjectival forms of the verb, equivalent to relative clauses where the subject is identical to the antecedent. They can be either active or passive.

27.1 Active participles

27.1.1 Morphology[222]

They are invariable in gender and number, and do not have any special endings.

Quite frequently they are preceded by a prosthetic yod  (example 3), sometimes written with the mouth sign (example 1). This prosthetic yod disappears, in principle, when the participle is nominalised and defined by an article or a demonstrative.

Active participles can be periphrased by the verb *iri*. This, in principle, is required for verbs which stem comprises more than three radicals,[223] for example: P. Turin 1875, 5, 1 (=*KRI* v, 356, 12):  *(i).iri w3w3* 'who plotted,' while it is optional for other verbs (example 2).

27.1.2 Syntax

The antecedent of the resulting relative clause must be **defined**, either by a proper noun, a personal pronoun, a noun defined by an article, a demonstrative, a possessive, a suffix or *nb*.[224]

The direct pronominal object, if there is one and it is pronominal, is, in general, indicated by the dependent pronoun (example 1), and a suffix pronoun attached to the infinitive if the participle is periphrased (example 2).

The negation having disappeared, *nty bwpwy.f sḏm* is used instead; see *infra* §29.7.

• **The active participle** of the verb *wnn*, *(i).wn*, **has a special role: it serves to transpose into the past sentences formed with *nty***, see below §30.2.

27.1.3 Values

The active participles of verbs with three, or fewer, radicals have a **past** temporal value in their **simple participial form** – the point of reference being, in the narrative, the time of the events narrated, and, outside the narration, the time of the statement. When **periphrased**, these participles possess the temporal value of the **habitual present** or of the **general present**. This distinction does not apply to verbs which require the use of a periphrastic construction.

27.1.4 Usage

With the value of a **relative clause** in real cleft sentences:

1. O. Nash 1, 8 (= *KRI* IV, 316, 2).

m-bi3 bn ink ***r(=i).iṯ3y se***

'No, it is not I who stole it.'

---

[222] See Winand, *o.l.*, p. 343-364.

[223] See *supra* §13.2. Some exceptions: *ṯṯṯ*, *smtr*, etc.

[224] See *supra* §1.2, 4.2 and §6.1.

2. P. Turin 1978/208, v° 1-2 (= Allam, *HOP*, pl. 97).

yꜣ bn ỉnn ***ỉ.ỉrỉ ẖn***.*w m-dwn ỉwnꜣ*

'For it is not us who usually transport them (= the goods).' In this example, the participle is periphrased and expresses the habitual present.

With the value of an attributive **adjective**:

3. Wenamun, 1, 20 (= *LES*, 62, 16-63, 1).

ỉr pꜣ ***ỉ.ṯꜣy tw*** *ntk se*

'As for the thief who robbed you, he belongs to you.'

4. Wenamun, 2, 38-39 (= *LES*, 70, 16-71, 1): narrative.

ỉw pꜣy.f ỉpwty **(ỉ).šm** *r kmt (ḥr) ỉy n.ỉ r ḫꜣr n (=m) ꜣbd* 1 *prt*

'His envoy who had gone to Egypt returned to me in Syria in the first month of the winter season.' Being a narrative context, the point of reference is the time of the events narrated.

As a **noun**:

5. P. BM 10383, 1, 5 (= *KRI* VI, 834, 2-3).

ḏd.f b(w)p(w)y.ỉ ptr ***pꜣ ḫpr*** *m-dỉ.f*

'He said: "I did not see what happened to it."'

27.2 Passive participles

They are fairly infrequent and, above all, only used with a limited number of verbs, the main ones being *ỉrỉ* 'make,' *rdỉ* 'give,' *ỉn* 'fetch,' and *gmỉ* 'find.' Contrary to what has been stated,[225] they are encountered in letters, and this only until the end of the 20th dynasty.

27.2.1 Morphology[226]

They show no distinction in gender and number.

They can have a prosthetic yod which, in principle, disappears after the article. This yod occurs less often than with the active participles.

They frequently have a characteristic ending 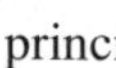 : 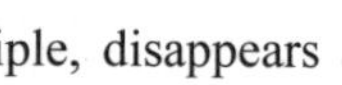 *ỉ.ỉryt* 'which was done' (P. Mayer A, 12, 12); 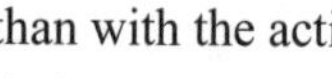 *ỉ.dyt* (P. Mayer A, 13, B1) or *ddy* (P. Turin 1880, r° 3, 2) 'which was given.'

They are never periphrased and, consequently, always possess a past temporal value.

27.2.2 Syntax

Unlike the active participles, the antecedent of passive participles can be undefined. The agent, if

225 Černý-Groll, *LEG*, p. 477-478.

226 See Winand, *o.l.*, p. 365-373.

it is expressed, is introduced by the preposition *ỉn*.

27.2.3 Usage

As attributive **adjective**:

6. P. Bologna 1086, 26 (= *KRI* IV, 81, 10-11): letter.

ḫr ỉr pꜣy ỉḥwty ḫꜣr ***ỉ.dyt*** *n.k*

'Now, as for this Syrian farmer who has been given to you.'

7. P. ESP, B, 15-16 (= *KRI* VI, 519, 4-5): letter.

wnn pꜣ wḫꜣ n pr-ʿꜣ ʿ.w.s pꜣy.k nb (ḥr) spr r.k ỉw.k (ḥr) šsp pꜣy msdmt ***ỉnyt*** *n.k*

'As soon as the letter of Pharaoh l.p.h., your lord, will reach you, you will receive this galena which is returned to you.'

8. P. Turin 1875, 6, 1 (= *KRI* V, 359, 14-16): statement's heading.

rmṯ ***ỉryt*** *n.w sbꜣyt m sꜣw fnd.w msḏr.w ḥr pꜣ ḫꜣʿ ỉ.ỉrỉ.w nꜣ mtrw nfrw* ***ḏdy*** *n.w*

'Individuals to whom a punishment has been inflicted, consisting of mutilation of the nose and ears, for having rejected (*lit.* 'because of the abandoning they had done') the excellent instructions that had been given (*lit.* 'said') to them.'[227]

As **noun**:

– in a thematisation:

9. P. Turin 1875, 3, 1 (= *KRI* V, 351, 6-7).

ỉr pꜣw ỉryt *nb ntw ỉ.ỉrỉ se*

'As for all that has been done, it is they who have done it.' Note the thematisation of the direct pronominal object, and the rhematisation of the subject through a true cleft sentence.

– in a pseudo-cleft sentence:

10. Mès, N 10 (= *KRI* III, 427, 4-5): deposition before the Court.

dnyt n ʿḏꜣ ***tꜣ ỉryt*** *r.ỉ*

'It is a false register that has been fabricated against me.'

[227] Another possible reading is: (*ỉ*).*ḏd.ỉ n.w* 'that I had given them,' relative form.

– in a statement’s heading where the participle is employed without the article:

11. P. Leiden I 350, v°, col. III, 11-12 (= *KRI* II, 810, 1-2): logbook.

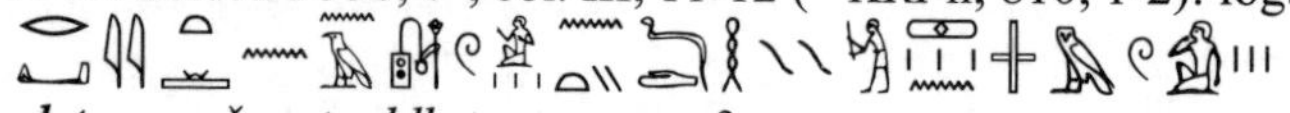

***rdyt** n nȝ sšw nty ḏdḥ.tw t n wnm 3*

‘What has been given to the scribes who are imprisoned: three loaves to eat.’

28. The relative forms

These are adjectival forms of the verb, equivalent to relative clauses where the subject is different from the antecedent. In principle, there are no passive relative forms.[228]

28.1 Morphology

Forms are invariable both in gender and in number, and do not have any particular ending.

They are frequently preceded by a prosthetic yod , which can be written with the mouth sign (this prosthetic yod, in principle, disappears when the relative form is nominalised and is defined by an article or a demonstrative).

Relative forms can be periphrased by the verb *iri*. In principle, this is required for verbs which stem has more than three radicals, but it is optional for the others.

28.2 Syntax

The antecedent of the resulting relative clause must be **defined**,[229] either by a proper noun, a personal pronoun, a noun defined by an article, a demonstrative, a possessive, a suffix or *nb*.[230]

This antecedent is always resumed by a resumptive pronoun, except when it is identical to the direct pronominal object of the relative form, providing that it is not periphrased. In other words, the direct pronominal object of the relative, if it there is one, is always expressed, except when the antecedent is identical to the non-periphrased relative form.

The subject of the relative form, being different from the antecedent, is always expressed.

The negation having disappeared, *nty bwpwy.f sḏm* is used instead; see *infra* §29.7.

▪ The relative form of the verb *wnn*, *(i).wn.f*, **has a special role: it serves to transpose into the past sentences formed with *nty***, see *infra* §30.3.

28.3 Values

The relative forms of verbs with three, or fewer, radicals have a **past** temporal value in their **simple form** – the point of reference being, in the narrative, the time of the events narrated, and outside the narration, the moment of the enunciation. When **periphrased**, these relative forms possess the temporal value of **habitual present** or **general present**. This distinction does not apply to verbs which require the use of a periphrastic construction.

28.4 Usage

28.4.1 As attributive adjective

1. P. BM 10053, 2, 9-10 (= *KRI* VI, 757, 3-4).

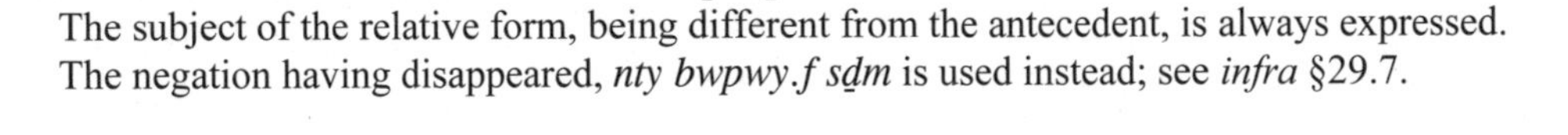

ḏd.tw n.f i.ḏd nbw nb ***i.qq.k*** *n pꜣ pr n nbw n nsw wsr-mꜣꜥt-rꜥ stp.n-rꜥ ꜥ.w.s.*

'They said to him: "Talk (about) all the gold that you stripped (*lit.* 'peeled') in the House of Gold of the King Usermaatra Setepenra l.p.h."'

[228] But see P. Turin 1896, 7 and 9 (= *KRI* VI, 734, 13 and 16); Gardiner, *EG*, §377.

[229] Except in statements' headings, see example 6 below.

[230] See *supra* §1.2, 4.2 and 6.1.

Being identical to the direct pronominal object of the relative, the antecedent, defined by *nb*, is not resumed in it, which, therefore, does not have an expressed direct pronominal object.

2. P. Northumberland I, 7-8 (= *KRI* I, 239, 9-10).

r-ḏd wḫꜣ pꜣy kr 2 ***i.di*** *n.f pr-ꜥꜣ ꜥ.w.s.*

'Saying: "Claim these two barges that Pharaoh has assigned to him."' Same scenario again, since the antecedent, defined by a demonstrative, is identical to the direct pronominal object of the relative.

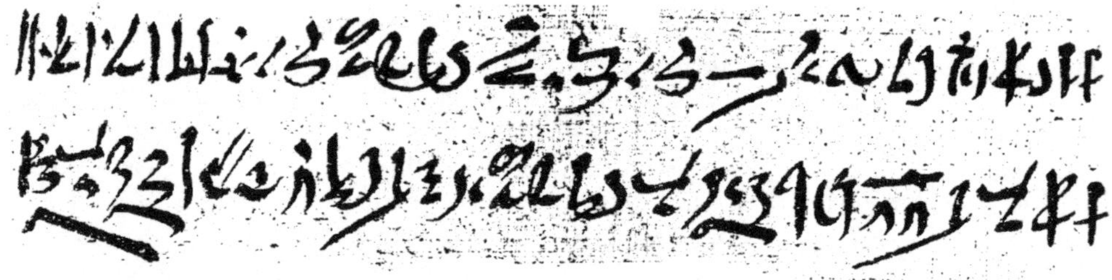

P. Northumberland 1, 7-8

3. P. Turin 1875, 4, 6 (= *KRI* V, 353, 13-15): narrative.

ḥrw ꜥꜣ pꜣ-ṯꜣw-m-di-imn (*i*)*.wn m rwḏw … in.tw.f ḥr pꜣ sḏm i.iri.f nꜣ mdwt* ***i.iri nꜣ rmṯ*** *wꜣwꜣ.w irm nꜣ ḥmwt* (*n*) *pr-ḫnr*

'The great criminal Patjauemdiamun, who had been controller ... if he was taken (before the Court) it is for having been aware of the conspiracies that individuals had devised with the women of the harem.' (*lit.* 'if he was brought, it is for having heard the words that people had whispered').[231]

Given that the verb is a quadriliteral one, the relative form is periphrased. The antecedent, *nꜣ mdwt*, although identical to the direct pronominal object of the relative, is resumed therein by a pronoun. Given the narrative context, the point of reference is the time of the events narrated.

4. P. Bologna 1086, 9 (= *KRI* IV, 79, 12-13).

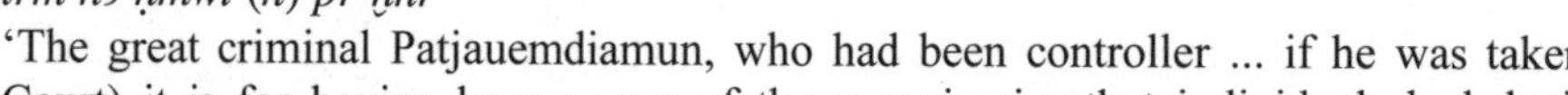

iry.i smtr pꜣ ḫꜣr n pr ḏḥwty ***i.ḥꜣb.k*** *n.i ḥr.f*

'I have examined the (case of the) Syrian of the temple of Thoth concerning which you wrote to me.' The antecedent, *pꜣ ḫꜣr n pr ḏḥwty*, being different from the direct pronominal object of the relative (that is not present), is resumed by a resumptive pronoun (*ḥr.f*).

---

[231] This is the last occurrence of the independent passive construction *in.tw.f* with a pronominal subject, successor of the second tense *sḏm.n.tw.f* of classical Egyptian. See *supra* §23.6 and Winand, *o.l* , §488, p. 310-312, and example 741.

5. P. Abbott, 7, 14 (= *KRI* VI, 481, 4-6).

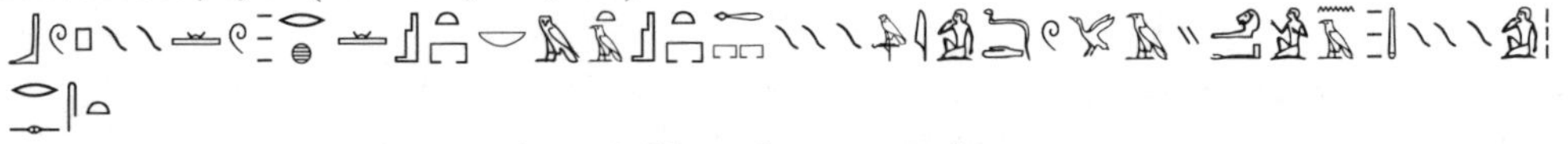

bwpw.w rḫ st nb m tꜣ st pr-ꜥꜣ ꜥ.w.s. ***i.ḏd*** *pꜣy ḥꜣty-ꜥ nꜣ mdwt r.s*
'They did not know any tomb in the necropolis of Pharaoh l.p.h., concerning which this Major had uttered the charges.'

The antecedent, being different from the direct pronominal object of the relative *nꜣ mdwt*, is resumed by a resumptive pronoun (*r.s*).

Exceptionally, the antecedent can be undefined, as in the case of headings:

6. P. BM 10068, 4, 22 (= *KRI* VI, 502, 15).

nbw ḥḏ ***i.di nꜣ iṯꜣw*** *n nꜣ rmṯ n niwt*
'Gold and silver that the thieves sold to the people of Thebes' (There follows the list of gold and silver objects stolen and then sold by the thieves).

Note. The relative form of the verb *iri* is regularly used to periphrase the infinitive, thus conferring it the value of a perfective. See above example 3: *pꜣ sḏm i.iri.f* and §13.3, §13.4.1.1 and §13.4.2.1.1.

28.4.2 As noun

In this case, as a general rule, the relative form is defined.

7. P. Turin 1875, 3, 2 (= *KRI* V, 351, 7-8).

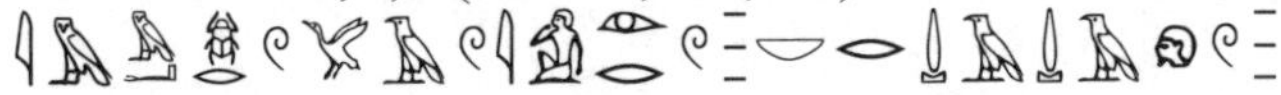

imi ḫpr ***pꜣw i.iri****.w nb r ḏꜣḏꜣ.w*
'Cause that everything that they have done falls (*lit.* 'happens') on their heads!'

In this example, the relative form plays the role of subject of the complement clause and, although defined, is preceded by a prosthetic yod, see above §28.1.

The nominalised and defined relative forms are frequently used in the second member of pseudo-cleft sentences to rhematise the objet of the predicative plain sentence (*Fr.* phrase plane sousjacente) (cf. *infra* §42.3).

8. P. BM 10052, 5, 23 (= *KRI* VI, 781, 6).

wꜥ st wꜥty ***tꜣ wn.n***
'It is one and only one tomb that we opened' (predicative plain sentence: **wn.n wꜥ st wꜥty*).

In legal texts, an archaic form is often used to introduce the statement of an individual to the court or that of the court itself, a unique survival in Late Egyptian of the perfective relative form of Middle Egyptian, expressing the neuter using the feminine:

9. P. Cairo J 65739, 19 (= *KRI* II, 802, 1), 19th dynasty.

ḏdt.n (*tꜣ*) *qnbt sḏmy n wꜥw nꜣḫy*

‘What (the) court said (*lit*. ‘chamber of hearings’) to the soldier Nakhy.’

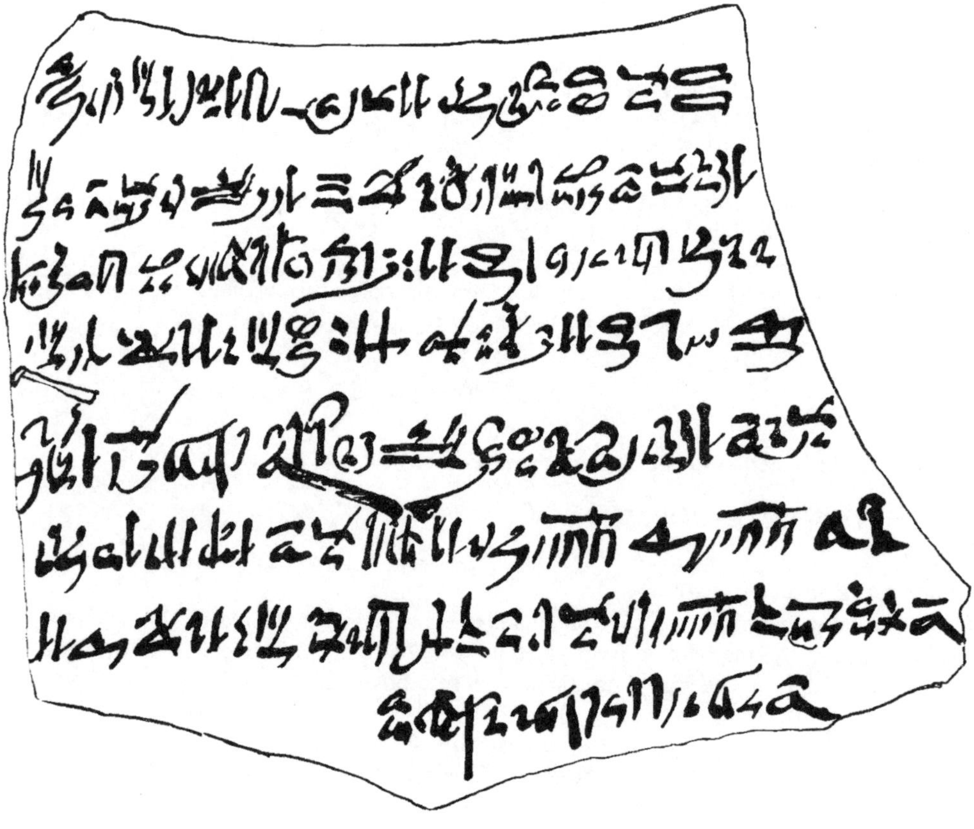

O. DM 592 (*cf*. p. 125)

29. Relative clauses introduced by *nty*

29.1 Syntax

Placed before an independent form, *nty*, invariable in Late Egyptian, turns it into a relative clause with adjectival value.

The independent forms most often preceded by *nty* are:
- the first present,
- the third future,
- the *bwpwy.f sḏm* form.

Theoretically, *nty* is not used before the perfective *sḏm.f*,[232] which is relativised through participles and relative forms, or before the prospective *sḏm.f*.

▪ Rarely it is also possible to find *nty* before a second tense, an existential sentence or the expression 'not yet' (*cf.* below §29.8).[233]

The antecedent of the relative clause must be defined,[234] either by a proper noun, a personal pronoun, a noun defined by an article, a demonstrative, a possessive, a suffix or *nb*.[235]

The direct pronominal object of the relative clause, if present, is always expressed even if identical to the antecedent.

29.2 Temporal values

The time of the relativised verb form is relative to the moment of the events narrated in a narrative context, and to the moment of the enunciation in the other instances[236] - shown in bold in the translation of examples 1-9.

29.3 Usage

The relative clauses constructed with *nty* can be employed as **attributive adjectives** or as **nouns**. In the latter case, they are often defined, especially in pseudo-cleft sentences (example 9), but they can also be undefined as, for example, is the case in headings (example 1).

29.4 *nty* + First Present, affirmative forms

29.4.1 The antecedent is the same as the subject of the relative clause

In this case *nty* functions both as relativiser and as subject. The subject of the relative clause is, therefore, unexpressed and the antecedent is not resumed in the relative by a resumptive pronoun.

---

[232] Examples of *nty* + *sḏm.f* are rare. They employ, above all, intransitive verbs and express the general present. See Vernus, *Or* 50 (1981), 439, n. 52 and 53; *l'Égyptologie en 1979, I*, p. 83, n..15, with references.

[233] *Nty* can also appear before nominal forms, for example O. Nash 2, v° 4-5 (= *KRI* IV, 319, 5).

[234] Except in headings.

[235] See *supra* §1.2, 4.2 and 6.1.

[236] Satzinger, *o.c.*, p. 129-130.

– *pꜣ* A … *nty dy* — the A ... who is there
– *pꜣ* A … *nty m-dỉ.k* — the A ... who is with you
– *pꜣ* A … *nty wꜣḥ.Ø* — the A ... who is placed
– *pꜣ* A … *nty ḥr wꜣḥ.(k)* — the A ... who places (you)
– *pꜣ* A … *nty m ỉy* — the A ... who comes (verb of motion)

1. Hittite Treaty, 36 (= *KRI* II, 232, 1): heading.
 ***nty m ḥry-ỉb*** *(n) pꜣ ꜥn n ḥḏ*
'**What is** in the middle of the silver tablet.' In this heading, the nominalised relative clause is not preceded by the article.

2. P. Turin 2021, 2, 2 (= *KRI* VI, 739, 7-8): non-narrative context.

ꜥnḫ-nw-nỉwt ỉnk-se-nḏm tꜣy st-ḥmt ***nty ꜥḥꜥ.tỉ m-bꜣḥ ṯꜣty***
'The lady Ineksenedjem, this woman **who stands** before the vizier.' In a non-narrative context the point of reference is the time of the enunciation.

3. Wenamun, 2, 77 (= *LES,* 75, 4-5): narrative context.
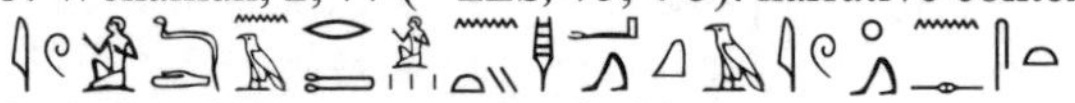
ỉw.ỉ (ḥr) ḏd (n) nꜣ rmṯ ***nty ꜥḥꜥ (r)-qr-n.s***
'I said to those **who stood** next to her ...' Given the narrative context, the point of reference is the moment of the events narrated.

4. P. Salt 124, 2, 9-10 (= *KRI* IV, 411, 11): non-narrative context.
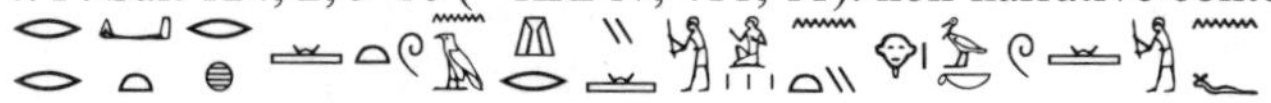
r rdỉt rḫ.tw nꜣ ḫryw ***nty ḥr bꜣk n.f***
'List of the quarrymen **who work** for him.' Description of habitual activity.

5. Doomed Prince, 4, 8 (= *LES,* 2, 4-5): non-narrative context.
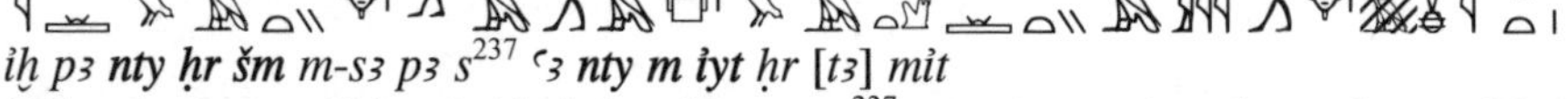
ỉḫ pꜣ ***nty ḥr šm*** *m-sꜣ pꜣ s*[237] *ꜥꜣ* ***nty m ỉyt*** *ḥr [tꜣ] mỉt*
'What is **that walking** behind the older man[237] **who is coming** down the road?' (*lit.* 'it is what this that walks ...'). Interrogative nominal sentence.

29.4.2 The antecedent is different from the subject of the relative clause

In this case *nty* only functions as relativiser, the subject of the relative is always expressed and the antecedent is taken up again in the relative clause by a resumptive pronoun.[238]

– *pꜣ* A … *nty tw.k m-dỉ.f* — the A ... with whom you are
– *pꜣ* A … *nty tw.k wꜣḥ.tw ỉm.f* — the A ... in which you are placed
– *pꜣ* A … *nty tw.k ḥr wꜣḥ.f* — the A ... that you place

[237] The article *pꜣ* shows that the text refers to a man and that the spelling is wrong, *cf. LES*, 2a, n. 4, 8a.
[238] Following *ỉm* the antecedent is sometimes not taken up again by a resumptive pronoun, *cf.* example 7.

6. P. Anastasi VI, 32 (= *LEM,* 75, 1): non-narrative context.

pꜣ rmṯ nty sw m-dỉ.f

'The man **with whom he is**' (And not 'the man who is with him,' that would be **pꜣ rmṯ nty m-dỉ.f*).

7. Wenamun, 1, 12-13 (= *LES,* 62, 3-4): narrative context.

*ỉw.ỉ (ḥr) šm r **pꜣ nty pꜣ wr ỉm***

'I went to the place **where the prince was**.' Note the absence of a resumptive pronoun as is sometimes the case with *ỉm*.

8. Wenamun, 2, 52-53 (= *LES,* 72, 7-8): non-narrative context.

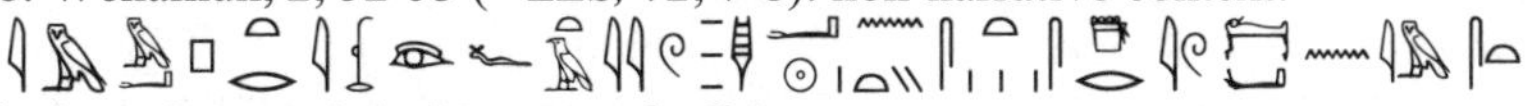

*ỉmỉ ptr.f pꜣy.w (m) ꜥḥꜥ **nty st sḏr.Ø** ỉm.s*

'Let him see the (*lit.* 'their') tomb **in which they are buried**' (*lit.* 'stretched out').

9. O. Gardiner 165, v° 4-5 (= *KRI* III, 549, 8-9): non-narrative context.

*tꜣ ꜥꜣt wꜥtỉ **tꜣ nty tw.k ḥr** wḫꜣ.s*

'It is only the she-ass **that you claim**.' Pseudo-cleft sentence.

29.5 *nty* + First Present, negative forms

The subject of the relative is always expressed, whether it is identical to the antecedent or not, which is always resumed in the relative clause by a pronoun.

10. *Giornale*, 12, 4 (= *KRI* VI, 569, 3-4).

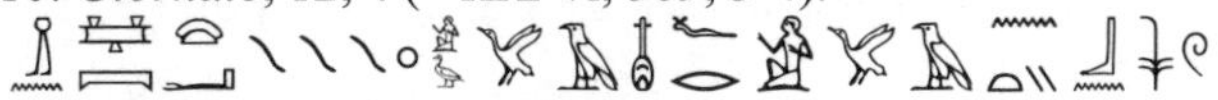

*ỉn-ḥr-ḫꜥw sꜣ pꜣ-nfr **pꜣ nty bn sw***

'It is Inherkhau, son of Panefer, who is not here.' Pseudo-cleft sentence where *bn sw* is the negative correlate of *sw dy* (*cf.* §16.2, example 7).

11. O. Mond 175, 1-2 (= *KRI* VII, 381, 8-9).

*ptr tw.ỉ ꜥm.k(wỉ) nꜣ mdwt qnwt ꜥšꜣt **nty bn mꜣꜥt ỉm.w ỉwnꜣ***

'See, I am aware of very many cases in which there is no justice' (*lit.* 'that justice is not in them').

12. O. DM 592, 6-7 (= *KRI* V, 593, 7-8) (fig. p. 122).

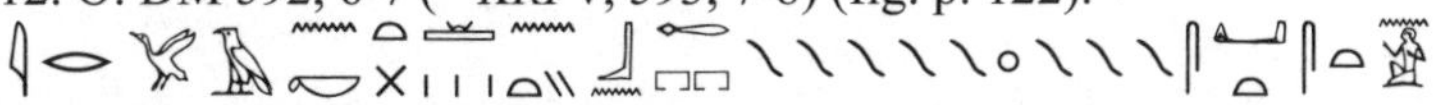

*ỉr pꜣ nkt **nty bn pr-ꜥꜣ ꜥ.w.s. (ḥr) dỉt** se n.ỉ*

'As for this (*lit.* 'the thing') that Pharaoh l.p.h. does not give me ...' Note the use of the dependant pronoun to express the direct pronominal object after the infinitive of *rdỉ* – a usage that will develop in demotic.

29.6 *nty* + Third Future

The subject of the relative is always expressed whether it is the same as the antecedent or not, which is always resumed in the relative by a pronoun.

– *pꜣ* A … *nty* (*bn*) *ỉw.f r wꜣḥ*	the A ... who will (not) place
– *pꜣ* A … *nty* (*bn*) *ỉw.k r wꜣḥ.f*	the A ... that you will (not) place
– *pꜣ* A … *nty* (*bn*) *ỉrỉ* B *r wꜣḥ.f*	the A ... that B will (not) place

▪ Note that in 'standard' Late Egyptian the *ỉw* following *nty* is always that of the third future and not the circumstantial *ỉw*. It is only later that the latter starts to be used after *nty*, heralding a usage that will develop during the Third Intermediate Period.[239]

13. P. Gardiner 4, 4-5 (= *KRI* VII, 339, 7-8).

pꜣ rmṯ ***nty ỉw.f r šm*** *r šsp nꜣ ỉt*

'The man who will go to receive the grain (*lit.* grains).'[240] The subject is identical to the antecedent.

14. P. Turin 2021, 2, 10 (= *KRI* VI, 740, 3-4).

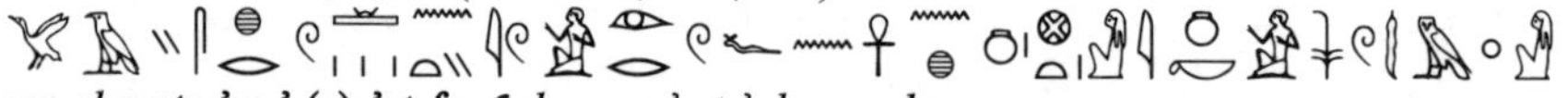

pꜣy sḫr ***nty ỉw.ỉ (r) ỉrt.f*** *n ꜥnḫ-nw-nỉwt ỉnk-se-nḏm*

'This arrangement that I will make in favour of the lady Ineksenedjem.' The subject is different from the antecedent, which is identical to the direct pronominal object. Similarly:

15. P. Mayer A, 1, 1-4 (= *KRI* VI, 803, 12-16).

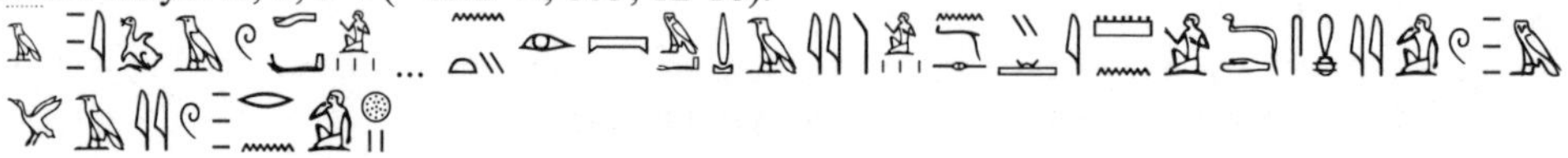

nꜣ ỉṯꜣw … ***nty ỉrỉ ḥry mḏꜣyw ny-se-ỉmn (r) ḏd smỉ.w*** *m pꜣy.w rnrn*

'The thieves ... of whom the chief of the medjay Nesamon will give a list.' (*lit.* 'that the chief ... will denounce by their list').

In the following examples the relative is nominalised and defined:

16. Hittite Treaty 30-31 (= *KRI* II, 230, 11-13).

ỉr nꜣy mdt nty ḥr pꜣy ꜥn n ḥḏ … ỉr ***pꜣ nty bn ỉw.f r sꜣw.sn***

'As for these clauses (*lit.* 'words') that are (engraved) on this silver tablet ... as for the one who will not respect them ...'

17 P. ESP, C, 29-30 (= *KRI* VI, 521, 8-9).

ỉr ***pꜣ nty ỉw.tn (r) ꜣty ỉm.f*** *ỉw.tn (r) hꜣb n.ỉ dỉ.ỉ ỉn.tw.f n.tn*

'As for that of which you will be lacking, you will write to me (so) that I have it brought to you.'

[239] See Vernus, *l'Égyptologie en 1979*, I, p. 82-84.

[240] See also *supra* §6.1, example 1.

29.7 *nty* + *bwpwy.f sḏm*

This syntagma serves as negation of the participles, if the subject of the relative is identical to the antecedent, otherwise it serves as the negation of the relative forms.

18. P. Ashmolean Museum 1945-95, 2, 7 (= *KRI* VI, 238, 2).

*ỉr pꜣ **nty bwpw.f dỉt** n.ỉ bn ỉw.ỉ r dỉt n.f m ꜣẖt.tw.ỉ*

'As for the one who has given nothing (*lit.* 'not') to me, I will not bequeath to him (*lit.* 'will not give') any of my property.' Negation of the participle. The affirmative sentence would be **pꜣ dỉ n.ỉ*.

19. P. BM 10326, 9-10 (= *LRL*, 17, 16): a letter (*šꜥt*) has not arrived to destination.

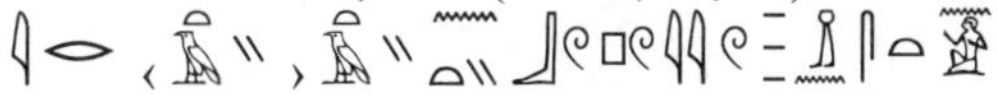

*ỉr ‹tꜣy› **tꜣy nty bwpwy.w ỉn.s** n.ỉ*

'As for this, this is what they did not bring to me.'[241] Negation of the relative form; the affirmative sentence would be **tꜣy ỉn.w se n.ỉ*.

29.8 *nty* + varia (examples are rare)

***nty* + second tenses**

20. Wenamun, 1, 43-45 (= *LES,* 65, 11-12).

*ỉn ntk **pꜣ nty ỉ.ỉrỉ.f** nw (ḥr) ỉy n.ỉ m-mnt r-ḏd rwỉ tw.k (m) tꜣy.ỉ mr(yt)*

'Are you (not) the one who spent time coming to see me daily with these words (*lit.* 'saying'): "Get away from my port!"?' In this example *nty* is followed by a modal second tense.

***nty* + existential sentence**

21. P. BM 10054, 2, 10-11 (= *KRI* VI, 493, 1-2).

*nꜣ wtw **nty wn nbw** ỉm.w*

'The coffins in which there was gold' (*lit.* 'that there was gold in them'). In principle, it is the existential *wn* that is found after *nty*.

***nty* + 'not yet' in the passive form**

22. P. Gurob, 2, 3-4 (= *RAD*, 14, 7-9).

*tꜣy wpt ꜥꜣt sb(q)ỉ ... **nty bw ỉry.t Ø** n pꜣ-rꜥ mỉ-qd.s*

'This great splendid work ... the like of which has not yet been done for Pre' (*lit.* 'that it has not yet been done for Pre like it').

---

[241] Here it is assumed that *tꜣy* was omitted due to a line change, see Amarna Border Stela U, 12, cited by Groll, *Non Verbal*, example 268, and P. Orbiney, 7, 7-8, where it is not a dittography.

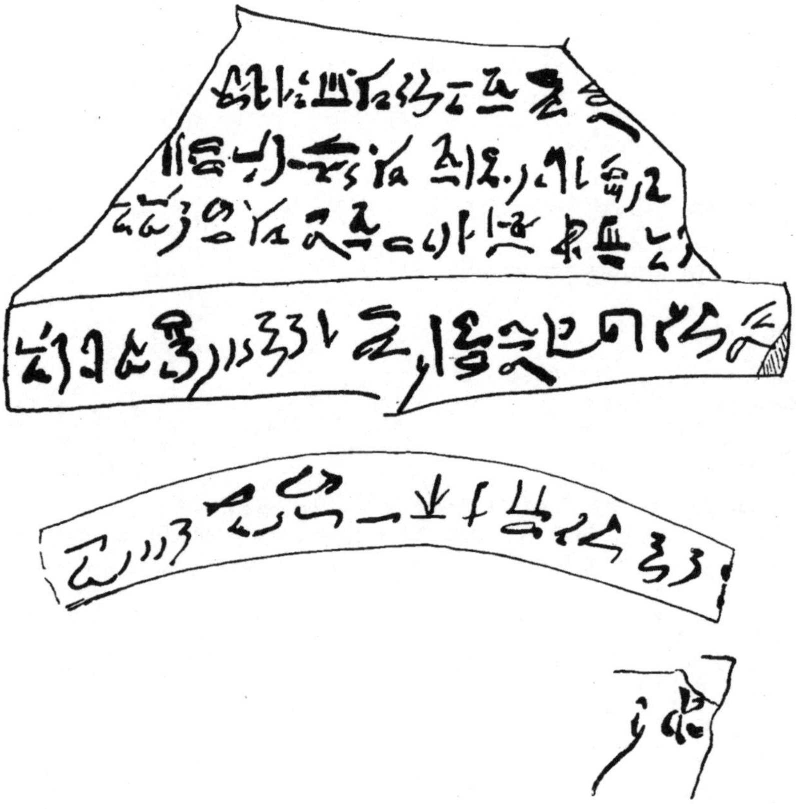

O. DM 563 (*cf.* p. 84)

30. Relative clauses introduced by (ỉ).*wn* or (ỉ).*wn.f*

30.1 Introduction

The participle or the relative form of the auxiliary verb *wnn* allows one to transpose into the past sentences formed with *nty*. These retain their 'unmarked' value, rendered in English with the past tense, which participles or relative forms, which are simply 'punctual,' do not have.

Compare

– *pꜣ A ... ỉ.wn ḥr wꜣḥ* the A ... who placed

with

– *pꜣ A ... nty ḥr wꜣḥ* the A ... who places

– *pꜣ A ... ỉ.wꜣḥ* the A who has placed, the A ... who placed

The syntax is exactly the same as for *nty*. The sentences thus transposed are almost always first present or, exceptionally, third future (example 5).

30.2 Relative clauses introduced by the participle (ỉ).*wn*

They are employed when the subject of the relative clause is identical to the antecedent:

Examples with the first present:

1. P. Turin 1977, 5-6 (= Bakir, *Epistolography*, pl. 26).

ỉw.k ḥr ḏd ỉmỉ dỉ.tw pꜣ ḥtr ***(ỉ).wn ḥr pr n.s*** *n tꜣy.ỉ snt*

'You said: "Cause that the income that was paid (*lit.* 'went out for her') to her (= 'to my mother') be given to my sister.'

2. P. Mayer A, 1, 9-10 (= *KRI* VI, 804, 9-11).

ỉḫ pꜣ sḫr (n) šm ỉ.ỉrỉ.k ỉrm nꜣ rmṯ ***(ỉ).wn ỉrm.k*** *ỉw.tn (ḥr) ỉrt hꜣw m nꜣ prw (n) sṯꜣ n nꜣ nsyw* ***(ỉ).wn wꜣḥ.Ø*** *m pr-ḥḏ n tꜣ ḥwt nsw wsr-mꜣꜥt-rꜥ mr-ỉmn ꜥ.w.s.*

'In what manner did you get (*lit.* 'it is what the way of going that you made') with the individuals who were with you when you grabbed the portable naoi of the kings that had been stored in the temple treasury of King Usermaatra Meriamun l.p.h. (Ramses III)?'

3. P. Turin 1875, 6, 2 (= *KRI* V, 360, 3).

ḫrw ꜥꜣ pꜣy-bs ***(ỉ).wn m wdpw***

'The great criminal Paybes, who had been cup-bearer.'

4. P. BM 10054, 2, 10 (= *KRI* VI, 492, 16-493, 1).

ỉ.ỉrỉ.n wn nꜣ ḏbꜣwt m nꜣ ẖl n ḥmt ***ỉ.wn m ḏrt.n***

'It is with the copper picks that we had in hand (*lit.* 'that were in our hands') that we opened the sarcophagi.'[242]

Example with the third future:[243]

5. P. Anastasi VI, 21-22 (= *LEM*, 74, 4).

ỉw.f ḥr ỉṯꜣ nꜣ nwt **(ỉ).wn ỉw.ỉ r ỉn.tw.w** *m-bꜣḥ pꜣ mr pr-ḥḏ*

'He seized the materials that I was going to deliver to the overseer of the treasury' (or 'that I should have delivered').

30.3 Relative clauses introduced by the relative form (*ỉ*).*wn.f*

They are used when the subject of the relative is different from the antecedent. Examples are found only in the first present.

6. P. BM 10054, 2, 8-9 (= *KRI* VI, 492, 13-15).

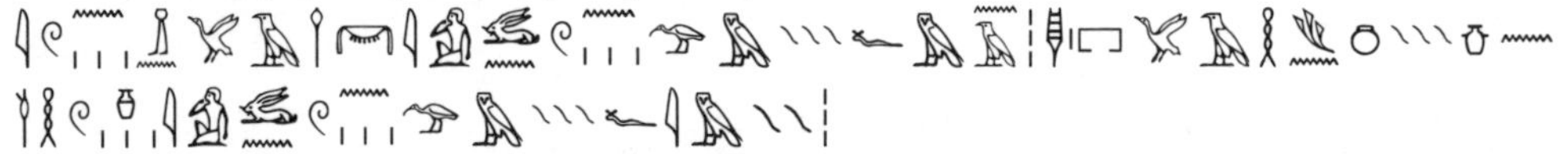

ỉw.n (ḥr) ỉn pꜣ ḥḏ pꜣ nbw ***ỉ.wn.n (ḥr) gm.tw.f*** *m nꜣ (m) ꜥḥꜥyt pꜣ ḥnw n wḏḥw* ***ỉ.wn.n (ḥr) gm.tw.f*** *ỉm.w*

'We carried away the silver and gold that we (habitually) found in the tombs, and the offering vessels that we (habitually) found there.'[244]

7. P. BM 10052, 15, 5-6 (= *KRI* VI, 800, 9-10).

ỉḫ ḫr.ṯ tꜣ mdt n pꜣy ḥḏ ***ỉ.wn nꜣ ỉṯꜣw (ḥr) ỉn.tw.f*** *n rꜥ-ms pꜣy.ṯ hꜣy*

'What have you to say (about) the matter (*lit.* 'it is what – you say – the matter') of this silver that the thieves brought to Ramose, your husband?'

8. P. Turin 1875, 4, 12 (= *KRI* V, 355, 8-9).

pꜣy ꜥꜣ n ꜥt ***(ỉ).wn.f r-qr-n.f***

'This Chamberlain with whom he had been.' Compare with Example 6 in §29.4.2, where the same construction is found with *nty*.

[242] It concerns habitual activity.

[243] See Silverman, *Festschrift Westendorf*, 1984, p. 191-196.

[244] Understand 'we carried away (this time) the same loot as in our previous expeditions.'

31. Table of relative clauses
(defined antecedent)

	antecedent = subject	*antecedent ≠ subject*
Present	*pꜣ A … nty ḥr wꜣḥ* who places *pꜣ A … nty bn sw ḥr wꜣḥ* who does not place	*pꜣ A … nty tw.ỉ ḥr wꜣḥ.f* that I place *pꜣ A … nty bn tw.ỉ ḥr wꜣḥ.f* that I do not place
Imperfect	*pꜣ A … (ỉ).wn ḥr wꜣḥ* who placed	*pꜣ A … (ỉ).wn.ỉ ḥr wꜣḥ.f* that I placed
Past	*pꜣ A … ỉ.wꜣḥ* who placed who has placed *pꜣ A … nty bwpwy.f wꜣḥ* who did not place who has not placed	*pꜣ A … ỉ.wꜣḥ.ỉ* that I placed that I have placed *pꜣ A … nty bwpwy.ỉ wꜣḥ.f* that I did not place that I have not placed
Future	*pꜣ A … nty ỉw.f r wꜣḥ* who will place *pꜣ A … nty bn ỉw.f r wꜣḥ* who will not place	*pꜣ A … nty ỉw.ỉ r wꜣḥ.f* that I will place *pꜣ A … nty bn ỉw.ỉ r wꜣḥ.f* that I will not place
Passive	*pꜣ A … nty wꜣḥ.Ø* who was placed who has been placed *pꜣ A … (ỉ).wn wꜣḥ.Ø* who had been placed	*pꜣ A … nty tw.ỉ wꜣḥ.Ø ḥr.f* on which I was placed on which I have been placed

32. Adverbial clauses introduced by *ỉw*

32.1 Introduction

The morpheme *ỉw* (called circumstantial *ỉw*) placed before an independent form (verbal or nominal) turns it into a non-independent, non-initial form, having the value of an adverb.

The independent verbal forms more frequently preceded by the circumstantial *ỉw* are:[245]

- the perfective *sḏm.f*: examples 1, 11, 13, 19, 20, 22, 23, 24;
- the *bwpwy.f sḏm* form: examples 1, 10;
- the first present[246] and its negation: examples 2, 3, 12, 14, 15, 16 (*wn*), 21;
- the negative aorist: example 4;
- the third future and its negation: examples 5, 6, 7, 17, 18;
- the second tenses: example 10;
- the existential sentences: examples 8, 9;
- the correlative system *ỉr ỉw.f* (*?*) *sḏm* within the protasis, see *infra* §33.2.3, example 20.

When the independent form possesses its **own** temporal value, the resulting sentences with *ỉw* take on a **relative** temporal value:

- **anteriority** (for example with the perfective *sḏm.f*);
- **concomitance** (for example with most forms of the first present);
- **posteriority** (for example with the third future).

The adverbial value of the resulting sentences allows them to take on the fundamental function of an adverbial clause that could be focused by a second tense. The adverbial clause introduced by *ỉw* most often follows the main clause, although it can sometimes precede it. In addition to their regular uses, they can also be found in place of relative clauses with an undefined antecedent (in the way specified above), or in place of a complement clause.

Remarks

1. It has been alleged that the circumstantial *ỉw* could not be employed before the prospective *sḏm.f*,[247] yet a few clear examples, because they appear in the negative form (*ỉw bn* (or *nn*) *sḏm.f*), have been identified.[248]

2. The morpheme *ỉw* that can be found before the imperative (almost always negative) is not the circumstantial *ỉw*, but the parenthetical *ỉw*, see *infra* §38.1.

---

[245] An example of *ỉw bw sḏm.t.f*: O. Florence 2625, v° 1 (= Allam, *HOP*, pl. 35).

[246] In the affirmative form the suffix pronoun replaces the proclitic pronoun, thus one finds *ỉw.f* and not *ỉw sw*. However, there is no change in the negative form, where one finds *ỉw bn sw*. See *supra* §16.1.1.

[247] Frandsen, *LEVS*, p. 15.

[248] Doomed Prince, 4, 6 (= *LES*, 1, 11-2, 1); P. Orbiney, 7, 4 (= *LES*, 16, 10); P. Turin 1880, v° 2, 10-14 (= *RAD*, 49, 5-8).

32.2 Used as adverbial clauses

32.2.1 The circumstantial is placed after the main clause (unmarked order, very frequent)

32.2.1.1 General case

1. P. Mayer A, 3, 18-19 (= *KRI* VI, 810, 1-3).

in sft p(ꜣ)-n-nswt-tꜣwy sꜣ bs ***iw ḏd ḏd-m-šnb pr-pꜣ-ṯꜣw*** *sḏm.i r-ḏd wn.f m nꜣ swt* ***iw b(w)p(w)y.i ptr.f*** *m irt.i*

'The butcher Paennesuttawy, son of Bes, was summoned (*lit.* 'brought') after the trumpeter Perpatchau had said: "I learned that he had been in the tombs, although I had not seen him, with my eyes."'

► *iw sḏm.f* perfective and its negation *iw bwpwy.f sḏm*.

2. P. Turin 1880, 3, 15 (= *RAD*, 57, 2-3).

iw.w (ḥr) ꜥš n pꜣ ḥꜣty-ꜥ n niwt ***iw.f m snn***

'They hailed the major of the City as he passed by.'

► *iw.f m ꜥq*, first present of verbs of motion.

3. P. Berlin P 3047, 10 (= *KRI* II, 803, 16-804, 1): concerning arable lands.

t

ṯꜣ sn n.f ḥry šnꜥ ny ḥnꜥ nꜣy.f snw ḥmn n rnpt r tꜣy ***iw bn st ḥr dit tꜣy.i psš***

'The chief of the storehouse Ny took for himself, together with his brothers, for some years until now, without giving (me) my share' (*lit.* 'without them giving (me) my share').

► *iw bn sw ḥr sḏm*, negative first present.

4. O. Berlin P 10627, 3-6 (= *KRI* VI, 155, 10-12).

yꜣ iḫ pꜣy.k ḫpr m pꜣy sḫr bin nty tw.k im.f ***iw bw iri mdt n rmṯ nb ꜥq*** *m msḏr.k*

'Well, how have you put yourself (*lit.* 'hey, it is what your happening') in this lamentable state in which you are, that no human word can penetrate into your ear? [249]

► *iw bw iri.f sḏm*, negative aorist.

[249] Understand 'to the point that you are no longer able to listen to reason.'

5. P. Turin 2021, 3, 13-14, 1 (= *KRI* VI, 741, 13-15).

tw.ỉ (ḥr) dỉt n.s pꜣy.ỉ ⅔ [ḥr pꜣ]y.s ⅓ ***ỉw bn ỉrỉ šrỉ šrỉt (r) mdw*** *m pꜣy sḫr ỉ.ỉrỉ.ỉ n.s m pꜣ hrw*

'I bequeath her my ⅔ in addition to her ⅓, so that no son or daughter shall contest this arrangement that I have made today in her favour.'

► *ỉw bn ỉrỉ N r sḏm*, negative third future with nominal subject.

6. O. Berlin P 10630, 6-7 (= *KRI* V, 565, 5-6).

ḥr dỉ ptḥ ỉry.k ꜥḥꜥw qꜣ ỉꜣwt nfr(t) ***ỉw.k m-dỉ.ỉ*** *m ỉt r nḥḥ* ***ỉw bn ỉw.ỉ (r) nmḥ*** *ỉm.k*

'And may Ptah cause that you to enjoy a long life and a happy old age, since you are to me a father for eternity and, thanks to you, I will never be an orphan!'[250] (*lit.* 'I will never be an orphan on your part').

► *ỉw.k m-dỉ.ỉ m ỉt*, first present with a prepositional phrase as predicate;

► *ỉw bn ỉw.f r sḏm*, negative third future with pronominal (suffixal) subject.

7. P. Turin 2021, 3, 3-4 (= *KRI* VI, 740, 11-13).

bn st [ꜣty] (m) pꜣ ỉn.‹ỉ› nb ỉrm tꜣy.w mwt ***ỉw wn ỉw.ỉ (r) dỉt*** *n.w m pꜣ ỉn.ỉ ỉrm ꜥnḫ-nw-nỉwt ỉnk-se-nḏm ḥr pr-ꜥꜣ ꜥ.w.s. (ḥr) ḏd*

'They are not deprived of any of what I acquired with their mother, still, I would have given them from what I acquired with the lady Ineksenedjem, but Pharaoh l.p.h. said ...'

► *ỉw wn ỉw.f r sḏm*, third future preceded by the past converter *wn*.

8. P. Turin 1887, 1, 10-11 (= *RAD*, 75, 7-8).

ỉw.f (ḥr) ꜥq ḥr pꜣ nṯr ***ỉw wn n.f 3 hrw n swr ḥsmn***

'He entered with the god although he (still) had three days of drinking natron' (*lit.* 'although there existed for him ...').

► *ỉw wn n.f A*, affirmative existential sentence.

9. O. DM 67, 3-5 (= *KRI* V, 536, 5).

ỉn.f n.ỉ (m) ꜣbd 1 šmw sw 15 ***ỉw mn ꜣḫt nb m-dỉ.f***

'He brought it (= the donkey) to me day 15 of the first month of the summer season, without having anything in the hand' (*lit.* 'while there was no property in his hand').

► *ỉw mn A m-dỉ.f*, negative existential sentence.

---

[250] Understand 'you will never abandon me.' For *nmḥ*, 'to be orphan,' see *Wb*, II, 268, 11-16.

10. P. BM 10052, 5, 18-19 (= *KRI* VI, 780, 14-781, 1).

ḏd.tw n sš t3t3-šrỉ ḥry ỉry-ʿ3 p3-k3w-m-p3-wb3 ***ỉw ỉ.ỉrỉ.n dỉt*** *n.w m-ḏr sḏm.*(*w*) *se* ***ỉw b(w)p(w)y.w šm*** *r t3y st ỉrm.n*

'(A share of the loot) was given to the scribe Tetisheri and the overseer of the porters Pakauempauba, although we gave it to them only after they had learned (of the looting) since they did not go to this tomb with us.'

► *ỉw ỉ.ỉrỉ.f sḏm* (= second tense) + rhematised circonstant;

► *ỉw bwpwy.f šm*, negation of *ỉw.f šm* (see *supra* §16.6.2.1).

32.2.1.2 Special cases

32.2.1.2.1 The adverbial clause is focalised by a second tense

11. P. Berlin P 8523, 5-6 (= Allam, *HOP*, pl. 76).

ỉ.ỉrỉ.ỉ ỉy r nỉwt ***ỉw ḏd.ỉ n.k*** *bn ỉw.ỉ* (*r*) *dỉt sk3.k gr*

'It is after I said to you: "I will not let you plough anymore" that I returned to Thebes.'

12. P. Mayer A, 2, 19 (= *KRI* VI, 808, 3).

ḏd.f ỉ.ỉrỉ.Ø ḫdb p3y.ỉ ỉt ***ỉw.ỉ m šrỉ***

'He said: "It was when I was a child that my father was murdered."'

See also example 20 below.

32.2.1.2.2 The adverbial clause is marked by the particle *ḫr*[251]

13. Horus and Seth, 10, 5-6 (= *LES*, 50, 14-15).

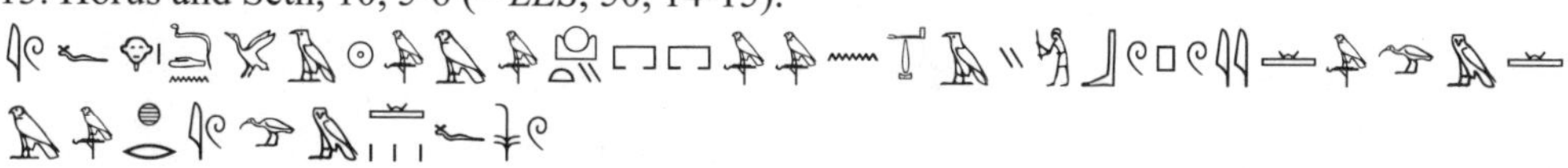

ỉw.f ḥr ḏd n p3-rʿ-ḥr-3ḫty n(=m) ʿḏ3 bwpwy.ỉ gm ḥr ***ḫr ỉw gm.f se***

'He said, falsely, to Pre-Horakhty: "I have not found Horus" – and this although he had found him!'

32.2.2 The adverbial clause is placed before the main clause (marked order, rare)

This produces a **correlative system** (or **hypotactic**) in which the adverbial clause, placed at the beginning (**protasis**), precedes the main clause (**apodosis**). The system is almost always preceded by an introductory morpheme which can be *ḫr* or *ỉr*.[252]

---

[251] For *ḫr ỉw* see Navailles-Neveu, *GM* 103 (1988), 56, o.

[252] Cases where the system, in non-initial position, is preceded by no morpheme are even rarer: P. Sallier I, 9, 6 (= *LEM*, 87, 12) and, perhaps, Wenamun, 2, 70-71 (= *LES*, 74, 9-10).

14. Mès, N 10 (= *KRI* III, 427, 4-6).[253]

r-ḏd dnyt n ꜥḏꜣ tꜣ ỉryt r.ỉ ***ḥr ỉw.ỉ smtr.kwỉ ḫr-ḥꜣt tw.ỉ gm.kwỉ ḥr wꜥrt***

'Saying: "It is a false register that has been fabricated against me because when my case was examined previously (*lit.* 'I was examined before'), my name was found (*lit.* 'I was found') on a document."'

For examples with *ỉr* + *ỉw* circumstantial, see *infra* §33.2.2.2.

32.3 Used in place of a relative clause

Relative clauses incorporating a participle, a relative form, *nty* or (*ỉ*).*wn*.(*f*) require a defined antecedent. When the antecedent is undefined, Egyptian replaces the relative clause with an adverbial clause.

Thus, to say 'a man who speaks,' one writes ***(wꜥ) rmṯ ỉw.f ḥr ḏd** (*lit.* 'a man, when he speaks') and not *(*wꜥ*) *rmṯ nty ḥr ḏd*.

15. Doomed Prince, 4, 7-8 (= *LES*, 2, 2-3).

ỉw.f ḥr gmḥ wꜥ n ṯsm ***ỉw.f m-sꜣ*** *wꜥ n s ꜥꜣ* ***ỉw.f ḥr šm*** *ḥr tꜣ mỉt*

'He glimpsed a dog that followed (*lit.* 'was behind') an older man who walked on the road.'

16. P. Leiden I 368, 8-9 (= *KRI* II, 895, 8-9).

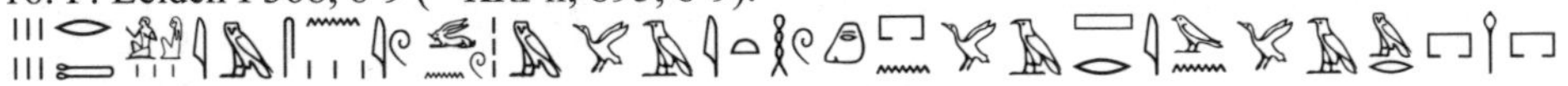

6 rmṯ ỉm.sn ***ỉw wn.w m*** *pꜣ ỉtḥ n pꜣ šrỉ n pꜣ mr pr-ḥḏ*

'Six of them (*lit.* 'individuals among them') who had been in the prison of the son of the overseer of the treasury.'

17. P. BM 10403, 3, 14-15 (= *KRI* VI, 832, 5-6).

ḥr mn rmṯ ***ỉw ỉw.f (r) sꜥḥꜥ.[ỉ]***

'And there is no one who will accuse me.'

18. P. Berlin 10494, v° 2-3 (= *LRL*, 24, 4-5).

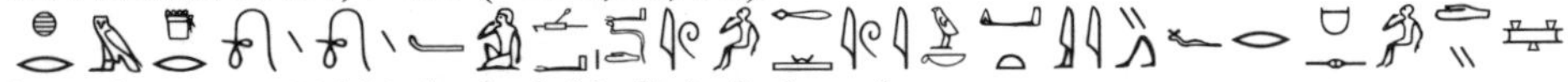

ḥr m dy wꜣwꜣ wꜥ ꜥḏd ꜥꜣ ***ỉw ỉw.k (r) dỉt*** *ỉy.f r ḥms dy*

'And do not give (time) to protest against (*lit.* 'and do nothing but whisper') an older teenager that you will cause to come to dwell here.'

In the following table are listed the adverbial clauses that replace relative clauses when the antecedent is undefined. Compare these with the table of true relative clauses in §31.

[253] Another example with the particle *ỉr*: P. Abbott, 7, 10-12 (= *KRI* VI, 480, 15-481, 2).

Circumstantial clauses that substitute relative clauses (undefined antecedent)

Present	(*wꜥ*) *A* … *ỉw.f ḥr wꜣḥ.*(*k*) who places (you) (*wꜥ*) *A* … *ỉw bn sw ḥr wꜣḥ.*(*k*) who does not place (you)
Imperfect	(*wꜥ*) *A* … *ỉw wn.f ḥr wꜣḥ.*(*k*) who placed (you)
Past	(*wꜥ*) *A* … *ỉw wꜣḥ.f* (*tw*) who placed (you) who has placed (you) (*wꜥ*) *A* … *ỉw bwpwy.f wꜣḥ.*(*k*) who did not place (you) who has not placed (you)
Future	(*wꜥ*) *A* … *ỉw ỉw.f r wꜣḥ.*(*k*) who will place (you) (*wꜥ*) *A* … *ỉw bn ỉw.f r wꜣḥ.*(*k*) who will not place (you)
Passive	(*wꜥ*) *A* … *ỉw.f wꜣḥ.Ø* who has been placed

32.4 Used in place of a complement clause

In Late Egyptian, the construction of a complement clause with a non-independent prospective *sḏm.f* is reserved to the verb *rdỉ*. Other 'operator' verbs, for example *gmỉ* (see Excursus below), use various constructions, including the adverbial clause in lieu of a complement clause.

19. P. Turin 1887, 1, 13 (= *RAD*, 75, 12).

ỉw.tw (*ḥr*) *smtr.f ỉw.tw* (*ḥr*) *gm* ***ỉw ḏd.f*** *se n*(*=m*) *mꜣꜥt*

'He was questioned and it was found that he had said it indeed.'

20. P. Turin 1972, 4-6 (= *LRL*, 7, 11-13).

yꜣ ỉ.ỉrỉ.ỉ gm ***ỉw dỉ.f ỉw wꜥ tsm r ṯꜣ.ỉ*** *ỉw.w (ḥr) gm.ỉ n(=m) mtrt n ḏbꜣ*
'For it is only when they met me in the vicinity of Edfu, that I realised that he had sent a boat to take me.' The first adverbial clause plays the role of a complement clause, while the second is focalised by a second tense.

32.5 Excursus: the construction of verbs called 'operators'[254]

These are the verbs that, in modern languages, admit as direct pronominal object a sentence subject + predicate (for example 'I find the sweetened apple'). In Late Egyptian the main ones among them are:

- *ꜥmꜣ* 'learn (that), understand (that),'
- *sḏm* 'find out (that),'
- *rḫ* 'know (that),'
- *ptr* 'see (that),'
- and especially *gmỉ* 'find (that),' but often 'realise (that).'

These verbs cannot be followed by a non-independent prospective, reserved to *rdỉ*, and are therefore, constructed in four different ways. Here are the possible syntagma that can be used to write in Late Egyptian the sentence:

'I found (out) that he was dead'

32.5.1 Verb + direct object pronoun + pseudo-verbal predicate[255]

gm.ỉ se mwt.Ø *lit.* 'I found him being dead'

In this construction, called 'embedded,' *se* is both the direct pronominal object of *gm.ỉ* and the subject of the pseudo-participle *mwt* (see *supra* §14.3.2).

21. P. Leopold-Amherst, 2, 9-10 (= *KRI* VI, 484, 5-6).

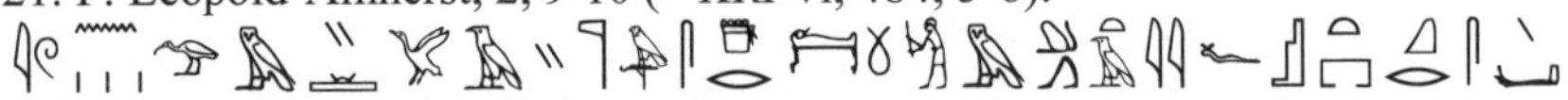

ỉw.n (ḥr) gm ***pꜣy nṯr sḏr*** *m pḥ tꜣy.f st-qrs*
'We found this god lying (*lit.* 'being stretched out') at the back of his grave.' In this example, *pꜣy nṯr* is both direct object of *gmỉ* and subject of *sḏr*.

32.5.2 Verb + direct object pronoun + adverbial clause

gm.ỉ se ỉw.f mwt.Ø *lit.* 'I found him when he was dead'

---

[254] See Vernus, *Or*, 50 (1981), p. 432-433 and n. 10.
[255] Pseudo-participle or preposition + infinitive.

22. P. Leopold-Amherst, 2, 5-6 (= *KRI* VI, 483, 13-484, 1).

ỉw.n (ḥr) gm ***pꜣ mr n nsw S ỉw bn se mỉ-qd*** *nꜣ mrw mỉḥꜥyt n nꜣ srw nty tw.n (ḥr) šm r ṯꜣwt ỉm.w m-dwn sp-sn ỉwnꜣ*

'We found that the pyramid of King S was not at all like the pyramids and tombs of the nobles in which we went to plunder very often.'

23. P. Abbott, 5, 5-6 (= *KRI* VI, 475, 4-5) (fig. p. 216).

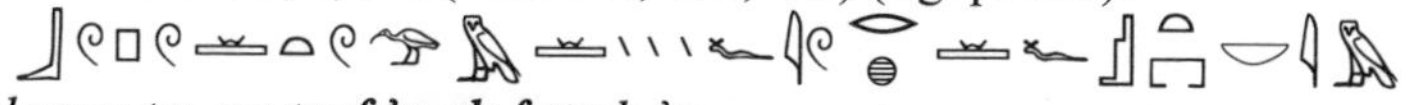

bwpw.tw gm.tw.f ***ỉw rḫ.f*** *st nb ỉm*

'It was not found that he had known of any tomb there.'[256]

32.5.3 Verb + adverbial clause (without direct object pronoun)

gm.ỉ ỉw.f mwt.Ø *lit.* 'I found (out) when he was dead'

This is the construction studied *supra* §32.4.

32.5.4 Verb + *r-ḏd* + independent form[257] (very frequent)

gm.ỉ r-ḏd sw mwt.Ø *lit.* 'I found (out): "he is dead"'

24. P. Turin 1875, 4, 2 (= *KRI* V, 352, 7-8).

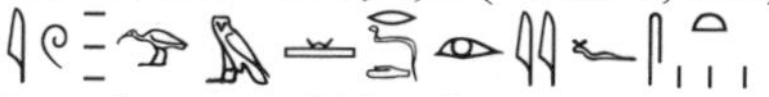

ỉw.w ḥr gm ***r-ḏd ỉry.f se***

'They found out that he had committed them (= major crimes).'

32.6 Remarks

Adverbial clauses can also be found in nominal sentences with adjectival predicate, see *infra* §40.5.

[256] See *supra* §15.2.2, example 17.

[257] See Sweeney, *Crossroads* I, 1986, p. 337-373.

33. Adverbial clauses introduced by *ỉr*

33.1 The particle *ỉr*

The fundamental property of the particle *ỉr* is to point out that an element, nominal or adverbial, of a predicative plain sentence, has been fronted. This results in two-member constructions of the type:

ỉr **+ fronted element / second member**

If the preposed element is nominal, one is dealing with a **thematisation** or **topicalisation** (see §12.4.2 and below Excursus A).

ỉr **+ noun (or equivalent) / independent form (verbal or not)**
marked theme = topic / rheme = comment

The thematised element is often resumed by a pronominal form in the second member. The sentence is usually translated: 'As for S ...'

If the element is adverbial, one has:

ỉr **+ circonstant** (= adverbial element) **/ non-subordinate verbal form**

The circonstant can be:
a. an **adverb** (see below Excursus B);
b. a **prepositional phrase** (see below Excursus C);
c. a **verbal form** with circumstantial function.

- These three categories can be combined in the order a, b, c.

Adverbial clauses introduced by *ỉr* belong to case 'c.' The particle is then shown in the protasis of correlative systems[258] of the type:

ỉr **+ verbal form** independent or not / **non-subordinate verbal form**
protasis / apodosis

The resulting systems can either be found in initial position, or be coordinated to the foregoing by means of the particle *ḫr*.

33.2 Correlative systems introduced by *ỉr*

33.2.1 The protasis incorporates *ỉr* + independent verbal form

The forms attested are the first present, the perfective and prospective *sḏm.f*, the third future, and the existential sentences.

Placed before these verbal forms, the particle *ỉr* converts them in non-independent forms

[258] Or even hypotactical. In these systems, the adverbial clause precedes the main one, see *supra* §32.2.2.

with adverbial function (or indicates that these forms have adverbial function).

33.2.1.1 The protasis incorporates *ỉr* + First Present

Examples are almost always found in narrative contexts.[259] In this case, the first present, introduced by *ỉr*, describes a process or a state more or less concomitant to the process of the apodosis, where the sequential is always present. The system has, in itself, no temporal nuance, it is the narrative context that confers it a past temporal value. In general, it is translated by 'when' or 'while.'

These systems are never found in an initial position – where other expressions, such as *ỉr m-ḏr sḏm.f …*, *ỉr ỉnk ...*, or the narrative infinitive, are used – but always at the beginning of a non-initial paragraph, systematically coordinated to the foregoing by the particle *ḫr*. This tends to indicate that for the Egyptians the narrative consisted of a unit without independent parts.

***ḫr ỉr* + first present / sequential**

33.2.1.1.1 The predicate of the First Present is a prepositional phrase (rare)

1. P. Orbiney, 16, 8 (= *LES*, 26, 10-11).

ḫr ỉr se ḥr rmn (n) nꜣ n rmṯ */ ỉw.f ḥr ktkt m nḥbt.f*

'But, while it was on the shoulders of the people, it moved its neck.'

33.2.1.1.2 The predicate of the First Present is (*ḥr*) + infinitive (frequent)

2. O. Cairo 25725, 1-3 (= *KRI* IV, 417, 6-8): deposition before the court.

ỉr ỉnk dỉ.‹ỉ› wꜥ n dꜣỉw n tꜣy.ỉ šrỉ(t) ỉw.s gb.[tỉ] ***ḫr ỉr st ḥr snb*** */ ỉw.ỉ ḥr hꜣb n.s ḥr ‹ḏd› ỉmỉ tw.f ỉw.s ḥr tm dỉ.tw.f*

'As for me, I gave a skirt to my daughter while she was ill, and, when she was recovering, I wrote to her saying: "So return it!" She did not return it.'[260]

This example illustrates the use of the system in non-initial paragraphs, and also shows that it can serve as support to other sequentials (here a negative sequential).

3. P. Turin 1880, 2, 17 (= *RAD*, 55, 13-14).

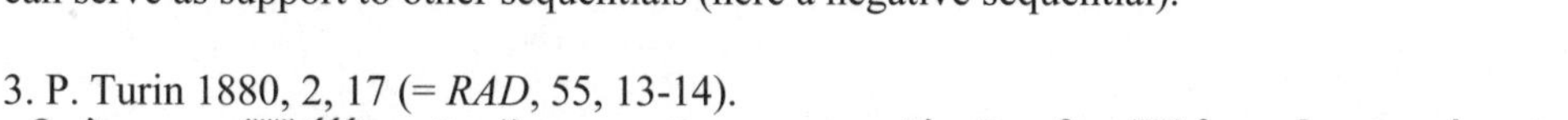

ḫr ỉr tw.n ḥr šm r sḏm r(ꜣ).w */ ỉw.w ḥr ḏd n.n ḏd.Ø se m mꜣꜥt*

'And when we went to hear their deposition, they said to us: "that has been, indeed, said"' (*lit.* 'it was said in truth').[261]

[259] Very rare exception is, for example, P. Anastasi VI, 38 (= *LEM*, 75, 8-9).

[260] See *supra* §25.2.2, example 3.

[261] See *supra* §15.2.1, example 12.

33.2.1.1.3 The predicate of the First Present is *m* + infinitive

This usage is limited to verbs of motion and indicates concomitance.

4. P. Mallet, VI, 6 (= *KRI* VI, 68, 1-2).

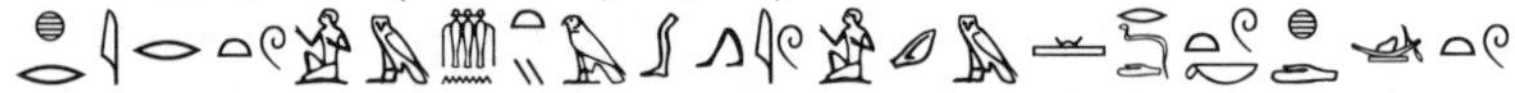

ḥr ỉr tw.ỉ m ḫnt */ ỉw.ỉ (ḥr) sḏm r-ḏd tw.k ḫd.tw*

'And while I was travelling south, I learned that you had arrived in the north.'

33.2.1.1.4 The predicate of the First Present is a stative

This usage seems limited to the semi-auxiliaries *ḫpr*, *ꜥḥꜥ*, *ḥmsỉ*.

5. P. BM 10053, v° 2, 16 (= *KRI* VI, 758, 2-3).

ḥr ỉr tw.n ꜥḥꜥ.tỉ (ḥr) pš.w */ ỉw šmsw nḫt-ỉmn-wꜣst*[sic] *{n} (ḥr) ỉy ỉw.f (ḥr) ỉṯꜣ ḥmt dbn 7*

'However, while we were sharing them, the servant Nakhtamunwaset came; he took seven copper debens.'

33.2.1.2 The protasis incorporates *ỉr + sḏm.f*

In these instances it will be necessary to distinguish carefully between *ỉr* + perfective *sḏm.f* and *ỉr* + prospective *sḏm.f.*

33.2.1.2.1 *ỉr* + perfective *sḏm.f* (rare)

In a narrative context this syntagma (either active or passive) constitutes a temporal protasis where the *sḏm.f* describes a process anterior to that of the apodosis, which always contains a sequential.

_ỉr_ + perfective _sḏm.f_ / sequential

6. P. Turin 1880, 3, 9-11 (= *RAD*, 56, 11-14).

'Saying by the foreman Khonsu to the crew..."Take the rations and go down to the quay..."

ḥr ỉr qn sš ỉmn-nḫt dỉt n.sn dỉw */ ỉw.w (ḥr) dỉt.w r mryt r-mỉtt-n pꜣ ḏd.f n.sn –* ***ḥr ỉr sn.w wꜥt ỉnbt*** */ ỉw sš ỉmn-nḫt (ḥr) šm ỉw.f (ḥr) ḏd n.sn m ỉr sn r mryt*

and, after the scribe Amennakht had finished distributing the rations to them, they set off (en route) to the quay in accordance with what he (= Khonsu) had told them, but when they passed a guard post, the scribe Amennakht went to say to them: "do not continue (*lit.* 'do not go towards') to the quay."'

33.2.1.2.2 *ỉr* + prospective *sḏm.f* (frequent)

In a non-narrative context this syntagma represents a protasis, usually a conditional one, expressing a process that has not yet occurred. In the apodosis, it is possible to find various independent forms (and, therefore, never the sequential). Depending on the probability of realisation of the process described in the protasis, the sentence is translated as 'if + present' or 'when + future.'

ỉr + prospective *sḏm.f* / independent form

7. O. Gardiner 310, 2-5 (= *KRI* III, 797, 11-12).

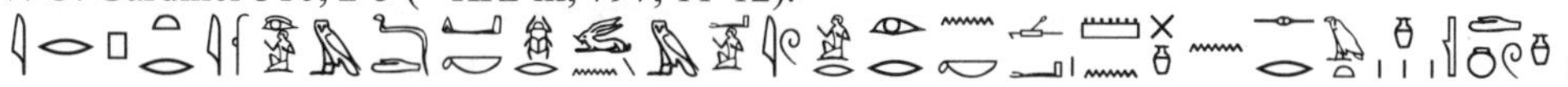 ***ỉr***

ptr.ỉ m-ḏd dỉ.k ḫpr (ỉ).wn m-dỉ.ỉ / *ỉw.ỉ r ỉrt n.k wꜥ mn n srmt qdy*

'If I see that you have made (re)appear what I owned (= 'that you make me find again my property'), I will allocate for you a measure of Cilicia *sermet*.'[262]

8. P. Orbiney, 10, 3 (= *LES*, 19, 16-20, 1).[263]

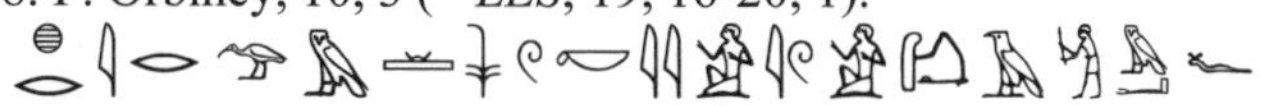

ḫr ỉr gm se ky / *ỉw.ỉ (r) ꜥḥꜣ m-dỉ.f*

'But if someone else finds it, I will fight with him.'

33.2.1.3 The protasis incorporates a Third Future (very rare examples)

9. P. Cairo 58059, 5-6 (= *KRI* III, 252, 6-7).

ỉr wn ỉw.k r ỉrt [*tꜣ*////] *ỉ.ḏd.k* / *ỉmỉ ỉn.tw.s dỉ.ỉ ỉṯꜣ.tw.s n.f*

'In the event that you would have done the ///// of which you spoke, have it sent so that I have it taken to him ...' Note the sequence *wn ỉw* characteristic of the third future in the protasis.

33.2.1.4 The protasis incorporates an existential sentence

10. O. DM 303, 3-4 (= *KRI* III, 534, 9-11).

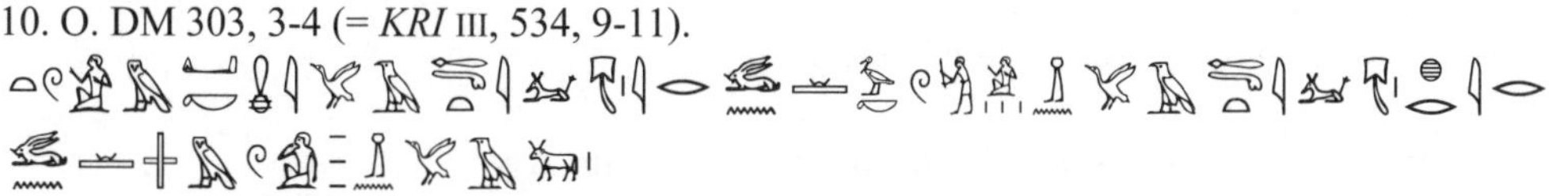

tw.ỉ m.dỉ.k mỉ pꜣ ꜥꜣ ***ỉr wn bꜣk*** / *ỉn pꜣ ꜥꜣ ḫr* ***ỉr wn wnm*** / *ỉn pꜣ ỉḥ*

'I am for you like the donkey: if there is work, one fetches the donkey (= me), but if there is food, one fetches the ox (= another)!'

33.2.2 The protasis incorporates *ỉr* + non-independent verbal form

33.2.2.1 The protasis incorporates a sequential[264] (examples are very rare and late)

---

[262] Beverage made from dates, see Valbelle, *Ouvriers*, p. 280.

[263] Another example: Hittite Treaty, 16-17 (= *KRI* II, 228, 7-8).

11. P. Strasburg 39, v° 3-6 (= Allam, *HOP*, pl. 105): 21st dynasty.

ỉr ỉw.k* (*ḥr*) *tm gm.tw.f* / *ỉw.k* (*r*) *ptr nꜣ rmṯ nty ỉrỉ ꜥnḫ.f* (*r*) *ḏd n.k ỉmỉ n.w ꜥnḫ mtw.k ṯꜣy.tw.w r pꜣ wbꜣ* (*n*) *pꜣy.w nṯr

'If you do not find it, you will see (= 'you will go and see') the people about which Ankhef will say to you: "Impose an oath on them" and you will bring them to the court of their god."'

33.2.2.2 The protasis incorporates a circumstantial First Present (examples are very rare)

12. O. Vienna 9, v° 1-2 (= *KRI* v, 563, 4-5).

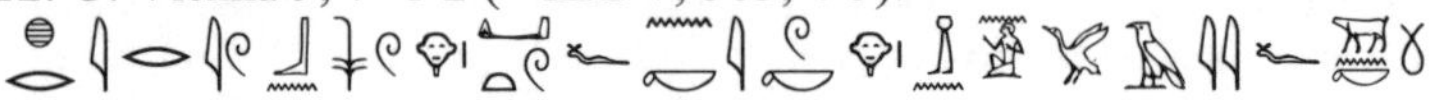

ḫr ỉr ỉw bn se ḥr dỉ.tw.f n.k** / **ỉw.k ḥr(=r) ỉn n.ỉ pꜣy.f ḫnk

'And if he does not give it (= the goat) to you, you will bring[265] me its coat.'[266] The sequence *ỉw bn se* is characteristic of a negative circumstantial first present.

13. P. BN 198, II, v° 6-7 (= *LRL*, 68, 9-10).

ỉr ỉw.k m ṯꜣty** / **bn ỉw.ỉ** (**r**) **hꜣy r nꜣy.k sktyw

'If you were the vizier, I would not venture (lit. 'would not go down') in your boats!'[267]

The presence of the first present in the protasis is very probable, because the predicate is a prepositional phrase built with *m*. The form in the apodosis is clearly a third future, unmistakable because in the negative form.

14. P. BM 10052, 3, 16-17 (= *KRI* VI, 774, 7-8).

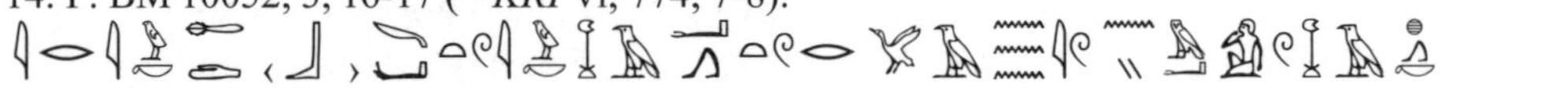

ỉr ỉw.k ẖdb.tw ỉw.k ḫꜣꜥ.tw r pꜣ mw** / **ỉw nỉm** (**r**) **wḫꜣ.k

'If you are killed and thrown in the water, who will seek you? (= 'will care about you').'

The double protasis contains two instances of the first present with a pseudo-participle[268] as predicate, while the apodosis contains a third future.[269]

33.2.2.3 The protasis incorporates *m-ḏr sḏm.f* or *m-ḫt sḏm.f*

In both cases, the construction preposition/adverb + prospective *sḏm.f*, produces, by grammaticalisation, a 'subordinate conjunctive,'[270] – a non-independent form also found in

[264] Another example: P. Boulaq 6, VI, 6 (21st dynasty). In reality, this construction is a precursor of the demotic 'conditional' *ỉw.f* (*tm*) *sḏm*, see Johnson, *The Demotic Verbal System*, p. 233-265, especially p. 235, n. 23.

[265] For the interpretation as a third future, see example 13 below.

[266] Another possible translation: 'And if he does not sell it to you, you will buy me its coat.'

[267] *Cf.* the Yiddish proverb quoted by F. Chandernagor, *L'archange de Vienne*, p. 78: 'If his word were a bridge, I would be afraid to go over.'

[268] The probability of this being a third future having a pseudo-participle as predicate – 'analogical' construction (see *supra* §19.4) – is very low.

[269] See the preceding example in the negative form. However, *ỉrỉ nỉm r sḏm* is also attested in the third future (P. Turin 2021, 3, 10).

[270] See Černý-Groll, *LEG*, §32 and §35, p. 410 and 418.

unmarked position, that is, after the main clause,[271] but obviously without *ỉr*. Examples are found only in narrative contexts.

Example with *m-ḏr sḏm.f*:

15. P. BM 10052, 12, 2-5 (= *KRI* VI, 793, 4-8).[272]

ḏd.f ỉr m-ḏr* ḫdb *ỉw.f-n-ỉmn *nꜣ snw n nꜣy.ỉ ḥryw / ỉw.ỉ (ḥr) hꜣ r pꜣ ỉmw ỉrm.f ỉw.ỉ (ḥr) šm r A ḥr ỉr se (ḥr) pḥ r dmỉ B / ỉw.w (ḥr) ḏd n.f nꜣy.k rmṯ (ḥr) ṯꜣy ỉmntt ỉw.f (ḥr) ḏd gr m ỉr ḏd.tw.f*
'He said: "'After Iuefenamun had killed the brothers of my superiors, I went into the boat with him and went to A, and, when he reached the town of B, he was told (*lit.* 'they said to him'): "'Your men plunder the West!" He replied: "'Shut up, do not say it!"'

In this example, an initial paragraph – consisting of a protasis with *m-ḏr* + *sḏm.f* and its apodosis – is followed by a second paragraph – consisting of a protasis with *ỉr* + first present and its apodosis – with the two paragraphs linked together by the particle *ḫr* (see *supra* §33.2.1.1.2).

Example with *m-ḫt sḏm.f*:

16. First Hittite marriage, 30-31 (= *KRI* II, 246, 1-7): Late Middle Egyptian.[273]

ḫr ỉr m-ḫt mꜣꜣ.se tꜣ.se *m sḫr pn qsn ḫr bꜣw ꜥꜣ nw nb tꜣwy nsw bỉtỉ R / ꜥḥꜥ.n ḏd pꜣ wr ꜥꜣ n ḫtꜣ n mšꜥ.f*
'But, when they saw their country in that pitiful state, (bowing) to the great power of the lord of the Two Lands, the King of Upper and Lower Egypt R(amses II), the great Chief of Hatti said to his army ...'

33.2.2.4 Remarks

There is a case where the construction preposition/adverb + independent verbal form is not grammaticalised: it is the syntagma *m-ḫt* + first present (limited to nominal subject + pseudo-participle, and confined to literary texts). This must be analysed as two units: adverb + independent form (and not a 'subordinate conjunctive'). It is found only after *ỉr*.

17. Doomed Prince, 4, 6-7 (= *LES*, 2, 1-2).

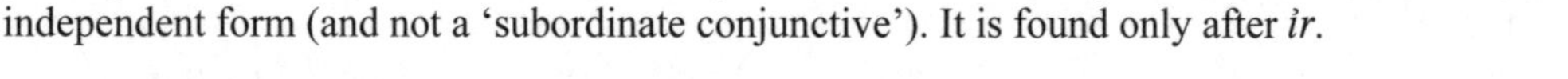

ḫr ỉr m-ḫt / pꜣ ẖrd ꜥꜣy */ ỉw.f ḥr ṯs r tꜣy.f tp-ḥwt*
'And later, the child having grown up, he went up to his terrace.'

---

[271] See *supra* §26.3. Examples of this usage after the main clause: with *m-ḏr* see P. Turin 1880, 2, 18-9, cited in §26.3, example 4; with *m-ḫt* see P. Abbott, 4, 13 (= *KRI* VI, 474, 3).
[272] Another example: Pentawer poem 205-207 (= *KRI* II, 66, 1-15).
[273] See Winand, *o.l.*, §22, p. 13.

18. P. Orbiney, 13, 6-7 (= *LES*, 23, 6-7).

ḥr ỉr m-ḫt / tꜣ ḥḏ.Ø / sn-nw n hrw ḫprw */ wn.ỉn.f ḥr ḫpr ḥr šm ḫr pꜣ ꜥš*
'And then, the earth having lit up, a second day having arrived, he began to walk under the pine.'

33.2.3 The protasis incorporates the ambiguous syntagma *ỉw.f* (*?*) *sḏm* (very frequent)

19. P. Geneva D 187, v° 1-4 (= *LRL*, 42, 2-6).

ỉr ỉw.ỉ (*?*) ***gm*** *r-ḏd mꜣꜥ.tw pꜣy rmṯ ỉst* [*ḥr nꜣ ?*] *qnqn ỉ.ỉrỉ.f pꜣy.ỉ šmsw / ỉw.ỉ* (*r*) *dỉt n.f* [*////*] *ḥr.w – ḫr* ***ỉr ỉw.ỉ*** (*?*) ***ꜥm*** *r-ḏd mꜣꜥ.tw pꜣy.ỉ* [*šmsw ỉw ỉrỉ.f?*] *qnqn.f m ḥwrꜥ / ỉw.ỉ* (*r*) *dỉt ptr.k pꜣ nty ỉw.ỉ* (*r*) [*ỉr.tw.f n.f*]
'If I find out that this (tomb) worker was right [about the] beatings that he inflicted to my servant, I will give him (= the servant) [others] in addition(?). – But, if I find out that my [servant] was right [when he (= the worker)] violently beat him,[274] I will let you see what I am going do to him (= the worker)!'

It is difficult to identify the *ỉw.f*(*?*) *sḏm* form because:
- it can be the third future, see above §33.2.1.3,
- the sequential, see above §33.2.2.1,
- or the circumstantial first present, see above §33.2.2.2.

Remark. It is possible to find examples where such a system is preceded by the circumstantial *ỉw*:

20. P. Mayer A, 8, 13-14 (= *KRI* VI, 818, 9-10): concerning gold and silver debens.

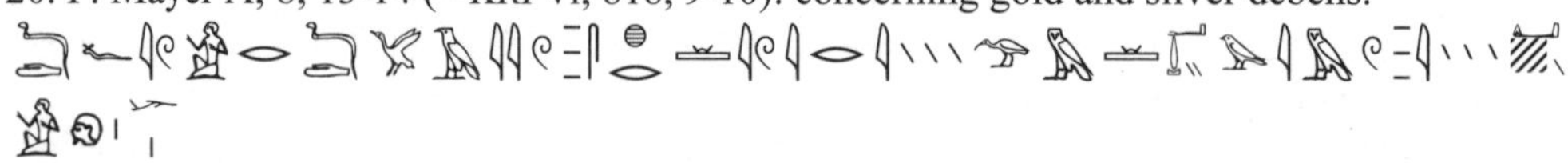

ḏd.f ỉw.ỉ r ḏd pꜣy.w sḫr ***ỉw ỉr ỉw.tw*** (*?*) ***gm*** *ꜥḏꜣ ỉm.w ỉw.tw* (*r*) *dỉt.ỉ tp ḫt*
'He said: "I will state their source[275] because, if it is found that it is irregular,[276] I will be put on the stake."'

33.3 Conclusion

The particle *ỉr* allows one to construct (among others) correlative systems containing in the protasis various verbal forms that take on a circumstantial function.

If these forms are not subordinate (independent or sequential forms), *ỉr* plays both the role of

[274] For the reading *ḥwrꜥ*, see Wente, *LRL*, p. 58, n. g.
[275] *Lit*. 'Their state, their situation.' The judges think it is 'dirty money' deriving from the plunder of graves.
[276] *Lit*. 'If something illegal is found in them.'

subordination converter and of signal of the marked order. Otherwise (circumstantial first present, *m-ḏr sḏm.f* ...), *ỉr* only fulfils the second function.

33.4 Excursus A: thematisations with *ỉr*

These are constructions that set up in marked theme or topic (see *supra* §12.4.2) any nominal element of an initial plain sentence (verbal or nominal). To do this, the element to be thematised is preposed (or topicalised) and the transposition is indicated by the particle *ỉr*. The result is a two-member construction:

***ỉr* + preposed element** (= topic) **/ rheme** (or comment)

The element thus thematised is frequently resumed in pronominal form in the comment.
When the element thematised is pronominal, the tonic independent pronoun is used, see *supra* §7.4.2 and below example 22.

33.4.1 Thematisation of the subject

21. O. Gardiner 55, v° 4 (= *HO*, pl. 66, 2).[277]

*ḫr **ỉr ꜣḫt nb sp-sn nty m pꜣy.‹ỉ› pr** / ỉw.w n tꜣy.‹ỉ› ḥmt ḥnꜥ nꜣy.s ẖrdw*
'And, as for all possessions, without exception, that are in my house, they will be for my wife and her children.'

22. O. Nash 1, 2-3 (= *KRI* IV, 315, 10-11).

*ḏdt.n rmṯ ỉst nb-nfr **ỉr ỉnk** / tms.‹ỉ› wꜥ ḫl ỉnk m pꜣy.‹ỉ› pr*
'What the worker Nebnefer said: "As for me, (I) buried one of my picks in my house ..."'

33.4.1 Thematisation of the direct object pronoun

23. P. Turin 1875, 2, 5 (= *KRI* V, 350, 16-351, 1).

***ỉr nꜣ mdwt ỉ.ḏd nꜣ rmṯ** / bw rḫ.ỉ se*
'As for the words that people have said, I do not know them.'

24. P. BM 10326, v° 21 (= *LRL*, 20, 14-15).

*ḫr **ỉr pꜣ ḫt ỉ.dỉ.k m-ẖnw šꜥt** / dỉ.‹ỉ› **se** ỉm ꜥn (r) dỉt ỉn.tw.f n.k ꜥn*
'And, as for the stick that you had placed inside a letter, I have put it back there again so that it is returned to you.'

---

[277] Another example (damaged): Mès, N 31-32 (= *KRI* III, 430, 15-16).

33.4.3 Thematisation of a noun (or equivalent) object of a preposition

25. P. Ashmolean Museum 1945.95 (Naunakht I), 2, 7 (= *KRI* VI, 238, 2).

ỉr pꜣ nty bwpw.f dỉt n.ỉ */ bn ỉw.ỉ r dỉt n.f m ꜣḫt.tw.ỉ*

'As for the one who has given nothing (*lit.* 'not') to me, I will not bequeath to him (*lit.* 'will not give') any of my property.'

26 O. Berlin P 1121, v° 1-2 (= *KRI* V, 525, 1-2).

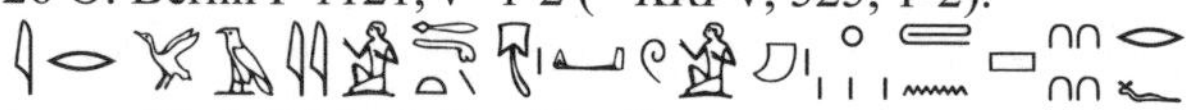

ỉr pꜣy.ỉ ꜥꜣ / dỉ.ỉ ḥmt dbn 40 r.f

'As for my donkey, I paid 40 debens for it' (*lit.* 'I gave 40 debens for it').

33.4.4 Thematisation of the subject of a complement clause

27. P. Mayer A, 9, 6-7 (= *KRI* VI, 820, 11-12).

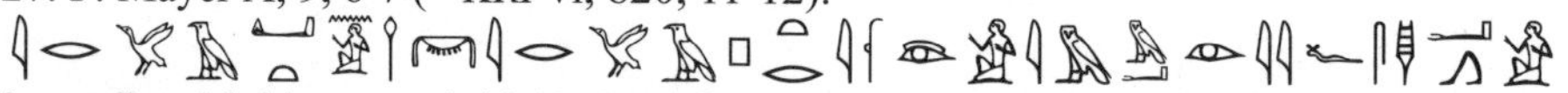

ỉr pꜣ dỉt n.ỉ ḥḏ ỉr pꜣ ptr (w)ỉ */ ỉmỉ ỉry.f sꜥḥꜥ.ỉ*

'As for the one who has given me silver, or as for the one who has seen me, cause (then) that he accuses me!' Note the double thematisation and the periphrasis of the quadriliteral verb of the complement clause.

Remark. It is possible to find, although less frequently, cases of thematisation through fronting without *ỉr*, especially after *mk*, *ptr*, or *ḫr*.

33.5 Excursus B: *ỉr* + adverb / verbal form

Adverbs thus constructed are often:

ḥr-sꜣ
(literary and daily life texts)

28. P. Leiden I 350, v° col. III, 1, 13 (= *KRI* II, 810, 3): logbook.

ḥꜣꜥ sš ptḥ-ms šmsw ptḥ-m-nw bꜣkỉ ḥr ***ỉr ḥr-sꜣ*** */ ỉw.tw ḥr ḥꜣꜥ sš ḥr-tl ḥr tr n mtrt*

'Release of the scribe Ptahmes, (along with) the servants Ptahmenu and Baki, and then the scribe Hortel was released at midday.'

m-ḫt
(only literary texts, and always with a prepositional phrase or a verbal form, see above §33.2.2.4)

29. P. Orbiney, 4, 3-4 (= *LES*, 13, 5-6).

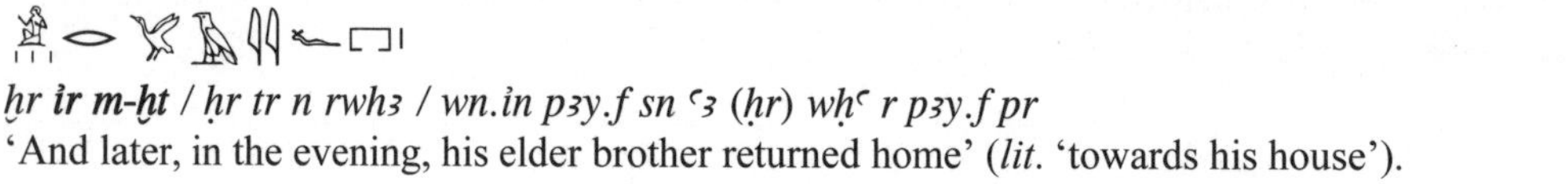

ḥr ỉr m-ḫt */ ḥr tr n rwhꜣ / wn.ỉn pꜣy.f sn ꜥꜣ (ḥr) wḥꜥ r pꜣy.f pr*

'And later, in the evening, his elder brother returned home' (*lit.* 'towards his house').

33.6 Excursus C: *ỉr* + prepositional phrase / verbal form

The most commonly used prepositions in this case are: *ḥr-sꜣ*, *ḥr*, *m*.

30. O. Gardiner 54, r° 6 (= *KRI* v, 473, 12).

***ḥr ỉr ḥr-sꜣ hrw* 2** / *ỉw.f ḥr ỉy r ḏd n.ỉ*
'And, two days later, he came to say to me ...'

31. P. Orbiney, 2, 2 (= *LES*, 11, 1-2).

ḥr ỉr ḥr tr n skꜣ / *ỉw pꜣy.f sn ꜥꜣ ḥr ḏd n.f*
'And, at the time of ploughing, his elder brother said to him …'

Remark. In example 31, the prepositional phrase *ḥr tr n skꜣ* is preposed, while in example 28 *ḥr tr n mtrt* is in its normal position at the end of the sentence. Thus, fronting (marked order) permits to highlight the adverbial, or to give it a slight emphasis, which is intermediate between the plain sentence and the second tense.[278]

O. DM 575 *(cf.* p. 219)

[278] In a narrative context, the fronting of the adverbial is practically the only way to emphasise it, the second tense being used only in a non-narrative context, but see Satzinger, *NÄS*, §2.7.1.3, p. 241-242: "Narrativierung der 'emphatischen' Form."

34. Adverbial clauses introduced by *wnn*

34.1 Introduction[279]

Adverbial clauses introduced by *wnn* are constructed from the first present (most often with *ḥr* + infinitive as predicate[280]). The auxiliary *wnn*, here as *mrr.f*, of which it is the only vestige in Late Egyptian, serves to nominalise the verbal phrase formed by the first present. This results in:

wnn.f*[281] *ḥr sḏm or ***wnn A ḥr sḏm***

This noun phrase then assumes adverbial function in the protasis of a correlative system which apodosis almost always contains a sequential (rarely an imperative[282] or a prospective[283]). In general, therefore, one has:

protasis /apodosis

wnn.f ḥr sḏm / ỉw.f ḥr (tm) sḏm

nominalised first present / sequential

Remarks

1. The system consists of two non-independent forms leaning on one another. They are independent sentences of higher order on which other non-independent forms, particularly the conjunctive, can lean.

2. The system is devoid of any temporality: it merely indicates that each realisation of the process of the protasis **automatically** brings about, and only once (hence the use of the sequential), the completion of the process of the apodosis:

A (protasis) ► **B** (apodosis)

In the much more frequent case where the process of the protasis is not a perfective (information provided by the co(n)text), the sentence is translated by a conditional system (**if**), or a temporal one (**when**, **as soon as**), depending on the **probability** of realisation of this process.

3. The system originated with the *Wechselsatz*:

A ◄► B *wnn pt / wnn.ṯ r.ỉ*[284]

and, by deterioration of the second member, one gets to the system studied:

---

[279] See Satzinger, *NÄS*, §1.4.1.1, p. 84-106; Vernus, *GM* 43 (1981), 77-83; *l'Égyptologie en 1979*, I, 1982, p. 86, n. g; *RdE* 34 (1982-1983), 119, (c); *Revue historique de droit français et étranger*, vol. 61, 1983, 75; Junge, *JEA* 72 (1986), 122-124.

[280] Very rarely a pseudo-participle or a prepositional phrase, see Satzinger, *o.c.*, §1.4.1.1.6, p. 94.

[281] Rare variants: *wnn ỉw.f ḥr sḏm*, for example Wenamun, 2, 50-51 (= *LES*, 72, 4-5).

[282] Satzinger, *o.c.*, §1.4.1.1.5, p . 93.

[283] Frandsen, *LEVS*, §98, example 6 (= O. Petrie 61, 6).

[284] 'As heaven exists, so you exist near me,' Urk. IV, 348, 9.

A ▶ B, where B is an independent verbal form.

4. The system can be coordinated with the foregoing by the particle *ḫr*.[285]

34.2 Examples[286]

The syntagma used in the first two examples is very frequent in letters.

1. P. BM 10412, 8-9 (= *LRL*, 55, 12-13).

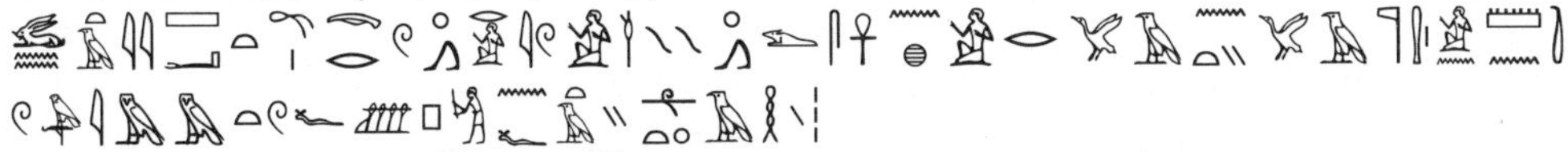

wnn tꜣy.(ỉ) šꜥt (ḥr) spr r.ṯ[287] ***/ ỉw.ṯ***[282] ***(ḥr) wḏ sbk-sꜥnḫ r pꜣ nty pꜣ ḥm-nṯr n mnṯw ỉm mtw.f šsp n.f tꜣy sṯꜣt ꜣḥt***

'As soon as my letter will reach you, you will send Sobeksankh to (*lit.* 'to the place where is') the priest of Montu, and he will receive from him this aroura of land.'

2. P. Berlin P 8523, 11-16 (= Allam, *HOP,* pl. 76).

wnn tꜣy.(ỉ) šꜥt (ḥr) spr r.k / ỉw.k (ḥr) dỉt ḥr.k n tꜣ(y) ꜣḥt mtw.k tm nnỉ n.s mtw.k ṯꜣy pꜣy.s qmꜣ mtw.k skꜣ.s

'As soon as my letter will reach you, you will take care of this field and you will not neglect[288] it, and you will pull off its reeds and you will plough it.'

3. P. BN 196, II, 7-9 (= *LRL*, 21, 11-13): letter.

ḫr wnn sš p(ꜣ)-n-tꜣ-ḥwt-nḫt (ḥr) ỉy n.t(n) r-ḏd ỉmỉ se ḥrỉ dd bꜣk.f / ỉw.tn (ḥr) tm dỉt.f *n.f* ***r-ḏd*** *‹ḏd› pꜣ mr mšꜥ ỉmỉ bꜣk.f nꜣ nỉwy mtw.tn dỉt n.f ḥmt r dỉt bꜣk.f nꜣ nỉwy*

'And if the scribe Pentahutnakht comes to tell you (*lit.* 'comes to you saying'): "Give it, (to) Hori who has been assigned to work!"[289] you will not give it to him, explaining (*lit.* 'saying'): "The general has said:[290] 'Have him forge the spears.' And you will give him (= to Hori) some copper to let him forge the spears."' Note the negative sequential in the apodosis of this last example.

---

[285] Note the article by Baer, *JEA* 51 (1965), 137-143, now outdated.

[286] The system is normally used in a discourse, in non-narrative contexts. Its use to report past events is an effect of style, for example: P. Salt 124, 2, 3-4; v° 1, 9; v° 1, 15.

[287] The text shows  instead of , but the context clearly indicates that this is a woman and that the scribe omitted the dot that, in hieratic, characterises the sign for the seated woman.

[288] *Lit.* 'And you will not be negligent towards it.'

[289] *Lit.* 'Who has been caused that he works.'

[290] Haplography.

34.3 Remark: another use of *wnn*

Although much more rarely, the 'nominalisation' converter *wnn* is attested in sentences where it transforms a verbal phrase A into a nominal sentence of the type B Ø, where B = *wnn* A (see *infra* §39.2.2.1).

4. Kuban Stela, 11 (= *KRI* II, 355, 7).[291]

wnn *bw ỉn.tw nbw ḥr ḫ3st tn m-ʿ ng3w mw*

'The fact is that gold was never brought back from this country due to lack of water.'

• In Middle Egyptian the construction is obviously *wnn A pw*, for example, P. Smith 8, 15-16:

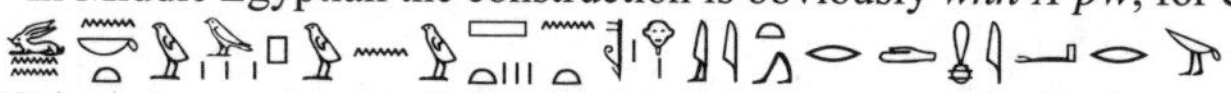

'It is that some bone splinters are coming into contact with the swab.'

[291] Other examples: P. Anastasi IV, 8, 2-1 (= *LEM*, 42, 14-16), cited *supra* §18.2, example 4; P. Anastasi IV, 12, 6 and 9 (= *LEM*, 48, 5-6 and 10), P. DM VI, 5 (= *KRI* VI, 267,1); P. Turin 1887 v° 1, 11 (= *RAD* 79, 10).

35. Adverbial clauses introduced by *ỉnn*

35.1 Introduction[292]

Placed before an independent form (verbal or otherwise), the particle  *ỉnn* 'if' converts it into an adverbial clause, always expressing a true condition.

▪ **Note**: the spelling  may also be that of the first person plural independent pronoun *ỉnn* 'we' (see *supra* §7.4.1); that of *ỉ.n.n* 'so we said' (see *supra* §12.3.2.2); that of the interrogative *ỉn* (see *supra* §11.2.1, *infra* §43 and example 5 below), or that of the morpheme meaning 'except.'[293]

Independent forms that can be converted by *ỉnn* are:
- the first present (example 2);
- the perfective *sḏm.f*;
- the *bwpwy.f sḏm* form (example 3);
- the third future (examples 4, 5);
- the affirmative (example 1) or negative (examples 2, 5) existential sentence;
- the second tenses;
- the cleft sentences (example 5).

35.2 Usage

The conditionals introduced by *ỉnn* always constitute the protasis of correlative systems whose apodosis contains a variety of independent forms, among which are:
- the third future (examples 3, 4, 5);
- the imperative (example 1, 2, 5);
- the prospective *sḏm.f*;
- the cleft sentences.

These conditionals can be found in an initial position, or after particles, such as *ḫr* or *ptr*. They are only found in the discourse, in a non-narrative context.

1. O. Brussels E 305, v° 2-4 (= *KRI* VII, 338, 14-15).

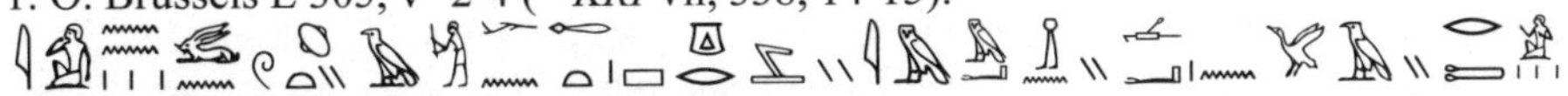

ỉnn wn wtyw n ꜥꜣt grg.tw / *ỉmỉ ỉn.tw wꜥ n pꜣy rmṯ*

'If there are hard stone sarcophagi that are ready, have one delivered to this man.'

2. O. Berlin P 12630, v° 1-2 (= *KRI* V, 595, 4-6).

ỉnn tw.ṯ ḥr dỉt pꜣ ỉḥ / *ỉmỉ ỉn.tw.f* – ***ḫr ỉnn mn ỉḥ*** / *ỉmỉ ỉn.tw pꜣ ḥꜥtỉ ḥnꜥ pꜣ wt*

'If you give the bull, have it brought; but if there is no bull, have the bed and the coffin brought back.'

---

[292] See Černý, *JEA* 27 (1941), 108-112, and *ZÄS* 90 (1963), 13-16; Satzinger, *NÄS*, §1.4.2.1, p. 106-108; Green, *Or* 49 (1980), 1-29; Depuydt, *JEA* 77 (1991), 69-78.

[293] See the excellent article by Černý, *loc. cit.*

3. P. BM 10100, 14-15 (= *LRL*, 50, 16-51, 2): concerning female servants.

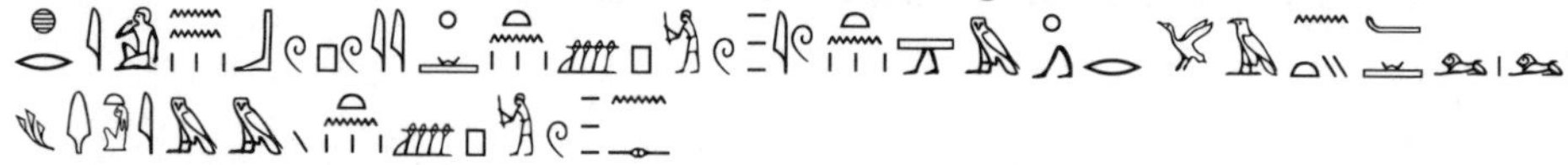

ḫr inn bwpwy.tn šsp.w */ iw.tn* (*r*) *šm r pꜣ nty ḥrrt im mtw.tn šsp.w n.s*
'And if you have not received them, you will go find Hereret and you will receive them from her.'

Example after thematisation:

4. P. Mayer B, 4-5 (= *KRI* VI, 515, 10-11).

ir nꜣ ḥḏ i.gm.k ***inn bn iw.k (r) dit n.i im.w*** */ iw.i* (*r*) *šm r ḏd.tw.f n pꜣ ḥꜣty-ꜥ*
'As for the silver (objects) that you found, if you do not give me some of them, I will go to tell it to the Major!'

5. P. Louvre E 27151, 7-11 (= *JEA* 64 (1978), pl. 14): concerning a honey jar of poor quality.

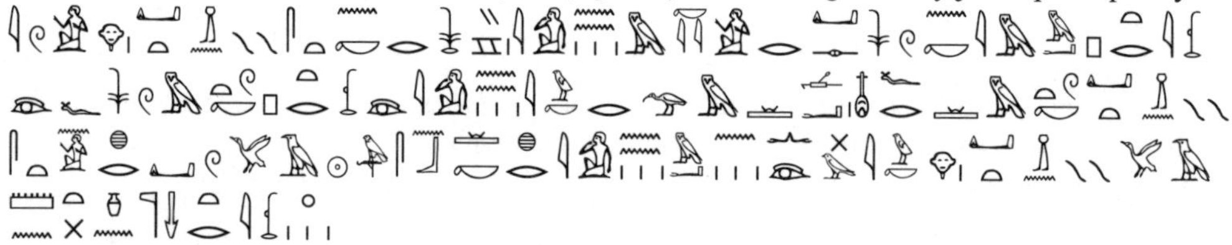

iw.i ḥr dit in.tw.s n.k r rsy ***inn m ky r(=i).di se n.k*** */ imi ptr.f se mtw.k ptr* in *iw.k r gm wꜥ*(*t*) *nfr*(*t*) *mtw.k dit in.tw.s n.i ḫr di pꜣ-rꜥ snb.k* ***ḫr inn mn Ø***[294] */ iw.k ḥr(=r?) dit in.tw pꜣ mn n snṯr*
'I have had it returned to you to the South. If it is someone else who supplied it to you, let him see it, and see whether you find a good one (*lit.* 'and see: "will you find a good one?"') and send it to me, and may Pre grant you good health![295] But if there is not, you will have the pot of incense brought (to me).'

Note that the second  in this example is not the particle studied in this chapter, but a writing of the interrogative morpheme *in* (see §11.2.1 and *infra* §43), that, in some cases, can also be translated as 'if, whether.'[296] Here it introduces an interrogative complement clause, transliterated in roman characters.

---

[294] See *supra* §22.2, example 5.

[295] Here the role of the particle *ḫr* is to allow the passage from the imperative (jussive) to the prospective (optative), and also to place the god and humans on a different level.

[296] For example: *I don't know whether it is true. Cf.* French '*Si.*' A similar example showing the current grapheme  of the interrogative *in* is: *mtw.k ptr (i)n sw iw ḥr ḫꜣr* 'And see whether he has come (back) from Syria,' P. Bologna 1094, 5, 5-6 (= *LEM*, 5, 7-8).

36. Adverbial clauses introduced by *hn*, *bsỉ* and *ḥl* (*ḥnr*)

36.1 Introduction

Placed in front of various independent forms (verbal or not), these three particles turn them into adverbial clauses expressing a condition that is already known to be unfulfilled:

‘if (but this is not the case) ... (‘Unreal Conditional’[297])

36.2 The conditional introduced by *hn*[298]

These are the more frequent of the three, and are mainly found in school texts. They are constructed from the following independent forms:

– the perfective *sḏm.f* (example 1);

– the *bw sḏm.f* form;

– the first present;

– the existential sentence (example 2);

– the nominal sentence (example 3).

Most often, they constitute the protasis of a correlative system which apodosis contains, almost always, the third future preceded by the past converter: *wn* (*bn*) *ỉw.f r sḏm* (see *supra* §19.2).

1. P. BM 10052, 4, 11-12 (= *KRI* VI, 776, 13-14).

ḏd.f b(w)p(w)y.ỉ ptr rmṯ nb ***hn ptr.ỉ*** */ wn ỉw.ỉ (r) ḏd.tw.f*[299]
‘He said: “I did not see anyone, if I had seen (someone), I would have said it.”’

2. Wenamun, 2, 29-30 (= *LES*, 69, 15-16).
‘As for what you said: “Former kings had silver and gold brought,”

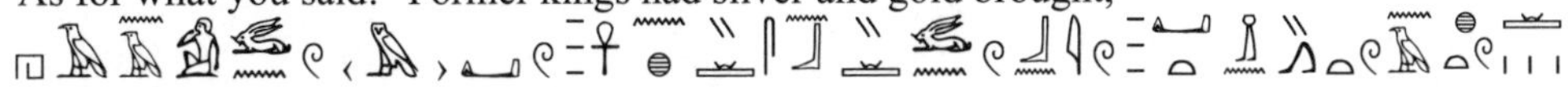

hn wn ‹m›-dỉ.w ꜥnḫ snb */ wn bn ỉw.w (r) dỉt ỉn.tw nꜣ ḫtw*
if they had had life and health, they would not have caused material goods to be brought!’

---

[297] Also termed ‘clauses of unfulfilled condition.’

[298] See Satzinger, *NÄS*, §1.4.2.2, p. 109-114.

[299] Note the variant: *hn wn ptr.ỉ / wn ỉw.ỉ (r) ḏd.tw.f* (P. BM 10403, 3, 31 = *KRI* VI, 776, 13-14).

3. Wenamun, 1, 18-19 (= *LES*, 62, 13-15).

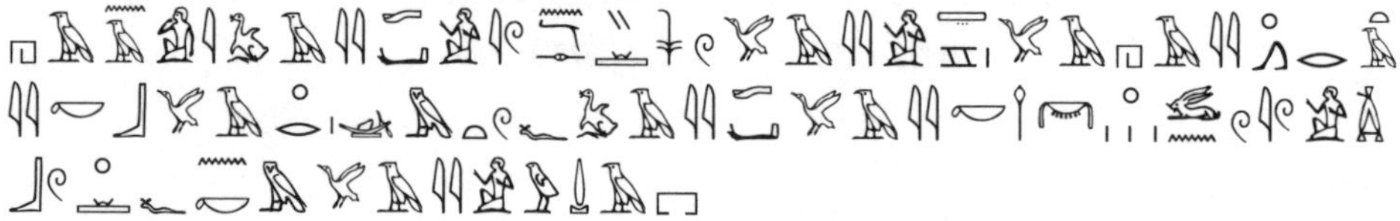

hn ỉṯꜣy ỉw ny-se pꜣy.ỉ tꜣ pꜣ hꜣy r tꜣy.k br mtw.f ṯꜣy pꜣy.k ḥḏ */ wn ỉw.ỉ (r) ḏbꜣ.f n.k m pꜣy.ỉ wḏꜣ*
'If it were a thief belonging to my country the one who went down into your ship and stole your silver, I would have reimbursed it to you from my treasury ... (but, as for the thief who robbed you, he is yours, he belongs to your ship).' In this example *hn* precedes a nominal sentence in which the second member is continued by a conjunctive.

36.3 The conditional introduced by  *bsỉ*[300]

The unreal conditional clauses introduced by *bsỉ always convey an optative nuance*: 'Ah, if only (but alas, this is not the case) ...,' unlike the previous one, which *could.*

When, and this is quite frequent, the independent form following *bsỉ* is a first present with a pronominal subject, the latter takes the suffixal form and is combined with *bsỉ* in the same way as with *ỉw* or *wn*, thus resulting in: *bsỉ.ỉ*, *bsỉ.k*, *bsỉ.f* etc.

Naturally, these conditionals may appear in correlative systems.

4. P. Lansing, 2, 8-9 (= *LEM*, 101, 11-12).
'And I have beaten you with all kinds of staffs, but you do not listen.

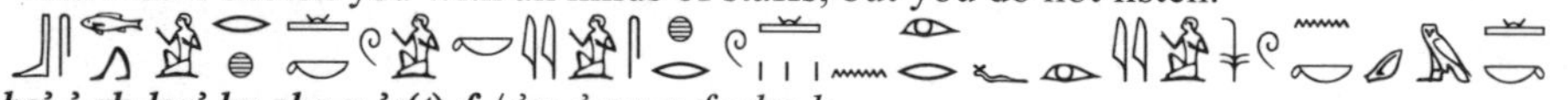

bsỉ.ỉ rḫ.kwỉ ky sḫr n ỉr(t).f */ ỉry.ỉ sw n.f sḏm.k*
Ah! If only I knew of another method to apply, I would apply it to you so that you listen!' The apodosis contains an independent prospective *sḏm.f.*

5. P. Leiden I 365, 6-7 (= *KRI* III, 233, 1).
'And, as for the letter you sent me (asking me) about the three young girls: they are well.

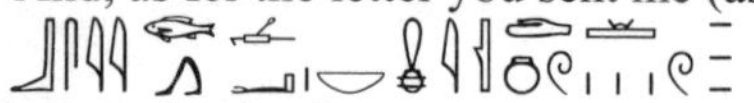

bsỉ wꜥ nb mỉ-qd.w
Ah! If only everyone (*lit.* 'each') was like them!'

6. P. Turin 1887, 1, 12-13 (= *RAD,* 75, 10-11).

bsỉ n.n ky 3 wꜥb */ dỉ.n ḫꜣꜥ pꜣ nṯr pꜣy šrỉ n pꜣy šwty r-bl*
'Ah! If only we had three other pure priests, we would ensure that the god cast out the son of this dealer! (*lit.* 'this son of this dealer').'

For an example with a nominal sentence, see *infra* §39.3.1, example 42.

---

[300] See Caminos, *LEM*, p. 150; Satzinger, *o.c.*, 1.4.2.3, p. 114-115.

36.4 The conditional introduced by  *ḥl* (*ḥnr*)[301]

They occur only in school or literary texts, and almost always in sentences expressing a wish *ḥl n.ỉ* 'Ah, if (only) I had!'

7. P. Sallier I, 8, 3-4 (= *LEM*, 86, 2).

***ḥl n.ỉ ḏḥwty** m ḥȝ.ỉ dwȝw*

'Ah, if only I had Thoth behind me (= 'as protector') tomorrow!'

In one example, the particle appears in the protasis of a correlative system where it introduces a first present:

8. Doomed Prince, 6, 2-3 (= *LES*, 4, 9-10).

***ḥl [bn]**[302] **tw.ỉ ḥr šnt rdwy.ỉ** / iw.ỉ ḥr(=r?) šm r pwy m-dỉ.tn*

'Ah, if only I did not suffer with my feet, I would go jumping with you!'

---

[301] See Satzinger, *loc. cit.*

[302] For the restoration see Wolf, *ZÄS* 68 (1932), 71.

37. The *ỉ.ỉrỉ.t.f sḏm* form

37.1 Introduction[303]

The *ỉ.ỉrỉ.t.f sḏm* form derives from the Middle Egyptian perfective *r sḏm.t.f* 'until he heard,' where the *r*, elided, is indicated by the prosthetic yod, and where the verb is periphrased by the auxiliary *ỉrỉ*, which is consistent with the evolutionary trend of the language. The *t* ending is usually indicated by  and variants, but sometimes it is omitted, which can cause confusion with a second tense. In the majority of cases the construction is:

37.2 Examples

1. O. Berlin P 12654, 10-11 (= *KRI* VI, 344, 16-345, 2).[304]

ỉw tꜣ qnbt ḥr ḏd ỉmỉ n.f 100 ‹n› sẖt šꜣt m-mỉtt 10 n ꜣbw mtw.tw dỉt.f r qḥqḥ m st-mꜣꜥt ***ỉ.ỉrỉ.t ṯꜣty ḥtp n.f***

'The court said: "Deal him a hundred blows with a staff, as well as ten burns, and put him to break stones (*lit.* 'hammer') in the Place of Truth until the vizier has pardoned him."'

2. P. BM 10052, 15, 8-9 (= *KRI* VI, 800, 13-15).

ḏd ṯꜣty ỉṯꜣy tꜣy st-ḥmt ỉmỉ se rmṯ sꜣw ***ỉ.ỉrỉ.t.tw gm ỉṯꜣw rmṯ*** *r sꜥḥꜥ.s*

'The Vizier said: "Take this woman and put her under guard (*lit.* 'place her as a guarded person') until one has found a thief (or another) man to accuse her."'

37.3 Remarks

1. Non-periphrased forms are still attested during the 19th dynasty:

3. O. Nash 1, v° 4 (= *KRI* IV, 316, 15): Seti II.

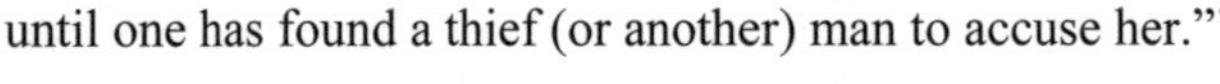

ỉw.tw ḥr wꜣḥ tꜣy.s mdt ***r ỉy.t ṯꜣty***

'Her case was suspended until the arrival of the vizier' (*lit.* 'until the vizier has come').

2. From the 21st dynasty onward, the syntagma is reinforced by the preposition *šꜣꜥ-(r)* 'until.' This resulted in the form *šꜣꜥ-ỉ.ỉrỉ.t.f sḏm*, often abbreviated as *šꜣꜥ.t.f*, ancestor of Coptic **ϣⲁⲧⲉϥⲥⲱⲧⲙ̄**.[305]

---

[303] See Gardiner, *JEA* 16 (1930), 231-234, which remains fundamental; Černý-Groll, *LEG*, §33 and 34, p. 415-417; Frandsen, *LEVS*, §56-59, p. 106-108; Winand, *o.l.*, §464-470, p. 292-297.

[304] Parallel example: P. Leopold-Amherst, 4, 10-11 (= *KRI* VI, 489, 3-8).

[305] See Gardiner, *o.c.*, 234 (4); Winand *o.l.*, §469, p. 296-297.

4. Wenamun, 1, 19-20 (= *LES*, 62, 15-16).
'If it were a thief belonging to my country the one who went down into your ship and who stole your silver, I would have reimbursed it to you from my treasury,[306]

šꜣꜥ.t.w gm pꜣy.k iṯꜣy
until your thief had been found' (*lit.* 'they had found').

[306] *Cf. supra* §36.2, example 3.

38. Recapitulation

38.1 The morpheme *ỉw* in the synchrony of Late Egyptian

Four different *ỉw* morphemes can be distinguished in Late Egyptian:

- the ***ỉw* of the third future** – *ỉw.f r sḏm* – which forms integral part of an independent, and therefore, initial, form. This *ỉw* can be preceded by *bn*, *wn* (past converter), *nty*, *ptr*, *mk*, *ỉr*, *yꜣ* and *ḫr*, or the circumstantial *ỉw*. It cannot be followed by any of these morphemes.
- the ***ỉw* of the sequential** – *ỉw.f ḥr* (*tm*) *sḏm* – which forms integral part of a non-independent, non-initial, but not subordinate form. It cannot be preceded or followed by any of the morphemes cited above.
- the **circumstantial *ỉw***, which transforms an independent form (verbal or nominal) in a non-initial, non-independent, subordinate form. It may be preceded – but not followed – by *ỉr*, *yꜣ* or *ḫr*, and can be followed – but not preceded – by *bn*, *wn* or the *ỉw* of the third future. It has no connection with *ptr* or *mk*.
- the much rarer **parenthetical *ỉw*,**[307] which transforms an independent form (almost always the vetitive) in a non-initial, non-independent, but not subordinate, form. It is used in additional distribution with the particle *ḫr*.[308] It is neither preceded, nor followed, by any morpheme.

There result the following combinations:

	bn* + *ỉw	*third future ỉw*
	nty* + *ỉw	
	wn* + *ỉw	
	ỉw* + *ỉw	
circumstantial ỉw	***ỉw* + *bn***	
	ỉw* + *wn	

There follows that:

– *ỉw bn ỉw* can only be a negative third future preceded by the circumstantial *ỉw*;[309]

– *ỉw wn ỉw* can only be a third future preceded by *wn* and the circumstantial *ỉw*;[310]

▪ The relationship between *bn* and *wn* is more difficult to establish because, if *wn bn ỉw r sḏm* (third future) appears well attested,[311] *bn wn.f* + first present is also known.[312]

---

[307] On this 'fourth' *ỉw* see Satzinger, *NÄS*, §2.6.2, p. 227-231.

[308] Compare: *ḫr m-ỉr šm r tꜣ ḳnbt* 'And does not go before the court' (O. Gardiner 109, 15) with *ỉw m-ỉr šm r wꜣḥ wꜥ wꜥty ỉm ỉm.w* 'And do not proceed to place a single one there among them' (P. BM 10100, 10 = *LRL*, 50, 12).

[309] O. Berlin P 10630, 6-7 (= *KRI* V, 565, 5-6), see *supra* §32.2.1.1, example 6.

[310] P. Turin 2021, 3, 3-4 (= *KRI* VI, 740, 11-13), see *supra* §32.2.1.1, example 7.

[311] P. BN 197, VI, v° 3 (= *LRL* 64, 13); Wenamun, 2, 29 (= *LES*, 69, 16).

[312] P. Mayer A, 3, 25 (= *KRI* VI, 810, 13).

From the foregoing there follows that the expression *ỉw.f* ( ) *sḏm* can be interpreted in four different ways:

			negative correlate
third future	*ỉw.f* (*r*) *sḏm*	he will hear	*bn ỉw.f* (*r*) *sḏm*
sequential	*ỉw.f* (*ḥr*) *sḏm*	he heard	*ỉw.f* (*ḥr*) *tm sḏm*
circumstantial first present	*ỉw.f* (*ḥr*) *sḏm* (active)	when he hears	*ỉw bn se* (*ḥr*) *sḏm*
	ỉw.f sḏm.Ø (passive)	when he was heard	*ỉw bwpw.tw sḏm*

38.2 The different values of *sḏm.f*

In Late Egyptian a ***sḏm.f*** form can be interpreted as:

- a **perfective** (in principle limited to transitive verbs), see §15;
- a **prospective** (open to all categories of verbs), see §20 and §26;
- an archaic **second tense** (especially intransitive verbs), see §23.6;
- a **relative form** without prosthetic yod, see §28;
- an **infinitive** with a suffixal direct pronominal object, see §13.2.

38.3 Uses of the prosthetic yod

The prosthetic yod, spelled as 𓇋𓀁 (very frequent) or 𓂋 (rare), which was pronounced *e*, occurs:

- **always** before the *i.ỉrỉ.t.f sḏm* form (see §37);
- **almost always** before second tenses (see §23);
- **sometimes** before the imperative (see §21), the participles (see §27), and the relative forms (see §28);
- **never** before the infinitive, except that of the verb *ỉrỉ*.[313]

38.4 The morphemes *wnn* and *wn*

The main function of *wnn* is to 'nominalise' a verbal sentence (see §34).

wn can be:

- either the morpheme *wn* used in the existential sentence (see §22.1), which subject is, in theory, never defined;
- or the morpheme *wn* used to transpose into the past the first present (see §16), the third future (see §19 and §36.2), rarely the second tenses (see §23, example 6), exceptionally the perfective *sḏm.f*.[314] This invariable morpheme (called 'past converter') is similar to the participle and the relative form of the verb *wnn*, which permit to transpose into the past constructions obtained with *nty* (see §30). The table above (§38.1) shows that the converter *wn* precedes the *ỉw* of the third future and follows the circumstantial *ỉw*.

▪ In principle, the past converter *wn* should not be found after *nty*, only the *wn* of existence can occupy this position.[315]

---

313 For example: O. Petrie 16, v° 2, see also Winand, *Morphologie*, §257-258 and 260, p. 151-152 and 154.
314 See note 299, p. 155.
315 But see Wenamun, 2, 28, cited in §16.2, example 7.

38.5 The negative morphemes

bn (formerly *nn*) is used to negate:
- the first present (see §16);
- the third future (see §19);
- the independent prospective *sḏm.f* (see §20);
- the nexus of the periphrased second tense (see §23.4.2) and the modal second tenses (see §23.5).

bw (formerly *n*) is used in the following constructions, which cannot be periphrased:
- *bw sḏm.n.f* (very rare), archaic form of the negative aorist (see §17.3);
- *bw sḏm.f* (quite rare), which can be the negation of the perfective *sḏm.f* (see §15.1.2.3, remark 2), or of the negative aorist (see §17.4);
- *bw sḏm.t.f* (very rare), expressing the nuance 'not yet' (see §18.1);
- *bw sḏmy.t N*, passive form corresponding to the previous one (see §18.2).

Or be periphrased by the auxiliary *ỉrỉ*:
- *bw ỉrỉ.f sḏm*, negative aorist (see §17.5);
- *bw ỉrỉ.t.f sḏm* expressing the nuance 'not yet' (see §18.1).

bwpwy is used only in the *bwpwy.f sḏm* form, which serves to negate the perfective *sḏm.f* (see §15.1.2), and the first present of some intransitive verbs (particularly verbs of motion) with a pseudo-participle as predicate (see §16.6.2.1).

mn (formerly *nn wn*) is the negative correlate of the *wn* of existence (see §22.2).

tm is used to negate:
- the infinitive, in its non-predicative uses (see §13), as well as the second tenses (see §23.4.2) and the continuative forms: sequential (see §25.2) and conjunctive (see §25.3);
- the non-independent prospective *sḏm.f* in purpose clauses (see §26.2).

NOMINAL FORMS

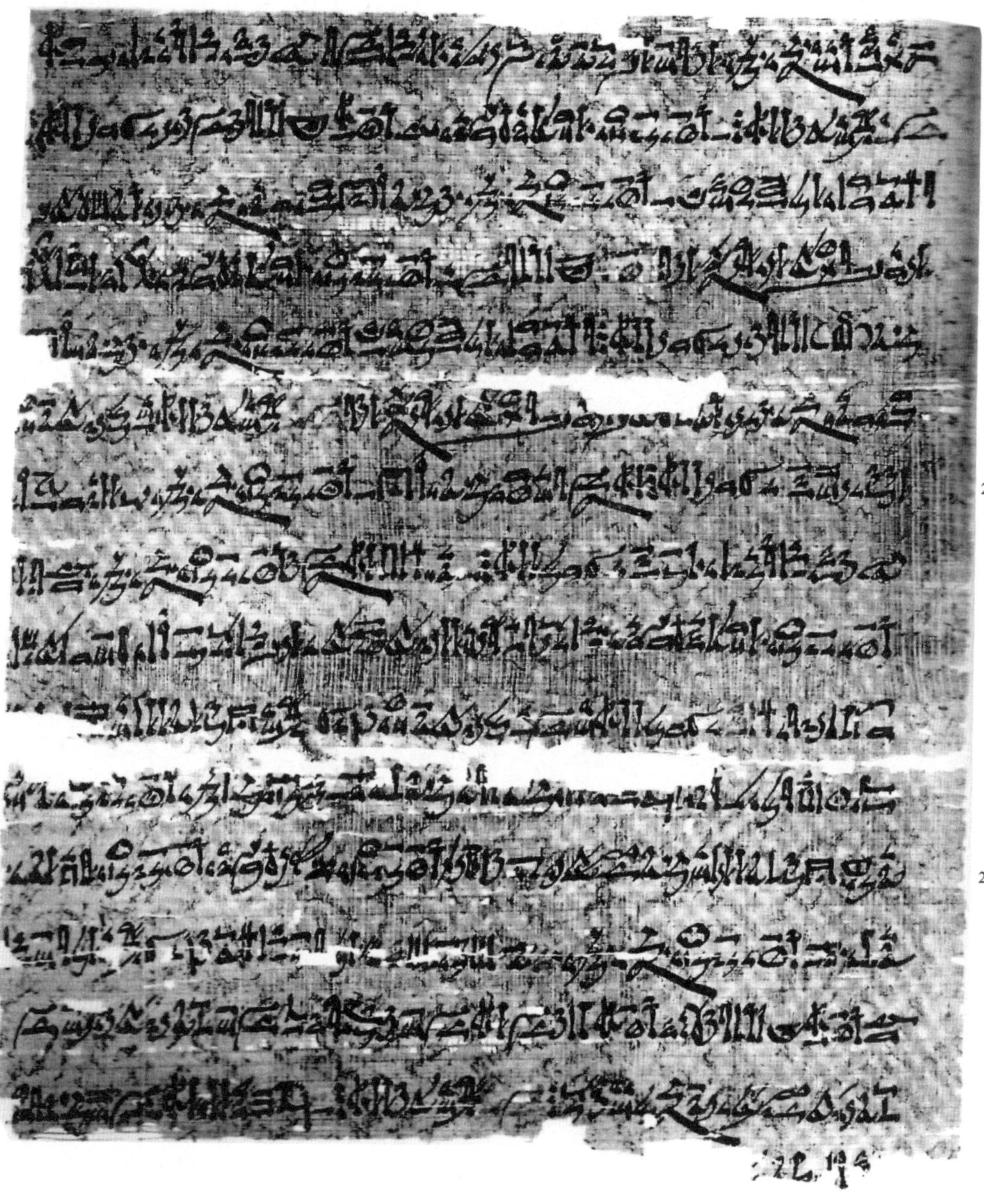

P. Cairo J 65739, 14-28 (*cf.* p. 79, 96, 122)

Nominal forms

Nominal forms (sometimes called 'non-verbal'[316]), theoretically, consist of three types of nominal sentences:

– nominal sentence with adverbial predicate,
– nominal sentence with nominal predicate,
– nominal sentence with adjectival predicate.

In practice, having been used as the basis on which new verb forms (first present and third future) were formed, the nominal sentence with adverbial predicate is integrated in these forms, and was studied at the same time as they were (see §16 and §19).

Therefore, the definition 'nominal' will be reserved for those sentences which predicate is either a noun (or equivalent) or an adjective (or equivalent).

Some of them, having the function of rhematiser, that is to say, to rank-shift to marked rheme a nominal element of a plain verbal sentence, will be called, in accordance with current usage, cleft sentences and will be studied separately.

[316] 'Un énoncé est ou nominal ou verbal,' Benveniste, *Problèmes de linguistique générale,* I, p. 157. See also D. Cohen, *La phrase nominale et l'évolution du système verbal en semitique*, Paris 1984, p. 14-15.

39. The nominal sentence with nominal predicate

39.1 Introduction

A nominal sentence with substantival predicate fundamentally articulates **the inclusion of a class of objects A in a class of objects B**. It corresponds to sentences formed using the verb 'to be' of the type: *birds are vertebrates*.

Its morphosyntactic analysis is complex because both subject and predicate are nouns, and it is not always possible to use purely morphological criteria to distinguish them.[317]

- Being the word order (also called 'morpheme order') the only criterion always applicable, especially in Middle Egyptian, a number of rigid and opposing systems where the order is always 'subject–predicate' or 'predicate–subject,' have emerged:[318]

– '*Prinzip: Im (Nichtverbal-) Satz des Ägyptischen, im Nominalsatz ebenso wie im Adverbialsatz, gilt die Reihenfolge Subjekt-Prädikat.*'[319]

– '*Der ägyptische Nominalsatz ist ... eine Satzkomtruktion ... mit einer festen Satzstellung Prädikat-Subjekt verbindet.*'[320]

In Late Egyptian, the existence of the opposition defined – undefined[321] permits to lay down, with D. Cohen, the following rule: **'the subject cannot be completely undefined, while the predicate is either undefined or defined.'**[322]

However, it can be observed that if the class included (A) is always defined, the inclusive class (B) can be either defined or not. Consequently, A is the subject and B the predicate. Hence the following definition: the nominal sentence asserts that **a class A (= subject) is included in a class B (= predicate),**[323] **$A \subset B$.**

39.2 Classification predication

In general, if the classes A and B do not have the same number of elements, the inclusion of A in B entails that **all the** elements of class A are **some** of class B,[324] or that **all** elements of class A **belong** to class B – **the converse is obviously false.**[325] The noun phrase is then a predication of inclusion in the mathematical sense of the term. To avoid confusion with constructions referring to possession,[326] the expression 'classification predication' has been preferred to that of 'inclusion predication.'

If class A contains only one element, the subject is singular, otherwise it is plural.

For the first two persons the pronominal subject is indicated with the independent pronouns

---

317 Particularly in classical Egyptian, where the opposition defined – undefined is not morphologically marked.

318 For critiques of these systems see Groll, *Non verbal* p. 28; Frandsen, *Crossroad*, I, 1987, p. 148-149.

319 Schenkel, Fokussierung, *Festschrift Westendorf*, p. 159.

320 Junge, 'Nominalsatz und Cleft Sentence im Ägyptischen,' Studies presented to H. J. Polotsky, ed. Young, 1981, 443. See also Roeder, *GM* 91 (1986), 31-32.

321 See *supra* §1.2 and 28.2.

322 D. Cohen, *La phrase nominale et l'évolution du système verbal en semitique*, Paris 1984, p. 33-34.

323 *Loc. cit.*

324 $(\forall x)\ (x \in A \Rightarrow x \in B)$.

325 Because then $(\exists x)\ (x \in B \text{ et } x \notin A)$, and there is at least one element of B that does not belong to A.

326 That is to say, membership in the legal sense of the term.

belonging to the **atonic series**, while in the third person it can be either unexpressed (*Ø*) or be represented by a demonstrative pronoun (*pꜣy*, *tꜣy*, *nꜣy*).[327]

The predicate B is **never defined**.

The construction is **unmarked**, with the subject carrying the theme and the predicate the rheme.

The base paradigm is the following:

Singular	1st person	***ỉnk B***	'I am a B'
	2nd person	***ntk / ntṯ B***	'you are (fem.) a B'
	3rd person	***B pꜣy / tꜣy*** or ***B Ø***	'it is a (masc./fem.) B'
Plural	1st person	***ỉnn B***	'we are B'
	2nd person	***nttn B***	'you are B'
	3rd person	***B nꜣy*** or ***B Ø***	'these are B'

The forms listed in the table are independent, but can be transformed into non-independent forms with the value of adverbial clauses using the converter *ỉw*. They are negated by means of the discontinuous negative morphemes *bn … ỉwnꜣ*.

Very important note. Since the classification predication expresses the **essence** of being, it is **timeless**: *ỉnk nṯr* 'I am a god' means 'I am of divine nature.' It is opposed to the 'locational predication' *tw.ỉ m nṯr* 'I am (like) a god' – but I am not of divine nature, and this is only a temporary situation.

39.2.1 Examples in the first two persons

39.2.1.1 General case: the predicate is a noun

1. Doomed Prince, 7, 2-3 (= *LES*, 4-6); *cf.* example 13.

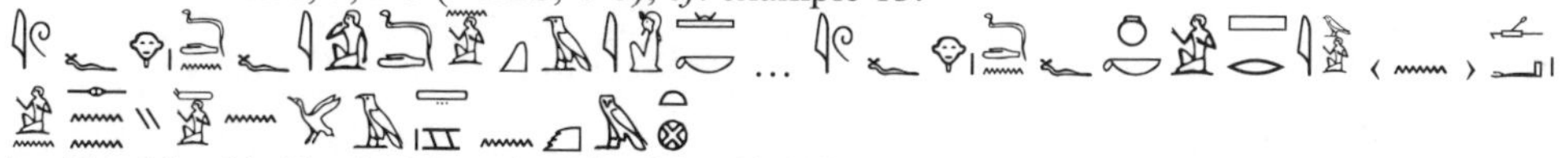

ỉw.f ḥr ḏd n.f ỉ.ḏd n.ỉ qỉ.k … ỉw.f ḥr ḏd n.f ***ỉnk šrỉ*** *‹n› wꜥ n snny n pꜣ tꜣ n kmt*

'He said to him: "Tell me (what is) your situation ..." He replied to him: "I am son of an officer of the land of Egypt."'[328]

Examples with the thematisation of the subject:

2. Mès, N 2 (= *KRI* III, 425, 4-5); *cf.* example 29.

ỉr ỉnk ***ỉnk šrỉ*** *n ḥwy sꜣ wrl* [*sꜣt*] *nšy*

'As for me, I am son of Huy, son of Werel, descendant (*lit.* 'daughter') of Neshy.'

---

[327] Consequently *ntf B*, *nts B*, or *ntw B* do not exist, see §7.4.

[328] That is to say, 'I belong to a class of Egyptian officers' sons.'

3. P. BM 10052, 1, 8 (= *KRI* VI, 767, 15-16).

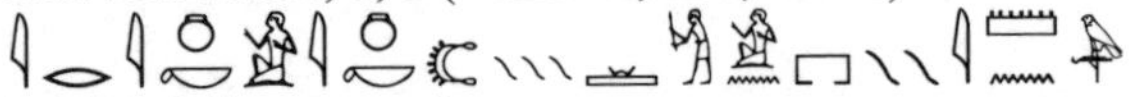

ỉr ỉnk ***ỉnk ỉḥwty*** *n pr ỉmn*

'As for me, I am a farmer of the temple of Amun.'

4. Wenamun, 2, 32 (= *LES*, 70, 4-5).[329]

ntk m-rꜥ ***ntk bꜣk*** *n ỉmn*

'You too, you are a servant of Amun.'

▪ If in these examples the second independent pronoun (the subject) belongs to the atonic series, by contrast, the first, the topic, belongs to the tonic series, as shown by Coptic: **ⲁⲛⲟⲕ ⲁⲛⲅ̄ ⲟⲩϣⲙ̄ⲙⲟ** 'Me, I am a stranger' (Ruth, II, 10).

Interrogative examples:

5. Wenamun, 2, 13 (= *LES*, 68, 7-8).

ỉn ***ỉnk bꜣk*** *n pꜣ ỉrỉ wḏ.k m-rꜥ*[330]

'Am I (also) servant of the one who sent you?'

6. P. Anastasi V, 10, 9 (= *LEM*, 61, 5).

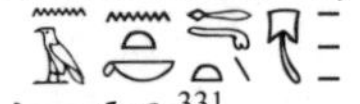

ỉn ***ntk ꜥꜣ***[331]

'Are you a donkey?'

Negative examples:

7. O. Berlin P 10627, 5-7 (= *KRI* VI, 155, 12-14).

bn ***ntk rmṯ*** *ỉwnꜣ yꜣ bw ỉrỉ.k dỉt ỉwr tꜣy.k ḥmt mỉ-qd pꜣy.k ỉry*

'You are no man, because you are not able to impregnate your wife like everybody else! (*lit.* 'like your similar').

8. O. Gardiner 273, 6 (= *KRI* VII, 355, 6-7).

bn ***ỉnk ỉwty ḥꜣty*** *ỉwnꜣ*

'I am not a heartless.'

---

[329] Another example: *ntk nḫt-ꜥ* 'You are one strong of arm,' P. Anastasi I, 10, 7.

[330] Note the spelling of *ỉn* and see next note.

[331] Note the spelling of *ỉn* and, for a parallel with the spelling , see Gardiner, *LEM*, 61a, n. 5c.

Circumstantial example:

9. Wenamun, 2, 81 (= *LES,* 75, 12).

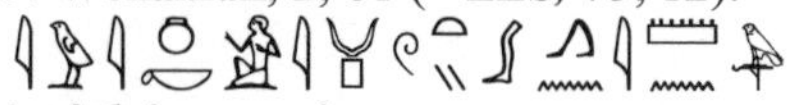

iw ***ink ipwty*** *n imn*
'While I am a messenger of Amun.'

39.2.1.2 Special case: the predicate is an interrogative pronoun

The pronouns employed in this case are ***nim*** 'who?' and ***iḫ*** 'what?'

10. P. Orbiney, 15, 9 (= *LES*, 25, 10); *cf.* example 18.

ntk[332] ***nim*** *tr*
'Who are you (then)?' (*lit.* 'you are who?[333]).

11. Qadesh Bulletin, 35 (= *KRI* II, 110, 3).

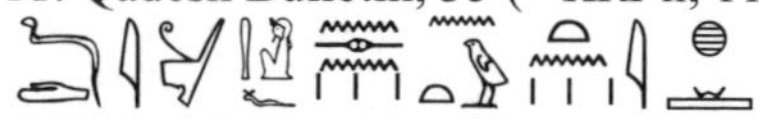

ḏd-in ḥm.f n.sn ***ntwtn iḫ***
'His Majesty said to them: "What are you?" (*lit.* 'You are what?'[334]).' Note the spelling of the atonic independent pronoun corresponding to ⲚⲦⲈⲦⲚ̄.

39.2.2 Examples in the third person

These constructions derive from the classical construction *B pw*, where *pw* disappeared, or rather, was actualised in *pꜣy*, *tꜣy*, *nꜣy*.

39.2.2.1 Examples of the form *B Ø*

In this case, the sentence is reduced to the single predicate, the subject being unexpressed.

12. P. Anastasi I, 10, 3-4:[335] concerning a strange animal.

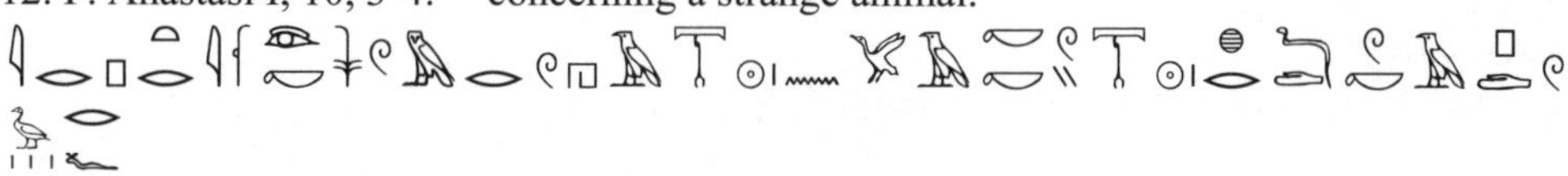

ir ptr.k se m rwhꜣ n(=m) pꜣ kkw ḫr-ḏd.k ***ꜣpd*** *r.f*
'If you see it in the evening, in the dark, you will have to say about him: "It is a bird!"' Note the aorist form *ḫr-sḏm.f* in the apodosis, see *supra* §17.6.

The nominal predicate can be followed by an indirect genitive:

---

332 should be deleted, see Gardiner, *ZÄS* 69 (1933), 70-71.
333 *Cf.* Coptic ⲚⲦⲞⲔ ϬⲈ ⲚⲦⲔ̄ ⲚⲒⲘ 'You then, who are you?' (John 1, 22). Note that **ntf nim* does not exist; the interrogative is always the rheme, while *ntf*, a tonic pronoun, cannot be the theme. The sentence, therefore, is written *nim Ø*, see example 18 below.
334 Not 'You are who?' – the individuals in question being not worthy of the status of human beings.
335 Parallel example: P. Ashmolean Museum 1945.96 (= P. Adoption), v° 6-7 (= *KRI* VI, 738, 1-3).

13. Doomed Prince, 6, 8-9 (= *LES,* 5, 3-5); *cf.* example 1.

wn-in pꜣ wr ḥr ndnd.f m-ḏd šri (n) nim m nꜣ n wrw – iw.tw ḥr ḏd n.f šri n wꜥ n snny
'The prince enquired of him, saying: "Of which great one is he son?" (*lit.* 'He is a son of whom among the great ones?). He was told: "He is a son of official" (*lit.* 'of an official').'

Examples where the nominal predicate is followed by an attributive participle and by an adverbial clause playing the role of a relative:

14. P. Bankes I, v° 2 (= *JEA* 68 (1982), 129).

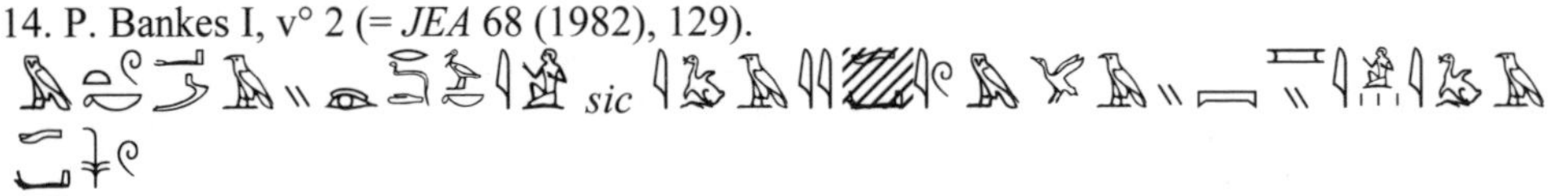

mtw.k ꜥm r-ḏd bꜣk(t) iṯꜣy iw m pꜣy ḥry mrt (i).iṯꜣ se
'And that you learn that it is a stolen servant, who was abducted precisely by this (person) in charge of the household servants' (*lit.* 'who was stolen, while it is this (person) in charge ... who stole her'[336]).

15. P. Geneva D 407, v° 18 (= *LRL*, 16, 8-9).

tw.n rḫ.tw r-ḏd rmṯ mr iw bwpw.f irt mšꜥ ///
'We know that it is a sick man who has not made the journey ///.'

Remark. The predicate can take the form *wnn* V, where V is an independent verbal form nominalised by *wnn*, see *supra* §34.3 and §18.2, example 4.

Circumstantial examples:

16. Dakhla Stela, 7 (= *JEA* 19 (1933), pl. v): 22nd dynasty; *cf.* example 22.

iw ḫnmt (n) nmḥyw
'While it is a private well' (*lit.* 'of private individuals').

17. P. Turin 2021, 3, 11-12 (= *KRI* VI, 741, 9-11); *cf.* example 44.

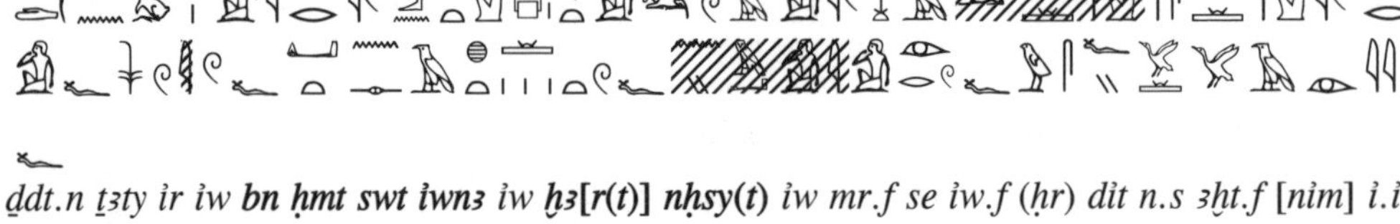

ḏdt.n ṯꜣty ir iw bn ḥmt swt iwnꜣ iw ḫꜣ[r(t)] nḥsy(t) iw mr.f se iw.f (ḥr) dit n.s ꜣḫt.f [nim] i.iri.f wsf pꜣ iry.f
'What the vizier said: "If this was not a wife of his,[337] (but) it was a Syrian (or) a Nubian, whom

---

[336] See Navailles-Neveu, *GM* 103 (1988), 58, n. v.
[337] That is to say 'a woman with whom he is married,' and not 'his woman,' which would be *tꜣy.f ḥmt*, see example 44 below, and *infra* §41.4.

he loved and bequeathed her his property, who would undo what he had done?"' (*lit.* 'it is who, who would undo ...').

The four circumstantials (two nominal and two verbal), placed at the beginning, form a quadruple protasis introduced by *ỉr*, while the apodosis includes a real cleft sentence.

Examples where the predicate is an interrogative pronoun:

18. P. BM 10052, 14, 14 (= *KRI* VI, 798, 14); *cf.* example 10 and 25.

ḏd.tw n.f ***nỉm sp-sn*** *ḏd.f*

'It was said to him: "Who is it? Who is it?" He replied ...'

19. P. DM IV, 5 (= *KRI* VI, 265, 1); *cf.* example 26 and 27.

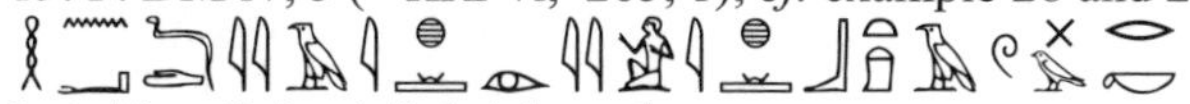

ḥnʿ ḏd ***yꜣ ỉḫ*** *ỉry.ỉ* ***ỉḫ*** *(m) btꜣ r.k*

'Another matter: Well, what? What kind of evil deed have I committed against you?'

39.2.2.2 Examples of the form B *pꜣy*[338]

20. Doomed Prince, 4, 8-9 (= *LES*, 2, 4-5)

ỉḫ pꜣ nty ḥr šm m-sꜣ pꜣ s ʿꜣ nty m ỉyt ḥr [*tꜣ*] *mỉt ỉw.f* (*ḥr*) *ḏd n.f* ***ṯsm pꜣy***

'What is that walking (*lit.* 'it is what that which walks') behind the older man who is coming down the road? He said to him: "It is a dog."'

21. P. Turin 2026, 18 (= *LRL*, 73, 1).

ỉḫ m mdt tꜣy

'What kind of matter is this?' (*lit.* 'it is what as matter?')

22. Dakhla Stela, 12 (= *JEA* 19 (1933), pl. VI): 22nd dynasty; *cf.* example 16.

ỉw ***mw (n) nmḥyw nꜣ(y)***

'While these are private waters.'

39.2.2.3 Extensions of previous constructions

In Middle Egyptian, the construction *B pw* gives, by explicature of *pw*, *B pw A* 'it is (a) *B*, *A*' – where *A* is in apposition to the subject *pw* – then, by thematisation (or topicalisation) of *A*, *ỉr A B pw* 'as for *A*, it is (a) *B*.'

[338] The negation *bn B pꜣy ỉwnꜣ* is not attested: *bn B ỉwnꜣ* is used instead, as is the case with *B Ø*.

The same constructions are found in Late Egyptian, except that *A*, perceived as the subject, is almost always defined, and *pw* disappears or is actualised in *pꜣy*, *tꜣy*, *nꜣy*. The thematisation can be done with or without *ỉr*, thus resulting in:

B pw A ► ***B Ø pꜣ A***
ỉr A B *pw* ► ***ỉr pꜣ* A B *pꜣy*** or ***ỉr pꜣ* A B *Ø*** or ***pꜣ* A B *pꜣy*** or ***pꜣ* A B *Ø***

39.2.2.3.1 Examples of the form *B Ø pꜣ A* (it is a B, the A)

Case where B is a noun (rare examples):

23. P. Turin 1979, v° 1-2 (= *LRL*, 43, 4).

***ḥr sn ỉnk pꜣy* [*rmṯ*]**
'Because this man is one of my brothers' (*lit.* 'Because it is a brother of mine, this man').

24. O. Nash 1, v° 1-3 (= *KRI* IV, 316, 13-14).

ꜥḥꜥ.n tꜣ qnbt ḥr ḏd ***ꜥḏꜣt ꜥꜣ(t) ꜥnḫ-n-nỉwt ḥry-ỉꜣ šꜣỉ (n) mwt***
'The court said: "The lady Herya is a great criminal deserving of death" (*lit.* 'It is a great criminal ... the lady Herya').

Case where B is an interrogative pronoun (frequent examples):

25. Mès, N 15 (= *KRI* III, 428, 8-9); *cf.* example 18.

ỉw ṯꜣty ḥr ḏd n nwb-nfrt ***nỉm pꜣy.ṯ ỉwꜥ***
'The Vizier said to Nebnefert: "Who is your heir?"' (*lit.* 'It is who, your heir?').

26. O. DM 446, 2-3 (= *KRI* II, 383, 9-10); *cf.* example 19.

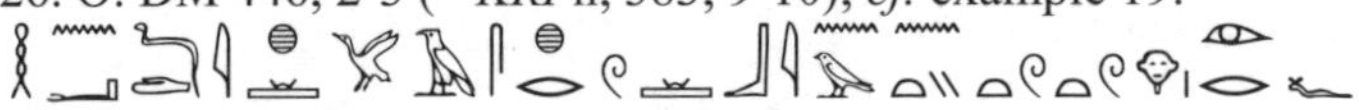

ḥnꜥ ḏd ***ỉḫ pꜣ sḫr bỉn*** *nty tw.tw ḥr ỉrỉ.f*
'Another thing: what is this bad thing that is being done?' (*lit.* 'It is what, this evil plan ...').

At the beginning of the nineteenth dynasty *pw* is sometimes still attested:

27. P. Cairo 58083, r° 3 (= *KRI* I, 322, 6-7): Seti I.

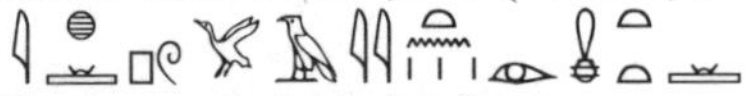

ỉḫ pw pꜣy.tn ỉrt (m)-mỉtt
'What is the meaning of your acting so?' (*lit.* 'It is what, your acting so?').

39.2.2.3.2 Examples of the form *ỉr pꜣ* A B *pꜣy* and variants

ỉr pꜣ A B pꜣy 'As for A, it is a B' (examples quite rare)

28. P. BM 10052, 5, 21-22 (= *KRI* VI, 781, 3-5).

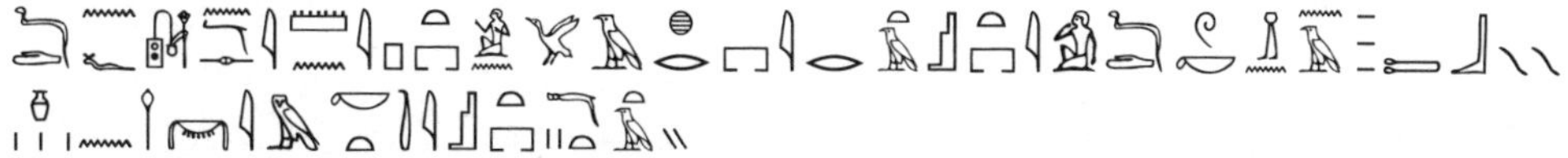

ḏd n.f sš ny-se-ỉmn-(m)-ỉpt n pꜣ ḫr ***ỉr tꜣ st ỉ.ḏd.k ỉn nꜣ ṯbw n ḥḏ ỉm kt st (ỉ).mḥ 2 tꜣy***

'The Scribe of the Tomb Nesamunemope said to him: "As for the tomb from which you said that the silver vessels had been taken away, is it another, a second grave?"' (*lit.* 'another tomb that completes the two').

ỉr pꜣ A B Ø 'As for A, it is a B' (frequent examples)

29 Mès, N 31 (= *KRI* III, 430,13); *cf.* example 2.

ỉr sš ḥwy šrỉ n wrl ḫr ỉr wrl šrỉt n nšy

'As for the scribe Huy, he is a son of Werel, and as for Werel, she is a descendant (*lit.* 'daughter') of Neshy.'

30. P. Berlin 10487, 9-v° 1 (= *LRL*, 36, 11).

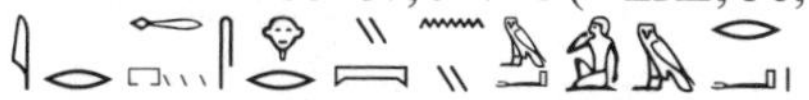

ỉr pr-ꜥꜣ ꜥ.w.s. ḥry (n) nỉm m-rꜥ

'As for Pharaoh l.p.h., of whom is he still master?' (*lit.* 'it is a master of whom, still?').

Example where *pꜣ* A is a tonic independent pronoun:

31. Doomed Prince, 4, 1 (= *LES*, 1, 1).

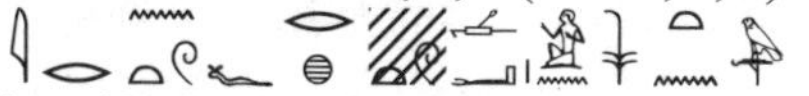

ỉr ntf *ḫr.*[*tw*] ***wꜥ n nsw***

'As for him – it was said – (it) was a king.'

pꜣ A B pꜣy 'The A, it is a B' (very rare examples)

32. O. DM 437, 1-3.

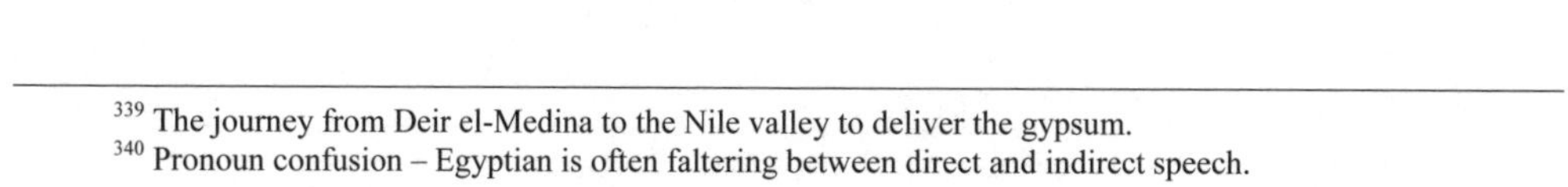

ỉr pꜣ ḏd ỉ.ỉrỉ.k ꜣbd n hrw r pꜣy m-ḏr ỉn.tw n.ỉ qḏ ***pꜣ hꜣy ỉ.ỉrỉ.k (=ỉ) bꜣk pꜣy*** *ptr tw.ỉ ḥr dit ỉn.tw n.k///*

'As for what you said (to me) a month ago, after the gypsum was brought to me: "the descent[339] that I have[340] made, it is a job!" – see, I have sent to you ////.'

[339] The journey from Deir el-Medina to the Nile valley to deliver the gypsum.

[340] Pronoun confusion – Egyptian is often faltering between direct and indirect speech.

pꜣ A B Ø 'The A, it is a B' (quite rare examples)

33. Amenemope, 8, 4-5.

ỉw pꜣy.f pr ḫft(y) n pꜣ dmỉ

'Because his house, it is an enemy of the city.'

Example where *pꜣ* A is a demonstrative pronoun:

34. P. Abbott, 6, 20-21 (= *KRI* VI, 479, 6-7).[341]

pꜣw btꜣ n pꜣy sš 2 n pꜣ ḫr pꜣy.w pḥ pꜣy ḥꜣty-ꜥ n nỉwt

'That, it is a wrongdoing on the part of these two scribes of the Tomb, (namely) for addressing (*lit.* 'their reaching') this Major of the City.'

39.3 Identification predication

In the specific case where the classes A and B have the same number of elements, the inclusion of A in B entails that all elements of class A belong to class B – but also, **the converse then being true**, that all the elements of B are elements of A. It follows that **classes A and B contain exactly the same elements** and are, therefore, **identical: A = B**.

The nominal sentence then corresponds to an **identification sentence** in which A and B denote the same object class, or the same object if they only contain one each – which implies that subject and predicate have the same degree of definition. Given that **the subject is always defined, so will the predicate be**.

The following are two examples in English (sentences with the verb 'to be'):
- **the** Bellifontains are **the** inhabitants of Fontainebleau;
- **the** Marseillaise is **the** national anthem of France.

There are two base paradigms:

– the first, isomorphic to the paradigm of the classification predication, is unmarked: the predicate *pꜣ B* carries the rheme, and the subject the theme. This paradigm employs as subject the atonic independent pronoun for the first two persons, and the demonstrative or *Ø* in the third person;

– the second is marked: it is the subject that becomes the rheme vector, while the predicate *pꜣ B* carries the theme. This paradigm uses the independent tonic pronoun as subject for all persons.

[341] Parallel example: P. Abbott, 6, 16-17 (= *KRI* VI, 478, 15-479, 1).

		Unmarked paradigm (atonic independent pronoun)		**Marked paradigm** (tonic independent pronoun)	
singular	1st p.	***ỉnk pꜣ B***	I am the B	***ỉnk pꜣ B***	it is me, the B
		ỉnk tꜣ B	I am the (fem.) B	***ỉnk tꜣ B***	it is me, the (fem.) B
	2nd p.	***ntk pꜣ B***	you are the B	***ntk pꜣ B***	it is you, the B
		ntṯ tꜣ B	you are the (fem.) B	***ntṯ tꜣ B***	it is you, the (fem.) B
	3rd p.	***pꜣ/tꜣ B Ø***	it is the (masc./fem.) B	***ntf pꜣ B***	it is him, the B
		pꜣ B pꜣy	it is the B		
		tꜣ B tꜣy	it is the (fem.) B	***nts tꜣ B***	it is her, the B
plural	1st p.	***ỉnn nꜣ B***	we are the B	***ỉnn nꜣ B***	it is us, the B
	2nd p.	***nttn nꜣ B***	you are the B	***nttn nꜣ B***	it is you, the B
	3rd p.	***nꜣ B Ø***	they are the B	***ntw nꜣ B***	it is them, the B
		nꜣ B nꜣy	they are the B		

In the texts, these two paradigms are differentiated only in the third person, where *pꜣ B* (*pꜣy*) is opposed to *ntf pꜣ B*. In pronunciation, the vocalisation (ⲁⲛ̄ versus ⲁⲛⲟⲕ) and supra-segmental features,[342] allows one to distinguish easily between all persons.

As before, all these constructions are independent and can be transformed into adverbial clauses by means of the converter *ỉw*. They are also negated using the discontinuous negation *bn … ỉwnꜣ*.

39.3.1 Examples in the first two persons

Neither paradigms are distinguished in writing, and the context does not always allow one to determine with which case one is dealing. In principle, all examples can be rendered either by marked or unmarked constructions.

35. P. Orbiney, 15, 9 (= *LES*, 25, 10-11); *cf.* example 10.

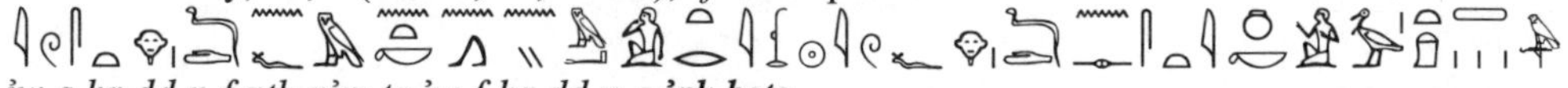

ỉw.s ḥr ḏd n.f ntk nỉm tr ỉw.f ḥr ḏd n.s ***ỉnk bꜣtꜣ***

'She asked him: "Who are you then?" He said to her: "I am Bata."' The question asked ('Who are you (then)?') shows that this is an unmarked paradigm. Otherwise the question would have been *nỉm bꜣtꜣ* 'Who is Bata?' – resulting in the marked response 'It is I (ⲁⲛⲟⲕ), Bata.'

[342] *Cf.* English, where 'I am the king' (unmarked construction where the subject corresponds to the theme) contrasts, through intonation, with '*I* am the king' (marked construction where the subject coincides with the rheme).

36. Graffito of year 34 of Ramses II, 4 (= *KRI* III, 436, 11): address to a god.

tw.ỉ r-gs.tn ***ỉnk pꜣy.tn bꜣk***

'I am close to you, I am your servant.' The first form is unmarked,[343] and it is likely that what we have here is also an unmarked paradigm.

37. Wenamun, 1, 13 (= *LES*, 62, 5).

ḥr ***ntk pꜣ wr n pꜣy tꜣ***

'Now, it is you, the prince of this country.' The sentence is certainly marked; Wenamun is addressing the prince in his official capacity.

38. P. Turin 1880, 4, 1-2 (= *RAD*, 57, 6-7).

ḏdt.n rmṯ ỉst p(ꜣ)-n-ꜥnqt n sš ỉmn-nḫt ꜥꜣ n ỉst ḫnsw – ***nttn nꜣy.ỉ ḥryw ḥr nttn nꜣ rwḏw n pꜣ ḫr***

'What the worker Penanuket said to the scribe Amennakht and the foreman Khonsu: "You are my superiors and you are the officials of the Tomb."'

But nothing in the co(n)text precludes translating the passage as: 'It is you my superiors and it is you the officials of the Tomb,' or again: 'You are my superiors because it is you, the officials of the Tomb' – *everything was down to the intonation.*

Negative example:

39. P. Leiden I 369, 8-9 (= *LRL*, 2, 1).[344]

ḥr ỉnk pꜣy.tn nfr ***bn ỉnk pꜣy.tn bỉn ỉwnꜣ***

'Because I am your friend, I am not your enemy.'[345] Or 'For it is I your friend, it is not I your enemy.'

Interrogative example with thematisation of the subject:

40. Wenamum, 2, 12-13 (= *LES*, 68, 7-8).[346]

ỉr ỉnk gr ỉnk ỉn ỉnk pꜣy.k bꜣk

'As for me, me too, am I your servant?'

Interro-negative example:

---

[343] Marked correlate: **ỉnk pꜣ nty r-gs.tn* 'it is I who is next to you,' pseudo-cleft sentence.

[344] Another example: P. DM IV, 6 (= *KRI* VI, 265, 2).

[345] *Lit.* 'I am your good, I am not your evil.'

[346] Another example: Horus and Seth, 4, 4 (= *LES*, 41, 12).

41. O. Berlin P 11247, v° 5 (= *KRI* III, 533, 7).

ỉs bn ỉnk p3y.k ỉt
'Am I not your father?' or 'Is it not I, your father?'

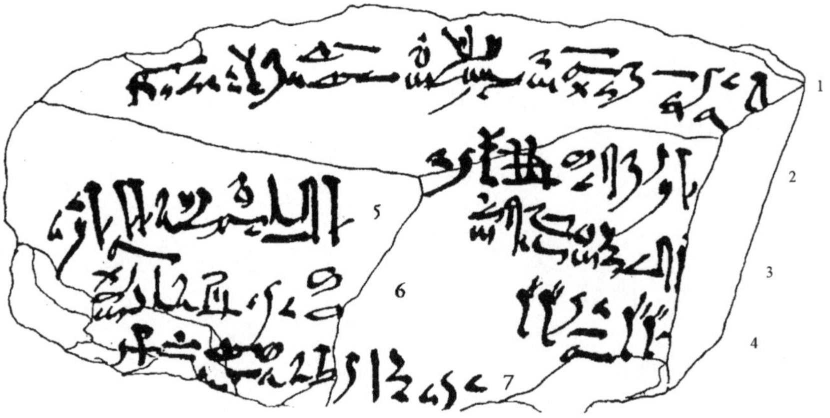

O. Berlin P. 11247, v° 5 *(cf.* p. 60, 81)

Example with the optative particle *bsỉ*, where *p3 B* is an independent pronoun:

42. P. Anastasi IV, 5, 1 (= *LEM*, 39, 10).
'Behold, my heart has gone furtively, it went south to see Memphis.

bsỉ ỉnk ntf
'Ah, if only I were it.'

The construction is unmarked because the predicate *ntf* can only belong to the tonic series (Ⲛ̄ⲦⲞϤ); it is this that carries the rheme. Consequently, the subject *ỉnk* is an atonic independent pronoun (ⲀⲚⲄ̄) corresponding to theme.[347]

39.3.2 Examples in the third person

39.3.2.1 Examples of the unmarked paradigm

The same constructions are found in the classification sentence (see above §39.2.2), except that the predicate B is now defined.

39.3.2.1.1 Examples of the form *p3 B Ø*

[347] The marked construction is attested in Middle Egyptian: *ỉnk pw sw* 'It is I (who is) him' (CT VII, 478, i).

43. P. Bankes I, 16-17 (= *JEA* 68 (1982), 128).

r-ḏd ***tꜣy.n snt*** *ḫr.w r.s*
'Saying: "It is our sister!" So they declared about it.'

Negative example:

44. O. DM 439, 1; *cf.* example 17.

ḫr bn ***tꜣy.ỉ ḥmt*** *ỉwnꜣ*
'For this is not my wife!'

Adverbial examples:

45. P. Ashmolean Museum 1945.96 (= P. Adoption), 21 (= *KRI* VI, 737, 3) (fig. p. 38).[348]

ỉw ***pꜣy.ỉ sn šrỉ***
'Given that it is my younger brother.'

46. P. Turin 2021 3, 1 + P. Geneva D 409, 3, 1 (= *KRI* VI, 740, 8-9).

ỉw ***pꜣ(y.ỉ) ⅔*** *ḥr* ***pꜣy.s ⅓***
'Given that these are my ⅔ over and above her ⅓.'

47. P. Bologna 1094, 6, 5 (= *LEM*, 6, 5).

ỉw bn ***pꜣy.ỉ ḥtr*** *ỉwnꜣ*
'Because it is not my tax.'

39.3.2.1.2 Examples of the form *pꜣ B pꜣy*[349]

48. Truth and Falsehood, 5, 7 (= *LES*, 33, 3-4).

wn.ỉn tꜣy.f mwt ḥr ḏd n.f tw.k (ḥr) ptr pꜣy kꜣmn nty ḥms r-gs pꜣ sbꜣ ***pꜣy.k ỉt pꜣy*** *ỉ.n.s ḥr ḏd n.f*
'His mother said to him: "You see this blind man who is seated by the door? He is your father" So she said to him.'

[348] Note, the text of *KRI* is incorrect since it omits the *ỉw*, see *JEA* 26 (1941), pl. VI and VIa.
[349] As in the case of *B pꜣy*, there is no attested negation **bn pꜣ B pꜣy ỉwnꜣ*; *bn pꜣ B ỉwnꜣ* is used.

49. P. BM 10052, 5, 17 (= *KRI* VI, 780, 12).

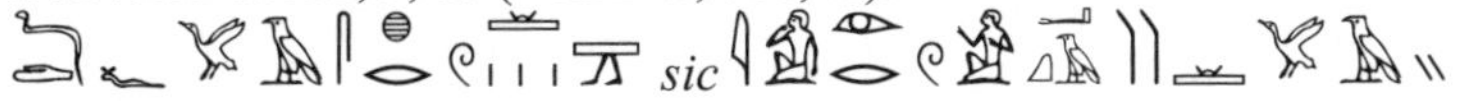

ḏd.f pꜣ sḫr (n) šm ỉ.ỉrỉ.ỉ ꜥqꜣ pꜣy

'He said: "This is exactly the manner (in) which I went"' (*lit.* 'the manner of going that I made exactly').

50. O. BM 5631, 12 (= *HO*, 88).

nꜣ n sdbḥw n tꜣ kꜣt (ỉ).wn r-ḫt pꜣ ỉt n pꜣy.ỉ ỉt nꜣ(y)

'These are the work-tools (*lit.* 'work, construction') which were under the responsibility of the father of my father.'

Example where the predicate is an independent pronoun:

51. P. BN 198, II, 11 (= *LRL*, 68, 1-2).[350]

ỉnk pꜣy pꜣ sbỉ ỉ.ỉrỉ.ỉ ỉrm.k pꜣy

'Such am I, and such is the joke that I have made on you.' (*lit.* 'it is I (ⲁⲛⲟⲕ) and it is a joke that I have made with you').

Circumstantial example:

52. P. Sallier I, 4, 1-2 (= *LEM*, 80, 4-6).

yꜣ ỉḫ pꜣy.k tm dỉt ỉn.tw mnḥt r ms n pr-ꜥꜣ ꜥ.w.s. ḫr ỉw pꜣ hrw (n) nꜣ ỉbw (n) nꜣ ꜥnḫw swḥwt ꜣpdw smw pꜣy

'Well, why have you not had presents brought to offer to Pharaoh l.p.h., and this although it is the day of the kids, goats, eggs, birds (and) vegetables?' (*lit.* 'well, it is what your not having had brought ...').

39.3.2.1.3 Examples of the form *ỉr pꜣ* A *pꜣ* B Ø[351]

53. P. Mayer A, 3, 23 (= *KRI* VI, 810, 9).

ỉr pꜣy rmṯ pꜣ ỉry n bw-ḫꜣꜥ.f

'As for this man, it is the accomplice of Bukhaaf.'

---

[350] Examples in Middle Egyptian: *ỉnk pw* 'It is I' (CT VI, 354, g), *ntf pw m mꜣꜥt* 'It is he, in truth' (Sinuhe B, 267).

[351] Example in Middle Egyptian: *ỉr sf wsỉr pw* 'As for yesterday, it is Osiris' (CT IV, 193).

54. Wenamun, 2, 10 (= *LES*, 68, 3-4).

ỉr pꜣ ḥqꜣ n kmt pꜣ nb n pꜣy.ỉ

'As for the ruler of Egypt, is he the master of my property?' The context shows clearly that this is a rhetorical question without an interrogative morpheme. Below will be found the marked form (*ỉr pꜣ* A *ntf pꜣ* B) of the last two examples (examples 57 and 58).

Circumstantial example:

55. O. Gardiner 55, v° 1-3 (= *HO*, 66, 2).[352]

*ỉw **ỉr nꜣ ḥnw ỉ.dỉ.f** [n.ỉ] **pꜣ ⅔ ddyt n.ỉ m-ḏr pš.f ỉrm tꜣy.w mwt***

'Whereas, as regards the property that he has given (me), these are the two-thirds which were attributed to me when he settled the division (*lit.* 'shared') with their mother.'

39.3.2.1.4 Example of the form *pꜣ* A *pꜣ* B Ø

56. P. Leiden I, 371, 2-3: letter to a dead person.

ỉrỉ.ỉ ỉḫ r.ṯ pꜣ ỉr.n.(ṯ) pꜣ(y).ṯ dỉt ḏrt ỉm.ỉ

'What have I done against you? What you have done is to lay (*lit.* 'your laying') a hand on me.'[353]

39.3.2.2 Examples belonging to the marked paradigm

They are of the form ***pꜣ ntf B***, where *ntf* is both subject and rheme, while *pꜣ B* is predicate and theme.

Circumstantial example:

57. P. Turin 1875, 1, 9 (= *KRI* v, 350, 10).

*//// ỉw **ntw nꜣ bwt n pꜣ tꜣ***

'(...) because it is they, the shame (*lit.* 'the abominations') of the country!'

Interrogative example:

58. O. DM 439, 1-3.[354]

ỉn nts tꜣy.ỉ ḥmt

'Is she my wife?'

---

[352] Similar example: P. Orbiney, 8, 3 (= *LES*, 17, 11-12).

[353] That is to say, 'torment me.'

[354] See *RdE* 33 (1981), 11-20.

Thematised examples (*ỉr pꜣ* A *ntf pꜣ* B):

59. Theban tomb n. 157 (*nb-wnn.f*) (= *KRI* III, 284, 1-3).

ỉr ỉt.ỉ ỉmn … ntf pꜣ nb psḏt

'As for my father Amun ... it is him, the master of the Enneade.'

60. Wenamun, 2, 30-31 (= *LES*, 70, 1-3).

ḥr ỉr ỉmn-rꜥ nsw nṯrw ntf pꜣ nb n pꜣ ꜥnḫ snb – ḥr ntf pꜣ nb (n) nꜣy.k ỉtyw

'And, as for Amun-Ra, king of the gods, he is the master of Life (and) Health; and it was him, the master of your ancestors!'

The unmarked form (*ỉr pꜣ* A B *Ø*[355]) of the last two examples has been given above (examples 53 and 54).

39.4 Important remark

In accordance with common practice, the two-member nominal forms having as second member a nominalised, defined relative clause, and which serve to rhematise a nominal element of a plain verbal sentence, are treated in the chapter devoted to cleft sentences.[356]

---

355 The unmarked correlate of example 60 would be **ḥr ỉr ỉmn-rꜥ nsw nṯrw pꜣ nb n pꜣ ꜥnḫ snb (pꜣy)*.

356 Example: *pꜣ ptr.ỉ pꜣ ḏd.ỉ* 'It is what I saw that I said' (P. BM 10052, 5, 8-9 = *KRI* VI, 779, 13); predicative plain verbal sentence: **ḏd.ỉ pꜣ ptr.ỉ* 'I have said what I saw.'

40. The nominal sentence with adjectival predicate

40.1 Introduction

The nominal sentence with adjectival predicate is a special case of the classification predication of the type ***B Ø***, where the predicate is a nominalised adjective, which is never defined.

nfr Ø 'it is good' ('belongs to the class of good ones'[357])

In this construction *nfr* is both the predicate and the rheme. The extension of the subject *Ø* can be either *se* or (*pꜣ*) A, A being almost always defined:[358]

nfr Ø se 'he is good' (it is a good (one), him)
nfr Ø (pꜣ) A 'the A is good' (it is a good (one, the) A)[359]

This nominal sentence,[360] expressing a **quality** of the subject, presented as intrinsic or permanent,[361] is also called '**predication of quality**' and is obviously timeless.

In Late Egyptian it tends to disappear and is only used with a small number of adjectives: ***nfr***, ***bỉn***, ***ꜥḏꜣ***, ***mꜣꜥ***, ***nḏm***, ***šꜣw***, etc., because it rivalled with the construction ***nfr sw Ø*** (first present whose predicate is a pseudo-participle). It is negated by the discontinuous negative morphemes *bn … ỉwnꜣ*.

40.2 *nfr Ø*

This type of sentence is quite frequent in daily life texts.

1. P. BM 10052, 5, 22 (= *KRI* VI, 781, 5).

ḏd.f ꜥḏꜣ
'He said: "It is false!"'

2. O. UCL 19614, 5 (= *KRI* V, 2, 3).

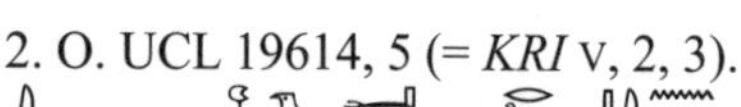

ỉw.tw ḥr ḫꜣꜥ.f r-ḏd bỉn
'It was rejected saying: "It is bad!"'

---

[357] Callender, *Middle Egyptian*, 1975, p. 68.

[358] The fact that A, which is only the extension of the real subject (*Ø*), is undefined does not contradict the 'Cohen Rule' (see *supra* §39.1): ***nfr Ø*** A 'it is a good (one, namely an) A,' the quality being true for all members of the class A.

[359] For the case when A is undefined, see the previous note.

[360] Probable origin of three sentences: *A pw*, *A pw sw*, *A pw B*, with *A = nfr* and *pw = Ø*. Example: *ḫns pw n wsḫ ỉs pw* 'It was narrow, it was not wide' (Eloquent peasant, R 45).

[361] The nominal sentence with adjectival predicate is used, in Late Egyptian, only in the third person – the **usual** paradigm of the predication of quality being: *ink nfr*, *ntk nfr*, *nfr Ø*, *nfr sw* 'I am good (I am a good [one]), you are good, it is good, he is good.' Note that *ntf nfr* is impossible in Late Egyptian – *nfr* is undefined – and that *nfr wỉ* and *nfr tw* are attested in the Coffin Texts.

Interrogative example:

3. P. Anastasi VIII, 1, 6-8 (= *KRI* III, 500, 6-9).

m-mitt sḏm.i r-ḏd ist mnš ꜣny … mwt ḥnꜥ nꜣy.f ẖrdw (i)n ***mꜣꜥ*** *(i)n* ***ꜥḏꜣ***

'And also: I heard that the bargeman[362] Any ... is dead, together with his children; is it true or is it false?'

Negative example:

4. O. Petrie 14, 6-7 (= *KRI* V, 524, 7-8).

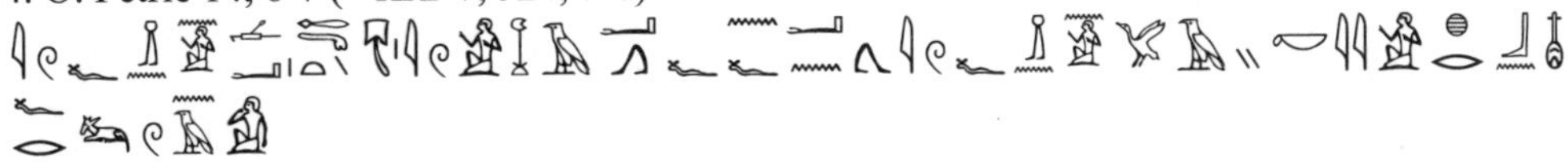

iw.f (ḥr) in n.i wꜥ ꜥꜣ iw.i (ḥr) ḥꜣꜥ.f n.f ꜥn iw.f (ḥr) in n.i pꜣy ky ḥr ***bn nfr iwnꜣ***

'He brought me a donkey, I sent it back to him. He brought me this other (one) – and it is not good!' (*lit.* 'it is not a good (one)').

40.3 *nfr Ø se*

Literary and infrequent.[363]

5. P. Lansing, 2, 2-3 (= *LEM*, 100, 12-13).

snsn n.k tꜣ ꜥwty pꜣ gsty ***nḏm se*** *r šdḥw ir sšw n pꜣ nty rḫ se* ***ꜣḫ se*** *r iꜣwt nbt*

'Take as companions[364] the papyrus-roll and the palette: they are more pleasant than pomegranate(?) wine. As for writing, to the one who masters it, they are more profitable than any other job!'

40.4 *nfr Ø (pꜣ) A*

Cases where the extension of the subject (*pꜣ*) A is undefined are very rare.[365]

6. P. BM 10052, 3, 18 (= *KRI* VI, 774, 9).

ḏd n.f ṯꜣty ***ꜥḏꜣ pꜣ ḏd.k***

'The vizier said to him: "What you said is false"' (*lit.* 'It is a false (thing), what you said').

---

[362] *Lit.* 'barge sailor.'

[363] Another example: *ꜥšꜣ se r šꜥw nw wḏbw* 'they are more numerous than the sand of the beaches,' Qadesh Bulletin, §50 (=*KRI* II, 112, 5-8).

[364] *Lit.* 'Fraternize with, socialise, adopt.'

[365] See above §40.1; for example: P. Leiden I 371, 36 *bn šꜣw dit iry se pꜣ nty mi-qd.i* 'it is not appropriate to cause that someone like me does it,' see Černý, *BIFAO* 41 (1941), 114.

7. P. Turin 1977, 9 (= Bakir, *Epistolography,* pl. 26).

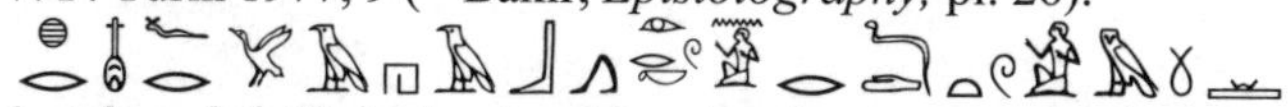

ḫr ***nfr pꜣ hꜣb (ỉ).ỉrỉ.k*** *n.ỉ r-ḏd tw.ỉ m šs*

'And the letter that you sent me (*lit.* 'the sending you made to me'), saying: "I am well," it is a good (thing)!'

Interrogative example:

8. O. IFAO 682 (= *BIFAO* 41 (1941), 15).

ỉn ***nfr pꜣ ỉḥ***

'The ox, is it good?'

Example after *nty*:

9. O. Nash 2, v° 4-5 (= *KRI* IV, 319, 5).

pꜣ nty ***bỉn pꜣy.f bꜣw*** *r mwt*

'He whose anger is more lethal (*lit.* 'bad') than death.'

Circumstantial example:

10. P. Anastasi IX, 2 (= *KRI* III, 505, 4).

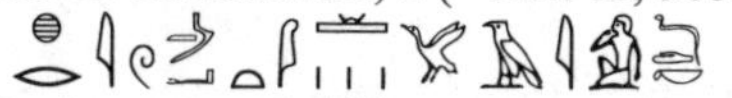

ḫr ỉw ***mꜣꜥ pꜣ ỉ.ḏd.k***

'And, although what you have said is true.'

Example where the sentence plays the role of a complement clause:

11. P. Anastasi IX, 11 (= *KRI* III, 506, 12).

ꜥm.k r-ḏd ***mꜣꜥ pꜣ ỉ.ḏd.ỉ***

'May you realise that what I said is true!'

Negative example:

12. P. DM v, v° 3 (= *KRI* VI, 266, 8).

bn nfr ỉwnꜣ pꜣ ỉ.ỉrỉ.k *r.ỉ m-dwn sp-sn sp-sn*

'What you have not ceased to do against me is not good' (*lit.* 'It is not a good (thing) what you have done continuously ...').

Example where the adjective contains the intensifying suffix *wsy*:[366]

13. P. Anastasi II, 5, 3 (= *LEM*, 15, 2-3): panegyric of Merneptah.

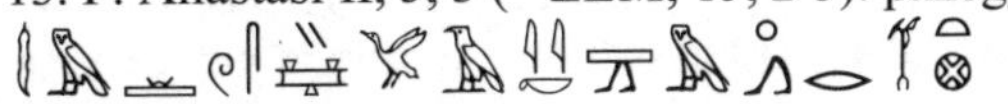

nḏm.wsy pꜣy.k šm r wꜣst

'How pleasant is your journey to Thebes!'

40.5 Special case

In some rare instances, the second member of the sentence with adjectival predicate contains a construction that seems to be a circumstantial first present:

14. O. DM 554, 5-6 (fig. p. 87).

***ỉs nfr ỉw.ỉ ḥr ḏd** n.f*

'Is it a good thing that I talk to him?' or 'Is it good that I talk to him?'

15. P. Turin 1971, 13 (= *LRL*, 32, 4).

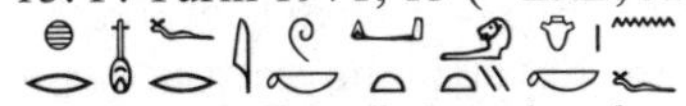

***ḫr nfr ỉw.k (ḥr) dỉt** ḥꜣty.k n.f*

'And it is good that you turn your heart to him.'

Based on the foregoing examples, one would have expected **ỉs nfr pꜣy.ỉ ḏd n.f* (example 14) and **ḫr nfr pꜣy.k dỉt hꜣty.k n.f* (example 15), whose second member contains a nominalised verbal sentence.

These two examples, where the circumstantial appears to be 'nominalised,' is reminiscent of cases where a circumstantial is used in place of a complement clause to take on the function of the direct object pronoun of an operator verb, see *supra* §32.4 and 5.

[366] This morpheme, deriving from Middle Egyptian *wy sy* (*nfr.wy sy* 'how beautiful is she!') is mostly found in school texts, and especially in panegyrics. Other examples: P. Anastasi III, 7, 3 (= *LEM*, 28, 10) with *nfr.wsy*; P. Lansing, 2, 4 (= *LEM*, 101, 1) with *ꜥꜣ.wsy*.

41. Expressing possession

The notion of **ownership** (to belong to, to be property of)[367] must be carefully distinguished from that of **possession**[368] or the concept of '**having**' something.[369] This notion is expressed in two different ways depending on whether the possessor is represented by a name (or an interrogative pronoun) or by a personal pronoun.

41.1 The possessor is represented by a name (or an interrogative pronoun)

In this case, being X an object and A an individual, an institution, an object or a country, to say that X is a property of A, belongs to A, or "is A's," the syntagma derived from the nominal sentence with adjectival predicate will be used:[370]

(ỉr) X ... ny-se A: (as for) X ... it is A's (it is a property of A)
ny-se A ... pꜣ X: it is A's ... the X

where *ny* is the genitival adjective playing the role of predicate,[371] while the subject ***se*** resumes (anaphora) or announces (cataphora) the object **X**. Thematisation (anterior or posterior) is required because the syntagma is grammaticalised, the genitival adjective having a nominal subject only in previous phases of the Egyptian language.[372] In Late Egyptian the construction is only used in the third person, without the pronoun's spelling necessarily corresponding to the gender and number of **X** – hence the transliteration ***se*** in conformity with the pronunciation.[373] The construction is negated by means of the negative morpheme *bn*.

The following are some of the attested spellings of *ny-se*:

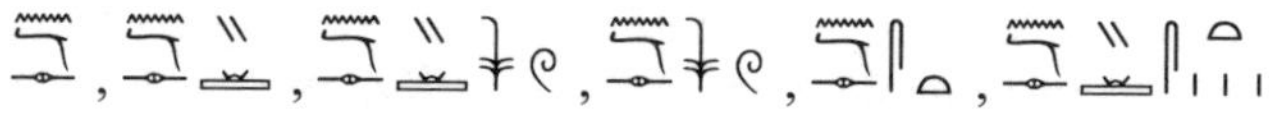

1. Personal names: frequent use.

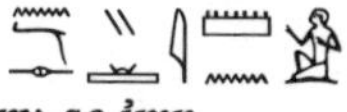

ny-se ỉmn
'Nesamun' (= he belongs to Amun), X being the individual himself.

Example with anterior thematisation:

---

[367] On Middle Egyptian see Gilula, *RdE* 20 (1968), 55-61.
[368] Expressed by *m-dỉ*; see Théodoridès, *RdE* 22 (1970) 139-154, and example 5 below.
[369] Expressed through the existential predication: *wn m-dỉ.f* A 'he has an A.' See *supra* §22.1, Černý-Groll, *LEG*, p. 392-395 and Benveniste, *Problèmes de linguistique générale* I, p. 196.
[370] See Černý-Groll, *LEG*, p. 24-27 and 542-543.
[371] See Gardiner, *EG*, §114, 2; Lefebvre, *Grammaire*, §182.
[372] *ny **X A*** 'X belongs to A,' construction frequently employed in proper names: *n(y)-mꜣꜥt-rꜥ* (Amenemhat III).
[373] See §7.2.1.

2. O. Berlin P 11239, 3-4 (= *KRI* III, 545, 3-5).

ptr nꜣ ḥmtyw n sm ỉw r-ḏd ***ỉr nꜣy ḥmt ny-se sm bn ny-se pꜣ ḫr***
'See, the coppersmiths of the *sem*-priest have come saying: "As for the copper objects, they belong to the *sem*-priest, they do not belong to the (institution of the) Tomb."'

Example with posterior thematisation:

3. P. Mayer A, 5, 14 (= *KRI* VI, 814, 6-7).

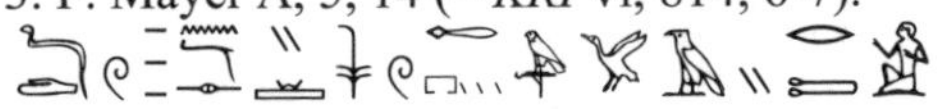

ḏd.w ***ny-se pr-ꜥꜣ ꜥ.w.s. pꜣy rmṯ***
'They said: "He belongs to Pharaoh l.p.h., this man."'

Example with the interrogative pronoun *ỉḫ* and posterior thematisation:

4. O. Leipzig 2, 5-6 (= *KRI* V, 467, 15-16) (fig. p. 238).

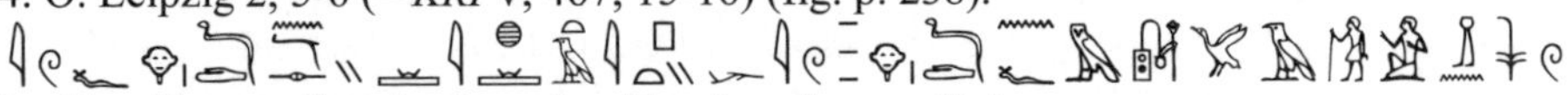

ỉw.f ḥr ḏd ***ny-se ỉḫ tꜣ ỉpt*** *ỉw.w ḥr ḏd n.f m sš pꜣ-sr (ỉ).ỉn se*
'He said: "To whom (= to which institution) does it belong, the measure?" They answered him: "It is the scribe Paser who brought it."'

Adverbial examples:

5. P. BM 10052, 3, 20-21 (= *KRI* VI, 774, 12-14).

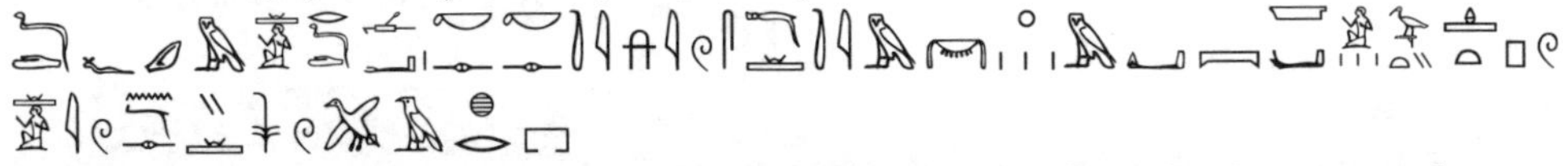

ḏd.f sḏm.ỉ r-ḏd ***wꜥ(t) kskst*** *ỉw.s mḥ.tỉ m nbw m-dỉ ḥry ỉryw-ꜥꜣ ḏḥwty-ḥtp ỉw* ***ny-se pꜣ ḫr***
'He said: "I have heard that a basket full of gold is in the possession of the chief porter Djehutyhotep, although it belongs to the Tomb."'[374] Note the contrast between the expression of possession (*m-dỉ*) and that of ownership (*ny-se*).

6. P. Mayer A, 3, 4-5 (= *KRI* VI, 808, 13-14).[375]

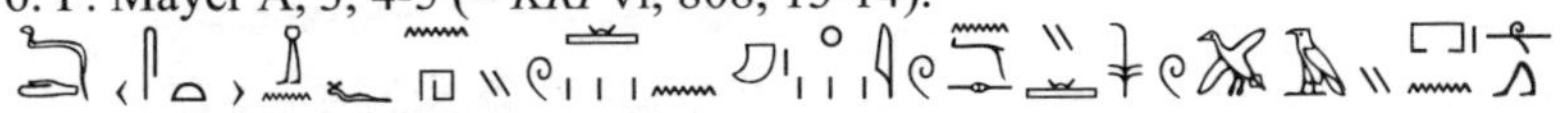

ḏd.‹s› ỉn.f ***nhꜣy n ḥmt*** *ỉw* ***ny-se pꜣy pr-n-stꜣ***
'She said: "He carried off copper that belonged to this portable shrine."'

---

[374] On *ỉry-ꜥꜣ* see Černý, Community, p. 161; on *kskst*, see Janssen, *CP*, p. 151. Note also the first present with indefinite subject.
[375] Also: P. Mayer A, 1, 12-3 (= *KRI* VI, 804, 15-16).

41.2 The possessor is represented by a personal pronoun

In this case a pronoun similar to the independent tonic pronoun,[376] or to the traditional independent pronoun,[377] functioning as adjectival predicate, is used.[378] Being X an object, the minimal sentence is:

ỉnk pꜣ X 'the X is mine, the X belongs to me' (my X)

X can be thematised, resulting in the following variants:

(ỉr)* X *... ỉnk se '(as for) X ... it is mine'

***ỉnk se ... pꜣ* X** 'it belongs to me ... the X'

As in the previous cases, this is negated using the negative morpheme(s) *bn* ... (*ỉwnꜣ*).

41.2.1 Examples with the new independent pronoun

7. Wenamun, 2, 24 (= *LES*, 69, 7-8).

ntf pꜣ ym *ḫr* ***ntf pꜣ lbln*** *nty tw.k* (*ḫr*) *ḏd* ***ỉnk se***

'The sea is his, and Lebanon – of which you never cease to say: "It is mine" – is his property.'

Examples with thematisation:

8. O. Turin 57472, v° 6-7.

ḫr ỉr pꜣy ky ***ỉnk se***

'And, as for this other (one), it is mine.'

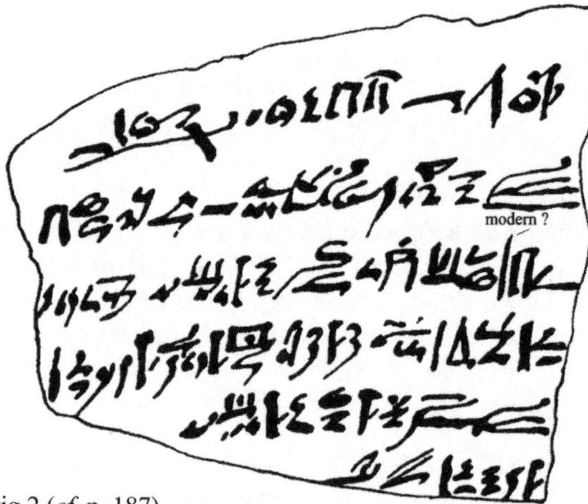

O. Leipzig 2 (*cf.* p. 187)

---

[376] Because the paradigm uses *ntf*.

[377] Use limited to the 2nd and 3rd persons: *twt* and *swt* for the two genders respectively, see §7.4.1.

[378] Gilula, *RdE* 20 (1968), 55-58.

9. P. Turin 2021, 2, 2 (= *KRI* VI, 739, 7): feminine proper noun.

ỉnk-se-nḏm
'Sweetness belongs to me' (*lit*. 'It is mine, the sweetness').

Negative example:

10. O. Nash 2, v° 14 (= *KRI* IV, 319, 13-14): oath.

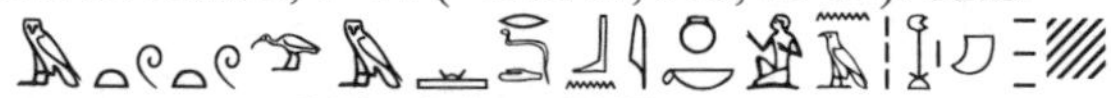

mtw.tw gm r-ḏd ***bn ỉnk nꜣ ẖl///***
'And if it is found that the picks are not mine …'

Example where the syntagma is used in a circumstantial clause in place of a relative clause:

11. P. Strasburg 39, 8-9 (= Allam, *HOP*, pl. 105).

ỉmỉ ḥn šmsw ỉw ***ntk se*** *m-sꜣ.f*
'Dispatch after him a servant that belongs to you (*lit*. 'Cause that a servant that is yours runs behind him').

Example with *nty*:

12. P. Strasburg 39, v° 2-3 (= Allam, *HOP*, pl. 105).

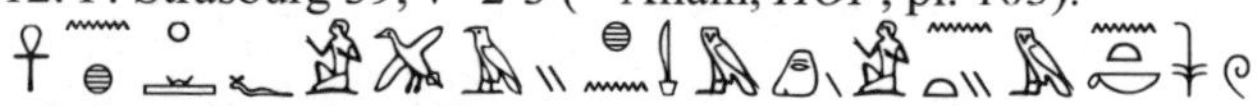

ʿnḫ.f pꜣy ḫnms nty ***ntk se***
'Ankhef, this friend of yours' (*lit*. 'who is yours').

41.2.2 Examples with the traditional independent pronoun

13. P. Turin 2021, 3, 10 (= *KRI* VI, 741, 8).

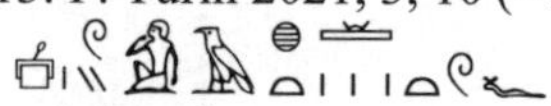

swt ꜣḫwt.f
'His property is his.'

Example with anterior thematisation:

14. P. Anastasi V, 26, 7-27, 1 (= *LEM*, 71, 11-12).

yꜣ ***ỉr nꜣ nty ḥr ḫꜣst twt sn*** *ḥr twt nꜣ nty ḥr kmt*
'Because, as for those who are in the desert, they belong to you (= 'they are under your authority'), and to you (also) belong those who are in the Valley.'

Negative example with *iw* circumstantial:

15. P. Salt 124, 1, 17 (= *KRI* IV, 410, 4): concerning tombs that the vile Paneb entered.

iw ***bn swt se***
'Although they did not belong to him.'

41.3 Examples using both modes of expressing possession[379]

16. O. Gardiner 103 A, 9-10 (= *KRI* V, 572, 1-2).

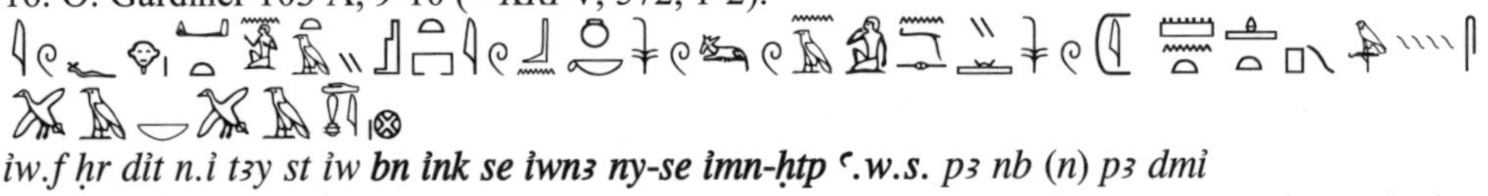

iw.f ḥr dit n.i tꜣy st iw ***bn ink se iwnꜣ ny-se imn-ḥtp*** *ꜥ.w.s. pꜣ nb* (*n*) *pꜣ dmi*
'He gave me this building, although it is not mine (because) it belongs to Amenhotep l.p.h., the lord (of) the village.'

17. O. Gardiner 143, 5-6 (= *KRI* VII, 376, 9-11).

iri.f ꜥnḫ n nb ꜥ.w.s r-ḏd ir pꜣy iḥ i.di.i n rmṯ ist pꜣ-rꜥ-ḥtp sꜣ mn-nꜣ ***ink se*** *n ḥꜥw.i* ***bn ny-se*** ***pꜣ ḥm-nṯr tpy***
'He swore an oath by the Lord l.p.h. saying: "As for the ox that I sold to the workman Prehotep son of Menna, it was my own, it did not belong to the high priest."'

18. Wenamun, 1, 20-21 (= *LES*, 62, 16-63, 2).

yꜣ ir pꜣ iṯꜣy i.ṯꜣy tw ***ntk se ny-se tꜣy.k br***
'Because, as for the thief who robbed you, he is yours, he belongs to your ship.'

41.4 Remark: the independent pronoun used as an attribute

(***wꜥ***) ***šmsw ink*** 'one of my servants (a servant of mine)'[380]

19. P. Anastasi V, 27, 3-4 (= *LEM*, 71, 16).

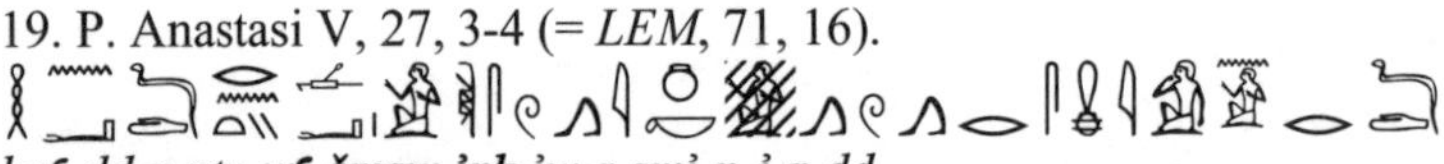

ḥnꜥ ḏd r-nty ***wꜥ šmsw ink*** *iw r smi n.i r-ḏd*
'Another matter: one of my servants came to report to me saying ...'

---

[379] Other examples: O. Nash 2, v° 1-3 (= *KRI* IV, 319, 1-3); Wenamun, 1, 14-17 (= *LES*, 62, 6-11).
[380] Sentence in which *šmsw* is undefined. Not to be confused with *pꜣy.i šmsw* 'my servant.'

20. O. Nash 1, 2-3 (= *KRI* IV, 315, 10-11).

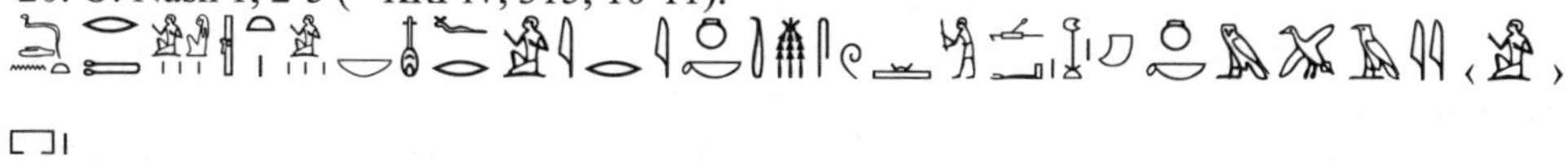

ḏdt.n rmṯ ist nb-nfr ir ink tms.‹i› ***wꜥ ẖl ink*** *m pꜣy.‹i› pr*
'What the worker Nebnefer said: "As for me, (I) buried one of my picks in my house."'

21. P. BN 197, II, 6- v° 1 (= *LRL*, 22, 14-15).

ẖr m di ḥꜣty.k [m-sꜣ] ***rmṯ nb twt*** *st m šs*
'And do not worry about any of your people, they are well.'

42. Cleft sentences

42.1 Introduction

The term **cleft sentence**[381] is normally used to describe Late Egyptian constructions employed to **rhematise** (that is, to shift to marked rheme[382]) any **noun phrase of a plain verbal sentence**,[383] as well as the verb itself in its nominal form, the infinitive. The order is always **marked rheme-theme**.

42.1.1 What is a cleft sentence?

Modern grammars carefully distinguish two types of clefting.[384]

Given the plain sentence:

'Paul likes tea'

a. It becomes, by **true clefting**:

'it is Paul *who likes tea*'

or

'it is tea *that Paul likes*'

following the extraction of '**Paul**' (subject) or of '**tea**' (direct object), and the relativisation of the rest of the sentence. In the resulting construction, which is a (**true**) **cleft sentence**, the relative is **not nominalised**, but simply embedded in the main clause. As a result, the relationship between the two clauses is one of **subordination**.

b. Through **pseudo-clefting** the same sentence becomes:

'it is Paul, *the one who likes tea*' = '*the one who likes tea*, is Paul'

or

'it is tea, *what Paul likes*' = '*what Paul likes*, is tea'

In this case, there is the **nominalisation** of the relative clause and the establishment of a predicative **relationship** between the extracted element '**Paul**' or '**tea**' on the one hand, and the **nominalised relative** on the other, that function as subject and predicate of a sentence constructed with the copula **be**. The resulting sentence is a pseudo-cleft sentence.

An excellent example of the method is provided by R. Chandler in his new *Trouble is my business*: **'I said "so what" and *"so what" is what I said.*'**

---

381 Or 'phrase coupée.'

382 See *supra* §12.4.2. Note that it is a 'functional' definition.

383 Remember: a plain verbal sentence is one that verifies the statistical affinities subject-theme and predicate-rheme, and is devoid of any syntactic turn of phrase explicitly designating one of its components as theme or rheme.

384 For example: Quirck *et al.*, *A Comprehensive Grammar of the English Language*, London and New York, 1985 §18.25-30, p. 1383-1389; Huddleston, *English Grammar, an Outline*, Cambridge, 1988, p. 184-188, *Dictionnaire de linguistique*, ed. Larousse, Paris, 1973, p. 91 and 399.

It follows that in Late Egyptian, where the copula 'be' does not exist, the sentence corresponding to the pseudo-cleft sentence is the **two-member noun phrase**: (*pꜣ*) ***B*** *pꜣ* ***A***, where A is a nominalised, defined relative clause.[385]

42.1.2 Cleft sentences in Late Egyptian

Although in Middle Egyptian there is only one type of cleft sentence, we distinguish two in Late Egyptian, corresponding to the two types mentioned above.[386]

42.1.2.1 The (true) cleft sentence (type I)

This is the cleft sentence of classical Egyptian which, in modern guise, continues to be used to rhematise the **subject** of a plain verbal sentence in the **active** voice, or the **agent**, of the process.

The first member, which is always the **marked rheme**, contains a **defined noun**[387] preceded by *m* (*ỉn* in a few texts closer to the classical stage of the language), a **tonic independent pronoun** or the interrogative pronoun *nỉm*.[388]

The second member, corresponding to the **theme**, contains an **active participle**, periphrased or not, or a **prospective** most often periphrased. This second member always agrees in **gender**, **number** and **person** with the first. There are three possibilities:[389]

		Late Egyptian		*Classical Egyptian*
I	**Past**	***m pꜣ A ỉ.stp (se)***	◄	*ỉn A sḏm* (*sw*) (perfective)
	or	***ntf ỉ.stp (se)***	◄	*ntf sḏm* (*sw*)
II	**Aorist**	***m pꜣ A ỉ.ỉrỉ stp.(f)***	◄	*ỉn A sḏm* (*sw*) (imperfective)
	or	***ntf ỉ.ỉrỉ stp.(f)***	◄	*ntf sḏm* (*sw*)
III	**Futur**	***m pꜣ A ỉ.ỉrỉ.f stp.(f)***	◄	*ỉn A sḏm.f* (*sw*) (prospective)
	or	***ntf ỉ.ỉrỉ.f stp.(f)***	◄	*ntf sḏm.f* (*sw*)

I 'it is the A / he who chose it'
II 'it is the A / he who chooses it (habitually)'
III 'it is the A / he who will choose it'

---

[385] See *supra* §39.2.2.3.1.

[386] On Late Egyptian, see Groll, *Non Verbal*; Černý-Groll, *LEG*, p. 525-541 and the fundamental article by Satzinger 'Nominalsatz und Cleft Sentence im Neuägyptischen,' in *Studies presented to H. J. Polotsky*, ed. Young, 1981, p 480-505.

[387] Very rare exceptions are: P. BN 198, II, v° 1-2 (= *LRL* 68, 4-5); see below example 41.

[388] *Nỉm* can be preceded, or not, by *m*, because the origin of *nỉm* = *ỉn* + *m* had been forgotten.

[389] Satzinger, *o.l.*, p. 492-493.

In this type of cleft sentence, the participle – which is never preceded by an article (or a demonstrative) – is **not nominalised**, but retains its **full verbal value.**[390] Consequently, the second member is not the equivalent of a noun, but a true relative clause[391] – which means that the relationship between the two members is not predicative in nature (= between a subject and a predicate), but a relationship of subordination between two clauses (more precisely the embedding of a relative clause in a nominal form of the type *B Ø*). This construction, therefore, corresponds perfectly to the definition of **true cleft sentence** of modern grammars, as noted above.

This true cleft sentence is negated by means of the negative morpheme *bn*, exceptionally by *bn … ỉwnꜣ*. It can be preceded by the circumstantial *ỉw*,[392] and/or the past converter *wn*.[393]

Remarks

a. In Late Egyptian the presence of the article makes it impossible to confuse it with a nominal sentence (as could happen in Middle Egyptian). Compare the two examples below:

1. P. Turin 1978/208, v° 1-2 (= Allam, *HOP*, pl. 97).

yꜣ bn ***ỉnn ỉ.ỉrỉ ẖn.w*** *m-dwn ỉwnꜣ*

'For it is not us **who** usually **transport them** (= the goods).' Given that it is not preceded by the article, the periphrased participle is not nominalised, thus, this is a true cleft sentence.

2. P. Anastasi V, 9, 6-7 (= *LEM*, 60, 9-10).

ntk[394] ***pꜣ ỉ.ỉrỉ sẖr*** *n pꜣ ỉwty mwt.f*

'It is you (you are) **the one who gives** guidance to one who has no mother.' Nominal phrase, marked or not,[395] where the nominalised participle is defined by the article.

▪ These two examples illustrate a key difference between the cleft sentence and the nominal sentence: while the unmarked correlate of the cleft sentence is a verbal sentence: **yꜣ bn tw.n ḥr ẖn.w* 'because we do not usually transport them' (first present, see below §42.2.1.4, example 40), the unmarked correlate of a marked nominal sentence 'It is you, the one ...' is still a nominal sentence externally identical in Late Egyptian:[396] 'You are the one ...'

b. Although most of the verbs encountered are transitive, the true cleft sentence remains, as in the classical period and in the Third Intermediate Period, open to intransitive verbs or verbs used

[390] View Doret *RdE* 40 (1989), p . 60: 'The participle ... in the cleft sentence ... will have a near verbal value' and *LingAeg* 1 (1991), 58: 'to the nominal phrase ... is opposed the cleft sentence where the participle will have its full verbal value.'

[391] In the case of the prospective we are dealing with a 'virtual relative clause.'

[392] It takes on a relative temporality.

[393] Examples with *ỉw wn*: P. Mayer A, 4, 10 (= *KRI* VI, 811, 14); O. DM 663, 8-9 (= *KRI* III, 161, 3-4).

[394] On the spelling of *ntk*, see *supra* p. 188, example 10 and n. 376.

[395] Depending on whether the independent pronoun is tonic (marked) or atonic (unmarked).

[396] See previous note.

intransitively.[397]

c. The object is most often expressed, exceptions occurring especially in the aorist.

d. There is a rare variant of this type where *m* is not found before *pꜣ A*.[398]

In conclusion, it can be seen that the true cleft sentence only allows the rhematisation of the **subject** (or **agent**) of a verbal sentence in the **active** voice, which verb is a **perfective** (past), a **prospective** (future) or an **aorist** (habitual present).

42.1.2.2 The pseudo-cleft sentence (type II)

It serves to extend the possibility of rhematising a nominal element of a verbal sentence (broadly defined),[399] in cases where the true cleft sentence cannot be used. Therefore, the pseudo-cleft sentence is additional to the true one, with which it is used in **complementary distribution**. In addition, the subject, the direct object and the verb itself – in its nominal form, the infinitive – can be rhematised in any voice and tense.

The first member, the **marked rheme**, includes either a **noun, defined or not**, a **tonic independent pronoun**, or the interrogative particle ***iḫ***.

The second member, the **theme**, **agrees with the first in gender**, **number and person** and contains a nominalised, defined (either by a defined article or by a demonstrative[400]) relative clause containing a **passive participle**, a **relative form**, ***nty*** **+ third future**, ***nty*** **+ first present**, or ***(i).wn*** **+ first present**.

Syntactically, this construction is, **to begin with**, nothing more than a **nominal sentence** which second member is a **nominalised relative clause**, **defined** by a definite article or a demonstrative, where *pw* is no longer present.[401] It thus complies with the definition that modern grammars give of the **pseudo-cleft sentence**, the term used in this book to designate it.

Afterwards, assuming, next to the true (and old) cleft sentence, the same function of rhematisation,[402] the pseudo (and new) cleft sentence was gradually **assimilated** while moving away from the nominal sentence.[403] At the end of the process, it became, by **grammaticalisation**, a fixed expression, irreducible to the analysis, where, as in the true cleft sentence, the second member agrees with the first in gender, number and **person**.

In Coptic, where the copula is again expressed and the development completed, the two syntagmas are clearly differentiated:

ⲟⲩⲙⲉ ⲧⲉϯϫⲱ ⲙ̄ⲙⲟⲥ ‘it is the truth that I speak’

---

[397] Examples in Middle Egyptian: CT VI, 401, o, with *iy*; *BIFAO* 85 (1985), 85, with *ʿq*; *CdE* 37 (1962), 253, with *spi*. Examples from the Third Intermediate Period: Urk. VI, 101, 4, with *mdw* and 145, 6, with *ḥwi r*. See Vernus, *RdE* 41 (1990), p. 188.

[398] See Vernus, *RdE* 38 (1987), p. 175-181.

[399] Including the various types of predicates of the first present.

[400] *Pꜣy*, *tꜣy*, *nꜣy* or *pꜣw*. In the absence of any systematic study (see however Satzinger, *o.l.*, p. 501, n. 50), it is unclear what rules the use of different morphemes obeys. Note the parallel use of *pꜣ* and *pꜣy*: tablets Rogers and Mac Cullum, line 7.

[401] The non-expression of the copula *pw* in nominal sentences is one of the characteristics of Late Egyptian.

[402] Remember that the usual definition of cleft sentences in Late Egyptian is a functional definition, not a syntaxical one.

[403] That continues to fulfil its functions of classification and identification.

pseudo-cleft sentence where the copula is not present, but in which the article defining the relative clause and the resumptive pronoun agree with the first member (in this case a feminine).

ⲟⲩⲙⲉ ⲡⲉ ⲡⲉϯϫⲱ ⲙ̄ⲙⲟϥ 'what I say is true'

nominal phrase in which the article defining the relative clause and the resumptive pronoun agree with the copula, here expressed.[404]

The pseudo-cleft sentence in Late Egyptian is, therefore, an original form, distinct from the true cleft sentence, and which is different from the nominal sentence not only in its function, but also because of the complete agreement existing between the two members. Its origin and evolution can be observed during the nineteenth dynasty.

3. P. Cairo 58053, 3 (= *KRI* I, 322, 6-7): Seti I.

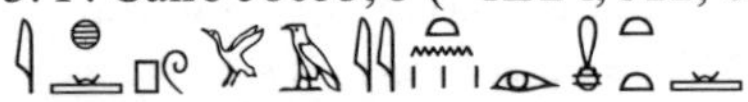

iḫ ***pw p3y.tn*** *ir̓t* (*m*)-*mitt*

'What is the meaning of your acting like (that)?' (*lit.* 'It is what, your acting so?'). 'Simple' nominal sentence with *pw*, where the second member, nominal by nature, is defined by the possessive.

4. O. Leipzig 16, 6-7 (= *HO*, 33, 2): date unknown.

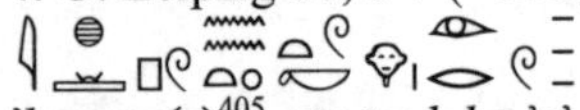

iḫ ***pw n(3)***[405] *nty tw.k ḥr ir̓.w*

'What are you going to do?' (*lit.* 'It is what, the (things) that you are going to do them?'). Nominal sentence where the second member is a nominalised relative clause, defined by an article, where *pw* is still expressed.

5. O. DM 126, 3 (= *KRI* III, 532, 3-4): Ramses II.

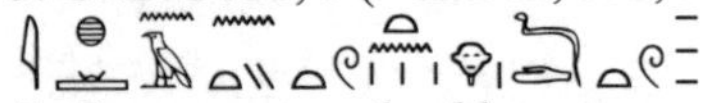

iḫ Ø n3 nty tw.tn ḥr ḏd.tw.w

'What is it that you are going to relate?' Following the disappearance of *pw*, the result is a pseudo-cleft sentence.

During this development, it can be observed that it is *pw* that disappears and, therefore, the morphemes *p3/t3/n3*, *p3y/t3y/n3y* or *p3w* – found in the pseudo-cleft sentences – are articles and demonstratives, not actualisations of *pw*.[406]

Remark. With regards to the translation, to comply with established practice and to distinguish them from nominal sentences, **both types of cleft sentences will be translated as true cleft sentences**.

The same evolution can be observed in the following examples:

---

[404] See the excellent exposition by Satzinger, *o.l.*, p. 480-481.

[405] For this spelling, see Wenamun, 2, 23.

[406] A different view is found in Satzinger, *o.l.*, p. 481 and n. 14, p. 491.

6. P. Cairo 58054, 3 (= *KRI* I, 323, 4-5): Seti I.

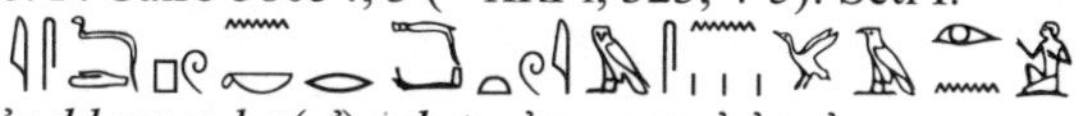

*ỉs ḏd **pw** n.k r(=ỉ).mḥ tw ỉm.sn **pꜣ** ỉrỉ.n.ỉ*

'Is saying to you "Stop them then!" **what I have done**?' Nominal sentence in which the second member is a nominalised relative clause and *pw* is expressed.

7. Theban tomb n. 19 (= *KRI* III, 395, 10-11): Ramses II.

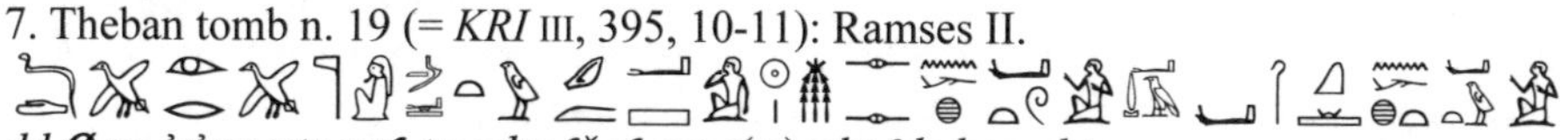

*ḏd **Ø pꜣ** ỉrỉ pꜣ nṯr mꜣꜥ.tw sḏm-ꜥš rꜥ-ms-s(w)-nḫt ꜥḏꜣ ḥqꜣ-nḫt*

'It is saying: "The worker Ramsesnakht is right, Heqanakht is wrong" **what the god has done**.' Pseudo-cleft sentence without *pw*.

Therefore, this type of nominal sentence and the pseudo-cleft sentence coexisted in Late Egyptian without being always possible, in the absence of *pw*, to distinguish them in writing – especially when pronouns are in the third person, or when the first member is a masculine singular. It is likely that the two sentences were distinguished only by suprasegmental features.[407] The following example can be analysed either as a nominal or as a pseudo-cleft sentence:

8. P. BM 10052, 5, 15-16 (= *KRI* VI, 780, 9-10).

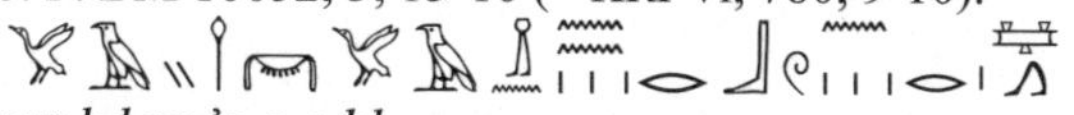

***pꜣy** ḥḏ pꜣ ỉn.n r-bl*

– 'It is this silver, **what we took** out' nominal sentence,

or

– 'It is this silver here **that we took** out' pseudo-cleft sentence.

Given that the first member is a masculine singular, it is impossible to distinguish between the two sentences. There follows that, each time there is **complete agreement** between the two members, the sentence will be taken, **somewhat arbitrarily**, as a pseudo-cleft sentence and will be translated accordingly,[408] otherwise the sentence will be deemed to be a nominal sentence.

The following are some examples where this distinction is possible:

9. P. Griffith, 5-6 (= *LRL*, 12, 6-7).

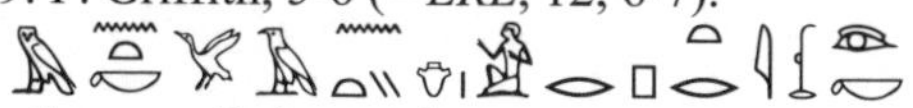

***ntk** pꜣ nty ỉb.ỉ r ptr.k*

'It is you that I desire to see' (*lit.* 'that my heart is towards seeing').

[407] It is the same in English where 'It is the wine I prefer' can indicate the vintage preferred by the speaker holding in his hand a bottle of Chateau Margaux (identification), or express its preference for the wine compared to beer, cider, etc. (restriction). In the first case, the construction is equivalent to a nominal sentence and in the second to a cleft sentence.

[408] As a cleft sentence, except when the resulting translation is awkward or likely to cause confusion.

10. Cairo Stela JE 48876, 26 (= *KRI* VI, 20, 4).

***ntk** pꜣ nty wn pḥty im.k*

'It is you who has strength' (*lit.* 'It is you that there exists strength in you').

These two indisputable pseudo-cleft sentences, in which both members agree **in person**,[409] contrast with the next construction where the lack of agreement between the pronouns shows that it is a nominal sentence:

11. P. Anastasi V, 27, 5 (= *LEM*, 72, 2).

***ink** pꜣ gm.tn r sꜥḥꜥ.f m tꜣ št r-ḏr.s*

'It is me (= I am) the one whom you have found in order to penalise him among all taxpayers!'

In the following examples the distinction is made on the basis of whether there is number agreement, or not:

12. P. BM 10052, 3, 18 (= *KRI* VI, 774, 9-10).

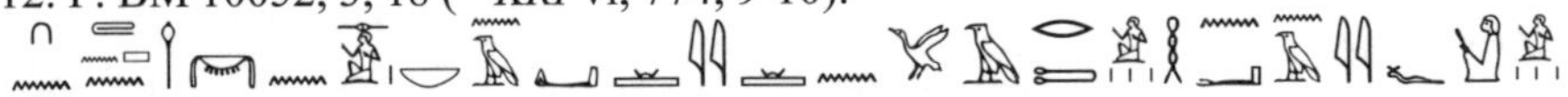

***10** n dbn n ḥḏ n s nb **nꜣ** dyt n pꜣ rmṯ ḥnꜥ nꜣy.f iryw*

'**These are** (the) ten silver debens per person **that were** given to the man and his accomplices.' Pseudo-cleft sentence in which the second member agrees in **number** with the first.[410]

13. O. DM 554, 6 (fig. p. 87).

***13** n rmw **pꜣ** iny (n).n*

'**It is** thirteen fish, **which** have been delivered to us.' Nominal sentence in which the second member remains in the **singular**, while the first is in the **plural**.[411]

The following example, where the second member agrees with the first, which is feminine, is a construction exactly like the Coptic pseudo-cleft sentence cited above:

14. O. Gardiner 165, v° 4-5 (= *KRI* III, 549, 8-9).[412]

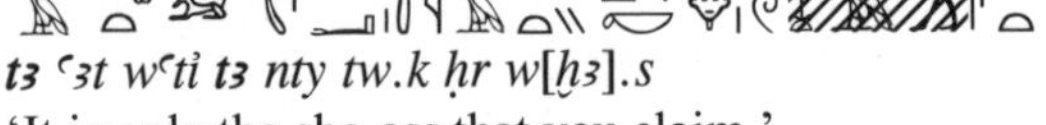

***tꜣ** ꜥꜣt wꜥti **tꜣ** nty tw.k ḥr w[ḫꜣ].s*

'It is only the she-ass that you claim.'

---

[409] Compare with the true cleft sentence cited in example 19 below.

[410] See below the parallel examples 57, 63 and 64.

[411] Parallel example: O. DM 576, 3-4: *bn it-m-it ḫꜣr* $6^1/_4$ *pꜣy in.f n.i* 'It is not $6^1/_4$ bags of barley what he brought to me.'

[412] See example 66 below.

The pseudo-cleft sentence is negated by the discontinuous negation *bn* … *ỉwnꜣ*, the latter term being inserted between the first and the second member;[413] it can also be preceded by the circumstantial *ỉw*.[414]

42.2 Rhematisation the subject of the predicative plain verbal sentence[415]

42.2.1 The sentence is in the active voice (type I or II)

42.2.1.1 Past (type I)

In this case it is always the true cleft sentence that is used:

stp A (*se*) ► ***m A ỉ.stp*** **(*se*)** non-periphrased active participle
stp.ỉ (*se*) ► ***ink ỉ.stp*** **(*se*)** non-periphrased active participle

Examples with nominal subject:

15. P. Chester Beatty I, 17, 1 and v° G, 2, 5.

m nbwt ỉ.wḏ se n.k

in nbwt ỉ.wḏ se n.k

'It is the Golden One who gave it to you.' These parallel examples clearly show the equivalence of *m* (recent form) and *in* (ancient form).

The following example employs both morphemes, the older one preceding the recent one:

16. Horus and Seth, 6, 14 (= *LES*, 45, 11-12).

in m r(ꜣ).k ỉ.ḏd se ḏs.k

'It is your own mouth which has said it.' Note the person agreement between the two members of this true cleft sentence.

17. O. Leipzig 2, v° 1 (= *KRI* V, 467, 16).

m sš pꜣ-sr (ỉ).in se

'It is the scribe Paser who brought it (= the measure).'

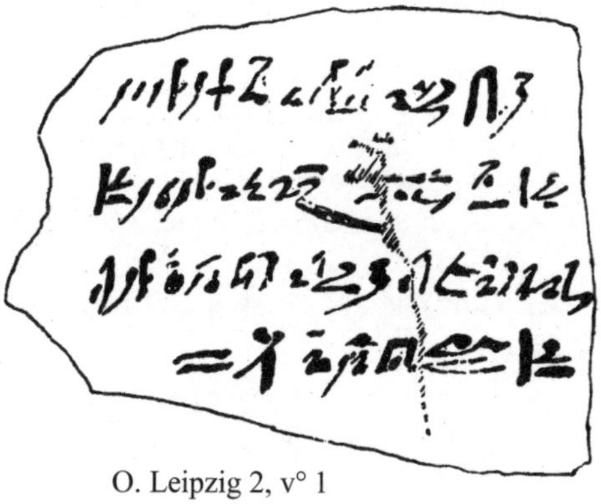

O. Leipzig 2, v° 1

Examples with the independent pronoun:

18. P. Mayer A, 4, 3 (= *KRI* VI, 811, 3).

ḏd.f ink. ỉ.wn pꜣy ḫr

'He said: "It is I who opened this tomb."'

---

[413] Whereas the same cannot happen in the case of the true cleft sentence (type I) where *ỉwnꜣ*, if present, is never inserted between the two members.

[414] In this case it takes on a relative temporality.

[415] The rhematised term is, therefore, the agent of the process.

19. Cairo Stela JE 48876, 24 (= *KRI* VI, 20, 1-2).

yꜣ ***ntk*** *ỉ.ḏd se m r(ꜣ)****.k*** *ḏs****.k***

'Because it is you who has said it with your own mouth.' Note again the person agreement between the two members.

Negative example:

20. O. Nash 1, 8 (= *KRI* IV, 316, 2).

m-bỉꜣ bn ỉnk r(=ỉ).ỉṯꜣy se

'No! It is not I who stole it!'

Interro-negative example:

21. O. DM 357, a, 3.

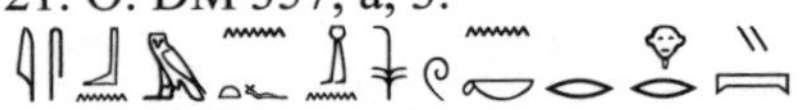

ỉs bn ntf (ỉ).ỉn se n.k r ḥry

'Is it not him who brought it to you up there (= Deir el-Medina)?'

Circumstantial example:

22. O. A. Gardiner 90, 7 (= *KRI* V, 571, 1).

ỉw bn ỉnk ỉ.hꜣb [*se*]

'While it is not I who sent it.'

Example with the thematisation of the direct object (= patient of the process):

23. P. Turin 1875, 3, 1 (= *KRI* V, 351, 6-7).

ỉr pꜣw ỉryt nb ntw ỉ.ỉrỉ se

'As for all that has been done, it is they who have done it.'

Example with the interrogative particle *nỉm*:

24. O. DM 582, 5-6 (= *KRI* V, 575, 15) (fig. p. 242).

ỉw.ỉ ḥr ḏd n.f m nỉm ỉ.dỉ n.k pꜣ ꜥꜣ

'I said to him: "Who (*lit.* 'it is who, who') gave you the donkey?"'

Example where the cleft sentence appears in the protasis of a correlative system introduced by *ỉnn*:

25. P. Louvre E 27151, 8-9 (= *JEA* 64 (1978), pl. XIV A): concerning poor quality honey returned to the sender.

ỉnn m ky r(=ỉ).dỉ se n.k ỉmỉ ptr.f se

'If it is someone else who supplied it to you, let him see it.'

The following are examples with intransitive verbs:

26. P. Orbiney, 4, 10 (= *LES*, 14, 1-2).

m nỉm (ỉ).mdw m-dỉ.ṯ

'Who (*lit.* 'it is who, who') has spoken (evil) with you?'

27. P. BM 10383, 1, 6 (= *KRI* VI, 834, 4).

m sš pr-ḥḏ swtḫ-ms (ỉ).wn m mr ꜣḥwt ỉ.ỉy

'It is the scribe of the Treasury Sethmose, the former (*lit.* 'who had been') Overseer of the Fields, who came.'

28. P. Anastasi V, 14, 1-2 (= *LEM*, 63, 8-9).

ỉs bn ntṯ ỉ.šm r-ḥꜣt nꜣ sšw ṯꜣty r pꜣy.s pr

'Is it not you who walked before the scribes of the vizier to her house (= that of a third person)?'

Remark. Some syntagmas (very few), containing the active participle of a verb of motion, could be interpreted as pseudo-cleft sentences. However, given that the speaker in this case could use a true cleft sentence, it follows that these are simply nominal sentence in which *pw* is unexpressed.

The following is an example found in the protasis of a correlative system introduced by *hn*:

29. Wenamun, 1, 18 (= *LES*, 62, 13-14).

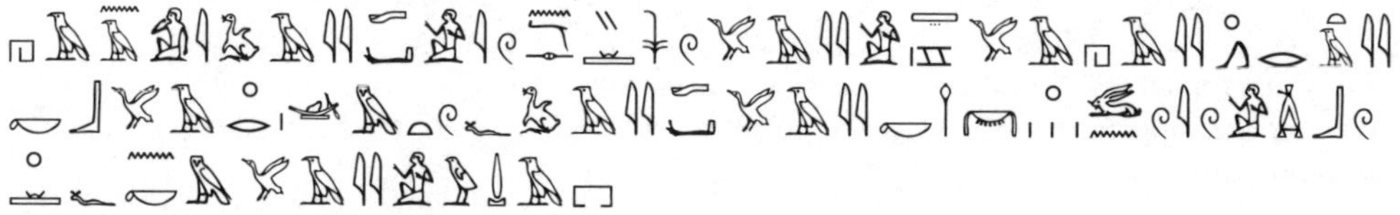

***hn ỉṯꜣy ỉw ny-se pꜣy.ỉ tꜣ pꜣ hꜣy r tꜣy.k br** mtw.f ṯꜣy pꜣy.k ḥḏ wn ỉw.ỉ (r) ḏbꜣ.f n.k m pꜣy.ỉ wḏꜣ*

'If it were a thief belonging to my country the one who went down into your ship and stole your silver, I would have reimbursed it to you from my treasury.'[416]

42.2.1.2 Present (type II)

This time it is the pseudo-cleft sentence that is employed:

A ḥr stp.(f) ► ***A pꜣ nty ḥr stp.(f)***

[416] Another example: P. BM 10052, 13, 8 (= *KRI* VI, 795, 14-15).

tw.ỉ ḥr stp.(f) ► ***ink pꜣ nty ḥr stp.(f)***[417]

This is an unmarked syntagma which expresses both the immediate and the habitual present. On the other hand, if it is a nuance of consuetude that one wants to convey, a marked form is used instead, the aorist.

Example containing a negative relative clause in which the adverbial predicate is implied:

30. *Giornale*, 12, 4-5 (= *KRI* VI, 569, 3-4).

ỉn-ḥr-ḫꜥw sꜣ pꜣ-nfr pꜣ nty bn sw (dy)
'It is Inherkhau, son of Panefer, who is not here.'

Example where the predicate of the relative clause is a prepositional phrase:

31. P. Turin A, v° 4, 1 (= *CLEM*, 508).

pꜣy.f gstỉ pꜣ nty m ḏrt.k
'It is his palette that is in your hand.'

Examples with a predicate of the form *ḥr* + infinitive:

32. P. Orbiney, 6, 5 (= *LES*, 15, 12-13).

pꜣy.ỉ nb nfr ntk[418] *pꜣ nty ḥr wp pꜣ ꜥḏꜣ r ‹pꜣ› mꜣꜥtw*
'Oh my good lord, it is you who judges between the guilty and (the) just!' Habitual present.

33. Kuban Stela, 9-10 (= *KRI* II, 355, 4-5).

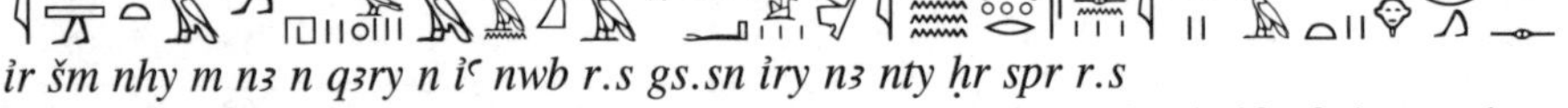

ỉr šm nhy m nꜣ n qꜣry n ỉꜥ nwb r.s gs.sn ỉry nꜣ nty ḥr spr r.s
'If some of the squads of gold washers go there, it is (only) half of them who reach there.' Habitual present.

34. Doomed Prince, 4, 8 (= *LES*, 2, 4-5).

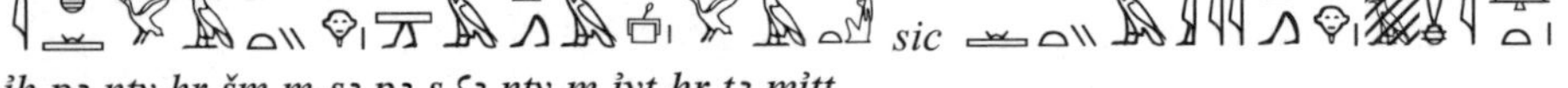

ỉḫ pꜣ nty ḥr šm m-sꜣ pꜣ s ꜥꜣ nty m ỉyt ḥr tꜣ mỉtt
'What is that walking behind the older man who is coming down the road?' Immediate present.

Examples where the predicate is a pseudo-participle:

[417] The same transformation takes place for other types of predicate of the first present. In the negative form the subject is resumed in the relative clause, see example 30.
[418] On this spelling see *supra* §39.2.1.1, example 10.

35. Graffito 1396, 3.
‘If (I) have come, it is to see the mountains (of the West) and to denounce the evil to Amun, Mut and Khonsu,

yꜣ ntw nꜣ nty rḫ ẖt ḥꜣp[419]
because they are the ones who know the true nature’ (*lit.* ‘the secret interior’).

36. Horus and Seth, 9, 11 (= *LES*, 50, 2). Isis turned herself into a headless statue (*rpyt*) and Pre asks Thoth:
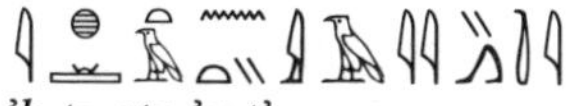
ỉḫ tꜣ nty ỉy.tỉ
‘Who is the one that has arrived?’ (*lit.* ‘It is who that has come (and who is there)?’). In this example, the pseudo-participle has a resultative value (unmarked) – Isis is there at the time the words are uttered – while in the example 27 the participle expresses a punctual past event (marked) unrelated to the moment of the enunciation.

42.2.1.3 Imperfect (type II)

This temporal nuance is obtained by transposing the previous sentence into the past, *nty* having been replaced by (*ỉ*).*wn*, the participle of the auxiliary *wnn*.

wn A ḥr stp.(*f*) ► ***A pꜣ* (*ỉ*)*.wn ḥr stp.*(*f*)**
wn.ỉ ḥr stp.(*f*) ► ***ink pꜣ* (*ỉ*)*.wn ḥr stp.*(*f*)**[420]

Example where the predicate of the relative clause includes an adverb and a pseudo-participle:

37. P. Mayer A, 1, 4 (= *KRI* VI, 803, 16-804, 1).

ntf pꜣ wn ỉm ʿḥʿ ỉrm nꜣ ỉṯꜣw
‘It is him who was over there attacking the thieves.’

Example where the predicate of the relative clause is a prepositional phrase:

38. P. BM 10052, 14, 18 (= *KRI* VI, 799, 2-3).
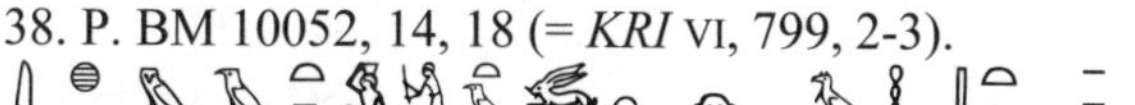
ỉḫ m ꜣtp tꜣ wn ‹ḥr› nḥbt.w
‘What kind of burden was (*lit.* ‘it is what as load that was’) on their neck?’

Example with a predicate of the form *ḥr* + infinitive:

[419] Other examples: *ỉnn nwỉ.tw nbw ntw nꜣ nty rḫ* ‘If one grabbed gold, it is they who know,’ P. Mayer A, 2 , 15 (= *KRI* VI, 807, 11 -12); *ṯꜣty pꜣ nty rḫ* ‘It is the vizier who knows,’ O. Nash 1, v° 14-15 (= *KRI* IV, 317, 12).
[420] The transformation is identical for other types of predicate of the first present.

39. Mès, N 11-12 (= *KRI* III, 427, 11-12): concerning a plot of land.

ỉw ḥry ỉḥꜣ ḥwy sꜣ pꜣ-rꜥ-ḥtp pꜣ wn ḥr skꜣ.s ḏr hꜣw N dỉ ꜥnḫ[421]

'While it was the Overseer of the Stables Huy, son of Prehotep, who cultivated it since the time of (king) N given life.'

42.2.1.4 Aorist (Type I)

It is a marked construction, specifying the repetition of the process or the general present, which derives from a Middle Egyptian cleft sentence containing an imperfective active participle. In Late Egyptian this participle is almost always periphrased:[422]

A ḥr stp.(f) ► ***m A ỉ.ỉrỉ stp.(f)***
tw.ỉ ḥr stp.(f) ► ***ink ỉ.ỉrỉ stp.(f)***

40. P. Turin 1978/208, v° 1-2 (= Allam, *HOP*, pl. 97).

yꜣ bn ỉnn ỉ.ỉrỉ ẖn.w m-dwn ỉwnꜣ

'For it is not us who usually transport them (the goods).' Consuetudinal present.

41. P. BN 198, II, v° 1-2 (= *LRL*, 68, 4-5).

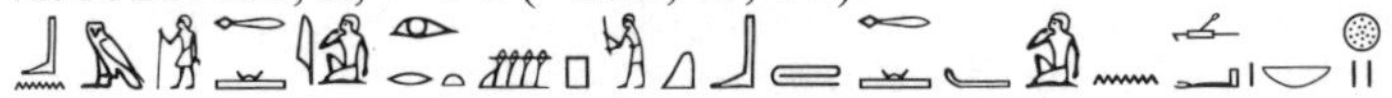

bn m sr ꜥꜣ ỉ.ỉrỉ šsp qbꜥ n wꜥ nb sp-sn

'This is not a great judge that accepts taunts from everyone!'[423] General present.

This example contains, quite exceptionally, an undefined subject. Therefore, what has been asserted[424] is valid for **the class** of great magistrates, the latter being designated by any of its components.[425]

Circumstantial examples:

42. P. BM 10403, 3, 25-27 (= *KRI* VI, 833, 1-3).

ḏd.tw n.s wn.ṯ m ḥnm m-dỉ wꜥb ỉṯꜣw tꜣtꜣ-šrỉ ỉw ntṯ ỉ.ỉrỉ wn n pꜣ nty ‹m› ꜥq ntṯ ỉ.ỉrỉ ḫtm n pꜣ nty pr

'They said to her: "You were a servant to the wab priest Tatisheri, (this) thief, so then it is you who opened to the one who came in, and you who closed behind the one that exited."' Relative

[421] The passage is much damaged.

[422] With non-periphrased participles: P. Chester Beatty IV, v° 3, 11-12; P. Orbiney, I, 3 (= *LES*, 9, 15-16); and probably P. Anastasi V, 26, 1 (= *LEM*, 71, 3-4). Except for the cleft sentence: P. Anastasi V, 9, 6-7 (= *LEM*, 60, 9-10). In any case, it is the sense that leads to see a non-periphrased imperfective participle, see Winand, *Morphology*, p. 360.

[423] See Groll, *RdE* 26 (1974), 172.

[424] 'That no great magistrate would accept taunts from anyone,' not that 'It is not a great magistrate the one who accepts taunts from anyone!' – which would be **bn sr ꜥꜣ **pꜣ** ỉ.ỉrỉ šsp qbꜥ n wꜥ nb sp-sn.*

[425] If in English one can say, ***a** duck is a bird*, it is because this is true of **all** ducks.

present expressing habitual activity.

43. P. Mayer A, 4, 10 (= *KRI* VI, 811, 14-15).

nby ỉw.f-n-mwt dbn 2 ỉw wn ntf ỉ.ỉrỉ wḏḥ n.n mtw.f pš m pš ꜥqꜣ ỉrm.n ꜥn

'The goldsmith Iuefenmut: 2 debens because it was he who smelted for us and shared in equal parts with us.' Note the presence of both the converters *ỉw* and *wn*.

Example with an intransitive verb:

44. P. Anastasi VI, 85-86 (= *LEM*, 78, 11).

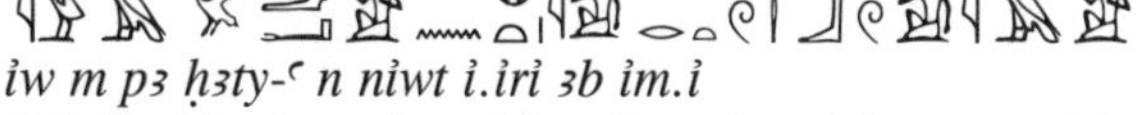

ỉw m pꜣ ḥꜣty-ꜥ n nỉwt ỉ.ỉrỉ ꜣb ỉm.ỉ

'While it is the major of the City who picks on me.' Habitual present.

42.2.1.5 Future (type I)

ỉw.ỉ r stp.(f) or stp.ỉ (se) ► ***ỉnk ỉ.ỉrỉ.ỉ stp.(f)***
ỉrỉ A r stp.(f) or stp A (se) ► ***m A ỉ.ỉrỉ.f stp.(f)***

The non-independent prospective appearing in the second member is often periphrased. Note that it is always the true cleft sentence (type I) that is employed to rhematise the subject of a future verbal sentence. Given that *ỉnk pꜣ nty ỉw.ỉ r stp.(f)* is apparently unattested, it is the old (and true) cleft sentence that expresses the modal future and the objective future.[426] There are many examples in the second person, where the construction serves to formulate a polite order.

45. P. BN 199, III, 6-7 (= *LRL*, 70, 14-15).

ntk ỉ.ptr pꜣ ỉꜣ//// ḥr ntk ỉ.ỉrỉ.k ꜥn smỉ n ṯꜣty ḥr.w

'It is you who has monitored the /////[427] and it is you who will report to the vizier about it.' Note the use of the two forms of the true cleft sentence (non-periphrastic participle first, then a prospective) to express first the past and then the future.

46. P. BM 10375, 26-27 (= *LRL*, 46, 11).[428]

ḥr ntk ỉ.ỉrỉ.k swḏ.w n pꜣy.k nb

'And it is you who will hand them over to your lord.'

---

[426] See Vernus, *Future*, p. 55-60; his conclusions extend also to Late Egyptian.
[427] The surviving determinative shows that the word in the lacuna referred to grain.
[428] Another example: Graffito 1396, 5: *ntk ỉ.ỉrỉ.k ḏbꜣ n.w ꜥn* 'It is you who will pay them too.'

47. P. Geneva D 407, v° 6 (= *LRL*, 15, 9).

ntk ỉ.ỉrỉ.k hȝb n.n ʿ.k
‘It is you who will send us your news.’

48. P. Bologna 1086, 6 (= *KRI* IV, 79, 8).

m pȝ-rʿ ptḥ ỉ.ỉrỉ.w nḏ-ḫrt.k
‘It is Pre and Ptah who will greet you.’

49. P. Turin 2021, 3, 11-12 (= *KRI* VI, 741, 10-11).[429]

[*nỉm ỉ*].*ỉrỉ.f wsf pȝ ỉrỉ.f*
‘[Who] will undo what he has done?’

Examples where the prospective is not periphrased:[430]

50. P. Anastasi I, 14, 1-2.
‘I am going to reveal you a decision of your master l.p.h.:

ntk pȝy.f sš nsw (*ỉ*)*.sb.k ẖry mnw wrw n ḥr nb tȝwy*
it is you, his royal scribe, who shall transport great monuments for Horus Lord of the Two Lands.’

51. Graffito of regnal year 50 of Ramses II, 4 (= *KRI* III, 437, 13-14).

ỉnn nȝ sšw n ptḥ pȝy.n ỉt ỉ.ḏd.n se n.f
‘It is us, the scribes of Ptah, our father, who will say it to him.’

42.2.2 The sentence is in the passive voice (type II)[431]

The second member of the pseudo-cleft sentence contains a **passive participle**. The construction is only attested in the **past** tense.

A stp or stp. Ø A ► ***A pȝ stpyt***

52. Mès, N 10 (= *KRI* III, 427, 4-5).

dnyt n ʿḏȝ tȝ ỉryt r.ỉ
‘It is a false register that has been fabricated against me!’

---

[429] Example where the interrogative pronoun was restored with a high probability.
[430] Other examples: Qadesh Poem, §330 (= *KRI* II, 97, 13), with *nỉm*, P. Anastasi V, 19, 2 (= *LEM*, 66, 9), with *ỉnk*.
[431] The term rhematised is now the patient of the process.

53. P. Anastasi IV, 7, 11 (= *LEM*, 42, 12-13): concerning a ship.

nhy n sꜥỉw n šnty nꜣ dyt n.f m ḥryt

'They are (only) acacia planks that he has put as gunwales.'

54. P. ESP, B, 13 (= *KRI* VI, 519, 2-3).

wꜥ dbn wꜥty n msdmt pꜣw gmyt ỉm.f

'It is one and only one deben of galena that was found therein.'

55. P. BM 10052, 3, 18 (= *KRI* VI, 774, 9-10).

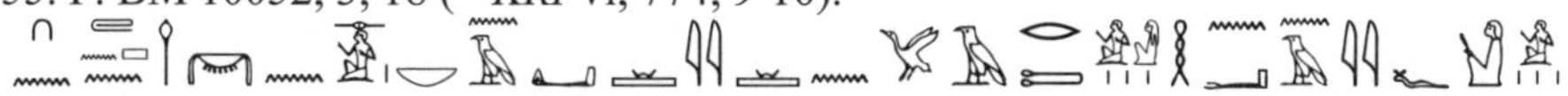

10 n dbn n ḥḏ n s nb nꜣ dy n pꜣ rmṯ ḥnꜥ nꜣy.f ỉryw

'These are 10 silver debens each that have been given to the man and his accomplices.'

Interrogative examples:

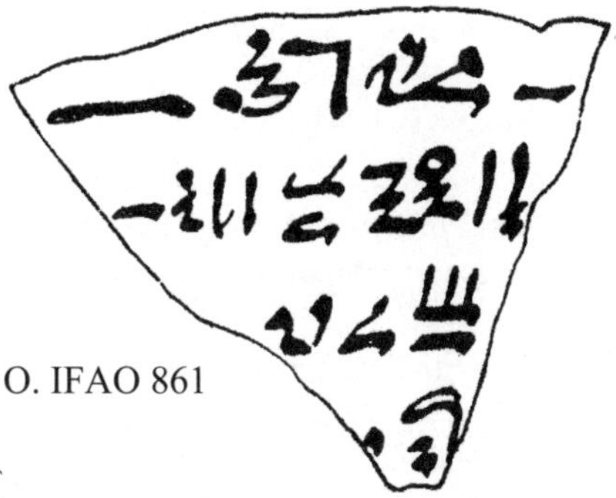

O. IFAO 861

56. P. Anastasi VIII, 1, 11-12 (= *KRI* III, 500, 14).

ỉḫ pꜣw ỉryt n.sn

'What has been done with it?'

57. O. IFAO 861 (= *BIFAO* 72 (1972), 53 and pl. XVII)

(ỉ)n pꜣ 5 dbn n ḥmt nꜣ dyt n p(ꜣ)-n-pꜣ-ḥꜥpy

'Are the five copper debens that have been given to Penpahapy?'

42.3 Rhematisation of the direct objet of the predicative plain sentence (type II)[432]

It is always the pseudo-cleft sentence that is employed for this purpose.

42.3.1 Past

The second member of the pseudo-cleft sentence contains a non-periphrased **relative form**, while the object, identical to the antecedent, is not resumed by a resumptive pronoun – in accordance with the rule studied above §28.1:

stp.ỉ (se) ▶ ***ntf pꜣ stp.ỉ***
stp.ỉ A ▶ ***A pꜣ stp.ỉ***

Example with pronominal object:

[432] The term rhematised here is also the patient of the process.

58. P. Mayer A, 2, 14 (= *KRI* VI, 807, 11).

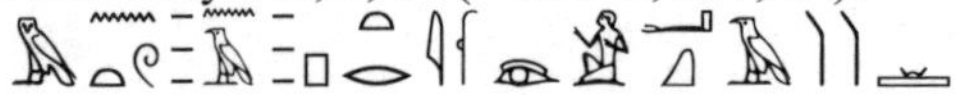

ntw nꜣ ptr.ỉ ꜥqꜣ
‘Those are exactly the ones that I saw.’

Examples with undefined object:

59. P. BM 10052, 5, 23 (= *KRI* VI, 781, 6).

wꜥ st wꜥty tꜣ wn.n
‘It is one and only one tomb that we opened.’

60. P. Turin 1880, v° 7, 7 (= *RAD*, 52, 2-3).

btꜣ ꜥꜣ pꜣw ỉ.ỉrỉ.f
‘It is a great crime that he has committed.’

61. P. Abbott, 6, 8-9 (= *KRI* VI, 478, 1-2) (fig. p. 238).

ḥr bn mdt šrỉt ỉwnꜣ tꜣy ỉ.ḏd pꜣy ḥꜣty-ꜥ n nỉwt
‘And this is not a small matter that this major of the City reported!’ (*lit.* ‘said’).

Examples with defined object:[433]

62 P. BM 10052, 5, 15-16 (= *KRI* VI, 780, 9-10).

pꜣ ḥḏ pꜣ ỉn.n r-bl
‘It is this silver that we brought out’ (*lit.* ‘brought outside’).

63 P. Mayer A, 2, 16 (= *KRI* VI, 807, 13).

pꜣy 3 rmṯ nꜣ ptr.ỉ ꜥqꜣ
‘It is exactly these three men that I saw.’

Circumstantial example:

64. P. Turin 1887, 1, 9 (= *RAD*, 75, 4-5).

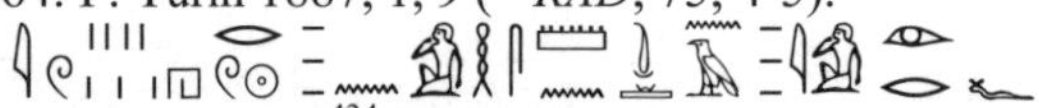

ỉw 7 hrw n swrỉ[434] *ḥsmn nꜣ ỉ.ỉrỉ.f*
‘While it is (only) seven days drinking natron that he had spent.’

[433] Another example: P. BM 10052, 5, 8-9 (= *KRI* VI, 779, 13) *pꜣ ptr.ỉ pꜣ ḏd.ỉ* ‘It is what I saw that I said.’
[434] The full spelling  is found in the lines following this.

42.3.2 Present

tw.ỉ ḥr stp.f ► ***ntf pꜣ nty tw.ỉ ḥr stp.f***
tw.ỉ ḥr stp A ► ***A pꜣ nty tw.ỉ ḥr stp.f***[435]

65. P. BN 198, I, 14 (= *LRL*, 66, 13).

ntk pꜣ nty ỉb.w r ptr.k
'It is you whom they wish to see.' Note the person agreement already pointed out in example 9 and 10 above.[436]

66. O. Gardiner 165, v° 4-5 (= *KRI* III, 549, 8-9).

tꜣ ʿꜣt wʿtỉ tꜣ nty tw.k ḥr w[ḫꜣ].s
'It is only the she-ass that you claim.'

Example with the interrogative particle *ỉḫ*:

67. O. DM 126, 3 (= *KRI* III, 532, 3-4).

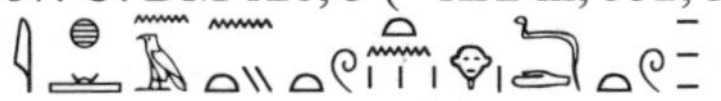

ỉḫ nꜣ nty tw.tn ḥr ḏd.tw.w
'What is it that you are going to relate?'

42.3.3 Future

ỉw.ỉ r stp.f ► ***ntf pꜣ nty ỉw.ỉ r stp.f***

68. P. Mayer A, 9, 15-16 (= *KRI* VI, 821, 8-9).

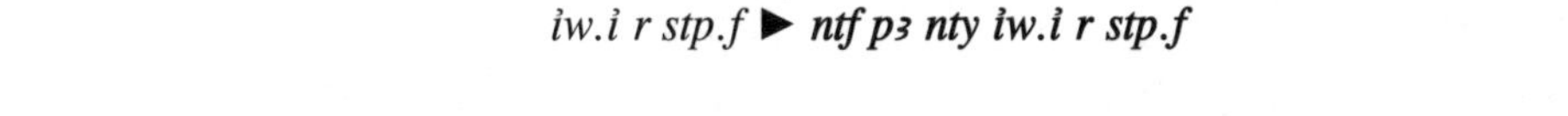

ỉr pꜣ pry nb m r(ꜣ).ỉ m tꜣ ḥꜣt ntf pꜣ nty ỉw.ỉ (r) ḏd.tw.f
'As for all that came out of my mouth from the beginning, that is what I will say (and nothing else).' In this example, the direct object of the verb (the patient of the process) is first thematised and then rhematised.

Example with the interrogative particle *ỉḫ*:

69. Horus and Seth, 16, 3 (= *LES*, 59, 15).

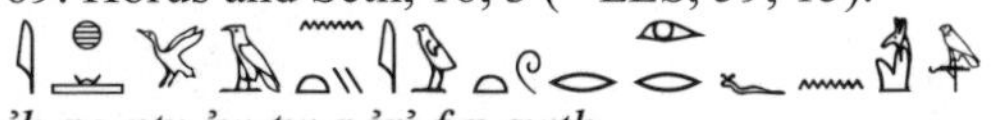

ỉḫ pꜣ nty ỉw.tw r ỉrỉ.f n swtḫ
'What will be done to Seth?'

---

[435] See p. 220, n. 464.
[436] Also P. Leiden I 369, 6 (= *LRL*, 1, 8-9), P. Griffith, 5-6 and 12 (= *LRL*, 12, 6-7 and 12), P. Turin 1974 + 1945 v° 4 (= *LRL*, 40 3), and P. Bologna 1094, 7, 5 (=*LEM*, 7, 4-5).

42.4 Rhematisation of the verb of the predicative plain sentence (type II)

The pseudo-cleft sentence also allows one to rhematise the verb itself in its nominal form, the **infinitive**.[437]

The latter, never defined and negated by *tm*, is found in the first member where it is always accompanied by a direct object and a dative, when they are present – which shows that the rhematisation does not affect the verb alone, but **the entire verbal sentence**.[438] It is periphrased in the second member by a defined relative clause always containing the auxiliary *ỉrỉ*. The resulting minimal sentence is:

stp pꜣ ỉ.ỉrỉ.f 'it is choosing what he did'
(*lit.* 'It is **an act of choosing** that he did.')

42.4.1 Past[439]

If the agent of the process is expressed, the second member of the pseudo-cleft sentence contains a relative form, or, otherwise, a passive participle.

70 P. Anastasi VIII, v° 4-5 (= *KRI* III, 504, 5-6).

ꜣtp.f m dḥꜣ [///]hb ꜥꜣ pꜣy ỉrỉ.k

'It is the loading of straw and large / / / / that you have done.'

Negative examples:

71 P. BN 197, VI, v° 4-5 (= *LRL*, 64, 14-15).

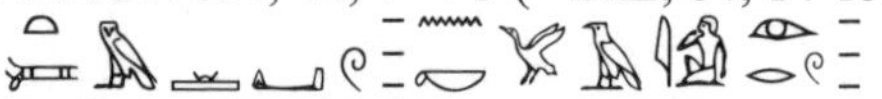

tm dỉt.w n.k pꜣ ỉ.ỉrỉ.w

'It is not giving them to you that they have done.'

72. P. Anastasi IV, 7, 10-11 (= *LEM*, 42, 12).

tm dỉt n.f ḥrỉt qꜣy pꜣ ỉryt

'It is not putting on it high gunwales what has been done.'

42.4.2 Imperfect

73. Wenamun, 2, 11-12 (= *LES*, 68, 6-7) .

nn(=ỉn) fꜣy mlk pꜣ wn.w (ḥr) ỉrỉ.f n pꜣy.ỉ ỉt[440]

'Was it offering royal gifts to my father what they did?'

---

[437] See Shisha-Halevy, *Or* 58 (1989), 33-35, and Quack, *RdE* 42 (1991), 201-206, for the examples and the origin of the construction. See also examples 6 and 7 above.

[438] Or **predicate construction**. See *Dictionnaire de linguistique*, ed. Larousse, p. 389 and 507.

[439] Other examples: P. BM 10052, 10, 8-9 (= *KRI* VI, 789, 9-10); P. Geneva D 407, v° 4 (= *LRL*, 15, 6-7) Tablets Mac Cullum and Rogers, 7; *KRI* III, 395, 10 (cited above, example 7); P. Anastasi IX, 7-8 cited incorrectly by Quack, *o.c.*, 202, after Satzinger, *o.c.*, 490, that is equally incorrect, and is to be dismissed – the relative form being undefined.

[440] Exceptionally, in this example the dative was left out after the second member.

42.4.3 Future

Example with nominal subject:[441]

74. P. Mayer A, 8, 5 (= *KRI* VI, 817, 14-15).

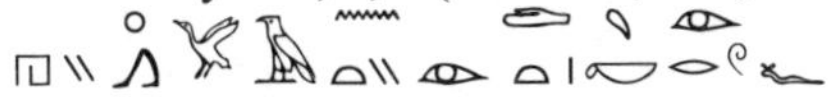

hꜣy pꜣ nty iri ḏrt.k (r) iri.f

'It is descend that your hand is going to do!'

Example with suffixal subject:

75. *URK* VI, 137, 8: ritual to repel the Aggressive.[442]

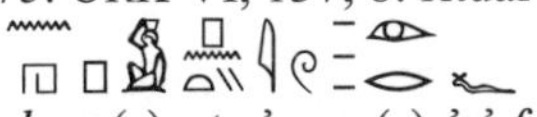

nhp p(ꜣ) nty iw.w (r) iri.f

'It is lamenting that they will have to do!'[443]

Example where the syntagma is found in an adverbial clause playing the role of a complement clause subject of *ḫpr*:[444]

76. Tablet Neskhons, 18-19 (= *JEA* 41 (1955), 102, 2).[445]

iw.i (r) dit ḫpr iw wḫꜣ n.f mdt nb(t) nfrt pꜣ nty iw.s (r) iri.f

'I will ensure that (*lit.* 'will cause to happen') it is claim for him all sorts of benefits (*lit.* 'all good things') what she will have to do!'

42.5 Special cases

Sometimes, it is possible to encounter constructions, apparently, having all the **syntactical** characteristics of a pseudo-cleft sentence: their first member contains an independent pronoun or a noun, and, the second, a defined, nominalised relative clause, where the preposition *m* (written *im*) is found, usually followed by a suffix,[446] resuming the pronoun or noun of the first member.

Is this a cleft sentence? Remember that the general definition of a Late Egyptian cleft sentence given above is a **functional** definition: a construction that allows for the rhematisation of a nominal element of a verbal sentence (in the broad sense, including the predication of location and existence). If the construction actually performs the function of rhematisation, it is a cleft sentence – or a pseudo-cleft sentence, as the case may be – otherwise it will be a nominal sentence.

The examples encountered are divided into two groups depending on whether the relative clause of the second member contains a verb or not, in other words, if it is or not strictly verbal.

---

[441] Found in a complement clause introduced by *r-ḏd*.

[442] On this text and its dating see Vernus, *RdE* 41 (1990), 206-207.

[443] Translation by Vernus, *o.c.*, 189 example 137.

[444] Example of an adverbial clause playing the role of a complement clause object of *ḫpr*: Doomed Prince 4, 5 (= *LES*, 1, 9).

[445] Another example: Tablet Neskhons, 18 (= *JEA* 41 (1955), 101, 24-102, 1).

[446] Sometimes implied, as may be the case with *im*.

42.5.1 The relative clause of the second member is strictly verbal

77. Horus and Seth, 9, 7 (= *LES*, 49, 10-11): Isis speaks to the iron of her harpoon.

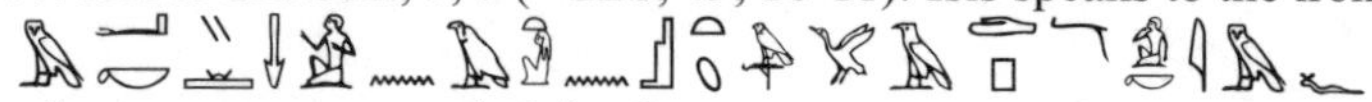

mk sn n mwt n ꜣst *pꜣ dp.k im.f*

'See, it is the maternal brother of Isis (= Seth), the one into which you bit' (*lit.* 'tasted').

This is a nominal sentence simply identifying the one that was harpooned. Take the corresponding verbal phrase: **dp.k m sn n mwt n ꜣst* – it can be seen that it would have been possible for the speaker to use a second tense to rank-shift to marked rheme the prepositional phrase containing the noun *sn n mwt n ꜣst*: **i.iri.k dp m sn n mwt n ꜣst* 'it is into the maternal brother of Isis (and into no-one else) that you have bitten.'

The same is true of the following example:

78. P. BM 10052, 5, 20 (= *KRI* VI, 781, 1-2).

iw wꜥ fꜣi šri n inr *pꜣ di.n n.w im.f iw bn pꜣ inr ꜥꜣ i.pš.n im.f iwnꜣ*

'But it was a small stone weight the one with which we measured their share (*lit.* 'given'),[447] it was not the big stone by means of which we shared.'

Nominal sentence indicating the inclusion of a given weight in the class of 'small stone weights.' Here again, the speaker had the opportunity to use a second tense: **iw i.iri.n dit nw n.w m wꜥ fꜣi šri n inr* … 'but it is with a small weight of stone that we have measured their share,' rhematising in this way also the adverbial phrase *m wꜥ fꜣi šri n inr*.

In addition, the second part of the sentence *iw bn pꜣ inr ꜥꜣ i.pš.n im.f iwnꜣ* is not a cleft sentence[448] – because the article does not appear before the relative form – but a nominal sentence of the type *bn B Ø iwnꜣ* preceded by the circumstantial *iw*, functioning as a relative clause qualifying the indefinite antecedent *wꜥ fꜣi šri n inr*.

42.5.2 The relative clause of the second member is non verbal

When the relative clause contains a location predication it works differently. If Middle Egyptian possessed the means to rhematise the adverbial phrase of such a predication, it was through the 'emphatic' converter *wnn*,[449] which is hardly ever used with this function in Late Egyptian.[450] It appears that the latter stage of the language no longer had the means to rhematise the adverbial element of a location predication.[451] Thus, it can be assumed that the pseudo-cleft sentence, through the rhematisation of the substantive in the adverbial phrase, would be a way to make up

---

447 Translation of a two-member nominal sentence referring to the inclusion into a class. It was preferred to 'But it is a small stone weight with which we measured their share,' which is a nominal sentence of the type B Ø expressing identity (**iw wꜥ fꜣy šri n inr iw di.n n.w im.f*).

448 For a different analysis see Satzinger, *o.l.*, example 22, p. 490.

449 See Vernus, *Future*, p. 45-51; *LingAeg* 1 (1991), 340.

450 Very rare examples: P. Anastasi I, 10, 2; P. Sallier I, 7, 1 (2 times) and 7, 8 – where *wnn* clearly serves as 'peg' providing an additional accentual unit to a text drafted in 'heptametrical couplets' (see Mathieu, *RdE* 39 (1988), 63-82).

451 For an exceptional case using the auxiliary *iri*, see Winand, *Morphologie*, p. 286-287.

for this.

In other words, if one cannot say '*it is in the house that I am*,' one will say '*it is the house, the place in which I am*.'

79. P. Turin A, v° 4, 10 (= *CLEM*, 510).

mwt[452] *pꜣ nty tw.i im.f m-di.k*

'It is Death in which I find (myself) (*lit*. 'I am') because of you.'

80. Wenamun, 2, 23 (= *LES*, 69, 5-6).

ꜥḏꜣ bn mšꜥ swgꜣ *iwnꜣ n(ꜣ) nty tw.i im.w*

'It is false! These are not foolish expeditions that I undertake! (*lit*. 'in which I am').'

81. P. BM 10052, 8, 5 (= *KRI* VI, 785, 16),

'He said: "Leave me be about the big tombs,[453] if I have to be executed because of the tombs of Imiotru,

ntw *nꜣ wn.i im*

(because) they are the ones (and not the first) in which I was!"' The rhematisation here appears very probable: the thief requests not to be questioned, and therefore not tortured, about the tombs of the Theban necropolis, because he has already been sentenced to death for theft in the tombs of Gebelein – the only ones where he has entered.

Finally, the relative clause may contain an existential predication. The pseudo-cleft sentence seems to be the only possible mode of rhematisation. In the following example the person agreement confirms it:

82. Cairo Stela, JE 48876, 26 (= *KRI* VI, 20, 4): hymn to Osiris.

ntk *pꜣ nty wn pḥty* ***im.k***

'It is you (and nobody else) who has strength[454] (*lit*. 'that there exists strength in you').'

42.6 Conclusion

In Late Egyptian the general term **cleft sentence** – designating constructions that allow for the rhematisation of a substantival term after a predicative plain verbal sentence – covers two different syntactic realities in complementary distribution: the true cleft sentence, successor of the classic cleft sentence, and the pseudo-cleft sentence, of recent formation, that remained close to the nominal sentence from which it derived.

Let us add some **syntactic** criteria learnt from this chapter, which, in some cases, allow one to distinguish between nominal and cleft sentences:

---

[452] Masculine word in Egyptian (Lefebvre, *Grammaire*, §115, b).

[453] *Lit*. 'Away from me, away from my body the great tombs.'

[454] The same sentence, non-rhematised, is also attested: *m-ḏd wn pḥty ꜥꜣ im.k* 'Saying: "you have great strength,"' P. Orbiney, 3, 5 (= *LES*, 12, 8).

a. A sentence whose second member contains a **nominalised, defined**[455] relative clause, formed with the **active participle**, or the non-independent **prospective** (periphrased or not) of a **transitive** or **intransitive** verb, is a **nominal sentence** – because the speaker, in this case, had the choice of using a true cleft sentence:

– *ntk pꜣ i҆.i҆ri҆ sẖr n pꜣ i҆wty mwt.f* 'You are / It is you the one who gives guidance to one who has no mother' (see above, example 2);

– *ḥn i҆ṯꜣy i҆w ny-sw pꜣy.i҆ tꜣ pꜣ hꜣy r tꜣy.k br mtw.f ṯꜣy pꜣy.k ḥḏ wn i҆w.i҆ (r) ḏbꜣ.f n.k m pꜣy.i҆ wḏꜣ* 'If it were a thief belonging to my country the one who went down into your ship and stole your silver, I would have reimbursed it to you from my treasury' (see above, example 29).

b. A sentence whose second member contains a **nominalised, defined** relative clause, formed with a **passive** participle, a **relative form,** ***nty*** **+ third future,** ***nty*** **+ first present**, or ***(i҆).wn*** **+ first present**, and **does not agree** (in gender, number, or person) with the first member, is a nominal sentence:

– *i҆nk pꜣ gm.tn r sꜥḥꜥ.f m tꜣ št r-ḏr.s* 'It is **me** / **I** am the one whom you have found in order to penalise **him** among all taxpayers!' (see above, example 11);

– *13 n rmw pꜣ i҆ny n.n* 'It is thirteen fish, **which** have been delivered to us' (see above, example 13).

c. A sentence whose second member contains a relative clause constructed with the same grammatical forms as in **b**, but is **undefined,**[456] is a **nominal sentence** where the relative clause plays the role of **attribute**. This noun phrase can also function as a one-member nominal sentence (*B Ø*):

– *bn pꜣ i҆nr ꜥꜣ i҆.pš.n i҆m.f i҆wnꜣ* 'It is not the big stone by means of which we shared' (see above, example 78): negative nominal sentence.

d. A sentence whose first member is **undefined**, and the second member is an **adverbial clause**, is not a cleft sentence, but a **one-member nominal sentence (*B Ø*)**, in which the adverbial clause functions as relative attribute of the undefined antecedent A:[457]

– *80 n rnpt r tꜣy i҆w.n m tꜣ qnbt* 'It is eighty years (*lit.* 'It is eighty years until this) that we are in the court,' Horus and Seth, 13, 12 (= *LES*, 55, 13-14).[458]

---

[455] By an article, a demonstrative, a possessive, etc.

[456] By an article, a demonstrative, a possessive, etc.

[457] Contrary to the interpretation of Černý-Groll, *LEG* (2nd ed.), p. 536 bottom ('Ø A + a virtual relative clause.' Note that the numbering of the paragraph is incorrect).

[458] Other examples: Horus and Seth, 14, 1 (= *LES*, 55, 15); P. BN 198, I, 15 (= *LRL*, 66, 13-14); O. IFAO 694 (= *BIFAO* 41 (1941), p. 18). These last two examples are cited as cleft sentences by Černý-Groll, *o.c.*, example 804 and 1586.

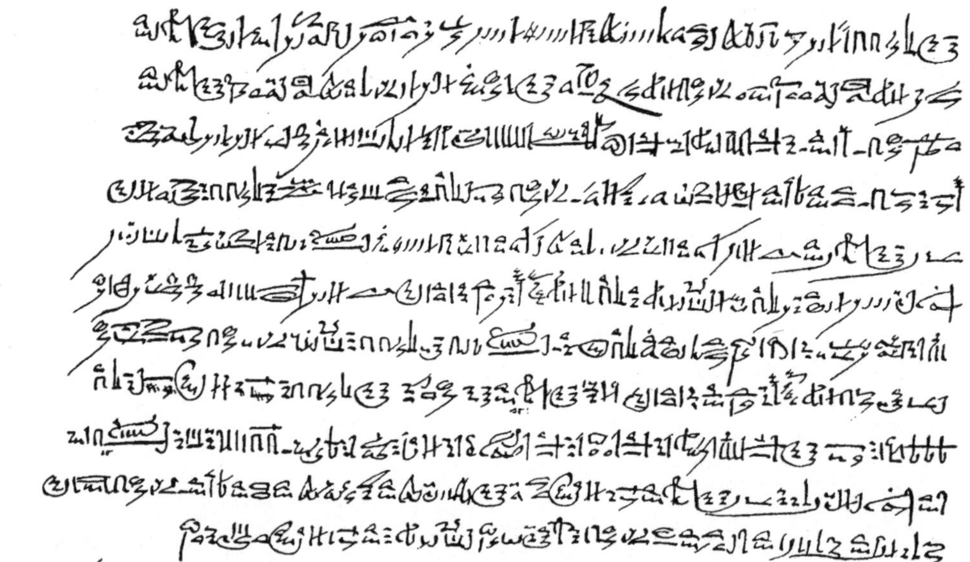

P. Abbott, 5 (*cf.* p. 55, 77, 139)

APPENDIX ONE

INTERROGATIVE SYNTAGMAS

43. Appendix one: interrogative syntagmas

43.1 Introduction

In Late Egyptian an interrogative syntagma generally includes a specific morpheme, which can be a particle, a pronoun or an adverb. However, besides the clearly identified constructions, it is possible to encounter sentences devoid of interrogative morphemes, thus it is only from the context that they can be interpreted as questions. These statements must have been uttered with a particular intonation.

43.2 Syntagmas introduced by an interrogative particle

A declarative sentence (affirmative or negative) becomes interrogative when preceded by one of the interrogative particles *ỉn*, *ỉs*(*t*), *ỉs bn*.

43.2.1 Syntagmas introduced by *ỉn*

Interrogative particle *par excellence*, *ỉn* can be placed before most independent forms, verbal or nominal. Questions thus obtained are true questions, likely to receive either an affirmative or a negative response.

The spellings, sometimes confusing, are the following:

 (frequent),  (quite rare),  (rare[459]),  (found exceptionally).

43.2.1.1 *ỉn* + *sḏm.f*

Without knowing the context, it is not always possible to choose between a *sḏm.f* perfective, referring to a past event, or a prospective *sḏm.f* expressing the modal future:

1. O. Clère (= *BIFAO* 72 (1972), 50 and pl. XV).

***ỉn** hꜣb.‹ỉ› ḥr.w n(=m) mꜣʿt*

– 'Have I really written about them?' (*lit.* 'Have I written about them, in truth?'): Perfective;
– 'Must I really write about them?' Prospective.

2. O. Brussels E 317 (= *BIFAO* 72 (1972), 52 and pl. XVI).

***ỉn** ỉṯꜣ se nꜣ rmṯ (n) pꜣ mšʿ*

– 'Have the people of the army stolen (or 'taken') it?:' perfective – people of the army are suspected of having stolen an object or carried away someone;
– 'Will the people of the army want to take it?' Prospective.

[459] But regularly so in Wenamun.

43.2.1.1.1 *ỉn* + perfective *sḏm.f*

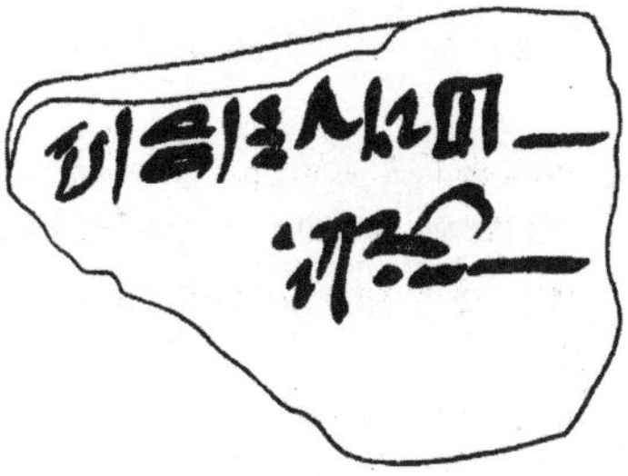

O. Clère

3. P. Turin 2026, v° 2 (= *LRL*, 73, 7).

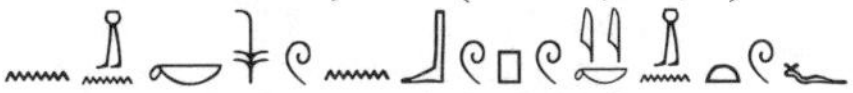

***ỉn** ỉn.k se **ỉn** bwpwy.k ỉn.*[*tw.f*]

'Have you gone to search for him, or have you not gone to search for him?'[460]

4. P. BM 10326, 8-9 (= *LRL*, 17, 14-15): concerning letters.

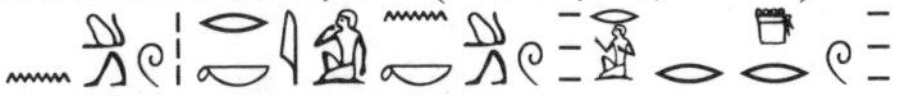

***ỉn** pḥ.w r.k ỉ.n.k pḥ.w r.ỉ r-ḏr.w*

'"Have they reached you?" you asked – "(Yes) they have reached me in (their) entirety."'

43.2.1.1.2 *ỉn* + prospective *sḏm.f*

5. O. IFAO 557 (= *BIFAO* 35 (1935), 46 and pl. II) (fig. p. 236).

***ỉn** ỉw.‹ỉ› n-bl*

'Do I have to go out?'[461]

O. IFAO 848

6. O. IFAO 848 (= *BIFA0* 41 (1941), 14 and pl. I).

***ỉn** tm.ỉ ỉn.tw.w*

'Need I not buy them?'

7. O. IFAO 851 (= *BIFAO* 72 (1972), 57 and pl. XIX).

***ỉn** tm.ỉ šm r pꜣ nty sw ỉm*

'Need I not go to the place where he is?'

In the last two examples, where it is the verb itself that is negated, the negative verb *tm* is used. If one simply wishes to ask an interro-negative question (which is equivalent to an assertion), the negative morpheme *bn* is used instead:

8. O. DM 575 (fig. p. 149).

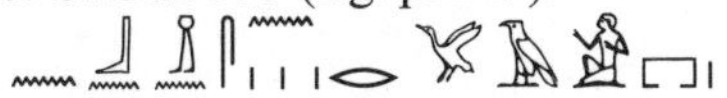

***ỉn** bn ỉn.‹ỉ› se r pꜣ(y).ỉ pr*

'Will I not bring them back to my house?'

[460] Another possible translation: 'Did you buy it or did you not buy it?'

[461] It is probably a prospective because the verb *ỉy / ỉw* is intransitive and does not have a perfective *sḏm.f*.

43.2.1.2 *ỉn* + *bwpwy.f sḏm*

9. P. BM 10052, 4, 2 (= *KRI* VI, 775, 13-14); see also example 3.

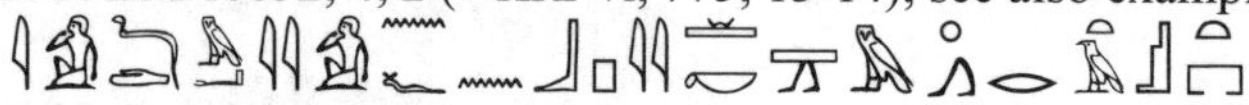

ỉ.ḏd my n.f ***ỉn*** *b(w)p(w)y.k šm r tꜣ st*

'Tell him (= me), please: did you not go to the tomb?'

43.2.1.3 *ỉn* + Third Future

10. O. IFAO 849 (= *BIFAO* 41 (1941), 15 and pl. I).

ỉn *ỉw.f r dỉt n.n ḥry m tꜣ wnwt*

'Will we give him a superior now?'

11. O. IFAO 691 (= *BIFAO* 41 (1941), 17 and pl. II).

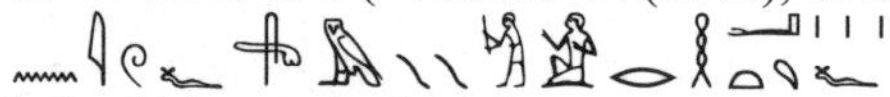

ỉn *ỉw.f (r) smtr.ỉ r-ḥꜥw.f*

'Will he interrogate me himself?'

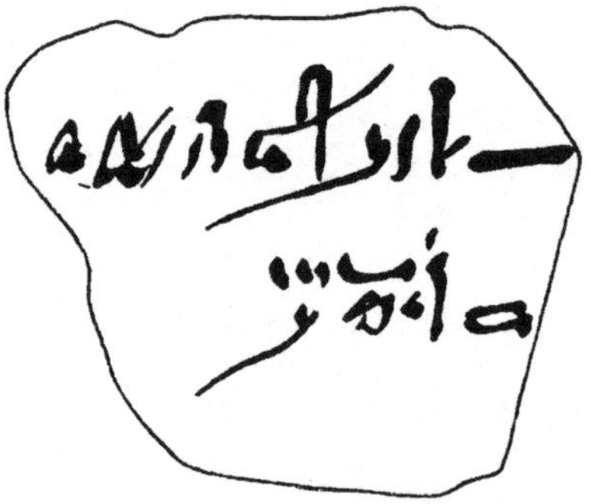

O. IFAO 691

12. O. IFAO 599 (= *BIFAO* 35 (1935), 46 and pl. II) (fig. p. 236).

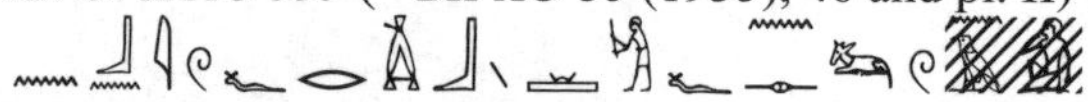

ỉn *bn ỉw.f r ḏbꜣ.f n.s ỉw[nꜣ]*

'Will he not pay it (to her)?'

13. O. IFAO 693 (= *BIFAO* 41 (1941), 17 and pl. II).

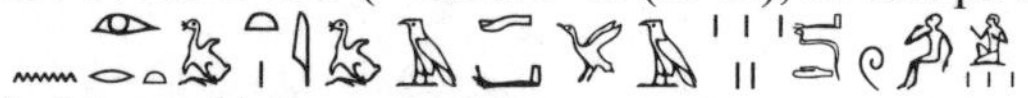

ỉn *ỉrỉ ṯꜣty (r) ỉṯꜣ pꜣ 5 ꜥḏd*

'Will the vizier take the five boys?'[462]

43.2.1.4 *ỉn* + First Present

14. O. IFAO 864 (= *BIFAO* 72 (1972), 54 and pl. XVII).

ỉn *st dy m sḫt ꜥꜣt r-ḥꜥw.s(?)*

'Are they here in the Great Field[463] itself?'

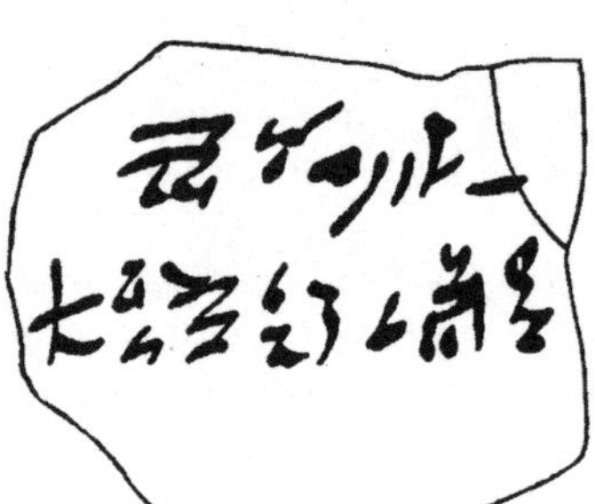

O. IFAO 849

15. P. Cairo 58056, 8 (= *KRI* III, 255, 9-10).

ḥr ***ỉn*** *bn ỉb.k r dỉt pꜣ kr*

'And do you not wish to send[464] the boat?'

[462] Either to use them as workers in the Tomb, or to send them to the army.

[463] The Valley of the Kings.

[464] *Cf.* Wente, *LRL*, p. 54, n. i.

16. P. BM 10375, 26 (= *LRL*, 46, 10).

***ỉn** bn tw.k m nꜥy ỉrm nꜣ ḥbsw*

'Are you not journeying with the clothes?'

17. P. Leiden I 365, v° 3-4 (= *KRI* III, 233, 7-8).

*ỉḫ pꜣy.tn tm ḫsf {f} n.ỉ tꜣy.ỉ šꜥt **ỉn** tw.tn wḏꜣ*

'What does it mean that you have not responded to my letter?[465] Are you well?'

43.2.1.5 *ỉn* + *bw ỉrỉ.f sḏm* (negative aorist)

18. Wenamun, 2, 66-67 (= *LES*, 74, 1-2).

*ḫr **ỉn** bw ỉrỉ.k ptr nꜣ ỉw r ḏdḥ.ỉ ꜥn*

'And can you not see those who have come again to arrest me?'

43.2.1.6 *ỉn* + Second Tense

19. Wenamun, 1, 44-45 (= *LES*, 65, 13).

***ỉn** ỉ.ỉrỉ.k ḏd smn tw m pꜣ grḥ r dỉt wḏ tꜣ br ỉ.gm.ỉ*

'Do you say "Rest (then) tonight" for the sole purpose of letting the boat that I found depart?' Periphrastic second tense.

20. O. Gardiner (= *BIFAO* 72 (1972), 51 and pl. XVI).

***ỉn** ỉrỉ.ỉ tꜣ mdt m sš dỉ.ỉ se n ṯꜣty*

'Is it in writing that I have to put the matter to submit it to the vizier?' Modal second tense.

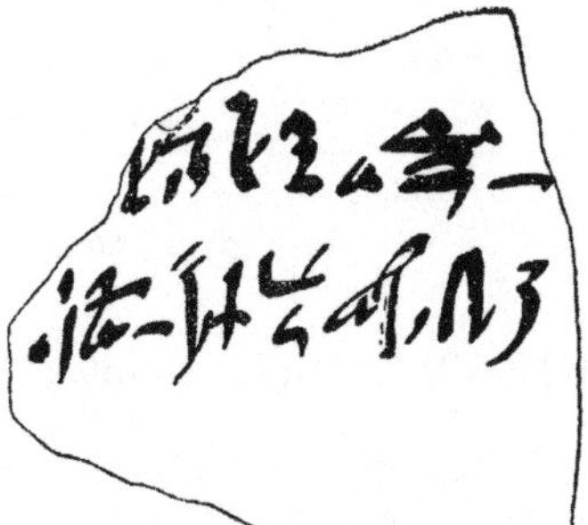

O. Gardiner

21. O. IFAO 1007 (= *BIFAO* 72 (1972), 59 and pl. XX).

***ỉn** ỉ.ỉrỉ.f r tꜣy*

'Is it against that one that he will want to act?' Modal second tense.

43.2.1.7 *ỉn* + existential predication

22. O. IFAO 884 (= *BIFAO* 72 (1972), 56 and pl. XVIII).

*ỉr nꜣ ỉḥw nty tꜣ rmṯ ḥr w[ḫꜣ.w] **ỉn** wn m-dỉ.s pš ỉ[m].w*

'As for the oxen that the woman claims, does she have a share in them?

[465] *Lit.* 'It is what your not having sent me back my letter?'

23. O. IFAO 862 (= *BIFAO* 72 (1972), 54 and pl. XVII).

ỉn *mn m-dỉ.s ỉm.w*

'Has she not got them?'

43.2.1.8 *ỉn* + nominal sentence with substantival predicate

24. O. IFAO 999 (= *BIFAO* 72 (1972), 57 and pl. XVIII).

ỉn *rmṯ ḏrḏrỉ*

'Is it a stranger?'

25. O. IFAO 857 (= *BIFAO* 72 (1972), 57 and pl. XIX).

ỉn *bꜣw n ꜣnynḫt*

'Is it a manifestation[466] of Anynakht?'

26. P. BN 198, II, 10-11 (= *LRL,* 67, 16-68, 1).

ỉn *pꜣ ꜥmꜣ ỉ.ỉrỉ.k pꜣy m tꜣy 20 n rnpt ỉ.ỉrỉ.ỉ m pꜣy.k pr*

'Is this the discovery that you have made during these twenty years that I have spent in your house?'

43.2.1.9 *ỉn* + nominal sentence with adjectival predicate

27. O. IFAO 682 (= *BIFAO* 41 (1941), 15 and pl. I).

ỉn *nfr pꜣ bḥs šsp.‹ỉ› sw*

'The calf, is it good for me to accept it?'

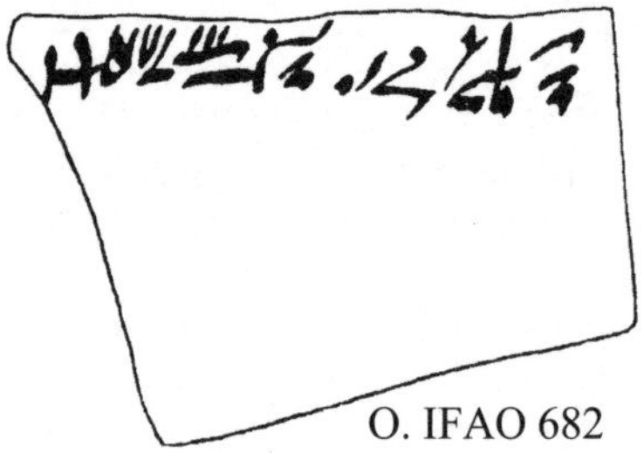

O. IFAO 682

43.2.1.10 *ỉn* + cleft sentence

28. O. IFAO 501 (= *BIFAO* 35 (1935), 43 and pl. I)

ỉn *ntf (ỉ).ỉṯꜣ pꜣy tmꜣ*

'Is it him who stole this mat?'

29. O. IFAO 870 (= *BIFAO* 72 (1972), 55 and pl. XVII).

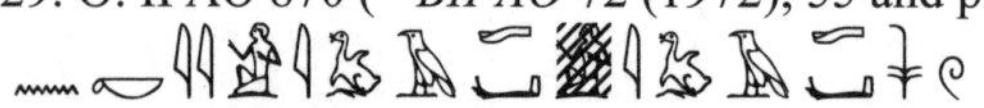

ỉn *ky ỉṯꜣ (ỉ).ỉṯꜣ sw*

'Is it another thief who stole it?'

[466] Or 'anger.'

43.2.1.11 Special case

The particle *ỉn* can also be found before the morpheme *m-bỉꜣ* 'not.' The resulting expression serves to strengthen an interrogative construction: (*ỉn*) X *ỉn m-bỉꜣ*.

30. Mès, N 11 (= *KRI* III, 427, 7-8).

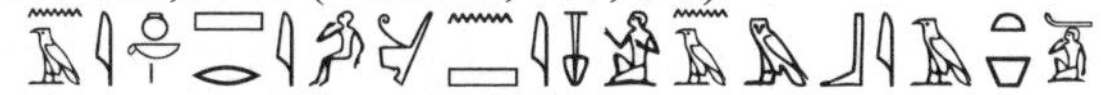

ỉn** ỉnk šrỉ n nšỉ **ỉn m-bỉꜣ

'Am I son of Neshi or not?'

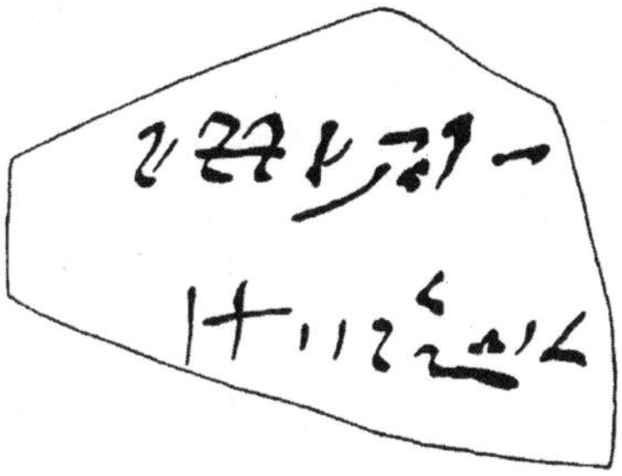

O. IFAO 501

31. O. DM 608, v° 1.

ỉn** ỉn.f n.k pꜣ gs n ꜥqw **ỉn m-bỉꜣ

'Has he brought you the half loaf or not?'

43.2.1.12 Remarks

In Late Egyptian the composite particle *ỉn-ỉw*, specific to Middle Egyptian, is only very rarely found:[467]

32. O. Nash 2, 5-8 (= *KRI* IV, 318, 3-6): 19th dynasty.[468]

ỉr nꜣ ḫl n pr-ꜥꜣ ꜥ.w.s. r(=ỉ).ḏd.k[469] *ṯꜣy se ḥwy m tꜣ st pr-ꜥꜣ ꜥ.w.s. **ỉn-ỉw** [wn m]-dỉ.k mtryw r.f **ỉn m-bỉꜣ** ḏdt.n nb-nfr wn m-dỉ.ỉ mtryw*

'As for the picks of Pharaoh l.p.h. of which you said Huy had stolen from the tomb of Pharaoh l.p.h., do you have any witnesses against him or not? – What Nebnefer replied: "(Yes) I have witnesses."' The absence of *ỉw* in the reply shows that this is the composite particle *ỉn-ỉw*.

33. P. Northumberland I, 2-3 (= *KRI* I, 239, 4-5): Seti I.

***ỉn-ỉw**.k m šs*

'Are you well?'

43.2.2 Syntagmas introduced by *ỉst*

This particle: , , or , and its variants , are used to ask questions, most often rhetorical, in a formal style.[470]

43.2.2.1 *ỉst* + *bw ỉrỉ.s sḏm* (negative aorist)

The particle *ỉst* is very frequently used with the negative aorist, and it is found in all textual genres.

---

[467] See Vernus *CdE* 57 (1982), 247. Example in literary idiom: Astarte, 2, x + 19 (= *LES*, 79, 6).

[468] Another example: *id.*, v° 3: *ỉn-ỉw swt Ø m-ḥꜥw.f* 'Does this belong to him alone?'

[469] For the spelling, see the table of the suffix pronouns §7.1.1.

[470] In literary texts it also retains its 'classical' role, the specification of an event in a narrative context (see Korostovtsev, *Grammaire*, p. 153).

34. P. BM 10375, 23 (= *LRL*, 46, 4-5): letter to a superior.

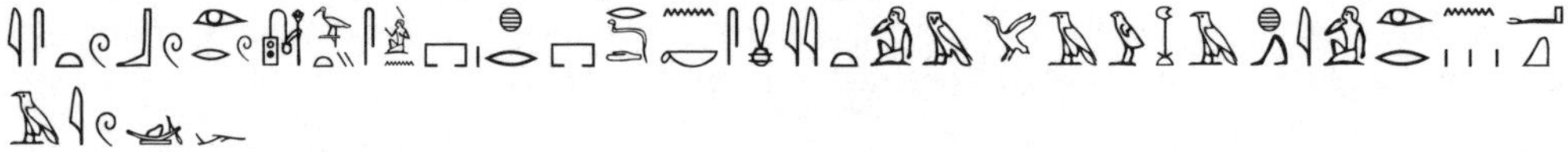

ỉst *bw ỉrỉ sš ḏḥwty-ms n pꜣ ḫr {r} ḏd n.k smỉ m pꜣ wḫꜣ i.ỉrỉ.n ꜥqꜣ*

'The Scribe of the Tomb Djehutymose, could he not report to you on account of the search for the barge that we made?'

35. P. Bologna 1094, 10, 1-2 (= *LEM*, 9, 8-10): school text, model letter.

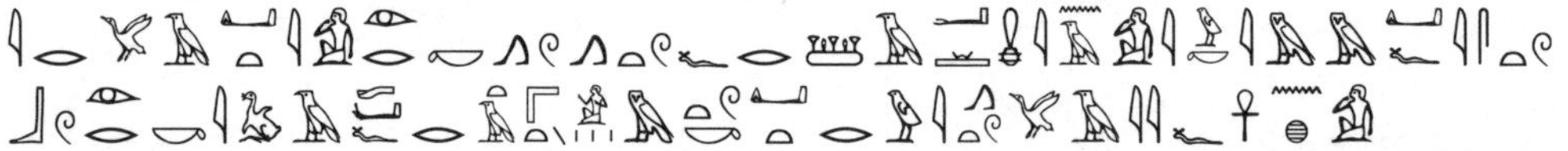

ỉr pꜣ dỉt i.ỉrỉ.k ỉwt.f r-šꜣꜥ-(r) mỉnꜣ ỉw.k ỉm m-dỉ.f ***ỉst*** *bw ỉrỉ.k ỉṯꜣ.f r tꜣ qnbt mtw.k dỉt rwỉꜣ.tw pꜣy.f ꜥnḫ*

'As for causing him to come[471] here, while you were there with him, could you not take him to the court and have his oath annulled?'

43.2.2.2 *ỉst* + First Present

36 O. DM 552, verso.

ḫr ỉr pꜣy.k ḏd sw ṯꜣy m br ***ỉs*** *sw ḥr rn.ỉ* ***ỉs*** *[sw]*[472] *bn sw ḥr rn.ỉ*

'And as for what you said: "It was stolen from a barge" – Is it in my name? Or is it not in my name?'[473]

43.2.2.3 *ỉst* + Second Tense

37. P. Turin 1880, 2, 20 (= *RAD*, 56, 1-2).

ỉst *i.ỉrỉ.ỉ tm ỉy n.tn m nkt*

'Is it for a trivial[474] reason that I did not come to you?'

38. Horus and Seth, 8, 5-6 (= *LES*, 47,14-15).

i.ỉrỉ.k qnd ḥr ỉḫ ***ỉst*** *bn i.ỉrỉ.tw m pꜣw ḏd tm nb tꜣwy ỉwnw ḥnꜥ pꜣ-rꜥ-ḥr-ꜣḫty*

'Why do you make yourself angry? Is it not in accordance with what Atum of Heliopolis, Lord of the Two Lands, and Pre-Horakhty have said that one must act?'

[471] *Lit.* 'As for the fact that you have caused that he come.'

[472] Unless 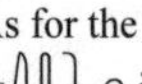 is a grapheme of *ỉs*.

[473] That is to say 'Is it or not under my responsibility?'

[474] *Lit.* 'Small thing, a trifle.'

43.2.2.4 *ỉst* + nominal sentence with substantival predicate

39. P. Turin 1880, 3, 2 (= *RAD*, 56, 4).

ỉs *ỉnk pꜣ ṯꜣty ddy r nḥm*

'Would I be the vizier who has (only) been appointed to take?'[475]

43.2.2.5 *ỉst* + nominal sentence with adjectival predicate

40. O. DM 554, 5 (fig. p. 87).

ỉs *nfr ỉw.ỉ ḥr ḏd n.f*

'Is it good that I talk to him?'

43.2.3 Syntagmas introduced by *ỉs-bn*

The existence of this composite particle[476] is certain, since it only occurs before sentences which negation does not employ the negative morpheme *bn*.[477]

43.2.3.1 Possible examples

41. P. Anastasi IV, 11, 3-4 (= *LEM*, 46, 13-14).

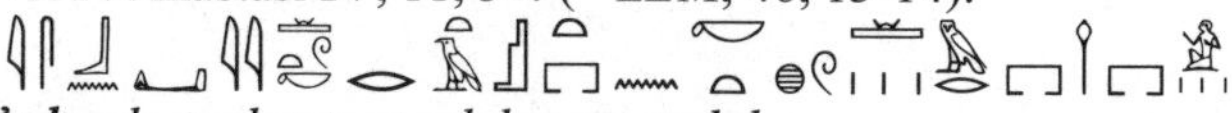

ỉs bn *dy.tw.k r tꜣ st n ktḫw mr pr-ḥḏ*

'Are you not going to be appointed in place of other overseers of the treasury?' One could hesitate here between *ỉs-bn* + prospective or *ỉs* + negative prospective.

42. O. DM 357, a, 3.[478]

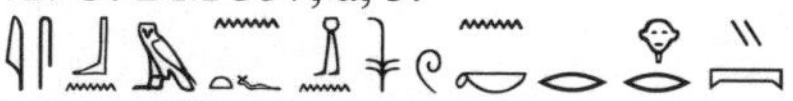

ỉs bn *ntf (ỉ).ỉn sw n.k r ḥry*

'Is it not him who brought it to you up there?' Again this can be *ỉs-bn* + cleft sentence or *ỉs* + negative cleft sentence.

43.2.3.2 Probable examples

43. O. Leipzig 16, v° 2-3 (= *HO*, XXXIII, 2).[479]

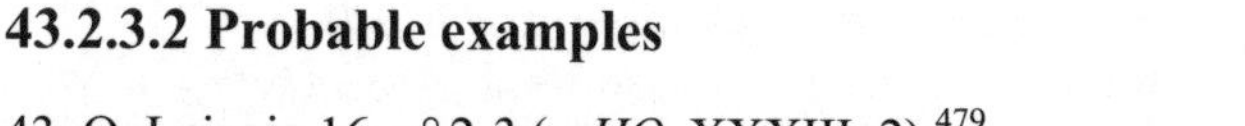

ỉs-bn *tw.ỉ rḫ.kwỉ pꜣ nty tꜣ ỉḥ(t) ỉm*

'Do I not know the place where the cow is?' The ordinary negative correlate of *tw.ỉ rḫ.kwỉ* is *bw rḫ.ỉ*,[480] therefore, it is very likely that this is the composite particle *ỉs-bn*.

---

[475] See Vernus, *RdE* 32 (1980) 122 -123, (d), who understands: 'who only gives to take back.'

[476] Not to be confused with *ỉs*(*t*) + *bn*.

[477] See Černý-Groll, *LEG*, §9.12, p. 151.

[478] Parallel example: P. Anastasi V, 14, 1-2 (= *LEM*, 63, 8-9).

[479] Parallel example: P. Anastasi V, 26, 4-5 (= *LEM*, 71, 7-8).

[480] See Černý-Groll, *LEG*, §20.5.4-10, p. 311-313, and Satzinger, *NÄS*, p. 188. Exceptions in P. Leiden I 371, 26 and 37.

44. Pentawer Poem, 95 (= *KRI* II, 35, 1-5).

is-bn *šm.n.ỉ ꜥḥꜥ.n.ỉ ḥr r(ꜣ).k*

'Is it not at your voice that I went where I stopped[481]?' Given that *bn* is hardly ever used before an emphatic *sḏm.n.f*,[482] it is highly probable that the one used here is the composite particle.

43.2.3.3 Examples certain

45. P. Anastasi V, 11, 4-5 (= *LEM*, 61, 12-13).

is-bn *wn m-dỉ.k sšw qnw ḫr wn m-dỉ.k šmsw qnw sp-sn*

'Have you not numerous scribes and have you not numerous servants?' Given that the negation of *wn m-dỉ.k* is *mn m-dỉ.k* and that *ỉs-bn* is not repeated after *ḫr* (factorisation), it is certain that the one used here is the composite particle.

46. Pentawer Poem, 98 (= *KRI* II, 36, 1-4).

is-bn *ỉry.ỉ n.k mnw ꜥšꜣw wrt*

'Have I not made for you countless monuments?' Before a perfective *sḏm.f*, which is negated with *bwpwy*, there is no doubt that the one used here is the composite particle.

47. P. Anastasi V, 26, 3-4 (= *LEM*, 71, 6-7).

is-bn *ḏd.‹ỉ› n.tn ḫsf n.tn pꜣ ỉmỉ-rn.f ḥr-ꜥ mtw.tn ỉṯꜣ.f*

'Did I not say to you: "Check the list immediately and take it?"'

48. P. Orbiney, 7, 5-6 (= *LES*, 16, 12-13).

is-bn *ỉr m-ḏr {wỉ} hꜣb.k‹wỉ› r ỉn n.n prt ỉw tꜣy.k ḥmt ḥr ḏd n.ỉ my ỉrỉ.n wnwt sḏr.n*

'Is it not (true) that, after having[483] (*lit.* 'that you had me') sent us to fetch some seeds, your wife said to me: "Come, let us spend an hour in bed"?'[484] In this example, the nuance conveyed by the composite particle *ỉs-bn* affects all of the following correlative system.

43.3 Syntagmas incorporating an interrogative pronoun

The interrogative pronouns (*ỉḫ*, *nỉm*, *ỉṯ*) can, in any sentence, play any of the roles of a noun. Thus they always occupy the place reserved to the noun which function they fulfill.

---

[481] That is to say: 'I have always followed your orders.'

[482] No examples given in Winand, *Morphologie*, p. 261.

[483] The reading *m-ḏr wỉ hꜣb.k(wỉ)* 'after I had been sent' would be possible, but if the prospective is attested after *m-ḏr*, the first present does not appear to be.

[484] *Lit.* ''being stretched out,' pseudo-participle in the first person plural.

43.3.1 Syntagmas with *ỉḫ*

This pronoun, meaning 'what,' is used especially for objects and animals. It originates from *ỉḫt* 'thing.'[485]

43.3.1.1 Nominal sentences

ỉḫ is very frequently found in nominal sentences, where it plays the role of predicate.

49. Qadesh Bulletin, 35 (= *KRI* II, 110, 3).

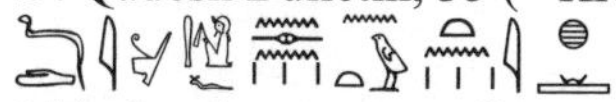

ḏd.ỉn ḥm.f n.sn ntwtn ***ỉḫ***

'His Majesty said to them: "What are you?"'[486]

In texts dating from the nineteenth dynasty one can still find examples with *pw*:

50. O. DM 321, 1.[487]

ỉḫ *pw pꜣ sḫr bỉn nty tw.k ỉm.f*

'What is this bad condition in which you wallow?' (*lit.* 'It is what this bad condition in which you are?').

However, as a general rule, *pw* is no longer found in this type of nominal sentence:

51. P. BM 10052, v° 9, 2-3 (= *KRI* VI, 788, 5-6).[488]

ḏd n.f ṯꜣty ***ỉḫ*** *pꜣ sḫr (n) šm ỉ.ỉrỉ.k r pḥ nꜣ swt ꜥꜣywt*

'The vizier said to him: "How did you get to reach the great tombs?"' (*lit.* 'It is what the manner of going you made to reach the great places?').

52. Wenamun, 2, 71 (= *LES*, 74, 10-11).[489]

ỉḫ *pꜣy.tn mšꜥ*

'What does (*lit.* 'it is what') your journeying mean?'

This sentence is very often reinforced by the particle *yꜣ*.[490]

---

485 Gardiner, *EG* §501

486 *Lit.* 'you are what,' not 'you are who' where *nỉm* would be used. Note the use of the atonic independent pronoun as subject. See also p. 188, n. 377.

487 Another example: P. Cairo 58083, 3 (= *KRI* I, 322, 6).

488 Another example: O. DM 446, 2-3 (= *KRI* II, 383, 9-10).

489 Another example: *id.* 2, 22 (= *LES*, 69, 4-5).

490 On *yꜣ* in this sentence, see Neveu, *SEAP* 11 (1992), 15-17.

53. O. DM 554, 1-2[491] (fig. p. 87).

yꜣ ***ỉḫ*** *pꜣy.k tm ḥn n mḏꜣy nb-mḥyt*

'Why then have you not gone (*lit.* 'Now, it is what your action of not having gone') to the medjay Nebmehyt?'

When *ỉḫ* is preceded by *yꜣ*, the construction can be reduced to *yꜣ ỉḫ Ø*:

54. P. DM IV, 5 (= *KRI* VI, 265, 1).[492]

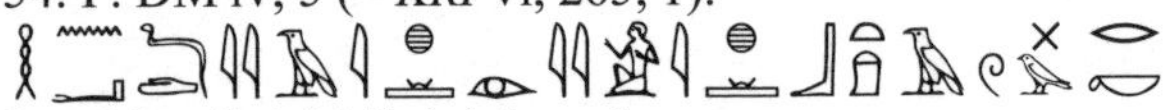

ḥnꜥ ḏd yꜣ ***ỉḫ*** *ỉrỉ.ỉ ỉḫ* (*m*) *btꜣ r.k*

'Another thing: "Well, what? What kind of evil deed have I committed against you?"'

There are also constructions of the type *ỉḫ Ø* + prepositional expansion:[493]

55. P. DM V, 2 (= *KRI* VI, 266, 1).[494]

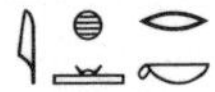

ỉḫ Ø r.k

'What's up with you?' (*lit.* 'It is what about you?').

56. First Hittite marriage, abridged version, 10 (= *KRI* II, 257, 6).

'It is every time that he shines that Re says to him:

ỉḫ m ỉb.k ỉry.ỉ se ḥr.k

'What do you wish that I perform for you?' (*lit.* 'It is what in your heart, so that I do it...').

Remark. *ỉḫ* can be found in a sentence constructed on the model of the nominal sentence with adjectival predicate denoting possession:

57. O. Leipzig 2, 4-6 (= *KRI* V, 467, 15-16) (fig. p. 188).

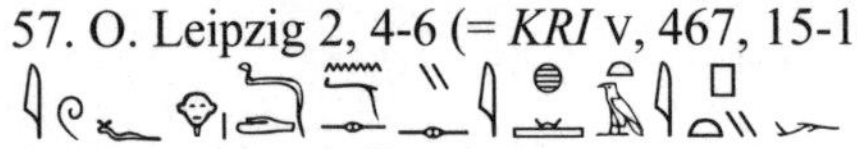

ỉw.f ḥr ḏd ny-se ***ỉḫ*** *tꜣ ỉpt*

'He said: "To whom (= 'to which institution') does it belong, the measure?"'

43.3.1.2 Cleft sentences

It is only the pseudo-cleft sentence that is encountered in this context, where *ỉḫ* is the rhematised direct object of a predicative plain sentence.

491 See also example 64 below.
492 Another example: P. Abbott, 6, 1 (= *KRI* VI, 477, 4).
493 Interpretation preferable to that as a first present having a prepositional phrase as predicate. See also Neveu, *o.c.*, example (5) where *yꜣ ỉḫ Ø* + prepositional expansion can be found (Wenamun, 2, 79-80 = *LES*, 75, 9-10).
494 Parallel example: Wenamun, 2, 65 (= *LES*, 73, 4).

43.3.1.2.1 Past[495]

58. P. Mayer A, 9, 11 (= *KRI* VI, 821, 2).

ỉḫ *pꜣ ỉn.tn ỉm*
'What have you brought therefrom?'

In the first member of a cleft sentence, *ỉḫ* can be accompanied by a prepositional expansion:

59. P. BM 10052, 5, 9-10 (= *KRI* VI, 779, 14-15).

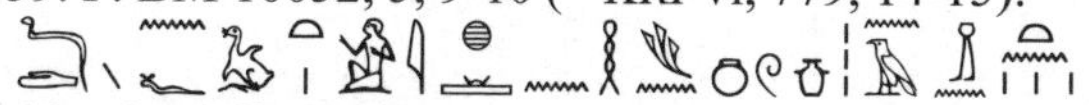

ḏd n.f ṯꜣty ***ỉḫ*** *n(=m) ḥnw nꜣ ỉn.tn*
'The vizier said to him: "What kind of vases did you bring (out)?" (*lit.* 'It is what as vessels ...').'

43.3.1.2.2 Present

60. O. DM 126, 3 (= *KRI* III, 532, 3-4).

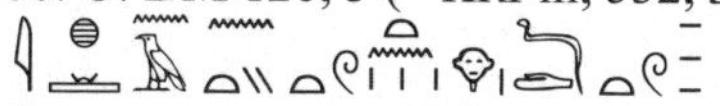

ỉḫ nꜣ nty tw.tn ḥr ḏd.tw.w
'What is it that you are going to relate?'

43.3.1.2.3 Future

61. Horus and Seth, 16, 3 (= *LES*, 59, 15).

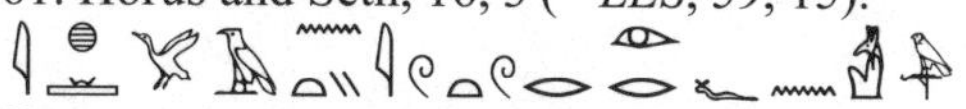

ỉḫ pꜣ nty ỉw.tw r ỉrt.f n swtḫ
'What will be done to Seth?

43.3.1.3 Verbal sentences[496]

In these sentences, *ỉḫ* can play the role of subject, object, or object of a preposition.

43.3.1.3.1 *ỉḫ* subject (very rare examples)

62. Doomed Prince, 4, 12 (= *LES*, 2, 12).

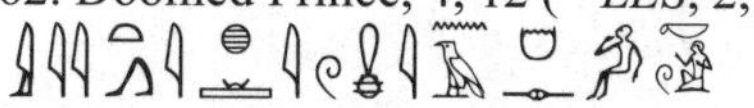

ỉyt ***ỉḫ*** *ỉw.‹ỉ› mỉnꜣ ḥms.kwỉ*
'What can happen as long as I remain seated here?'[497] Prospective;

but it can also be understood as:

(r)-ỉy.t ***ỉḫ*** *ỉw.‹ỉ› mỉnꜣ ḥms.kwỉ*
'Until happens what will I remain seated here?' *r sḏm.t.f* form.[498]

---

[495] For a passive example: P. Anastasi VIII, 1, 11-12 (= *KRI* III, 500, 14).
[496] In a broad sense, including all types of predicate of the first present.
[497] *Lit.* 'Will come what, while I am here being seated?'
[498] See Winand, *Morphologie*, §468, example 696.

Compare with the following example:

63. Wenamun, 2, 66 (= *LES*, 73, 16-74, 1).

šꜣꜥ.tw ***ỉḫ*** *ỉy (= šꜣꜥ-ỉ.ỉrỉ.t* ***ỉḫ*** *ỉy) ỉw.ỉ dy ḫꜣꜥ.tw*
‘Until happens what will I be left here?’ *šꜣꜥ-ỉ.ỉrỉ.t.f sḏm* form or ϣⲁⲧⲉϥⲥⲱⲧⲙ̄.

43.3.1.3.2 *ỉḫ* direct object

64. P. DM xviii, 5-6 (= *KRI* vii, 384, 2-4).[499]

ḥnꜥ ḏd yꜣ ỉḫ pꜣy.‹t› tm hꜣb n.ỉ pꜣy.ṯ snb ỉrỉ.ỉ ***ỉḫ*** *r.ṯ*
‘Another thing: why have you not sent me (news) of your health? What have I done against you?’ Perfective.

65. O. DM 328, 8-10 (= *KRI* iii, 535, 13-14).

ỉ.ḏd n.f ỉry.k ***ỉḫ*** *(m) pꜣ hrw*
– ‘Tell him: “What have you done today?”’ Perfective, or:
– “What will you do today?” Prospective.

66. P. BM 10052, 6, 3-4 (= *KRI* vi, 782, 2).

ỉw.ỉ (ḥr) ḏd n.w ỉw.ỉ (r) wnm ***ỉḫ*** *m-dỉ.tn*
‘I said to them: “What will I eat with you[500]?”’ Third Future.

67. Horus and Seth, 5, 12 (= *LES*, 43, 15).

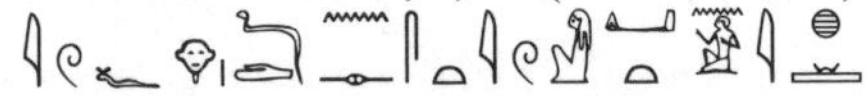

ỉw.f ḥr ḏd n.s ỉw.ṯ (r) dỉt n.ỉ ***ỉḫ***
‘He asked him: “What will you give me?”’ Third Future.

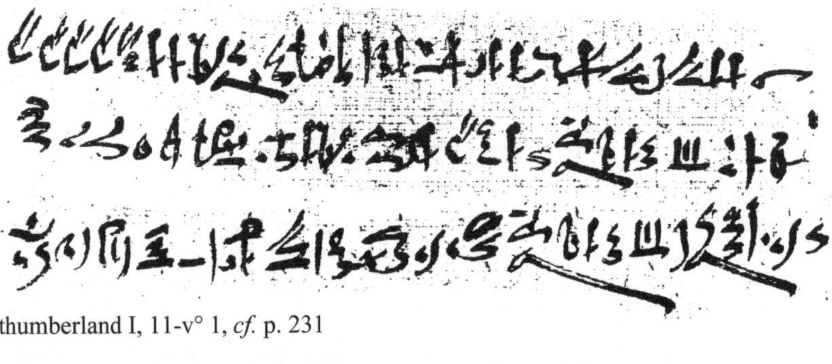

P. Northumberland I, 11-v° 1, *cf.* p. 231

[499] See also example 57 above.
[500] That is to say: ‘What will my share of the booty be?’

43.3.1.3.3 *iḫ* object of a preposition

The main combinations are: ***r iḫ*** 'why, until when' (*lit.* 'until what'); ***mi iḫ*** 'how, by means of what;' ***ḥr iḫ*** 'why, for what reason.'

68. Horus and Seth, 5, 13 (= *LES*, 44, 1).

iw.s ‹r›[501] ***iḫ*** *n.i tȝy.ṯ wḫȝt*

'What should I do with your food?' (*lit.* 'It will be what for me ...').

69. P. Northumberland I, 11- v° 1 (= *KRI* I, 239, 13-15) (fig. p. 230): it is a woman speaking.

tw.k ***mi iḫ*** *sp-sn sp-sn sp-sn sp-sn ib.i r ptr.k* ***r iḫ*** *sp-sn iw irty.i mi ʿȝ mn-nfr pȝwn tw.i ḥqr.k(wi) m ptr.k*

'How are you, oh you, you, you, you? Until when will I languish thus for you?[502] – while my eyes are as big as Memphis so hungry am I (*lit.* 'because I am famished') for the sight of you!'

Most often, these interrogative syntagma are rhematised by second tenses:[503]

70. P. BM 10052, 1, 16-17 (= *KRI* VI, 768, 12-14).

ir tȝ st i.ḥn.k r.s i.iri.k gm.s ***mi iḫ***

'As for the tomb where you went, how (= 'in what condition') did you find it?'

71. O. DM 580, 4-5 (= *KRI* V, 575, 2-3).

i.iri.k iṯȝ ȝḫt.i ***ḥr iḫ***

'Why have you stolen my things?'

72. Wenamun, 2, 3 (= *LES*, 67, 9-10).

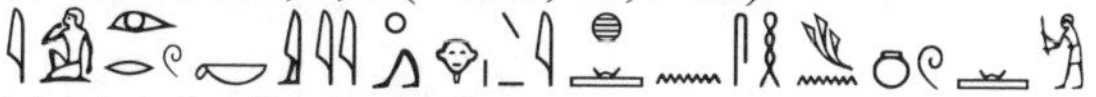

i.iri.k iy ***ḥr iḫ*** *n(=m) sḥn*

'On what kind of mission have you come?' (*lit.* 'About what as mission ...').

43.3.2 Sentences with 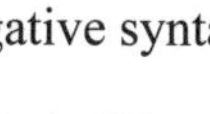 *nim*

This pronoun, used for persons, derives from  *in* + *m*, where *in* is the Middle Egyptian particle used in cleft sentences, and *m* the interrogative particle of this stage of the language. Its origin having been forgotten, scribes sometimes used in cleft sentences *m nim*, where *m* is the

[501] See Gardiner, *LES*, p. 44, note 5, 13a. See also this part of the Story of the Revenant (= *LES*, 93, 8): *iw.w r iḫ nȝ i.iri.k* 'What is the point of what you have done?' (*lit.* 'They will be what the (things) that you have done?').

[502] *Lit.* 'My heart is towards seeing you until what.'

[503] Another non-rhematised example: P. BM 10052, 8, 13 (= *KRI* VI, 786, 12) *iw.w m-di.i n iḫ*; the meaning is obscure.

diachronic successor of *ỉn*;[504] *cf.* examples 79, 80, and 81 below.

43.3.2.1 Nominal sentences

In these sentences ***nỉm*** often plays the role of predicate:

73. P. BM 10052, 14, 14-15 (= *KRI* VI, 798, 14).

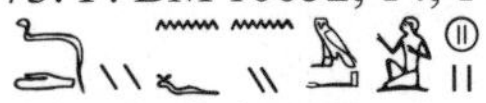

*ḏd.tw n.f **nỉm nỉm***

'He was asked: "Who then?"' (*lit.* 'It is who? It is who?'). Nominal sentence *B Ø*.

74. Truth and Falsehood, 5, 5 (= *LES*, 32, 16-33, 1).

***nỉm** rn n pꜣy.ỉ ỉt*

'What is the name[505] of my father?' Nominal sentence *B Ø pꜣ A*.

75. Mès, N 15 (= *KRI* III, 428, 9-10).

***nỉm** pꜣy.ṯ ỉwꜥ m[m] nꜣ ỉwꜥw nty ḥr tꜣ dnyt 2.t nty m ḏrt.[n]*

'Who is your heir[506] among the heirs who are (listed) on the two registers that we have in our hand?' Nominal sentence *B Ø pꜣ A*.

76. P. Orbiney, 15, 9 (= *LES*, 25, 10).

*ntk **nỉm** tr*

'Who are you (then)?' Nominal sentence *ntk B*.

In addition, *nỉm* can also be used with a genitive (direct or indirect):[507]

77. Doomed Prince, 6, 8-9 (= *LES*, 5, 4-5).

*šrỉ (n) **nỉm** m nꜣ n wrw ỉw.tw ḥr ḏd n.f šrỉ n wꜥ n snny*

'Of which prince is he son?[508] They answered him: "He is a son of official."' Nominal sentence *B Ø*.

78. Truth and Falsehood, 5, 3 (= *LES*, 32 , 14).

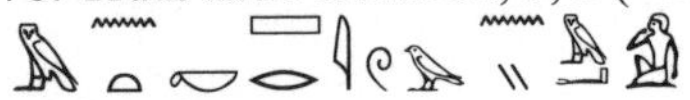

*ntk šrỉ **nỉm***

'Whose son are you?' (*lit.* 'You are son of who?'). Nominal sentence *ntk B*.

---

[504] See Gardiner, *EG*, §227 and 496.
[505] *Lit.* 'It is who, the name …'
[506] *Lit.* 'It is who, your heir.'
[507] Given the spelling, we can assume that only one *n* has been written: (*n*) *nỉm*.
[508] *Lit.* 'It is a son of whom among the great ones?'

43.3.2.2 Cleft sentences

43.3.2.2.1 Past

79. O. DM 582, 5-6 (= *KRI* v, 575, 15) (fig. p. 242).

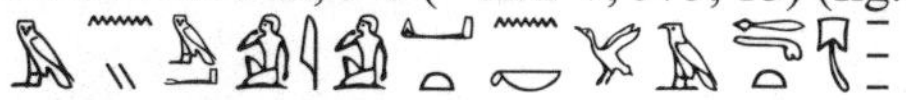

m ***nỉm*** *ỉ.dỉ n.k pȝ ʿȝ*

'Who (*lit.* 'it is who, that') gave you the donkey?'

80. P. Orbiney, 4, 10 (= *LES*, 14, 1-2).

m ***nỉm*** *(ỉ).mdw m-dỉ.ṯ*

'Who has spoken (evil) with you?'

43.3.2.2.2 Future

81. Pentawer poem, 330 (= *KRI* II, 97, 13).

m ***nỉm*** *tȝy.f tw hrw qnd.k*

'Who will resist you on the day of your anger?'

82. P. Turin 2021, 3, 11-12 (= *KRI* VI, 741, 10-11).

[***nỉm ỉ***]*.ỉrỉ.f wsf pȝ ỉrỉ.f*

'[Who] will undo what he has done?'

43.3.2.3 Verbal sentences

43.3.2.3.1 *nỉm* subject

83. P. Turin 2021, 3, 10 (= *KRI* VI, 741, 7-8).

ỉr pȝ ỉry.f ỉrỉ [***n***]***ỉm*** *(r) rḫ mdt ỉm.f*

'As for what he has done, who will be able to contest it?' Third Future where *nỉm* is treated as a noun.

84. P. BM 10052, 3, 16-17 (= *KRI* VI, 774, 7-8).

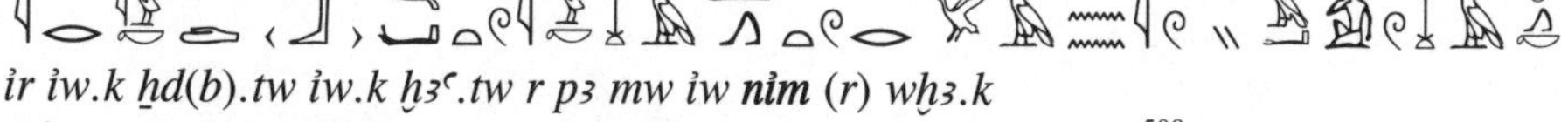

ỉr ỉw.k ḫd(b).tw ỉw.k ḫȝʿ.tw r pȝ mw ỉw ***nỉm*** *(r) wḫȝ.k*

'If you are killed and thrown in the water, who will seek you?'[509]

43.3.2.3.2 *nỉm* genitive

85. P. Anastasi IV, 10, 11-12 (= *LEM*, 46, 8-9).

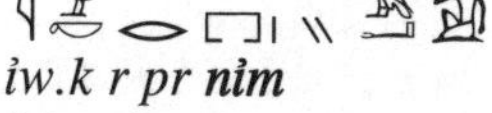

ỉw.k r pr ***nỉm***

'To whom are you going?' (*lit.* 'You are towards the house of whom?)'

---

[509] Third future, despite the previous example. It appears that with *nỉm* the third future can be constructed with *ỉrỉ* or *ỉw*.

43.3.2.3.3 *nỉm* object of a preposition

86. P. Anastasi VIII, 1, 9-11 (= *KRI* III, 500, 10-13).

ỉr nꜣ sʿrt n pꜣ nṯr ... dỉ.tw.w m sbwt n ***nỉm***

'As for the wool (pl.) of the god ... to whom has it been given as cargo?' (*lit.* 'they were given in the capacity of cargo to whom?').

The resulting adverbial phrase can be rhematised by a second tense:

87. Wenamun, 1, 56-57 (= *LES*, 66, 16-67, 2).

wn ỉ.ỉrỉ.w wḫꜣ pꜣ nṯr m-dỉ ***nỉm*** *ntk m-rʿ ỉ.ỉrỉ.w wḫꜣ.k m-dỉ m-rʿ*

'From whom would the god be sought? And you too, from whom would you be sought?'

43.3.3 Sentences with  *ỉṯ*

This interrogative pronoun, meaning 'what, who, which,' is very rare.

88. P. BM 10052, 13, 7-8 (= *KRI* VI, 795, 14-15).

ỉṯ *šmsw n ỉw.f-n-ỉmn pꜣ ỉy n.k*

'Which servant of Iuefenamun is it, the one who came to you?' Nominal sentence.[510]

89. P. Anastasi V, 20, 4 (= *LEM*, 67, 7).

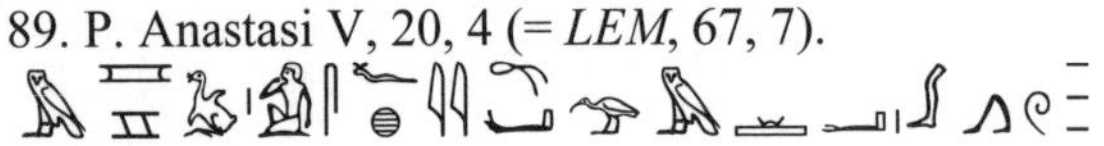

m ***ỉṯ*** *sfḫy (ỉ).gm ʿ.w*

'Which is the patrol[511] (*lit.* 'It is which patrol') who found their tracks?' True cleft sentence.

43.3.4 Sentences with  *wr*

Although classified by Černý-Groll[512] among adverbs, this term, derived from the adjective meaning 'great' (from the adjective verb *wrr* 'to be great'), and which is generally rendered by 'how,' appears to behave like a pronoun[513] whose meaning would be: 'what greatness, what amount.'

90. Wenamun, 1, 50-51 (= *LES*, 66, 7).

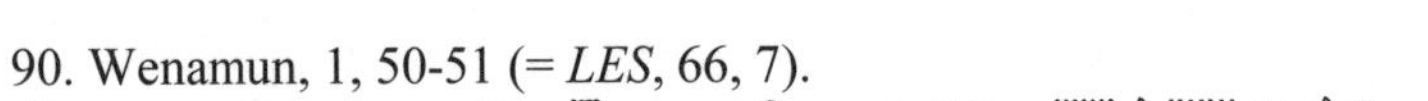

wr *r pꜣ hrw m-ḏr ỉw.k n(=m) pꜣ nty ỉmn ỉm*

'How long has it been since you left the place where Amun resides?' (*lit.* 'It is what amount (of

[510] And not a cleft sentence, because in this case one would have had: *(*m*) *ỉṯ šmsw n ỉw.f-n-ỉmn ỉ.ỉy n.k*, that is to say, a cleft sentence of type I (see following example), in which can appear verbs of motion. See *supra* §42.1.2.1, note b.

[511] Rare word that Janssen in Ship's Logs, p. 46, renders – like other translators – as 'guard, body guard.' Here it refers to surveillance units travelling across the desert and controlling the nomads.

[512] *LEG*, §8.2.2, p. 136.

[513] Vicychl, *Dictionnaire étymologique de la langue copte,* p. 236.

days) until today since you came from where Amun is?').

91. P. Anastasi V, 20, 5 (= *LEM*, 67, 8).

di.tn ḥn ***wr*** *(n) rmṯ m-sꜣ.w*

– 'How many men have you dispatched (*lit.* 'made run') in their pursuit?' Perfective, or:

– 'How many men are you going to dispatch ...? Prospective.

92. P. Anastasi I, 27, 8.

se ḥr ir͗t ***wr*** *n i͗trw m šm r-šꜣꜥ-(r) qḏt*

'How many leagues does he have to travel until Gaza?' (*lit.* 'He does what amount of leagues walking ...').

43.3.5 Remarks

There is still an interrogative pronoun written *ḫy*  or *ḫr* ,[514] that is only found in the formulaic sentence: *ḫy qd.k* 'How are you?' (*lit.* 'What is your (present) condition?'), in the eighteenth[515] and nineteenth[516] dynasties.[517] The expression becomes: *ḫy ꜥ.k* in the nineteenth dynasty,[518] and then, in the twentieth dynasty, *ḫr ꜥ.k* with the same meaning.

93. P. Leiden I 369, 5 (= *LRL*, 1, 7).

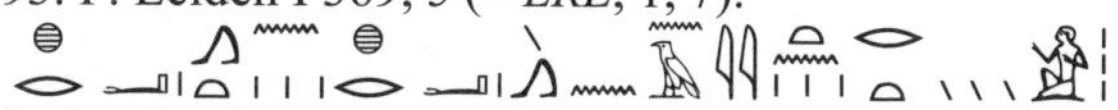

ḫr *ꜥ.tn* ***ḫr*** *ꜥ n nꜣy.tn rmṯ*

'How are you? How are your people?'

43.4 Syntagmas incorporating an interrogative adverb

The only representative of this category is:  (and variants) *tnw* 'where?' 'whence?'

94. Truth and Falsehood, 5, 6 (= *LES*, 33, 2).[519]

s(w) ***tnw*** *pꜣy.k i͗t*

'Where is your father?' (*lit.* 'Where is he, your father?'). First present.

95. Doomed Prince, 5, 10-11 (= *LES*, 3, 15-16).[520]

i͗y.k ***tnw*** *pꜣ šri͗ nfr*

'From where have you come, beautiful child?' Second tense.

---

[514] Not to be confused with the coordinating particle *ḫr*, see §10.1.

[515] P. Louvre 3230 A, 4 (= *JEA* 12 (1926), pl. XVII); P. BM 10103, 4 (= *JEA* 14 (1928), pl. XXXV).

[516] P. Northumberland I, 2 (= *KRI* I, 239, 4); P. Sallier IV, v° 1, 3 (= *LEM*, 89, 3).

[517] See Barns, *JEA* 34 (1948), 38, n. 2.

[518] P. Leiden I 365, 4 (= *KRI* III, 232, 14-15); P. Sallier IV, v° 2, 2 (= *LEM*, 90, 2).

[519] Parallel examples: *id.*, 8, 6 (= *LES*, 34, 15); Wenamun, 1, 51-52 and 54-55 (= *LES*, 66, 9-10 and 13-14); Qadesh Bulletin, §12 and 38 (=*KRI* II, 105, 2 and 110, 11); P. Anastasi I, 27, 8.

[520] Parallel example: Astarte, 2, x + 18 (= *LE5*, 79, 4-5).

96. P. Anastasi IV, 10, 11 (= *LEM*, 46, 8).

ỉw.k r ***tnw***
'Where will you go?' Third future.

43.5 Questions without interrogative morphemes

97. P. BM 10052, 14, 16-17 (= *KRI* VI, 798, 16-799, 1).

ḏd.tw n.f ***ptr.k tꜣy.w ꜣtp*** *ḏd.f b(w)p(w)y.ỉ ptr*
'He was asked: "Did you see their cargo?" He replied: "I did not see (anything)."'

98. O. Gardiner 4, v° 4-6 (= *KRI* VI, 142, 11-13).

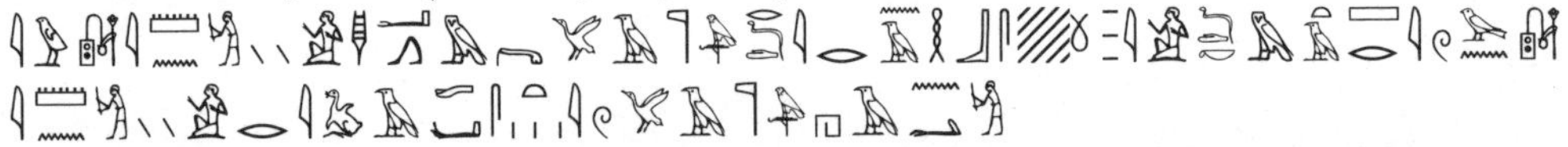

ỉw sš ỉmn-nḫt (ḥr) ꜥḥꜥ m-bꜣḥ pꜣ nṯr r-ḏd ỉr nꜣ ḥbsw ỉ.ḏd.k ***m tꜣ šrỉ(t) n sš ỉmn-nḫt r(=ỉ).ỉṯꜣ se*** *ỉw pꜣ nṯr (ḥr) hn*
'The scribe Amunnakht stood before the god saying: "As for the clothes of which you spoke, is it the daughter of the scribe Amunnakht who stole them?" The god assented.'

99. Horus and Seth, 15, 12-13 (= *LES*, 59, 5-8).

wn.ỉn tm ḥr ḏd n.f ỉ.ỉrỉ.k tm dỉt wḏꜥ.tw.tn ḥr ỉḫ ***ỉw.k (r) nḥm n.k tꜣ ỉꜣt n ḥr*** *wn.ỉn swtḫ ḥr ḏd n.f m-bỉꜣ pꜣy.ỉ nb nfr*
'Atum asked him: "Why have you prevented that you be judged? Are you going to take for yourself the office of Horus?" Seth replied him: "No, my good lord!"'

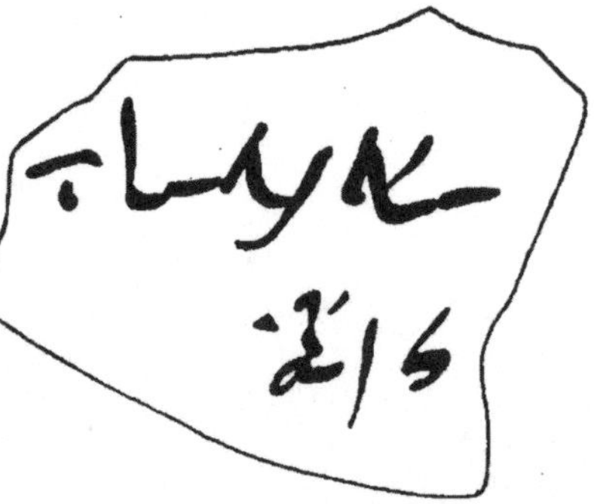

O. IFAO 557 (*cf.* p. 219)

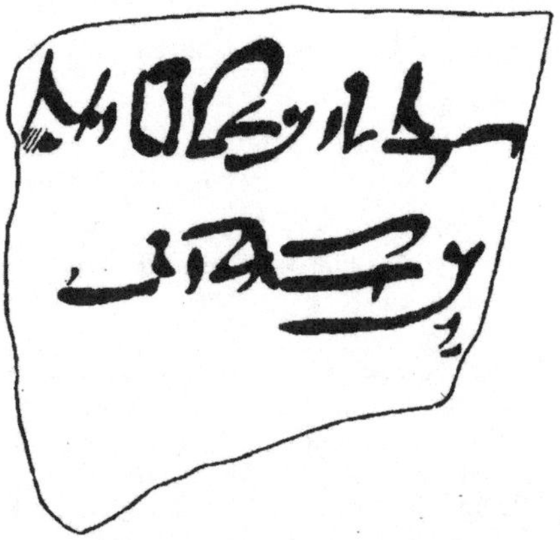

O. IFAO 599 (*cf.* p. 220)

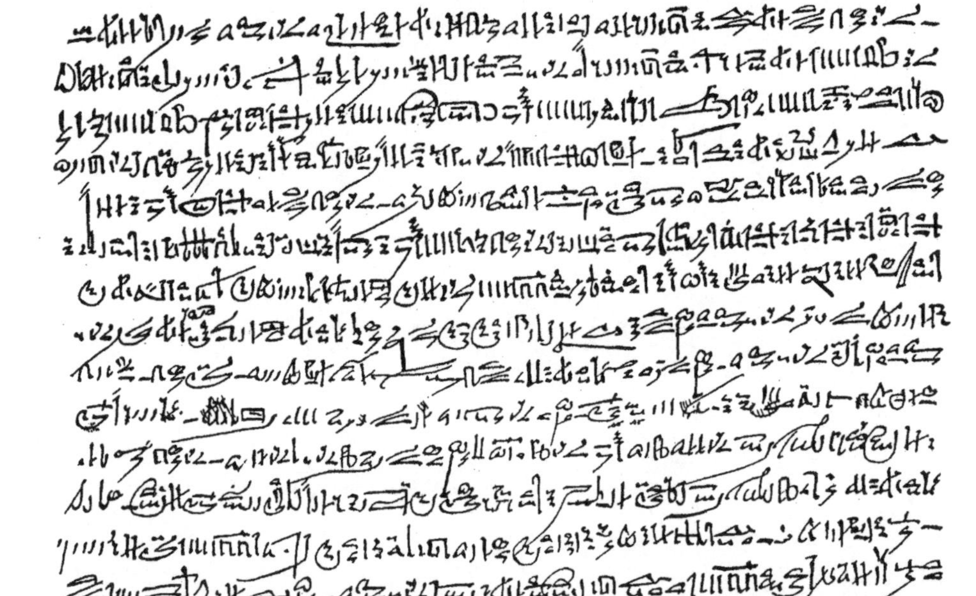

P. Abbott, 6 (*cf.* p. 208)

APPENDIX TWO

SYLLABIC WRITING

44. Appendix two: Syllabic Writing

44.1 Introduction[521]

Syllabic writing, or, more accurately, 'group writing,' is a very flexible system, purely phonetic (never ideogrammatic), used whenever the scribe is not linguistically driven, that is, whenever he cannot relate the word to a known root.

Although employed since the 11th dynasty, the system experienced considerable development during the New Kingdom when Egypt, through its conquests, found itself in contact with many foreign countries. Syllabic writing allowed one to write many foreign words (names of countries and cities, people, new objects), but also new Egyptian words that had never been written out, old words which etymology was forgotten, or that one, perhaps, wanted to write in a new way.

The system consists of 'groups,' each with the value of consonant + vowel. Each group can contain a biliteral sign, possibly accompanied by a determinative, and/or one or more uniliteral signs, or can simply consist of uniliteral signs.

Examples of the first type:

- Biliterals only (sometimes with a determinative):

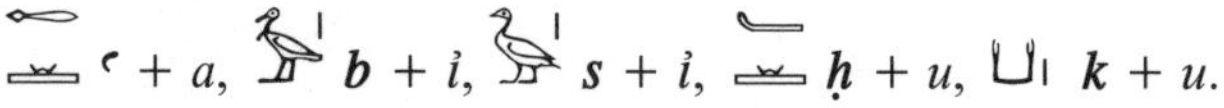
ʿ + *a*, *b* + *i͗*, *s* + *i͗*, *ḥ* + *u*, *k* + *u*.

- Biliterals + uniliterals:

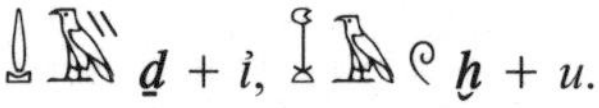
ḏ + *i͗*, *ḫ* + *u*.

Examples of the second type:

k + *a*, *k* + *i͗*, *k* + *u*, *k* + *ê*,[522] *r* + *i͗*, *r* + *ê*, *h* + *u*.

Important remark: If each group has a certain consonantal value, the same is not true for its vocalic value.[523] In these instances, it may be best to retain in transliteration only the consonantal value of the group.

44.2 Usage

44.2.1 Writing foreign words

(*KRI* II, 230, 8) ***qḏwdn*** 'Qizzuwadna'[524]

---

[521] See Schenkel, *LÄ* VI, 114-121; Helck, *SAK* 16 (1989), 121-143; Hoch, *Semitic Words in Egyptian Texts*, 1994, p. 487-504.

[522] The value ê for [hieroglyphs] seems well attested.

[523] With the exception of ê, see previous note.

[524] Name of country.

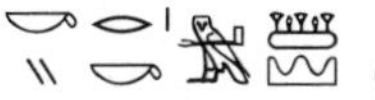 (*KRI* II, 4, 8) ***krkmš*** ‘Carchemish’

 (*LES*, 61, 10) ***ḫr*** ‘Khar, the Hurrian countries (Syria)’

 (*KRI* II, 105, 7) ***ḫlb*** ‘Aleppo’

 (*KRI* IV, 19, 7) ***ỉsrêl*** ‘Israel’

 (*LES*, 62, 10) ***ṯkrbꜥl*** ‘Tjekerbaal’[525]

 (*KRI* IV, 19, 3-4) ***šlm*** ‘shalom’ or ‘salam’

44.2.2 Writing words of foreign origin (loan words)

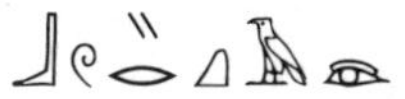 (*LEM*, 35, 8) ***brq*** ‘sparkle, shine’

 (*KRI* VI, 805, 8) ***bḏn*** ‘staff, cudgel’

 (*LEM*, 53, 3) ***mrkbt*** ‘chariot’

 (*KRI* IV, 411, 9-10) ***ḫnr*** or ***ḫl***[526] ‘chisel (of quarry-worker)’

 (*KRI* IV, 411, 10) ***qrḏn*** ‘hoe’ or ‘pick (of quarry-worker)’

 (*LEM*, 32, 6) ***kṯn*** ‘charioteer, chariot driver’

 (*LEM*, 47, 8-9) ***gwš*** ‘become bent, become twisted’

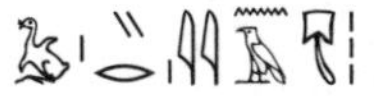 (*KRI* II, 28, 13) ***ṯryn*** ‘cuirass’

44.2.3 Writing Egyptian words

– **recent** (new words or loan-words of unattested origin):

---

[525] Name of person.

[526] Note the frequent combination of *n* + *r* = *l*. The word is often abbreviated as .

 ***ỉrm*** 'with'

 ***bnr*** or ***bl*** 'outside'[527]

– **traditional** (re-written in a new way?)

 (*LES*, 19, 16) ***ḥrrt*** 'flower,' *cf.*  (*URK* IV, 775, 16)

Remark

Syllabic writing is also used to write diminutives:

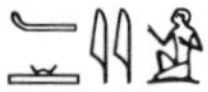 ***ḥwy***, diminutive of 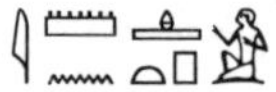 ***ỉmn-ḥtp***

 ***ỉpy***, diminutive of 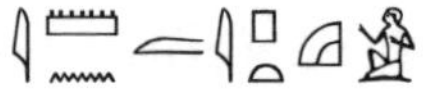 ***ỉmn-m-ỉpt***

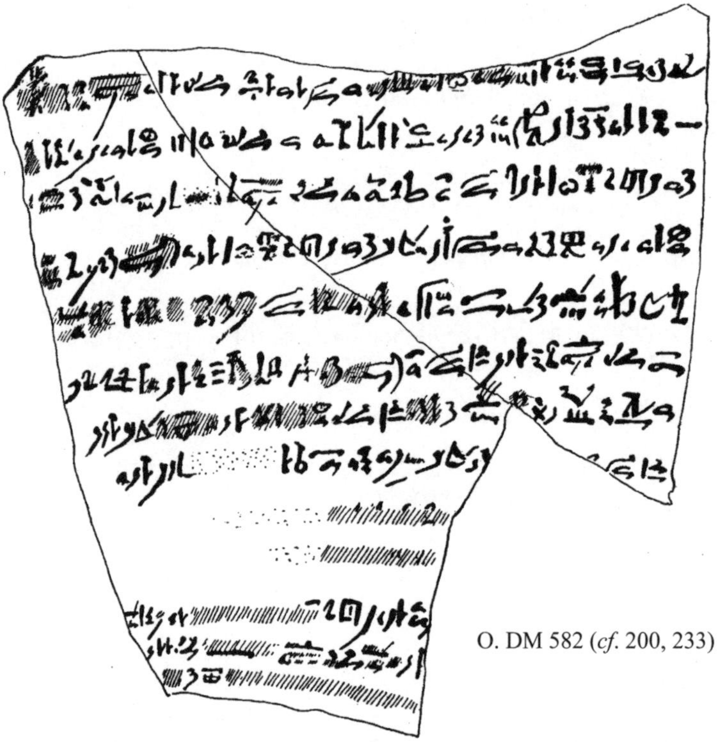

O. DM 582 (*cf.* 200, 233)

[527] Coptic: ⲂⲞⲖ.

INDEXES

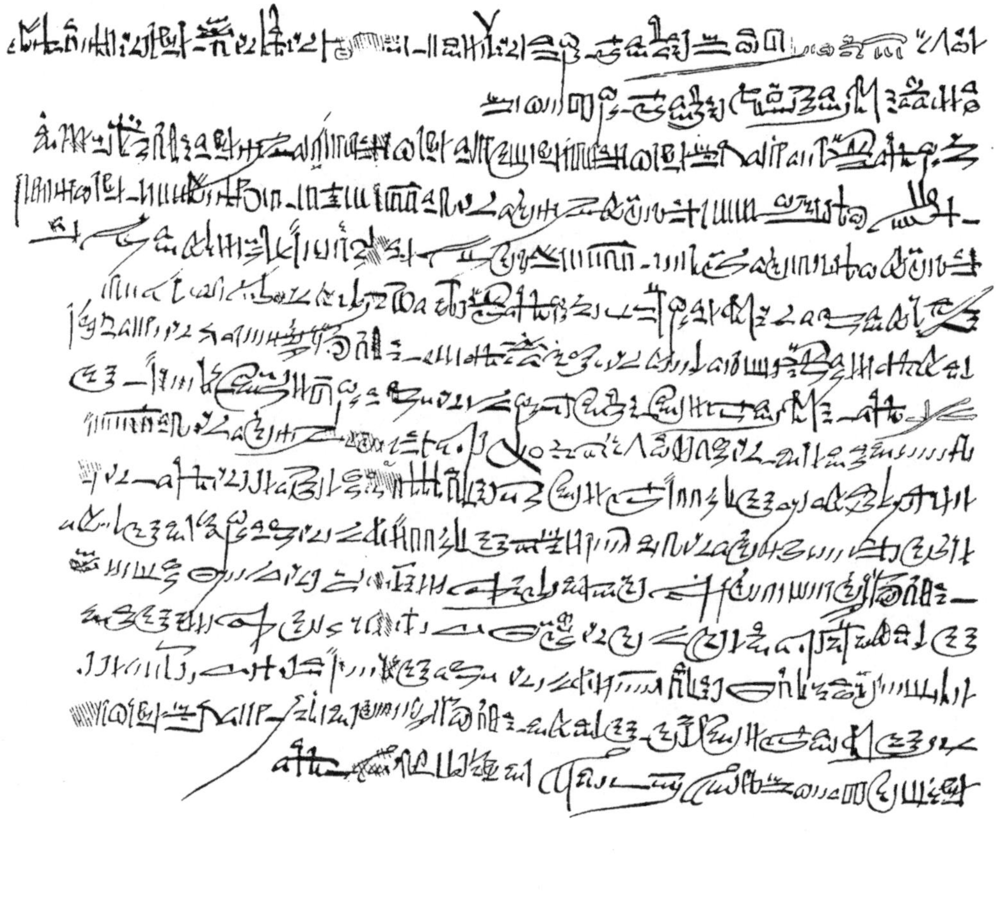

P. Abbott, 7 (*cf.* p. 54)

Grammar index[1]

Adverbs, 9;
– interrogative, 11.2.3; 43.4;
– used as predicate of the First Present, 16.2.
Adverbial clauses
– introduced by *ỉw*, 32;
– substituting relative clauses, 32.3 (table);
– substituting complement clauses, 32.4;
– introduced by *ỉr*, 33.2;
– introduced by *wnn*, 34.1 and 2;
– introduced by *ỉnn*, 35;
– introduced by *hn*, 36.2;
– introduced by *bsỉ*, 36.3;
– introduced by *ḥl* (*ḥnr*), 36.4.
Aorist, 16.4, note 2; 42.1.2.1; 42.2.1.4.
Aorist (demotic), 17.6.
Aorist (negative), 16.4.4;
– remark; 17; 24.4;
– preceded by *ỉw*, 32.1;
– preceded by *ỉn*, 43.2.1.5;
– preceded by *ỉst*, 43.2.2.1.
Articles, 2;
– definite, 2.1;
– indefinite, 2.2.
Autonomy, 12.1.

Cleft sentences, 12.4.2; 27.1.4; 28.4.2; 35.2; 42;
– preceded by *ỉn*, 43.2.1.10;
– preceded by *ỉnn*, 35.1;
– true cleft sentence, 42.1.2.1;
– pseudo-cleft sentence, 42.1.2.2.
Comment, 12.4.2.
Complement clauses
– after *rdỉ*, 26.1;
– after ‘operator’ verbs, 32.5.
Continuative forms, 25.
Conjunctive, 25.3; 34.1.
Converters, 11.3.
Correlative system, definition, 32.2.2;
– introduced by *ỉw*, 32.2.2;
– introduced by *ỉr*, 33.2;
– introduced by *wnn*, 34.1 and 2;
– introduced by *ỉnn*, 35;
– introduced by *hn*, 36.2;
– introduced by *bsỉ*, 36.3;
– introduced by *ḥl* (*ḥnr*), 36.4.

Demonstratives, 3; 39.2.
Deontic, 19.1.
Discourse, 12.3.2.2.

Enunciation, 12.3.
Expressing possession, 41.

Focalisation, 12.4.2.
Focus, 12.4.2.
Forms
– independent and subordinate, 12.1;
– initial and non-initial, 12.2;
– narrative and non-narrative, 12.3.1.
Future, 16.5.1.
(Third) Future, 19; 35.2; 38.1;
– preceded by *wn,* 19.2; 36.2;
– preceded by *nty,* 29.6;
– preceded by *ỉw,* 32.1;
– preceded by *ỉn,* 43.2.1.3;
– preceded by *ỉnn,* 35.1;
– preceded by *ỉr*, 33.2.1.3.

Imperative, 21; 34.1; 35.2.
Indefinites, 6.
Infinitive, 13; 16.4; 16.5; 28.4.1, Note; 38.2.
Initiality, 12.2.
Interrogative pronouns, 11.2.2; 39.2.1.2.
Interrogative sentences, 43.

Narrative, 12.3.1.
Negative (morphemes), 11.1.
Nominal sentences with adjectival predicate, 40;
– preceded by *ỉn*, 43.2.1.9;

[1] The table of contents should also be consulted, since the indexes do not list all of the various sections. The numbers refer to chapters and paragraphs.

– preceded by *ìst*, 43.2.2.5.
Nominal sentences with adverbial predicate, 16.1.
Nominal sentences with substantival predicate, 39;
– type *B Ø*, 34.3;
– preceded by *ìn*, 43.2.1.8;
– preceded by *ìst*, 43.2.2.4.
'Not yet' form, 18;
– preceded by *nty*, 29.8.
Numerals, 5;
– cardinal, 5.1;
– ordinal, 5.2.

Participles, 27;
– active, 27.1; 42.1.2.1;
– active periphrased, 27.1.1; 27.1.3;
– passive, 27.2; 42.1.2.2.
Particles, 10;
– interrogative, 11.2.1.
Passages
– narrative, 12.3.1; 16.6.2.1; 16.6.2.2;
– non-narrative, 12.3.1; 16.6.2.1; 16.6.2.2.
Plain sentence, 12.4.2.
Possessives, 4.
Predication of classification, 39.2.
Predication of identification, 39.3.
Predication of existence, 22;
– preceded by *nty*, 29.8;
– preceded by *ìw*, 32.1;
– preceded by *ìr*, 33.2.1.4;
– preceded by *ìn*, 43.2.1.7;
– preceded by *ìnn*, 35.1;
– preceded by *hn*, 36.2.
Prepositions, 8.
Present, 16.4;
– unmarked, 16.4;
– general, 16.4; 16.4.3; 24.4;
– habitual, 16.4; 16.4.2; 24.4;
– immediate, 16.4; 16.4.1;
– synchronic, 16.4.
(First) Present, 16;
– preceded by *nty*, 29.4 and 5;
– preceded by *ìw* (= circumstantial), 32.1; 38.1;
– found in the second member of a nominal sentence with adjectival predicate, 40.5;
– preceded by *ìn*, 43.2.1.4;
– preceded by *ìr*, 33.2.1.1;
– preceded by *ìst*, 43.2.2.2;
– preceded by *wnn*, 34.1;
– preceded by *ìnn*, 35.1;
– preceded by *hn*, 36.2;
– preceded by *bsì*, 36.3.
Personal pronouns, 7;
– new direct object pronouns, 7.3; 21.1;
– dependent, 7.2; 21.1;
– independent, 7.4; 39.2; 39.3; 41.2; 41.4; 42.1.2.1; 42.1.2.2;
– prefixes of the First Present, 16.1.1;
– suffixes, 7.1.
Pseudo-participle, 14; 16.6; 19.4; 32.5.1; 33.2.2.4.

Narrative, 12.3.2.1.
Relative forms, 28; 42.1.2.2;
– periphrased, 28.1; 28.2; 38.2.
Relative clauses (table), 31.
Rhematisation, 12.4.2; 42.1.
Rheme, 12.4.1; 12.4.2;
– marked, 12.4.2; 23.1; 23.2; 42.1.

Second tenses, 12.4.2; 23;
– periphrased 23.4;
– modal (non-periphrased), 23.5;
– archaic, 23.6; 38.2;
– preceded by *nty*, 29.8;
– preceded by *ìw*, 32.1;
– preceded by *ìn*, 43.2.1.6;
– preceded by *ìnn*, 35.1;
– preceded by *ìst*, 43.2.3.3.
Sequential, 25.2; 33.2.1.1; 33.2.1.2.1; 34.1; 38.1;
– preceded by *ìr*, 33.2.2.1.
Substantive, 1;
– defined, 1.2; 42.1.2.1;
– undefined, 1.2.
Syllabic writing, 44.

Thematisation, 12.4.2; 33.1; 33.4.
Theme, 12.4.1; 12.4.2; 23.1; 23.2; 42.1.

Theory of the three points of view, 12.4.1.
Topicalisation, 12.4.2; 33.1.
Topic, 12.4.2; 33.4.

Utterances (marked and unmarked), 12.4.2.
Verbal forms
– independent, 15 to 24;
– subordinate, 25 to 37.
Verbs
– intransitive, 14.2;
– of motion, 16.5; 16.6.2.1; 24.3.1;
– other, 16.6.2.2; 24.3.2;
– 'operator,' 32.5.

Egyptian grammar index

i, see 'prosthetic yod.'
i.ỉrỉ.f sḏm.(f) + adverbial, 23.1 and 4.
i.ỉrỉ.t.f sḏm, 37.
i.sḏm (se), 21.1.
i.sḏm (se) + adverbial, 23.1 and 5.
ỉw (circumstantial), 7.1.2; 11.3; 32; 38.1;
– preceding the First Present with pronominal subject, 16.1.1;
– preceded by *ỉr*, 33.2.2.2;
– before a nominal sentence, 39.2; 39.3.
ỉw (of the Third Future), 19; 38.1.
ỉw (parenthetical), 32.1, remark 2; 38.1.
ỉw (of the sequential) 25.2; 38.1.
ỉw.f (?) sḏm, 33.2.3; 38.1.
ỉw.f r sḏm, see Third Future.
ỉw.f ḥr (tm) sḏm, see Sequential.
ỉw sḏm.f passive, 15.2.1.
ỉw sḏm.n.f, 15.1.
ỉmỉ (imperative of *rdỉ*), 21.1.
ỉn (preposition introducing the agent of the process), 13.2; 13.4.2.2.2; 27.2.2.
ỉn (interrogative particle), 11.2.1; 35.2 (*in fine*); 43.2.1.
ỉn-ỉw, 43.2.1.12.
ỉnn, 35.
ỉr, 10.2; 12.4.2; 33.
ỉr + ỉw (circumstantial), 33.2.2.2.
ỉrỉ (auxiliary), 13.2; 27.1.1.
ỉrỉ (before the Third future with nominal subject), 19.3.
ỉḫ (particle preceding the prospective *sḏm.f*), 20; 25.3, example 9.
ỉḫ (interrogative pronoun), 11.2.2; 39.2.1.2; 42.1.2.2; 43.3.1.
ỉs-bn, 43.2.3.
ỉst, 11.2.1; 43.2.2.
ỉṯ, 11.2.2; 43.3.3.

yꜣ, 10.4.

ꜥḥꜥ.n sḏm.f, 25.2.4.
ꜥḥꜥ.n.f ḥr sḏm, 25. 2.4.

wꜥ, 2.2.
wn (past converter), 7.1.2; 11.3; 38.1; 38.4;
– before the First Present, 16.2; 16.3;
– before the First Present with pronominal subject, 16.1.1;
– before the Third Future, 19.2; 36.2;
– before the Second Tenses, 23.4.1.
wn (of existence), 22.1; 38.4.
(ỉ).wn (participle), 27.1.2; 30.1 and 2; 42.1.2.2.
(ỉ).wn.f (relative form), 28.2; 30.1 and 3.
wn.ỉn.f ḥr sḏm, 25.2.4.
wnn, 7.1.2; 11.3; 18.2; 34; 38.4.
wr, 43.3.3.

bw, 11.1; 38.5.
bw ỉrỉ.f sḏm, 17.1; 17.5; 24.4;
– preceded by *ỉn*, 43.2.1.5;
– preceded by *ỉst*, 43.2.2.1.
bw ỉrỉ.t.f sḏm, 18.1; 24.4.
bw sḏm.f, 15.1.2.3, remark 2; 17.1; 17.4; 24.4; 36.2.
bw sḏm.n.f, 17.1; 17.3.
bw sḏm.t.f, 18.1.
bw sḏmy.t N, 18.2.
bwpwy, 38.5.
bwpwy.Ø sḏm, 15.2.2.
bwpwy.f sḏm, 15.1.2; 16.6.2.1 (*bwpwy.f ꜥq*); 24.4;
– preceded by *nty*, 29.7;
– preceded by *ỉw*, 32.1;
– preceded by *ỉn*, 43.2.1.2;
– preceded by *ỉnn*, 35.1.
bwpwy.tw sḏm, 15.2.2; 16.1.1.
bn, 11.1; 38.1; 38.5;
– negation of the First present 16.2; 16.3; 16.4.4; 16.5; 16.6.1; 16.6.2.2;
– negation of the Third Future, 19.2; 19.3;
– negation of the independent prospective, 20;
– taking on the predication alone, 22.3;
– negation of the second tense nexus, 23.4.2;
– negation of the expression of possession, 41.1.
bn ... ỉwnꜣ, 11.1;
– negation of the First Present, 16.3;
– negation of the Second Tense nexus, 23.4.2;
– negation of nominal sentences, 39.2; 39.3.

bsi, 36.3.
p3, 2.1.
p3y, 3.1; 39.2; 39.2.2.2; 39.2.2.3; 39.3; 39.3.2.1.2.
p3y.f, 4.1.
p3w, 3.1.3; 39, example 34.
p3wn, 10.3.
pw, 34.3; 39.2.2; 39.2.2.3; 42.1.2.2.
pn (demonstrative), 3.1.3.
pn (abbreviation of ***p3-n***), 3.2.1; 3.2.2, example 8.
ptr, 10.5.

m (imperative of the negative verb *imi*), 21.2.1; 21.2.2.
m (morpheme introducing a true cleft sentence), 42.1.2.1.
m (preposition), 42.5.
m-bi3, 43.2.1.11.
m-ḫt sḏm.f, 26.3; 33.2.2.3.
m-ḏr sḏm.f, 26.3; 33.2.2.3.
my (imperative of *iw/iy*), 21.1.
my (imperative reinforcing particle), 21.1.
mn, 22.2; 38.5.
mk, 10.5.
mtw.f (tm) sḏm, see Conjunctive.

n (negation), 11.1.
n … is, 11.1.
n p3.f sḏm, 15.1.2.1.
n sḏm.f, 15.1.2.3, remark 2; 24.4.
n sḏm.n.f, 15.1.2.3, remark 2; 17.1; 24.4.
n.sḏm.t.f, 18.1.
n3 (n), 2.1.
n3y, see ***p3y***.
nim, 11.2.2; 19.3; 39.2.1.2; 42.1.2.1; 43.3.2.
ny (genitival adjective), 41.1.
ny-se, 41.1.
nʿy (auxiliary of the First Future), 16.5.1.
nb, 1.2; 6.1.
nn, 11.1.
nh(3)y n, 2.2.
nkt, 6.3.
nty, 11.3; 27.1.2; 28.2; 29; 30.1; 38.1; 42.1.2.2.

r sḏm.t.f, 37.1; 37.3.
r-tnw sḏm.f, 26.3.
r-ḏd (introducing a complement clause), 32.5.4.
rḫ,16.7.

hn, 19.2; 36.2.

ḥnʿ ntf (tm) sḏm, 25.3.
ḥl (ḥnr), 36.4.

ḫy, var. ***ḫr***, 43.3.5.
ḫr, 10.1; 33.2.1.1; 34.1; 38.1.
ḫr ir.f sḏm, 17.6.
ḫr-sḏm.f, 17.6; 24.4.
ḫr.f sḏm, 17.6.

se, 7.2.1.
sw im, 16.2.
sw m p3 pr, 16.3.
sw ḥr sḏm, 16.4.
sw m ʿq, 16.5.
sw w3ḥ, 16.6.1.
sw ʿq, 16.6.2.1.
sw sḏr, 16.6.2.2.
swl, 7.4.1; 41.2.
sḏm.f (various values), 38.2.
sḏm.f perfective, 15; 16.6.2.2; 24.4; 38.2;
– active, 15.1;
– passive, 15.2;
– preceded by *iw*, 32.1;
– preceded by *in*, 43.2.1.1.1;
– preceded by *inn*, 35.1;
– preceded by *ir*, 33.2.1.2.1;
– preceded by *hn*, 36.2.
sḏm.f prospective, 38.2; 42.1.2.1;
– independent, 20; 34.1; 35.2;
– non-independent, 26;
– preceded by *iw*, 32.1, remark 1;
– preceded by *in*, 43.2.1.1.2;
– preceded by ir, 33.2.1.2.2;
– in purpose clauses, 26.2.
sḏm.f 'emphatic,' 15.1.1, remark; 23.6.
sḏm.n.f, 15.1.1; 23.6.
sḏm-ḫr.f, 17.6.

š3ʿ.t.f sḏm, 37.3.

šꜣꜥ-i.iri.t.f sḏm, 37.3.
ky, 6.2.

gr, 7.4.2.

tꜣ, 2.1.
tꜣy, see *pꜣy*.
tw.f (new direct object pronoun), 7.3.
twt, 7.4.1; 41.2.
tm, 11.1; 38.5;
– negation of the infinitive, 13.2;
– negation of the verb of second tenses, 23.4.2;
– negation of continuative forms, 25.1;
– negation of the sequential, 25.2;
– negation of the conjunctive, 25.3;
– negation of the subordinate prospective in purpose clauses, 26.2.
tnw, 11.2.3; 43.4.1.

Coptic Index

ⲁⲛⲅ̂ and ⲥⲓⲙ., 7.4.1; 39.3.
ⲁⲛⲟⲕ and ⲥⲓⲙ., 7.4.1; 39.3.
ⲉⲃⲟⲗ, 9, n. 48, p. 26.
ⲟⲛ, 9, n. 46, p. 26.
ⲙ̂, 11.1.
ⲙⲉϥⲥⲱⲧⲙ̂, 17.1.
ⲙ̂ⲡⲁⲧϥ̂ⲥⲱⲧⲙ̂, 18.1.
ⲙ̂ⲡϥ̂ⲥⲱⲧⲙ̂, 15.1.2.1.
ⲛ̂, 11.1.
ⲛ̂...ⲁⲛ, 11.1.
ⲛⲁ, ⲛⲟⲩ, 16.5.1
ⲛ̂ⲧⲉⲧⲛ̂, 39.2.1.2.
ⲧⲙ̂, 11.1.
ϣⲁⲧⲉϥⲥⲱⲧⲙ̂, 37.3; 43.3.1.3.1.
ϣⲁϥⲥⲱⲧⲙ̂,17.6.

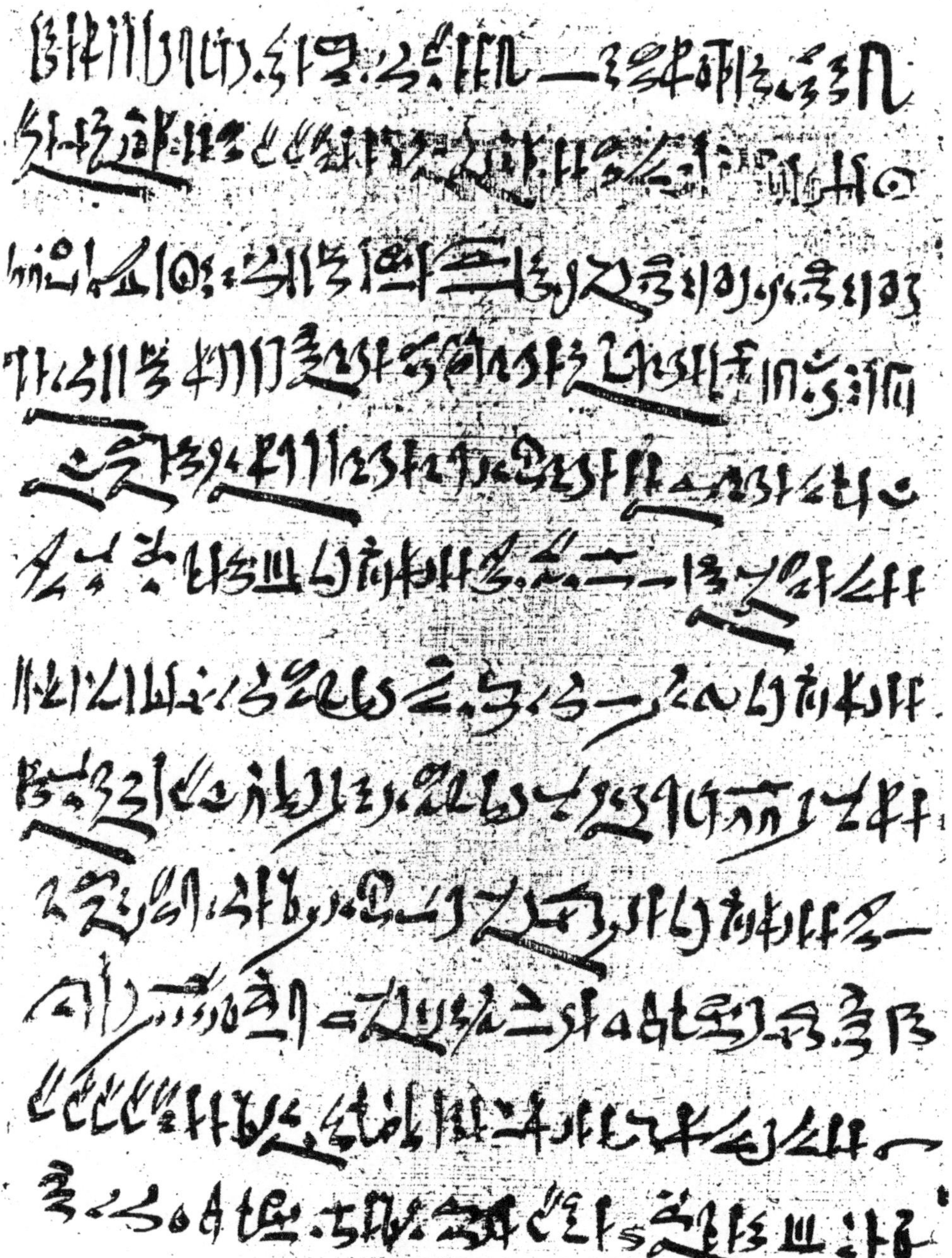

P. Northumberland 1, r°

Index of sources cited[1]

A

Abydos Osireion, Hieratic ostraca n. 2 44

Amenemope
27, 7 ...13
8, 4-5 ...174

C

Cairo Stela JE 48876
24 ...200
26 ...198, 213

D

Dakhla Stela
12 ...171
7 ...170

Doomed Prince
4, 1 ...55, 173
4, 3-6 ...109
4, 5 ...224
4, 6 ...140
4, 6-7 ...145
4, 7-8 ...136
4, 8 ...124, 202
4, 8-9 ...7, 171
4, 12 ...229
5, 10-11 ...96, 235
6, 2-3 ...157
6, 8-9 ...170, 232
7, 2-3 ...167

F

First Hittite marriage
30-31 ...145
abridged version, 10 ...228

G

Giornale
12, 4 ...125
12, 4-5 ...202

Graffito 1396, 3 ...203

Graffito of regnal year 34 of Ramses II
3 ...43
4 ...58
Graffito of regnal year 47 of Ramses II
1 ...45
Graffito of regnal year 50 of Ramses II
4 ...206

H

Hittite Treaty
13 ...18
15 ...17
22 ...77
30-31 ...126
36 ...124

Horus and Seth
3, 12 ...85
5, 2-3 ...110
5, 12 ...230
5, 13 ...231
6, 14 ...199
8, 5-6 ...224
9, 11 ...203
9, 7 ...212
10, 5-6 ...135
13, 12 ...214
15, 12-13 ...94, 236
16, 3 ...209, 229

K

KRI I
128, 14 ...44
238, 7 ...64
238, 11-12 ...21
238, 12 ...58, 86
238, 14-15 ...61
239, 4 ...59

[1] The numbers refer to the pages in the book.

239, 4-5 ... 223
239, 9-10 ... 120
239, 13-15 ... 231
239, 15 ... 57, 67
240, 4 ... 81
322, 6-7 ... 172, 196
323, 4-5 ... 197
409, 5-6 ... 78
KRI II
4, 8 ... 241
28, 13 ... 241
35, 1-5 ... 226
36, 1-4 ... 226
65, 1-4 ... 76
97, 13 ... 233
105, 2 ... 57
105, 3-4 ... 58
105, 7 ... 241
108, 6-9 ... 57
110, 3 ... 169, 227
111, 2 ... 65
115, 9-14 ... 43
118, 8 and 9 ... 65
227, 15 ... 18
228, 3 ... 17
229, 4 ... 77
230, 8 ... 241
230, 11-13 ... 126
232, 1 ... 124
240, 1-6 ... 110
246, 1-7 ... 145
257, 6 ... 228
355, 4-5 ... 202
355, 7 ... 152
381, 10 ... 62
381, 11-12 ... 44
383, 9-10 ... 172
383, 15-16 ... 63
800, 9-10 ... 11, 111
800, 11 ... 60
801, 12 ... 79
802, 1 ... 122
802, 13-14 ... 96
803, 16-804, 1 ... 133
810, 1-2 ... 118
810, 3 ... 148
810, 3-4 ... 108
895, 8-9 ... 136
895, 11 ... 76
910, 11-12 ... 61
911, 1-2 ... 67
KRI III
148, 4-6 ... 45
233, 1 ... 156
233, 7-8 ... 221
252, 6-7 ... 143
255, 9-10 ... 220
284, 1-3 ... 181
395, 10-11 ... 197
425, 4-5 ... 167
427, 4-5 ... 117, 206
427, 4-6 ... 136
427, 7-8 ... 223
427, 11-12 ... 204
428, 8-9 ... 172
428, 9-10 ... 232
430,13 ... 173
431, 6-7 ... 111
436, 8-9 ... 43
436, 11 ... 58, 176
437, 13-14 ... 206
500, 6-9 ... 183
500, 10-13 ... 234
500, 14 ... 207
504, 5-6 ... 210
505, 3-4 ... 52
505, 4 ... 184
506, 12 ... 184
532, 3-4 ... 196, 209, 229
532, 6-7 ... 66
533, 5 ... 81
533, 7 ... 177
533, 8 ... 60
534, 9-11 ... 143
535, 13-14 ... 230
545, 3-5 ... 187
549, 8-9 ... 125, 198, 209
797, 11-12 ... 143
KRI IV
19, 3-4 ... 241
19, 7 ... 241
79, 8 ... 206
79, 8-10 ... 93
79, 12-13 ... 120
80, 5-7 ... 65
80, 16-81, 2 ... 86

81, 1-2 ... 51
81, 10-11 ... 117
302, 15-303, 1 ... 66
315, 10-11 ... 147, 191
316, 2 ... 115, 200
316, 13-14 ... 172
316, 15 ... 158
317, 9-10 ... 77
317, 9-13 ... 113
318, 3-6 ... 223
319, 5 ... 184
319, 8-9 ... 48
319, 13-14 ... 189
410, 4 ... 190
410, 12-13 ... 8
411, 9-10 ... 241
411, 10 ... 241
411, 11 ... 124
413, 11-13 ... 90
417, 6-8 ... 108, 141
KRI v
2, 2 ... 84
2, 3 ... 182
2, 3-4 ... 64
350, 10 ... 180
350, 16-351, 1 ... 147
351, 6-7 ... 117, 200
351, 7-8 ... 121
352, 7-8 ... 139
353, 13-15 ... 120
355, 8-9 ... 130
359, 14-16 ... 117
360, 3 ... 129
360, 3-4 ... 54
436, 7 ... 5
458, 1-3 ... 80
467, 15-16 ... 187, 228
467, 16. ... 199
473, 11 ... 83
473, 12 ... 149
475, 2-3 ... 9
477, 6-7 ... 64
524 , 7-8 ... 183
525, 1-2 ... 148
536, 5 ... 134
542, 10-11 ... 42
560, 3-5 ... 60
560, 6-7 ... 62
563, 4-5 ... 144
565, 5-6 ... 134
571, 1 ... 200
572, 1-2 ... 190
573, 15-16 ... 96
575, 2-3 ... 231
575, 15 ... 200, 233
593, 7-8 ... 125
595, 3-4 ... 90
595, 4-6 ... 153
KRI vi
20, 1-2 ... 200
20, 4 ... 198, 213
67, 15 ... 13
68, 1-2 ... 142
142, 11-13 ... 236
155, 10-12 ... 133
155, 12-13 ... 71
155, 12-14 ... 168
155, 14-156, 1 ... 72
238, 2 ... 127, 148
259, 13 ... 45
265, 1 ... 228
266, 1 ... 4, 85, 113, 228
266, 3 ... 71
266, 8 ... 184
267, 7-8 ... 5
268, 4 ... 18
344, 16-345, 2 ... 158
470, 3-4 ... 64
470, 15-16 ... 53
472, 1-2 ... 14
474, 5-6 ... 14
474, 8-9 ... 59
475, 4-5 ... 55, 139
476, 9 ... 77
478, 1-2 ... 208
479, 6-7 ... 174
481, 4-5 ... 16, 54
481, 4-6 ... 121
483, 13-484, 1 ... 139
484, 5-6 ... 47, 138
487, 6 ... 55
489, 9 ... 15
490, 9-10 ... 7
492, 13-15 ... 130
492, 16-493, 1 ... 130
493, 1-2 ... 127

494, 7 11
502, 15 121
515, 10-11 154
515, 12-13 23
516, 2-4 112
517, 10 78
517, 12-13 18
519, 2-3 207
519, 4-5 117
520, 11 82
521, 8-9 126
564, 2 and 4 89
569, 3-4 .... 125, 202
599, 9-11 93
671, 5 44
671, 7 58
672, 8 44
737, 3 178
738, 1-3 82
739, 7 189
739, 7-8 124
740, 1-2 65
740, 3-4 126
740, 5-7 61
740, 8-9 178
740, 11-13 134
740, 13-14 61
740, 16-741, 4 10
741, 7-8 .... 78, 233
741, 8 189
741, 9-11 170
741, 10-11 .... 206, 233
741, 13-15 134
757, 3-4 119
758, 2-3 142
758, 16-759, 1 79
760, 2-3 71
760, 3 18
767, 15-16 168
768, 12-14 231
768, 14-15 .... 81, 83
769, 11-12 59
773, 8-9 13
774, 7-8 .... 144, 233
774, 9 183
774, 9-10 .... 198, 207
774, 12-14 187
775, 13-14 220
776, 13-14 .... 77, 155
777, 13 94
777, 15-16 54
779, 14-15 229
780, 3 17
780, 9-10 .... 197, 208
780, 12 179
780, 14-781, 1 135
781, 1-2 212
781, 3-5 173
781, 5 182
781, 6 .... 12, 121, 208
782, 2 230
782, 11 84
782, 15-16 12
784, 4-8 52
785, 10 14
785, 16 213
787, 10-13 80
788, 5-6 227
789, 12 55
793, 4-8 145
793, 7-8 86
795, 14-15 234
796, 12-13 113
798, 14 .... 171, 232
798, 16-799, 1 236
799, 2-3 203
800, 12 .... 14, 17
800, 9-10 130
800, 13-15 158
803, 12-16 126
803, 16-804, 1 203
804, 9-11 129
805, 2-5 107
805, 8 241
806, 3 15
807, 11 208
807, 13 208
807, 6-7 57
808, 3 135
808, 13-14 187
808, 15-16 4
809, 16 47
810, 1-3 133
810, 13 59
810, 9 179
811, 3 199

811, 4-5 7
811, 14-15 205
814, 6-7 187
814, 12-13 65
816, 12-14 67
817, 14-15 211
818, 9-10 146
820, 11-12 148
821, 1-2 55
821, 2 229
821, 8-9 209
823, 12-13 7
832, 5-6 .... 89, 136
833, 1-3 204
833, 3 85
834, 2-3 116
834, 4 201
835, 1 13
835, 7-8 94

KRI VII

338, 14-15 153
339, 6-8 108
339, 7-8 126
339, 8-9 .... 51, 83
339, 11 67
355, 6-7 168
376, 9-11 190
381, 8-9 125
384, 2-4 230
384, 3-4 51

Kuban Stela

9-10 202
11 152

L

LEM

2, 13-14 62
6, 5 178
9, 8-10 224
15, 2-3 185
17, 1-3 62
18, 1-3 71
29, 1-2 70
30, 16-31, 1 62
32, 6 241
35, 8 241
39, 10 177
41, 7-8 70
42, 12 210
42, 12-13 207
42, 14-16 75
46, 8 236
46, 8-9 233
46, 13-14 225
47, 8-9 241
53, 3 241
60, 9-10 194
61, 5 168
61, 12-13 .... 88, 226
61, 14-15 89
63, 8-9 201
67, 7 234
67, 8 235
67, 15-16 74
71, 6-7 226
71, 11-12 189
71, 16 190
72, 2 198
74, 4 130
75, 1 125
75, 13-14 75
78, 11 205
80, 4-6 179
84, 17-85, 2 71
86, 2 157
100, 12-13 183
101, 11-12 156

LES

1, 1 173
1, 1-2 55
1, 5-10 109
2, 1-2 145
2, 2-3 136
2, 4-5 .... 124, 171, 202
2, 5 7
2, 12 229
3, 15-16 .... 96, 235
4, 9-10 157
5, 3-5 170
5, 4-5 232
10, 15-16 48
11, 1-2 149
12, 8 88

13, 5-6 148
14, 1-2 .... 201, 233
14, 6.... 10
15, 1.... 14
15, 12-13 202
16, 12-13 226
19, 16.... 242
19, 16-20, 1 143
23, 6-7 146
25, 10.... 169, 232
25, 10-11 175
26, 10-11 141
32, 6.... 48
32, 14.... 232
32, 16-33, 1 232
33, 2.... 235
33, 3-4 178
41, 2-3 85
42, 16-43, 1 110
43, 15.... 230
44, 1.... 231
45, 11-12 199
47, 14-15 224
49, 10-11 212
50, 2.... 203
50, 14-15 135
55, 13-14 214
59, 5-8 236
59, 6.... 94
59, 15.... 209, 229
61, 5.... 9
61, 10.... 241
62, 3-4 125
62, 4-5 64
62, 5.... 176
62, 10.... 241
62, 13-14 201
62, 13-15 156
62, 15-16 159
62, 16-63, 1 116
62, 16-63, 2 190
63, 4-5 53
65, 1.... 21
65, 11-12 127
65, 13.... 221
66, 7.... 234
66, 16-67, 2 234
67, 9-10 231
68, 3-4 180
68, 6-7 210
68, 7-8 .... 168, 176
68, 15-69, 4 93
69, 5-6 213
69, 7-8 188
69, 12-13 58
69, 14-15 61
69, 15-16 .... 77, 155
70, 1-3 181
70, 4-5 168
70, 16-71, 1 116
72, 7-8 125
72, 8-9 87
73, 16-74, 1 230
74, 1-2 221
74, 10-11 227
74, 14.... 85
75, 1.... 8
75, 4-5 124
75, 7-9 95
75, 12.... 169

LRL

1, 7.... 235
2, 1.... 176
2, 2.... 81s
2, 8.... 59
4, 6.... 5
7, 11-13 138
8, 7-8 86
10, 8-9 88
12, 6-7 197
15, 9.... 206
16, 8-9 170
17, 10-12 108
17, 14-15 219
17, 16.... 127
19, 15-16 16
20, 4-5 21
20, 14-15 147
21, 11-13 151
22, 14-15 191
23, 11.... 58
24, 4-5 136
28, 4-5 114
28, 8-9 16
30, 8-9 .... 45, 71

32, 4 185
34, 14 81
35, 13 6
35, 15 63
36, 11 173
40, 6 82
42, 2-6 146
43, 4 172
45, 5-6 81
46, 4-5 224
46, 10 221
46, 10-11 63
46, 11 205
48, 16 4
50, 16-51, 2 154
50, 16-51, 3 111
55, 12-13 151
64, 9-10 82
64, 14-15 210
66, 13 209
67, 16-68, 1 222
68, 1-2 179
68, 4-5 204
68, 9-10 144
70, 14-15 205
73, 1 171
73, 7 .... 53, 219

M

Mès
N 2 167
N 10 .... 117, 136, 206
N 11 223
N 11-12 204
N 15 .... 172, 232
N 31 173
N 35 111

N

P. Naunakht I, (P. Ashmolean Museum 1945.95), 2, 7 148

O

O. Ashmolean 1945-37 + 1945-33
13-14 62
O. Ashmolean 1945-37
15 44

O. Berlin P 1121, v° 1-2 148
O. Berlin P 10627
3-6 133
5-7 168
6-8 71
9-11 72
O. Berlin P 10630
6-7 134
O. Berlin P 10655
5-7 96
O. Berlin P 11239
3-4 187
O. Berlin P 11247
v° 1 81
v° 5 177
v° 7 60
O. Berlin P 12630
6 90
v° 1-2 153
O. Berlin P 12654
10-11 158

O. BM 5631
12 179

O. Brussels E 317 218
O. Brussels E 305
v° 2-4 153

O. Cairo 25530, 1-3 42
O. Cairo 25556
4-5 66
O. Cairo 25589
2 5
O. Cairo 25725
1-3 .... 108, 141

O. Clère 218

O. DM 67, 3-5 134
O. DM 108, 4-5 78
O. DM 126
3 .... 196, 209, 229
5-6 66
O. DM 303, 3-4 143
O. DM 321, 1 227

O. DM 328, 8-10 ... 230
O. DM 357, a, 3 ... 200, 225
O. DM 364, 2-3 ... 9
O. DM 437, 1-3 ... 173
O. DM 439
1 ... 178
1-3 ... 180
O. DM 446
2-3 ... 172
8-9 ... 84
v° 6-7 ... 63
O. DM 552
verso ... 224
v° 1-2 ... 44
O. DM 554
1-2 ... 228
5 ... 225
5-6 ... 185
6 ... 67, 198
v° 3-4 ... 54
v° 5 ... 4
O. DM 563, 4 ... 84
O. DM 575 ... 219
O. DM 580, 4-5 ... 231
O. DM 582, 5-6 ... 200, 233
O. DM 587, 5-6 ... 5
O. DM 592, 6-7 ... 125
O. DM 607, 2 ... 60
O. DM 608, v° 1 ... 223

O. A. Gardiner 90, 7 ... 200
O. Gardiner 4, v° 4-6 ... 236
O. Gardiner 54
5 ... 83
r° 6 ... 149
O. Gardiner 55
v° 1-3 ... 180
v° 4 ... 147
v° 4-6 ... 79
O. Gardiner 103 A, 9-10 ... 190
O. Gardiner 143, 5-6 ... 190
O. Gardiner 165, v° 4-5 ... 125, 198, 209
O. Gardiner 273, 6 ... 168
O. Gardiner 310, 2-5 ... 143
O. Gardiner (no number) ... 221

O. IFAO 501 ... 222
O. IFAO 557 ... 219
O. IFAO 599 ... 220
O. IFAO 682 ... 184, 222
O. IFAO 691 ... 220
O. IFAO 693 ... 220
O. IFAO 848 ... 219
O. IFAO 849 ... 220
O. IFAO 851 ... 219
O. IFAO 857 ... 222
O. IFAO 861 ... 207
O. IFAO 862 ... 222
O. IFAO 864 ... 220
O. IFAO 870 ... 222
O. IFAO 884 ... 221
O. IFAO 999 ... 222
O. IFAO 1007 ... 221
O. IFAO 1296, 7 ... 67

O. Leipzig 2
4-6 ... 228
5-6 ... 187
v° 1 ... 199
O. Leipzig 16
6-7 ... 196
v° 2-3 ... 225

O. Mond 175, 1-2 ... 125

O. Nash 1
2-3 ... 147, 191
8 ... 115, 200
v° 1-3 ... 172
v° 4 ... 158
v° 12 ... 77
v° 12-16 ... 113
O. Nash 2
5-8 ... 223
v° 4-5 ... 184
v° 8-9 ... 48
v° 14 ... 189

O. OIC 16991
11- v° 3 ... 60
v° 4-7 ... 62
O. Petrie 14, 6-7 ... 183
O. Petrie 60, 1-v° 2 ... 111
O. Petrie 61, 7- v° 3 ... 78

O. Prague 1826, 6-7 ... 88

O. Turin 57093, v° 4 74
O. Turin 57173, 3-5 80
O. Turin 57472, v° 6-7 188

O. UCL 19614
4 84
5 182
5-6 64

O. Vienna 9, v° 1-2 144

P

P. Abbott
2, 15 53
2, 7 64
3, 10 14
4, 14 14
4, 16 59
5, 18 77
5, 5-6 .... 55, 139
6, 8-9 208
6, 20-21 174
7, 13-14 .... 16, 54
7, 14 121

P. Adoption (P. Ashmolean Museum 1945.96)
21 178
v° 6-7 82

P. Anastasi I
10, 3-4 169
14, 1-2 206
27, 8 235
P. Anastasi II
5, 3 185
7, 6-7 62
9, 3-4 71
P. Anastasi III
7, 8 70
v° 3, 2-3 62
P. Anastasi IV
5, 1 177
6, 9 70
7, 10-11 210
7, 11 207
8, 1-2 75
10, 11 236
10, 11-12 233
11, 3-4 225
P. Anastasi V
9, 6-7 194
10, 9 168
11, 6 89
11, 4-5 .... 88, 226
14, 1-2 201
20, 4 234
20, 5 235
21, 2-3 74
26, 3-4 226
26, 7-27, 1 189
27, 3-4 190
27, 5 198
P. Anastasi VI
21-22 130
32 125
42 75
85-86 205
P. Anastasi VIII
1, 6-8 183
1, 9-11 234
1, 11-12 207
v° 4-5 210
P. Anastasi IX
1-2 52
2 184
11 184

P. Ashmolean Museum 1945.95
2, 7 .... 127, 148
P. Ashmolean Museum 1945.96
21 178
v° 6-7 82

P. Bankes I
16-17 178
v° 2 170

P. Berlin P 3047, 10 133
P. Berlin P 8523
5-6 .... 93, 135
8-11 85
11-16 151
P. Berlin 10487, 9-v° 1 173

P. Berlin 10494
6 58
v° 2-3 136
P. Berlin P 10496, 12-13 64

P. BM 10052
1, 8 168
1, 16-17 231
1, 17 .... 81, 83
2, 1 59
3, 7-8 13
3, 16-17 .... 144, 233
3, 18 .... 183, 198, 207
3, 20-1 187
4, 2 220
4, 11-12 .... 77, 155
4, 21 94
4, 22 54
5, 9-10 229
5, 12 17
5, 15-16 .... 197, 208
5, 17 179
5, 18-19 135
5, 20 212
5, 21-22 173
5, 22 182
5, 23 .... 12, 121, 208
6, 3-4 230
6, 9 84
6, 12-13 12
7, 5-7 52
8, 1 14
8, 5 213
8, 21-22 80
v° 9, 2-3 227
10, 9 55
12, 2-5 145
12, 5 86
13, 7-8 234
13, 17-18 113
14, 14 171
14, 14-15 232
14, 16-17 236
14, 18 203
15, 5-6 130
15, 7 .... 14, 17
15, 8-9 158
P. BM 10053
2, 9-10 119
v° 2, 16 142
v° 3, 5 79
v° 3, 12 .... 18, 71
P. BM 10054
2, 8-9 130
2, 10 130
2, 10-11 127
3, 6 11
v° 1, 6 7
P. BM 10068, 4, 22 121
P. BM 10083, 2, 5 94
P. BM 10100
14-15 154
14- v° 1 111
P. BM 10284, 7 4
P. BM 10326
5-8 108
8-9 219
9-10 127
v° 10-11 16
v° 14 21
v° 21 147
P. BM 10375
13-14 81
23 224
26 .... 63, 221
26-27 205
P. BM 10383
1, 5 116
1, 6 201
2, 2 13
P. BM 10403
3, 14-15 .... 89, 136
3, 25-27 204
3, 27 85
P. BM 10412, 8-9 151
P. BM 10417
v° 3 114
v° 6-7 16

P. BN 196, II, 7-9 151
P. BN 197
II, 6- v° 1 191
III, v° 3 81
V, 3 6
V, v° 2, 3 63
VI, 7-8 82

VI, v° 4-5 210
P. BN 198
I, 14 209
II, 10-11 222
II, 11 179
II, v° 1-2 204
II, v° 6-7 144
P. BN 199, III, 6-7 205

P. Bologna 1086
6 206
6-7 93
9 120
14-15 65
20-21 .... 51, 86
26 117
P. Bologna 1094
2, 4-5 62
6, 5 178
10, 1-2 224

P. Cairo 58053, 3 196
P. Cairo 58054, 3 197
P. Cairo 58056, 8 220
P. Cairo 58057
3 64
6 21
6-7 86
7 58
8 61
P. Cairo 58059, 5-6 143
P. Cairo 58083, r° 3 172
P. Cairo J 65739
4-5 111
5 11
6 60
17 79
19 122
27 96

P. Chester Beatty I, 17, 1 and v° G, 2, 5 199
P. Chester Beatty V, v° 5, 1 13
P. Chester Beatty VII, v° 1, 7 96
P. DM II, 1 45
P. DM IV, 5 .... 171, 228
P. DM V
2 .... 4, 228
2-3 .... 85, 113
4 71
v° 3 184
P. DM VI, v° 2-3 5
P. DM VII
1 5
v° 6 95
P. DM VIII
1 44
3 58
P. DM IX, 3 44
P. DM XVI, v° 1 18
P. DM XVIII
5-6 230
6 51
P. DM XXVIII
10-11 17
9-10 8

P. ESP, A
7 78
9-10 18
P. ESP, B
13 203
15-16 117
P. ESP, C
16 82
29-30 126

P. Gardiner 4
4-5 .... 108, 126
5-6 .... 51, 83
v° 1 67

P. Geneva D 187, v° 1-4 146
P. Geneva D 407
v° 18 170
v° 6 206

P. Griffith, 5-6 197

P. Gurob
2, 1-2 76
2, 3-4 127
2, 6-8 112

P. Lansing, 2
2-3 183

8-9 156

P. Leiden I
350, VI, 9 72
350, v° col. III, 1, 13 148
350, v°, col. III, 11-12 118
350, v°, col. III, 13-14 108
365, 6-7 156
365, v° 3-4 221
366, 2-3 61
366, 7 67
368, 11 76
368, 8-9 136
369, 5 235
369, 8-9 176
369, 9 81
369, v° 4 59
370, 18 88
371, 2-3 180

P. Leopold-Amherst
2, 5-6 139
2, 9-10 .... 47, 138
3, 16 55
4, 12 15

P. Louvre E 27151
7-11 154
8 17
8-9 201

P. Mallet
VI, 4 13
VI , 6 142

P. Mayer A
1, 1-4 126
1, 4 203
1, 9-10 129
1, 14-16 107
1, 23 15
2, 12 57
2, 14 208
2, 16 208
2, 19 135
3, 4-5 187
3, 6 4
3, 17 47
3, 18-19 133
3, 23 179
3, 28 59
4, 3 199
4, 4 7
4, 10 205
5, 14 187
5, 18-19 65
6, 21-22 67
8, 5 211
8, 13-14 146
9, 6-7 148
9, 11 229
9, 15-16 209
10, 22-3 7
v° 9, 10-11 55

P. Mayer B
4-5 154
5-6 23
8-9 112

P. Nevill, v° 3-4 74

P. Northumberland I
2 59
2-3 223
7-8 120
11- v° 1 231
v° 1 .... 57, 67
v° 3-8 110
v° 6 100

P. Orbiney
2, 1-2 48
2, 2 149
3, 5-6 88
4, 3-4 148
4, 10 201
5, 2 10
5, 8 14
6, 5 202
7, 5-6 226
10, 3 143
13, 6-7 146
15, 9 .... 169, 175, 232
16, 8 141

P. Phillipps, v° 6-7 .... 45, 71

P. Pushkin 127, 4, 12-13 47

P. Sallier I
4, 1-2 179
7, 6-7 71
8, 3-4 157

P. Salt 124
1, 17 190
2, 1 8
2, 9-10 124
v° 1, 9-10 90

P. Smith 8, 15-16 152

P. Strasburg 39
8-9 189
v° 2-3 189
v° 3-6 144

P. Turin 1875
1, 9 180
2, 5 147
3, 1 .... 117, 200
3, 2 121
4, 2 139
4, 6 120
4, 12 130
6, 1 117
6, 2 .... 54, 129
P. Turin 1880
1, 1 43
1, 5 43
2, 2-3 89
2, 17 .... 54, 141
2, 18-19 113
2, 20 .... 95, 224
3, 15 133
3, 2 225
3, 4-5 76
3, 9-11 142
4, 1-2 176
v° 6, 4-5 .... 13, 96
v° 7, 7 208
P. Turin 1887
1, 9 209
1, 10-11 134
1, 12-13 156
1, 13 .... 45, 137
v° 1, 5 18
v° 1, 10 109
v° 2, 10 89
v° 3-7 61
P. Turin 1971, 13 185
P. Turin 1972
4 86
4-6 138
P. Turin 1973, v° 5 5
P. Turin 1974 + 1945, v° 7 82
P. Turin 1976, v° 1-6 93
P. Turin 1977
4-6 84
5-6 129
9 184
P. Turin 1978/208, v° 1-2 .... 116, 194, 204
P. Turin 1979, v° 1-2 172
P. Turin 2009 + 1999, v° 1, 9 and 10 89
P. Turin 2021, 2, 2 .... 124, 189
2, 8-9 65
2, 10 126
2, 11-12 61
3, 1 178
3, 3-4 134
3, 4 61
3, 6-8 10
3, 10 .... 78, 189, 233
3, 11-12 .... 170, 206, 233
3, 13-14, 1 134
P. Turin 2026
18 171
v° 1 53
v° 2 219
P. Turin A
v° 1, 6-7 73
v° 4, 1 202
v° 4, 10 213

P. Valençay I, v° 6-7 17

Pentawer poem
95 226
98 226
202 72
330 233

Q

Qadesh Bulletin
12 57
14 58
27 57
35 .... 169, 227
40 65
65-67 43
78-79 65

R

RAD
14, 5-6 76
14, 7-9 127
14, 11-15, 2 112
48, 11-12 96
48, 12 13
52, 2-3 208
52, 14-15 43
53, 2-3 43
53, 15-54, 1 89
55, 13-14 .... 54, 141
55, 15-16 113
56, 1-2 224
56, 2-3 95
56, 4 225
56, 6-7 76
56, 11-14 142
57, 2-3 133
57, 6-7 176
73, 6-7 17
75, 4-5 208
75, 7-8 134
75, 10-11 156
75, 12 137
75, 12-13 45
78, 12-13 18
79, 7-8 109
80, 16 89
82, 3 61

T

Tablet Neskhons, 18-19 211

Theban tomb
n. 157 181
n. 19 197

Truth and Falsehood
4, 5 48
5, 3 232
5, 5 232
5, 6 235
5, 7 178

U

URK
IV, 775, 16 242
VI, 137, 8 211

W

Wenamun
1, 2 42
1, 4 9
1, 12-13 125
1, 13 .... 64, 176
1, 18 201
1, 18-19 156
1, 19-20 159
1, 20 116
1, 20-21 190
1, 22 53
1, 37-38 21
1, 43-45 127
1, 44-45 221
1, 50-51 234
1, 56-57 234
2, 3 231
2, 10 180
2, 11-12 210
2, 12-13 89
2, 13 168
2, 19-22 93
2, 23 213
2, 24 188
2, 27-28 58
2, 28-29 61
2, 29-30 .... 77, 155
2, 30-31 181
2, 32 168
2, 38-39 116
2, 52-53 125
2, 53 87

2, 66 230
2, 66-67 221
2, 71 227
2, 73 85
2, 75 8
2, 77 124
2, 78-79 95
2, 81 169

List of figures

O. Berlin P 11247, HP Berlin, III, Taf. 35

v° 1 82

v° 5 177

v° 7 60

O. Bruxelles E 317, *BIFAO* 72, pl. XVI 12........ 12

O. Clere, *id*, pl. XV........ 219

O. DM 552, v°, *Doc. de fuilles*, V1, pl. 2a........ 45

O. DM 554, r°, *id*, pl. 3a........ 87

O. DM 554, v°, *id*, pl. 3a........ 103

O. DM 563, *id*, pl. 8a 128

O. DM 575, *id*, pl. 12a 149

O. DM 582, *id*, pl. 17a 242

O. DM 592, *id*, pl. 22a 122

O. Gardiner, *id*, pl. XVI 221

O. IFAO 501, *BIFAO* 35, pl. I........ 223

O. IFAO 557, *id*, pl. II........ 237

O. IFAO 599, *id*, pl. II........ 237

O. IFAO 682, *BIFAO* 41, pl. II 222

O. IFAO 691, *id*, pl. I........ 220

O. IFAO 848, *id*, pl. I........ 219

O. IFAO 849, *id*, pl. I........ 220

O. IFAO 861, *BIFAO* 72, pl. XVII........ 207

O. Leipzig 2, *Ho*, pl. 34, 4 188

O. Leipzig 2, v°, *id*, pl. 34, 4........ 199

P. Abbott, Select Papyri in the Hieratic character from the Collection of the Bristish Museum, IInd series, 1860, pl. I-VII

1 50

2 98

3 104

4 106

5 217

6 239

7 245

P. Adoption, r° II, 15-26, *JEA* 26, pl. VI 34........ 32

v° II, 1-13, *id*, pl. VII 40

P. Cairo, J 65739, 1-14, *JEA* 21, pl. XIV 2

P. Cairo J 65739, 14-28, *id*, pl. XVI........ 164

P. Northumberland I

1, *JEA* 34, pl. IX........ 249

2, *id*, pl. IX 42

7-8, *id*, pl. IX........ 120

11- v° 1, *id*, pl. IX-X........ 230

v° 1, *id*, pl. X........ 57

v° 3-8, *id*, pl. X........ 38

v° 6, *id*, pl. X........ 82

P. Valençay I, v°, *RdE* 6, 17........ 30

Caning of Hittite scouts taken prisoner at the Battle of Qadesh:

pꜣ ỉy ỉr.n pꜣ ḥꜣpỉtw n pr-ʿꜣ ʿ.w..s. ỉw ỉn.f ḥꜣpỉtw 2 n pꜣ ḫrw n ḫtꜣ m-bꜣḥ pr-ʿꜣ ʿ.w.s. ỉw.tw (ḥr) qnqn.sn m-bꜣḥ r dỉt ḏd.sn pꜣ nty pꜣ ḫrw n ḫtꜣ ỉm.

'The arrival of (*lit.* 'the coming he has done') the scout of Pharaoh l.p.h. leading two scouts of the Hittite enemy in the presence of Pharaoh l.p.h.. They were beaten in the presence (of Pharaoh) to make them confess (*lit.* 'to cause that they said') where the Hittite enemy was.'

Great Temple of Abu Simbel, north wall of the hypostyle hall, after DestochesNoblecourt, Donadoni and Edel, 'La Bataille de Qadesh,' Cairo, 1971.